COLORADO'S CLASSIC
MOUNTAIN TOWNS

FIRST EDITION

Colorado's Classic Mountain Towns

Evelyn
Spence

The Countryman Press
Woodstock, Vermont

Dedication
To my parents, Alexander and Marie Spence, who deserve all credit for my lifelong love affair with the mountains.

ISBN 978-1-58157-036-6

Front cover photo © Whit Richardson
Interior photos by the author unless otherwise specified
Book design by Bodenweber Design
Page composition by Melinda Belter
Maps by Mapping Specialists, Ltd., Madison, WI, © The Countryman Press

Published by The Countryman Press, P.O. Box 748, Woodstock, Vermont 05091
Distributed by W. W. Norton & Company, Inc., 500 Fifth Ave., New York, NY 10110

Printed in the United States of America

10 9 8 7 6 5 4 3 2 1

GREAT DESTINATIONS TRAVEL GUIDEBOOK SERIES

Recommended by *National Geographic Traveler* and *Travel & Leisure* magazines.

[A] CRISP AND CRITICAL APPROACH, FOR TRAVELERS WHO WANT TO LIVE LIKE LOCALS.
— *USA Today*

Great Destinations™ guidebooks are known for their comprehensive, critical coverage of regions of extraordinary cultural interest and natural beauty. The authors in this series are professional travel writers who have lived for many years in the regions they describe. Each title in this series is continuously updated with each printing to insure accurate and timely information. All the books contain more than one hundred photographs and maps.

Current titles available:

THE ADIRONDACK BOOK

AUSTIN, SAN ANTONIO & THE TEXAS HILL COUNTRY

THE BERKSHIRE BOOK

BIG SUR, MONTEREY BAY & GOLD COAST WINE COUNTRY

THE CHARLESTON, SAVANNAH & COASTAL ISLANDS BOOK

THE CHESAPEAKE BAY BOOK

THE COAST OF MAINE BOOK

COLORADO'S CLASSIC MOUNTAIN TOWNS: GREAT DESTINATIONS

THE FINGER LAKES BOOK

THE HAMPTONS BOOK

THE HUDSON VALLEY BOOK

THE NANTUCKET BOOK

THE NAPA & SONOMA BOOK

PALM BEACH, MIAMI & THE FLORIDA KEYS

PLAYA DEL CARMEN, TULUM & THE RIVIERA MAYA: GREAT DESTINATIONS MEXICO

THE SEATTLE & VANCOUVER BOOK: INCLUDES THE OLYMPIC PENINSULA, VICTORIA & MORE

THE SANTA FE & TAOS BOOK

THE SARASOTA, SANIBEL ISLAND & NAPLES BOOK

THE SHENANDOAH VALLEY BOOK

TOURING EAST COAST WINE COUNTRY

If you are traveling to, moving to, residing in, or just interested in any (or all!) of these enchanting regions, a Great Destinations guidebook is a superior companion. Honest and painstakingly critical, full of information only a local can provide, Great Destinations guidebooks give you all the practical knowledge you need to enjoy the best of each region. Why not own them all?

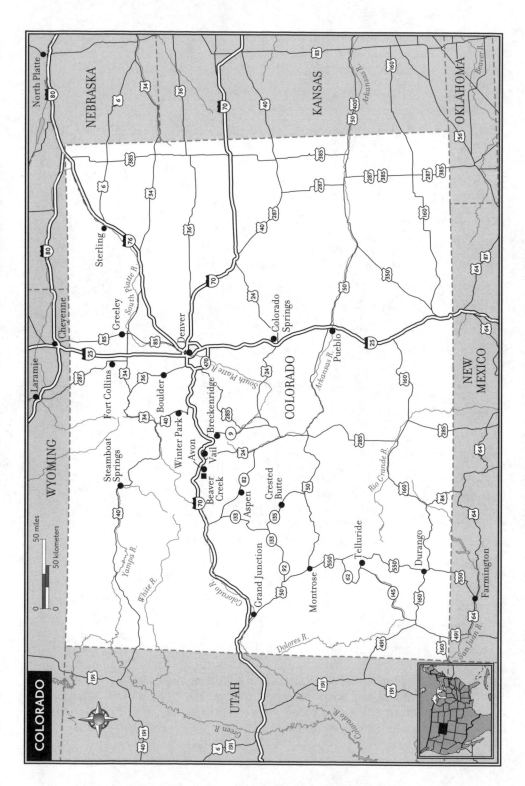

Contents

ACKNOWLEDGMENTS

Putting together a guidebook is a daunting proposition, and I couldn't have done it without the generous help of many people. First thanks go to my colleagues at Countryman Press: Kermit Hummel, for approaching me with this idea; Jennifer Thompson, for her steady organization; and Philip Rich, for spit-shining my words. I'm especially grateful to my contacts at the Colorado ski resorts I was lucky enough to visit: Kristin Rust, Nicky DeFord, Katie Coakley, Erin Lentz, Christina Schleicher, Jen Brown, Maryhelyn Kirwan, April Prout, Jennifer deBerge, Mike Lane, and Riley Polumbus. And, lastly, to a whole list of friends and family: There are too many of you to count, but your words of encouragement, open ears, and flattery kept my head above water.

Introduction

I only went out for a walk, and finally concluded to stay out till sundown,
for going out, I found, was really going in. —John Muir

When I first moved to Colorado in 2001, I was utterly overwhelmed: Should I pick up fly-fishing? Learn how to ice climb? Plan my backpacking trips around when the aspens in the San Juans turn to quivering gold? Try to telemark ski into as many backcountry huts as possible? Pledge to play hooky on every single powder day? For someone with a pervasive passion for all things outdoors, someone who—growing up in Seattle in the glacial shadow of Mount Rainier, going to college in the rolling Berkshire Hills of Massachusetts, moving to San Francisco and spending every possible weekend in the Sierra—never had a shortage of chances to recreate (to use the stilted term), I was close to paralyzed. How could one state contain so many summits, passes, rivers, valleys, wilderness expanses? How could so many peaks get folded into one place? And, really, in the face of so much natural beauty to explore, where does one begin?

For me, it began in ski towns: I moved here to join the staff of *Skiing* magazine and spent many winters on the slopes and powder-dusted streets of Vail, Steamboat, Telluride, and Aspen. When the snow melted, I started returning—to head up to a high alpine lake for a few days, to lean back in a camp chair and listen to bluegrass, to attend film festivals, to look for wildflowers. And each creek I crossed, every dive bar and swanky restaurant and pioneer museum and coffee shop I ducked into, I realized how much more these ski towns have to offer than just skiing. They have storied mining and railroad histories. They have world-class ballet, jazz, literature. They have food that ranges from breakfast burritos the size of Duraflames and pizzas 2 inches thick to elk carpaccio and Hudson Valley foie gras atop brioche french toast. And, ever anchoring it all is an almost insatiable love for being outside.

So, yes, writing this book was a tough assignment: Visit seven quintessential Colorado mountain towns. Find the best and quirkiest and oldest and newest B&Bs, resort hotels, cafés, and nightspots. Figure out where to catch a brown trout, where to climb a 14,000-foot peak, where to ker-splash down a Class IV rapid. Read about gold rushes and silver busts. Pick the top seasonal festivals, whether they celebrate music, mushrooms, beer, antiques, comedy, food, or—in the case of Telluride—Nothing. And then, in the end, put it all together in one big guide. These pages represent what I wish I knew when I first came to Colorado, and everything I have gleaned since.

Here's to staying overwhelmed.

—Evelyn Spence, Boulder, Colorado

THE WAY THIS BOOK WORKS

Organization

This book is divided into seven chapters, one for each town. Within each chapter, the organization is the same, with information on history, lodging, dining, culture, recreation, shopping, and more—all in the same order and the same format. At the end of each chapter, an extra section, "Nuts and Bolts," lists contact numbers for police, fire, libraries, medical facilities, avalanche reports, media, and other useful categories. There's also a bibliography if you want to do some homework.

Lodging and dining entries all start with a block of specific information (Web site, phone, credit cards taken, price range, whether pets or children are allowed, whether the place is handicap accessible) for easy reference. All information was rechecked as close to publication as possible, but since these details can change unexpectedly, it's always a good idea to call ahead. Ski towns are notorious for ins and outs, especially in the restaurant business.

In each town, a few hotels, inns, night spots, and cultural sights stand out as being either incredibly luxurious, or quirky, or historic, or they just capture the character of the place. I've marked them with a star—which means they're highly recommended, especially if they fit within your budget. If they don't, they're worth stopping by—if only to gawk.

Prices

Within each chapter, lodging prices are noted as the range between the cheapest low-season room to the most expensive high-season room at a given accommodation. Keep in mind that rates fluctuate wildly—winter holidays are generally the most expensive, and the so-called shoulder seasons (April and May, mid-September to early November) are usually much more reasonable. Guest ranches often charge per week; this is noted accordingly. Since many restaurants have a wide range of options from cheap tapas to $50 steaks, I've simply listed dining prices as the range for entrées. Watch out for shoulder-season specials at dining spots, too.

Credit cards are abbreviated as follows:

AE: American Express
D: Discover
MC: MasterCard
V: Visa

Man casting in stream Dan Bayer

1

ASPEN

Haute Paradise

Don't let stories about Jack Nicholson, Goldie Hawn, Cher, Kevin Costner, Ringo Starr, Arab princes, billionaires, heiresses, ocelet coats, Fendi bags, *Town & Country*, or Manolos keep you away from Aspen. Yes, home prices average close to $4 million (and recently one hit the market for over $120 million), and the boutiques, galleries, restaurants, bars, and hotels are world class (often with tabs to match). But none of this can change a few simple facts: The four ski hills here—Aspen Mountain, Snowmass, Aspen Highlands, and Buttermilk—have some of the best and most varied terrain in the state, if not the country; despite its snooty CV, the town is actually very open-minded and inclusive, with competitions like the Winter X Games (teenage ski punks), events like Gay Ski Week (needs no explanation), and landmarks like the Woody Creek Tavern (made famous by beloved local gonzo Hunter S. Thompson); and with all that money, worldliness, and intellectual curiosity, the local art, culture, and music scene matches that of some international cities.

The Utes first inhabited the Aspen area, calling it "Shining Mountain"—but it really exploded when silver miners arrived during the 1870s. Thanks to the passage of the Sherman Silver Purchase Act in 1878, Colorado's mining boom kicked off in a big way: The legislation required that the Fed buy silver every month and have it coined into silver dollars. Prospectors branched out from Leadville (a nearby high-mountain town where silver was discovered in 1878) in all directions: William Hopkins and company to the Roaring Fork Valley, between Glenwood Springs and Aspen; Charles E. Bennett to what is now Independence Pass; and Henry Staats to Hunter Creek. Those first winters brought heavy snowfall—and early settlers learned quickly from a few natives of Sweden in camp to use the "Norwegian snowshoe," or ski. Aspen's fate, perhaps, was already sealed.

In 1880, B. Clark Wheeler arrived from Leadville (then a 17-day journey on those Norwegian snowshoes), surveyed the area, and changed the name from Ute City to Aspen, after the telltale white-barked tree. By 1882, mines around town had produced $44 million in silver and lead ores, and by 1890, the population had rocketed to 10,000. At one point, Aspen was the third-largest city in the entire state behind Denver and Leadville. Jerome B. Wheeler (no relation to B. Clark), a president of Macy's who moved to Colorado in 1882 for his wife's health, took full advantage of the boom and established himself as the father of Aspen: On top of being a rancher, he built the area's first smelter, founded a bank, and built an opera house and a hotel—both of which still stand. After the Denver & Rio Grande and Colorado Midland railroads arrived in 1887 and 1888, no fewer than 14 trains rolled in a day.

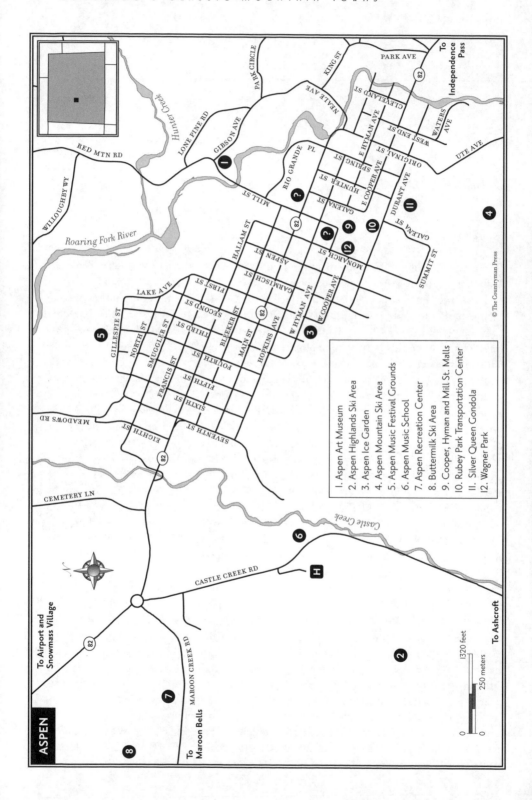

ASPEN

1. Aspen Art Museum
2. Aspen Highlands Ski Area
3. Aspen Ice Garden
4. Aspen Mountain Ski Area
5. Aspen Music Festival Grounds
6. Aspen Music School
7. Aspen Recreation Center
8. Buttermilk Ski Area
9. Cooper, Hyman and Mill St. Malls
10. Rubey Park Transportation Center
11. Silver Queen Gondola
12. Wagner Park

© The Countryman Press

Tree blossoms frame the historic Wheeler Opera House.
Burnham W. Arndt

But even back then, Aspen was different from the typical bawdy mining camp: There were four daily newspapers. A race track. Polo grounds. Literary meetings. Wives of mine bosses shopped in Paris and New York, bringing high fashion into the high mountains. As is true today, all the cash led to an unusual sophistication and intellectual diversity.

Everything came crashing down with the repeal of the Sherman Silver Purchase Act in 1893: Men like Jerome Wheeler lost their fortunes literally overnight, mines closed, buildings started sagging, and population stats dropped from 12,000 at Aspen's peak to 700 by World War II. A few hardscrabble ranchers stuck it out, herding sheep and cattle, growing potatoes, and watching the natural beauty return to the hills. City lots were available for $5 in the 1930s. These days, locals look back and call it "The Quiet Years."

Despite the somewhat depressing conditions, locals still managed to come up with the idea to start a ski area, though: Highlands Bavarian—the first ski area in Colorado—opened in 1936 near the now-abandoned town-site of Ashcroft, and Swiss skier André Roch put up a boat tow (two mine hoists, a Ford Motel T motor, and a pair of sleds that each fit eight people) on Ajax Mountain in 1937. His "Roch Run" hosted National Alpine championship races in 1941, putting the nascent ski resort on the winter recreational map. Austrian-born ski instructor Friedl Pfeifer moved to town after the war, and soon persuaded Chicago cardboard-box tycoon Walter Paepcke to develop a world-famous, European-style resort. And Paepcke went at it with a vengeance: He organized an international Goethe Bicentennial in 1949, with a tent designed by Eero Saarinen and performances by the Minneapolis Symphony Orchestra, establishing Aspen's cultural legacy (and the ever-widening idea of the mountain summer festival). He brought in the World Alpine Ski Championships in 1950. He gave people paint to spruce up their houses. He renovated the Hotel Jerome and the Wheeler Opera House.

And his vision paid off. The Kennedy family came. John Denver came. Hunter S. Thompson came. Chevy Chase. Private jets lined up at the airport. Despite the big names, it was—and still is—an extremely liberal place: As one writer said, Aspen was "a strange mix of hedonism, industry, liberality, athleticism, and unpretentiousness." People smoked pot on the street. The police had long hair. Skiers soon had three more mountains to choose from—Buttermilk, Aspen Highlands, and Snowmass. Legendary racers like Billy Kidd and Ingemar Stenmark made appearances in alpine races. In cultural, pop-cultural, and athletic senses, with its radical-chic sensibility, Aspen captured the nation's imagination—and continues to hold its fascination. All sappiness aside, it's a must-stop. Save up and splurge. Dirtbag it, or just drive through. It's well worth it.

Lodging

Aspen

✪ Annabelle Inn
Innkeeper: Charley Case
877-266-2466, 970-925-3822
annabelleinn.com
info@annabelleinn.com
232 W. Main St., Aspen
Price Range: $100–$399, including
    breakfast
Credit Cards: AE, D, MC, V
Children: Y
Pets: N
Handicap Accessible: Y

*A nod to old-school skis on the Annabelle Inn's
clock tower.* Evelyn Spence

The new Annabelle (which used to be the Christmas Inn, founded in 1948) has the mining shack–chic feeling that pervades many new homes in Crested Butte and greater Aspen and has now been brought to Main Street: It's a blend of rough-hewn salvaged timber, rusty corrugated metal, railroad tie–like beams, and old skis from different eras (there's an ancient pair of Olins next to the inn's clock tower). The 35 rooms—either standard, deluxe, or premium (on the third floor, away from the road noise and overlooking the beautiful garden of a local)—are all decorated and named differently: The Spruce has a whimsical, curly-cued wrought-iron bed and handmade quilt; Karen's has a bent birchwood four-poster canopy; Norway has a white peeled-paint queen and a Tiffany lamp; and Cloud Nine has one wall with logs and chinking. The courtyard in the middle of the inn has a Japanese-style waterfall, a stream garden, and a fire pit; there are also two hot tubs (and they screen ski movies alongside one of them every evening). Don't want to watch another Warren Miller flick? Nosh on complimentary cookies and cocoa in the lounge.

Hearthstone House
Innkeeper: Tracy Lofgren
888-925-7632, 970-925-7632
hearthstonehouse.com
info@hearthstonehouse.com
134 E. Hyman Ave., Aspen
Price Range: $119–$409, including break-
    fast
Credit Cards: AE, D, MC, V
Children: Y
Pets: N
Handicap Accessible: N

This 19-room, L-shaped inn is one of Aspen's most distinctive and understated, thanks to a Frank Lloyd Wright–inspired architecture and decor that extends all the way down to the light fixtures in the hallways and the chairs and coffee tables in the common areas. The windows are all large and look up to Aspen Mountain. The Hearthstone has the amenities of a larger property, too: herbal steam room, concierge, complimentary afternoon wine and cheese by the fireside, complimentary townie bikes for cruising around town, wireless Internet, video and book libraries, and a Jacuzzi that's in the corner of a below-street-level courtyard (and is lit up by tiki torches at night). All the rooms are true to Wright as well: simple and spacious, with light woods, beige colors, and matching furniture. There's a great spread for breakfast: cereals, piles of fruit, baskets of baked goods, a variety of fresh juices, and all the coffee you can drink.

✪ Hotel Jerome

800-331-7213, 970-920-1000
hoteljerome.com
330 E. Main St., Aspen
Price Range: $265–$1,530
Credit Cards: AE, D, MC, V
Children: Y
Pets: Y
Handicap Accessible: Y

This historic hotel was built by Aspen's founding father, Jerome Wheeler, in 1899, with the intention of surpassing great European and New York hotels (like Claridge's). The exterior, made of sandstone and a rich red brick from nearby quarries, was stunning enough for the times—but there were also 15 bathrooms with indoor plumbing and hot and cold running water, and it was one of the first buildings west of the Mississippi to be lit by electricity. Take note: Rooms were $3 a night back then. From 1918 to 1941, known as Aspen's "Quiet Years," they were $10 a

The front facade of the landmark Hotel Jerome. Evelyn Spence

month. It wasn't until Walter Paepcke (see introduction, page 15) entered the picture that the Jerome reclaimed its former glory: Over several decades, it was restored carefully and conscientiously. A hundred and fifteen antique light fixtures were repaired. Cut glass and ceramic doorknobs were fixed. Victorian wallpaper was re-created. Fireplaces were donated from other historic mansions. The latest step of its evolution? A $20 million facelift (with one eye on a five-star rating), including a new spa, an updated fitness center, a remodeled restaurant, and contemporary additions like plasma TVs—all of which means the Jerome will be closed from April until December 2007. Book early to find out if it still walks the line between updated and genuine—or if it has left history behind.

Hotel Lenado

800-321-3457, 970-925-6246
hotellenado.com
info@hotellenado.com
200 S. Aspen St., Aspen
Price Range: $125–$325, including
    breakfast
Credit Cards: AE, D, MC, V
Children: Y
Pets: Y
Handicap Accessible: N

The most dramatic part of the Hotel Lenado is its Great Room—the 28-foot fireplace is made of concrete and dotted with large red rocks and framed by long timbers, all of which came from the town-site of Lenado (down the valley and up Woody Creek). In fact, *lenado* means wood in Spanish, and there are riffs on that theme throughout the place. The couches are made from willow branches, and they're covered in plaid down cushions. Each of the 19 rooms has hickory or carved applewood beds and custom cherrywood armoires; the ones on the second floor have high, polished-wood

vaulted ceilings; some even have wood-burning stoves and private balconies. There's a small library/reading room in the back and an outdoor hot tub if you want to chill out on-site—and the breakfast room, which serves a full spread of pancakes and fruit plates and eggs cooked to order in the morning, is converted to Markham's Bar in the afternoon (and serves booze and complimentary nibblies).

Independence Square

800-633-0336, 970-920-2010
indysquare.com
reservations@indysquare.com
404 S. Galena St., Aspen
Price Range: $120–$470, including
    continental breakfast
Credit Cards: AE, MC, V
Children: Y
Pets: N
Handicap Accessible: N

If you want to stay in the center of it all, this 28-room lodge—in a brick building built in 1889—is the closest thing you'll come to urban accommodations: It's right on the pedestrian mall above a few first-floor shops with green awnings, a block away from the gondola and a block away from the transit center. But it's easy to walk right by and miss the entrance. And though the outside looks historic, the interior is much more modern: Most of the rooms have bright white walls, wooden ceilings, track lighting, modern furniture (futons, cushy couches), and angular layouts. There are two rooms that are particularly unusual: 205 and 206, which adjoin, are painted into an over-the-top Italian theme (one has a Botticelli-esque mural behind the bed, and the other has a mural of marble arches against a blue sky). Continental breakfast includes fresh danishes, fruit, and yogurt—nothing fancy, but enough to fuel you for a few hours of skiing or shopping.

A view of the chimneys on L'Auberge D'Aspen's cottages. Evelyn Spence

L'Auberge d'Aspen

970-925-8297
preferredlodging.com/lauberge.html
435 W. Main St., Aspen
Price Range: $99–$369
Credit Cards: AE, D, MC, V
Children: Y
Pets: N
Handicap Accessible: Y

A row of colorful dollhouselike cabins tucked off Main Street behind aspen trees, L'Auberge is like some kind of Candy Cane Lane: You feel cute just walking by. Each of the dozen or so cottages is done up differently, but all mix the rustic and romantic with the purely charming: The Alpine has beds made from wood branches. The Pinon, a Southwestern-style room, is hung with chili peppers and garlic strands. The Club Cottages, a moniker for the newest buildings of the lot, have vaulted ceilings, canopy beds, Jacuzzi tubs for two, and antler chandeliers. All of the accommodations have kitchen facilities (so there's no breakfast included), and they're about a 15-minute walk from the gondola. Catch the shuttle bus at the stop right outside if you'd rather not hoof it.

The Little Nell

970-920-4600
thelittlenell.com
675 E. Durant Ave., Aspen
Price Range: $270–$4,600
Credit Cards: AE, D, MC, V
Children: Y
Pets: Y
Handicap Accessible: Y

One recent guest of the Little Nell raved, "Making guests happy is a religion here." That means twice-a-day maid service, five drivers to take you around town, a regular concierge, a ski concierge, and even a laundry concierge. Such service comes at a price (Yes, you can get a suite for $4,600 a night!), but if you can afford it, this Aspen legend won't let you down. It's just a few steps from the Silver Queen gondola, it has a stellar in-house restaurant (see Montagna, page 28), and the staff won't bat an eye if you ask them to walk eight blocks to pick up a meal at Matsuhisa because you're too sore to get out of bed. It's understandable if you don't want to stir: The beds are oversized, piled high with down, and the rooms all have Belgian wool carpeting, marble bathrooms, gas fireplaces, and huge walk-in closets. The mountain-view rooms are more expensive, and the ultimate suite, the Pfeifer, is 2,000 square feet, with a full wet bar, a dining room, two bathrooms, two fireplaces, and two decks looking right out at Aspen Mountain.

✪ The Little Red Ski Haus

Innkeper: Beverly Fiore
866-630-6119, 970-925-3333
littleredskihaus.net
info@littleredskihaus.net
118 E. Cooper Ave., Aspen
Price Range: $89–$615, including breakfast
Credit Cards: AE, D, MC, V
Children: Y
Pets: N
Handicap Accessible: Y

There's no mistaking the Little Red Ski Haus: Its scarlet paint job, with bright white trim, speaks for itself. Built in 1888 by a silver miner, it became Aspen's first (admittedly dormlike) B&B in 1961—its first guest was "a cowboy who worked at the Red Onion, paying 50 cents a night"—and it gained a reputation for being a cheap place to crash. Over the years, however, it became more and more dilapidated, until in 2003 new owners put in $1 million to refurbish it. And refurbish they did: The room count was reduced from 23 to 13, making for much more space. Whirlpool baths and steam showers were added to the bathrooms. The original woodwork and fixtures—an arched Victorian staircase, a

The Little Red Ski Haus. Evelyn Spence

library with built in shelves, wingback chairs, crystal chandeliers, and beaded-fringe lampshades—were all restored. The biggest change? They dug down below the house to build an underground pub and breakfast area dubbed Prospector's Cellar, with a mesquite dining room table, leather high-backed chairs, and a dark wood bar with copper panels. If you want one of the three original rooms, request Ruthie's Run (up a spiral staircase, overlooking the garden), Spar Gulch, or Silver Bell (with an octagon window and cathedral ceiling).

✪ St. Regis Aspen

888-454-9005, 970-920-3300
stregisaspen.com
315 E. Dean St., Aspen
Price Range: $495–$2,000

Credit Cards: AE, D, MC, V
Children: Y
Pets: Y
Handicap Accessible: Y

Everything about the St. Regis—which was constructed of 800,000 Colorado red bricks—is top-of-the-line, whether it's the marble bathrooms (with double vanities) that are stocked with Bijan toiletries, or the ivory Pratesi linens on the beds, the 30-inch flat-screen TVs, the Godiva chocolates on the pillows at turndown, the bowls of fruit, the fresh flowers. As you enter, the lobby is just a sign of things to come—original bronzes of horses, Native Americans, and cowboys (not to mention the massive elk out front, called "Standing Watch"); oil paintings of mountain scenes; overstuffed leather couches and leather-topped tables;

The St. Regis Aspen is one of the most opulent—and convenient—spots in town. St. Regis Aspen

Turkish, Tibetan, and Persian rugs; a two-way fireplace that's always warm and crackling; richly striped curtains and wood-paneled walls. The hotel, built in 1991, makes up in service and amenities what it lacks in history: If you have a pet, they'll provide a pet sitter for you. Have a kid? They'll get a baby sitter for you. You can leave your shoes overnight to be shined or sign up for a golf-conditioning consultation. The Remède Spa has vapor caves and steam rooms, warm and cold waterfalls, a 24-hour fitness center, and even an oxygen bar if you're feeling the effects of being at 8,000-plus feet. New this winter: You can take two-hour cooking classes in Olives Restaurant through the Cooking School of Aspen. One last reminder: Be sure to take your time and look at the art throughout the hotel. The collection is acclaimed, with artists like Herman Herzog, Michael Coleman, and Frederick Ferdinand Schaffer.

Sardy House Residence & Carriage House Inn
800-321-3457, 970-920-2525
sardyhouse.com
128 E. Main St., Aspen
Price Range: $115–$1,075
Credit Cards: AE, MC, V
Children: Y
Pets: N
Handicap Accessible: Y

The red-brick Victorian Sardy House has gone through a few different renditions since it was built in 1892—it was a private residence, then a 20-unit inn, and now is a hybrid of the two: You can rent the entire house itself (the turret, the porches, the ironwork, the flagstone terrace), which has six bedrooms, nine and a half baths, 9,000 square feet of space, and an included staff of 10, with a four-night minimum and "rates available upon request." Or you can settle for one of the eight rooms in the renovated carriage house out back—which aren't too shabby, with heated towel racks, polished wood ceilings, cozy terry robes, bay windows, and thick down comforters.

Snow Queen Lodge

Innkeepers: Norma Dolle and Larry Ledingham
970-925-8455
snowqueenlodge.com
sqlodge@rof.net
124 E. Cooper Ave., Aspen
Price Range: $115–$315, including breakfast
Credit Cards: AE, MC, V
Children: Y
Pets: Y, call for details
Handicap Accessible: N

Innkeeper Norma Dolle is an Aspen institution—and her funny claim to fame is this: She and her sister, Marge, were one set of twins for Toni Home Permanents' "Which twin has the Toni?" campaign. Trivia aside, the family-run Snow Queen—built in 1886 and now divided into rooms named after famous silver mines—is an unpretentious and friendly place to hang your beanie. Whether you opt to crash in the Aspen Belle, the Fancy Lady, the Best Friend, or the Good Luck, you'll get Victorian lamps and flowered bedspreads or handmade quilts; some rooms have private decks or kitchens. Breakfast is basic but good: bread, muffins, cereals, juice, coffee. And don't miss the Snow Queen's version of happy hour: hot spiced wine by the fireplace.

Tyrolean Lodge

Innkeeper: Pierre Wille
888-220-3809, 970-925-4595
tyroleanlodge.com
stay@tyroleanlodge.com
200 W. Main St., Aspen
Price Range: $66–$190
Credit Cards: AE, D, MC, V
Children: Y
Pets: N
Handicap Accessible: N

As one of the cheapest places to stay in all of Aspen, you'd think the 16-room Tyrolean would lack character. Not so. Built by Lynne and Lou Wille, who met in art school in Aspen in the late 1940s (he was a teacher, and she was a student), it has been around since 1970. By character we mean, say, the enormous eagle perched on top of the chimney that Lou made out of chrome car

The Tyrolean Lodge's telltale eagle, poised for takeoff.
Evelyn Spence

them—the mixed grill fajita is a combo of buffalo, chorizo, and chicken, and the mixed veggies come with asparagus, carrot, zucchini, and tofu.

Cache Cache

970-925-3835
cachecache.com
info@cachecache.com
205 S. Mill St., Aspen
Meals Served: D
Price Range: $22–$60
Full Bar: Y
Reservations: Y
Credit Cards: AE, MC, V
Handicap Accessible: N

The decor of Cache Cache (French for "hide and seek") subtly evokes the mood of Provence: summer squash—colored walls, beaded amber pendant lights, a few mirrors, a few photos, and some worn-out wooden chairs. And the mood goes with the food: Everything on this French-American bistro's menu is lovely, simple, and sophisticated. This is where you come for escargots, calf's liver with caramelized onions, calf's liver with spinach and smoked bacon, terrines of foie gras or pork or rabbit. The Marseille seafood stew comes topped with aioli and croutons; the sea scallops are joined by a poached egg; the pasta sheets are complemented by roasted garlic, mushrooms, spinach, and brown butter; and the New York strip, from Brandt Farms, has a bright Dijon-peppercorn sauce. The restaurant, tucked down a few steps from street level, is often crowded (even on weeknights), but the feeling is always cozy rather than hectic.

The Cantina

970-925-3663
411 E. Main St., Aspen
Meals Served: L, D
Price Range: $11–$25
Full Bar: Y
Reservations: Y
Credit Cards: AE, D, MC, V
Handicap Accessible: Y

This huge—and hugely popular—Mexican restaurant keeps people coming back for several reasons: When drinks are on special, the margaritas are $2.50 and the Coronas are $2. The portions are outrageously huge. There are 130 tequilas available. And the food prices are more down-to-earth than you can find almost anywhere else in town (unless you're fine with a 12-inch meatball from Subway). The dining area, with its scarlet, hand-troweled walls, slightly tacky palm-tree-painted mirrors, hanging stars, and abundance of plant life, has some extra-long tables for large groups, and the patio stays nice and shaded on hot summer days. The menu itself is huge, too, and offers Mexican standards and then some: nachos piled with cheddar, chicken, beans, guacamole, and sour cream; soft tacos, huevos rancheros, enchiladas, burritos, flautas, quesadillas, chili rellenos, tamales, and chimichangas; drinks made with prickly pear juice; fajitas of duck, elk, or buffalo; and even flan and brownie sundaes.

✪ D19

970-925-6019
305 S. Mill St., Aspen
Meals Served: L, D
Price Range: Entrées $25–36
Full Bar: Y
Reservations: Y
Credit Cards: AE, D, MC, V
Handicap Accessible: Y

One of the newest and hottest hotspots in Aspen, D19—so named because a lot of big things have happened to the restaurateurs, Craig and Samantha Cordts-Pearce, on that "Date"—is what the duo calls New Italian: gnocchi with braised wild boar, an Italian-style donut with San Daniele prosciutto, bread served with saffron oil, rabbit stew, ravioli with fresh pea shoots, minestra soup with tiny meatballs, osso bucco that melts in the mouth (and is served with a surprisingly perfect spiced popcorn), and octopus salad. The menu is divided into D1 through D6, a slightly gimmicky designation for different courses and sides; the cover of the wine book is made of cork and one wall is completely stacked with wine; the antique chandelier is covered in feathers and tassles; and the building—a tunnel-like shape with a copper band—is totally unique. It doesn't even have a sign (and, with all the hype, doesn't need one). The Cordts-Pearces also run The Wild Fig (see page 30), and whatever they're doing, it's working: Locals rave that they've had some of their best meals ever at D19, and this in a town where restaurants come and go like the seasons.

Elevation

970-544-5166
elevationaspen.com
304 E. Hopkins Ave., Aspen
Meals Served: D
Price Range: $24–$32
Full Bar: Y
Reservations: Y
Credit Cards: AE, D, MC, V
Handicap Accessible: N

With a dining room that features modern art—including a huge Warholesque portrait of Claudia Schiffer—along with buff-colored walls, blond-wood furniture and floors, and white tablecloths, Elevation is a hip spot, and the food synchs flavors of South America, Asia, California, and the American South with an underlying French technique. Chef Drew Scott is nothing if not playful: His Sleepless in Aspen dessert is a warm chocolate torte with vanilla ice cream, caramel mousse, chocolate-covered espresso beans, and—no kidding—a Red Bull reduction. Each presentation is a work of art, whether it's pistachio gnocchi with

sweet corn, fava beans, prosciutto, and sage; or caramelized black cod with lemongrass risotto and cashew vinaigrette; or crispy Thai basil veal sweetbreads. Come summer, you can sit al fresco under big red umbrellas—but the Cosmos are strong all year long.

Little Annie's Eating House

970-925-1098
517 E. Hyman Ave., Aspen
Meals Served: L, D
Price Range: Dinner entrées $13–$25
Full Bar: Y
Reservations: N
Credit Cards: AE, MC, V
Handicap Accessible: N

One of the best things about Aspen: There's an abundance of posh, high-quality restaurants. The downside? Sometimes it seems impossible to find a decent, down-home meal with a come-back-to-earth price. Locals swear by Little Annie's, a rustic log cabin with red trim and flower boxes—you can start your meal with onion rings, potato latkes, or shrimp cocktail, and then move on to spaghetti with meatballs, reuben sandwiches, messy barbecued ribs, or Colorado lamb. The tables are covered in red-and-white checkered tablecloths and the walls are packed with photos of wildlife, sports teams, and historical scenes.

✪ Matsuhisa

970-544-6628
nobumatsuhisa.com
303 E. Main St., Aspen
Meals Served: D
Price Range: Sushi $5 and up; entrées
    $12–$37
Full Bar: Y
Reservations: Y
Credit Cards: AE, D, MC, V
Handicap Accessible: Y

A sister to Nobu Matsuhisa's restaurants in L.A., New York, Tokyo, and London, the

Aspen version adopts his same philosophy—he puts his heart, or *kokoro*, into his cooking. What does that mean for you? The best sushi in Aspen, where there are a several places to get your unagi fix. All the fish (Spanish mackerel, Norwegian salmon, abalone, toro, kampachi) is superb, and flown in from L.A. every day. You can get almost anything you want fried in light tempura batter (pumpkin, crab claws, oysters, sea urchin). The sake, Hokusetsu, is one of Japan's best; and the cold and hot main dish menu is extensive. You can't go wrong with the toro tartare with caviar, the Kobe beef sashimi, the lobster ceviche, the broiled black cod with miso, the halibut cheek with pepper sauce, or the thick udon noodle soups. For $100 a head, Matsuhisa (or, more likely, one of his peons) will bring you a whole slew of dishes—perfect for a big night out . . . or for those of us who are painfully indecisive at the sight of so much incredible food.

✪ Montagna
970-920-6330
thelittlenell.com
675 E. Durant Ave., in the Little Nell, Aspen
Meals Served: B, L, D
Price Range: Dinner entrées $14–$37
Full Bar: Y
Reservations: Y
Credit Cards: AE, D, MC, V
Handicap Accessible: Y

The in-house restaurant at a hotel like the Little Nell (see page 20) better be great, if not epic—and Montagna is. For starters, it has a 20,000-bottle wine cellar, but still offers over 50 wines under $50 (which is actually amazing for the Aspen demographic). The cuisine highlights local ingredients, sometimes taking "local" to the utmost: Chef Ryan Hardy makes his own cheese, and he has converted a broom closet into an aging room for charcuterie.

The dining room has multi-level seating, with rich wood columns and railings, and butter-colored walls lit up by sconces. Every meal of the day is outstanding and just one step over the top—for breakfast, the warm banana bread is studded with molten chocolate chips, the omelets can be mixed in with prosciutto and forest mushrooms, and the french toast is made with pecan sticky buns. Come dinnertime, the seasonal cuisine really dazzles: Hungarian elk salumi crostini with pickled fiddlehead ferns; hand-cut pasta with spring tomatoes; chicken from local farms that's served with fava beans, radish, and pecorino; and local spring lamb braised in milk with a spring pea risotto. The Montagna Bar brings the high-brow down a notch (and the prices accordingly) with pizettas, cheese plates, mini cheeseburgers, and hand-cut fries with homemade mayo.

✪ Piñons
970-920-2021
pinons.net
pinons@sopris.net
105 S. Mill St., Aspen
Meals Served: D
Price Range: $25–$38
Full Bar: Y
Reservations: Y
Credit Cards: AE, D, MC, V
Handicap Accessible: Y

Located on the top floor of a Victorian and steps away from the Hotel Jerome, Piñons is the epitome of the Colorado dining experience: leather-wrapped banisters and leather-bound menus, log pillars, a painted tin ceiling, a ranch-house vibe, and views of Aspen Mountain through willow-twig shutters. It's a hands-down local favorite, and by that we mean it's the hardest reservation in town—even though it's been open since 1988. (You can call up to 30 days in advance.) Credit its success to the simple, flavorful, and elegant preparations of chef

Rob Mobilian: pheasant quesadilla with herbed goat cheese, Maytag Blue Cheese salad with sun-dried cranberries and orange-vanilla vinaigrette, almond-seared barramundi, pistachio-crusted rack of Colorado lamb, and chocolate bread pudding made with cake (not bread) swimming in bittersweet custard and topped with chocolate chip ice cream.

Syzygy

970-925-3700
syzygyrestaurant.com
520 E. Hyman Ave., Aspen
Meals Served: D
Price Range: $22–$65
Full Bar: Y
Reservations: Y
Credit Cards: AE, D, MC, V
Handicap Accessible: Y

An *Aspen Times* reviewer compared the food at Syzygy to jazz—"a combination that lets each flavor run around the palate for a bit, making a riff or two before settling into the mix and awaiting another taste's solo." It takes its name from the astronomical term for heavenly bodies in alignment. Its signature decorative element is a set of glass-enclosed waterfalls, which separate different parts of the dining room. And yes, it does have jazz acts—good ones—every Friday and Saturday night. The food is creative and creatively displayed: the Syzygy salad, for example, comes topped with raspberries, beet chips, champagne poppyseed dressing, and edible flowers. The ravioli is filled with Maine lobster and shined with black truffle vinaigrette. The wild mushroom soup is rich with foie gras and crème fraîche. The Black Angus beef short ribs are braised in shiraz. And desserts include strawberries marinated in dark rum. After dinner, settle into a plush black U-shaped booth under the black-and-white photos of musicians and listen to the real riffs of Nelson Rangell, Frank Todaro, and Jessica Cox.

Takah Sushi

970-925-8588
takahsushi.com
320 S. Mill St., Aspen
Meals Served: D
Price Range: Sushi $4–$22, entrées $18–$32
Full Bar: Y
Reservations: Y
Credit Cards: AE, D, MC, V
Handicap Accessible: N

If the beautiful people make their reservations at Matsuhisa (see page 27), the just-as-beautiful-but-not-as-rich people make theirs at Takah, a below-ground Japanese restaurant and sushi bar occupying a space where a cheesy nightclub used to be. Though it has no windows, it's hardly cave-like: The mustard-colored walls are accented by light bamboo, the bar has red chairs and metal accents, the ceilings are slightly arched, and the layout is open. Come winter, it feels positively cozy. The fish here is just as good as any other spot in town, with a range of melt-in-your-mouth sashimi, and nigiri that runs from the standards (yellowtail, unagi) to the more unusual (jumbo clam, fluke). Entrées include tempura, pad Thai, crispy Chinese duck, and New York steak teriyaki.

Wienerstube

970-925-3357
633 E. Hyman Ave., Aspen; 305 Gold Rivers Court, Basalt
Meals Served: B, L
Price Range: $8–$20
Full Bar: N
Reservations: N
Credit Cards: AE, D, MC, V
Handicap Accessible: Y

"The 'Stube," which has been around since 1965, is a perennial favorite with old-timers, new locals, tourists, and Klaus Obermeyer alike: It serves lunch (bratwursts, Dover sole, sauerbraten), but breakfast is what draws the crowds. We dare you to start your day with the Austrian apple bread pudding with warm vanilla sauce—or even better, with wiener schnitzel (you may have to be rolled out of the restaurant). They also make homemade waffles, omelets, and scads of Viennese pastries.

The Wild Fig

970-925-5160
315 E. Hyman Ave., Aspen
Meals Served: D
Price Range: $14–$35
Full Bar: Y
Credit Cards: MC, V
Handicap Accessible: Y

An intimate spot (a mere 50 seats) just across the street from the Wheeler Opera House, the Wild Fig completes Samantha and Craig Cordts-Pearce's monopoly over the happening corner of Hyman and Mill: This little mustard-colored building, with a raised patio and an embarrassment of flowers spilling from boxes on the railing, feels like a cross between a Parisian brasserie and a sleek New York eatery. But the food is much closer to Mediterranean, with hints of Spain and Greece: You can start the meal with the Butcher's Board, a spread of thin-cut charcuterie with mustard and parmesan, then order a bowl of the delicious clams and chorizo to share. If you're a fig fan (and if you aren't, this will convert you), try the fig-glazed pork chop with port reduction—or finish your meal with warm figs. Occasionally, the menu heads south to Morocco (say, chicken in a chili-tomato broth), but that doesn't change the food mood here: sunny, light, and consistently excellent.

Zocalito

970-920-1991
420 E. Hyman Ave., Aspen
Meals Served: D
Price Range: $17–$26
Full Bar: Y
Reservations: Y
Credit Cards: AE, MC, V
Handicap Accessible: Y

Zocalito, a Latin bistro, is a product of the game of Musical Restaurants: Chef Michael Beary, who spent 10 years at Cache Cache, opened Zocalito in Carbondale—then opened a second branch in an underground space in Aspen where Takah Sushi used to be and sold the original restaurant, then set up a small patio (open in summertime). Eating here is a small education for mind and palate alike: Many items on the menu have a short description of what they are, why they're there, or where they came from. Which means you'll learn what amontillado and chihuacle sauces are, why the fried calamari comes with annatto seed, and where Beary has purchased his supply of dried chilies. To go along with entrées like a Peruvian chicken wrapped in a banana leaf and served with chorizo, or a chicken mole with chayote squash and Oaxacan peppers, there's a good list of Central American and Spanish wines. As of press time, Zocalito was one of the few places in the States to offer white-streaked, thinly sliced Iberico ham (after a long fight with the FDA), made from pigs who feasted on a lifetime of acorns in Spain.

SNOWMASS

Il Poggio

970-923-4292
73 Elbert Lane, Snowmass Village
Meals Served: D
Price Range: $13–$35
Full Bar: Y
Reservations: Y
Credit Cards: AE, D, MC, V
Handicap Accessible: Y

People who live or stay in Aspen tend to rip on the dining options up in Snowmass—and yes, there are a lot fewer choices up here for

Summertime at Krabloonik: when sleeping sled dogs lie. Evelyn Spence

a good meal. Il Poggio is by far the best of them (if you don't want to ride a sled dog to get there, à la Krabloonik): There's a 500-degree brick oven in one corner, where pizza cooks crank out the likes of the pizetta (roasted whole garlic and Cambozola spread onto rosemary flatbread), the funghi (portobello mushrooms with fontina, sage, and truffle oil), and the pollo affumicato (smoked chicken, fontina, mushrooms, and peppers). If the oven doesn't make things cozy enough, there are rough-hewn ceilings, rustic floors, and rope-seated chairs. The homemade pastas are all hearty and unpretentious: duck ragu with cherries and pine nuts, gnocchi with veal tenderloin, chicken grilled with rosemary and lemon and served alongside artichoke ravioli. Even if you're down in town, Il Poggio is worth the trek—and by trek we mean about 15 minutes.

✪ Krabloonik

970-923-3953
krabloonik.com
krabinc@rof.net
4250 Divide Rd., Snowmass
Meals Served: L, D
Price Range: Lunch entrées $14–$20,
    dinner entrées $22–$70
Full Bar: Y
Reservations: Y
Credit Cards: AE, MC, V
Handicap Accessible: N

To get to Krabloonik—the word comes from the Inuit for "big eyebrows" and was the name of owner Dan MacEachen's first lead sled dog—you can drive up from Snowmass Village, ski down the Dawdler Catwalk through Snowmass's campground parking lot, or take a two-hour dogsled ride before pulling up for lunch or dinner (it'll cost you

The Pine Creek Cookhouse in Ashcroft. Evelyn Spence

$225 to $295, and includes a multi-course meal). From the dining room, you can see teams of dogs (there are over 200 canines here) as well as views of Capitol Peak and Mount Daly. And Krabloonik does Western-rustic to a T: There's a sunken fire pit, exposed chinking, worn-in leather chairs, and black-and-white photos. All the meat is smoked in-house, and game is the thing here, whether it's pheasant hash strudel, caribou tartare, buffalo Bolognese, noisettes of caribou wrapped in bacon, or rack of venison. Whether you come for lunch or dinner, be sure to try the hearty wild mushroom soup—it comes with sour cream and sweet herbs and never fails to hit the spot.

Lynn Britt Cabin

970-923-0460
stayaspensnowmass.com
On Snowmass Mountain
Meals Served: D, only during ski season
Price Range: $79 for adults, $45 for
    children
Full Bar: N
Reservations: Y
Credit Cards: AE, MC, V
Handicap Accessible: Y

The Lynn Britt experience, in a nutshell: Jump in a snowcat that picks you up at the Snowmass Village Mall; rumble up into aspen groves to views of the Snowmass Valley; and look out for the cozy mountain cabin all lit up with white Christmas lights. Then sit down to a multi-course meal of soup, organic baby field greens (perhaps topped with asiago and sautéed pears), and an entrée like elk meatloaf, roast duckling, or cedar plank–roasted salmon—along with the included wine. Over dessert, tap your feet to music from a local bluegrass duo like John Livingston and Kevin Glenn of the Frying Pan Bluegrass Band. A couple hours later, catch your snowcat ride back home.

FARTHER AFIELD

✪ Pine Creek Cookhouse

970-925-1044
pinecreekcookhouse.com
11399 Castle Creek Rd., Aspen (12.5 miles
   up Castle Creek Rd.)
Meals Served: L, D
Price Range: á la carte $10–$28, prix fixe
   dinner $90–$110
Full Bar: Y
Reservations: Y
Credit Cards: AE, D, MC, V
Handicap Accessible: Y

Having a meal at the Pine Creek Cookhouse is an entire experience, especially if you come in winter: You have to cross-country ski, snowshoe, or take a sleigh ride to get here. (In summer, you can ride your bike all the way from Aspen or, by God, just drive.) Whatever your mode of transportation, you'll get a just reward: a rustic cabin with picture windows, cathedral ceilings, log beams, antler chandeliers, and a central fireplace. If you want panoramic sunlit views, reserve a spot for lunch—or opt for dinner if you'd rather get cozy and wrapped up in the black of night. Chef Kurt Boucher started here as a line cook just after high school. He went east for culinary school and then returned in 1996—bringing with him big ideas for mountain gourmet cuisine. Lunches (there are two daily seatings) may include the Cookhouse Decker—a sandwich with smoked turkey, Jarlsberg, bacon may-

The Battle of Aspen
Writer Hunter S. Thompson (1937–2005) was one of Aspen's most beloved, confounding, brilliant, and famous personalities—and his very first article in ROLLING STONE, published on October 1, 1970, was titled "The Battle of Aspen," an account of his attempt to run for Pitkin County sheriff on the "Freak Power" ticket. The party's hot-button issues? Decriminalizing drugs, turning the streets into green pedestrian parks, and changing Aspen's name to "Fat City." Thompson lost, but went on to wreak decades of havoc (and write some of RS's most remembered stories).

onnaise, and veggies on six-grain bread—or a grilled quail salad with candied pistachios, Cambozola, green apples, and a maple balsamic vinaigrette. Dinner steps things up a couple levels: elderberry-marinated caribou with wilted dandelion greens, cinnamon-scented elk tenderloin, diver scallops with tomato jam and butternut squash fondue. The signature dessert? Brownie Grilled Cheese, with vanilla bean ice cream, chocolate and caramel sauces, melted mascarpone, and whipped cream. Calories be damned—you most likely came here on foot, after all.

✪ Woody Creek Tavern

970-923-4585
0002 Woody Creek Plaza, Woody Creek
Meals Served: L, D
Price Range: $8–$18
Full Bar: Y
Reservations: N
Credit Cards: N
Handicap Accessible: Y

The Woody Creek Tavern is just a few minutes away from Aspen, but it feels like another universe: Slightly grungy (but completely endearing), it's best known as the hangout of the late gonzo writer Hunter

The interior of Woody Creek Tavern, with photos celebrating the exploits (some drunken) of loyal patrons.
Evelyn Spence

S. Thompson. It's also been frequented, over the years, by John Oates, Don Johnson, and Don Henley. Its floors are covered in wall-to-wall leopard-skin carpeting. There are stuffed boars' heads above the bar. Every inch of the wall is covered with newspaper clippings, paraphernalia, photos of drunk visitors, and Hunter memorabilia. At one point, there was a jar on top of the bar to collect funds for defending late Enron CEO Kenneth Lay (the donations included string, rubber bands, condoms, screws, and a couple pennies). A lot of people ride their bikes here from Aspen on the Rio Grande Trail—and there's a service to drive you home if you've had one too many margaritas (made with blue-agave tequila and fresh-squeezed lime juice). There's good grub here, too—burgers made from lean Colorado beef, barbecue ribs, veggie soups, burritos and fajitas, and organic green salads.

Food Purveyors

Bakeries

Main Street Bakery and Café (970-925-6466, 201 E. Main St., Aspen) The baked goods at this quaint café, which is decorated with shelves of cookie jars and biscuit tins, are wonderful—whether you're craving a tart, a cookie, a brick-size brownie, or a loaf of fresh bread. But the breakfasts and lunches are worth sitting down to (which is obvious when you see the crowds waiting to get in on weekends): omelets, pancakes, home fries, granola packed with cashews and sesame seeds, and bottomless cups of coffee.

Paradise Bakery (970-925-7585, 320 S. Galena Ave., Aspen; 970-923-4712, Silvertree Plaza, Snowmass Village) In summer, there's usually a line out the door for ice cream flavors like mandarin orange cream, cappuccino coffee crunch, and toasted coconut macadamia. Paradise also sells cider, chai, cocoa, huge cinnamon rolls, gigantic muffins, quiche, croissants, bagels, and carrot cake.

Coffee Shops

Fuel (970-923-009, Snowmass Village Mall, Snowmass) Worn wood floors, bright red walls, paninis, great coffee, and smoothies with names like Tofu Cloud, Banana Blues, and Almond Madness—if you're staying or skiing in Snowmass, this is the best place to stop for caffeine.

Ink! Coffee (970-544-0588, 520 E. Durant Ave., Aspen) This popular local joint roasts its own beans and makes its cups strong and hot.

World Link Café (970-544-0001, worldlinkcafe.com, 720 E. Durant Ave., Aspen) Aspen's only true Internet café, World Link serves hot and cold drinks, snacks—and Web access in 15-minute increments.

Zele Café (970-925-5875, 121 S. Galena St., Aspen) An often-crowded quick stop with original artwork on the walls, Zele offers a big selection of smoothies, coffee concoctions, muffins, and cookies. You can also get good sandwiches and wraps: The New Delhi is stuffed with curried chicken salad, red onions, and grapes; the Venezia packs in chicken breast, roasted red peppers, pesto, pine nuts, and fresh mozzarella.

Cooking Classes

Aspen Fresh & Wyld (970-309-0510, freshandwyld.com) This local organic produce cooperative puts together weekly boxes for delivery and sells everything from goat milk to bison to snapdragons to apricots. Fresh & Wyld also offers healthy cooking classes—baking, fast family meals, Indian curries.

Cooking School of Aspen (970-920-1879, cookingschoolofaspen.com, 414 E. Hyman Ave., Aspen) In a town with so much good food, it's no surprise that there's a high-caliber culinary school here, and one with a ton of variety: Courses include high-altitude bread baking, raw foods, sushi, vinaigrettes, cooking with kids, and master classes with top-notch chefs.

Delis

Aspen Bagel Bites (970-920-3489, 300 Puppy Smith St., Aspen) Aspen's only bagel shop also sells breakfast burritos, sandwiches, salads, smoothies, and various baked sweets.

The Big Wrap (970-544-1700, 520 E. Durant Ave., Aspen) If you'd rather that everything be swaddled in a big tortilla, The Big Wrap's your answer: They pack—and we mean pack—their wraps to bursting. The Rock Your World has nothing less than roast turkey, lettuce, jicama, carrot, cucumber, green onion, guacamole, dill ranch dressing, and sprouts, all somehow contained in a whole-wheat tortilla. Other fillings include hummus, grilled chicken, roasted potatoes, grilled portobellos, and spicy peanut sauce.

Butcher's Block (970-925-7554, 424 S. Spring St., Aspen) The oldest and best true deli in town, Butcher's Block sells sandwiches with liverwurst, corned beef, prosciutto, bologna, and turkey. It also serves a mean meatball. You can get aged meats and even caviar to go.

A rare sight: empty seats at Café Zele. Evelyn Spence

Johnny McGuire's Deli (970-920-9255, johnnymcguires.com, 730 E. Cooper St., Aspen) A narrow countertop and a few outside bench seats, a sizzling grill, and a wall covered with photos and stickers: Johnny McGuire's is a local favorite, with messy sandwiches (in skinny, regular, and fatty sizes) like the Trucker (grilled turkey, bacon, BBQ sauce, cheddar, and mayo), the Reuben Carter (roast beef, swiss, sauerkraut, onions, and honey mustard), and the Manhattan (corned beef, swiss, coleslaw, Thousand Island, and tomato). Johnny's sister deli at Snowmass, **The Little Dill** (970-923-9410, Snowmass Village Mall), serves up the same fare.

Jour de Fete (970-925-5055, 710 E. Durant Ave., Aspen) Fresh pastries and coffee in the morning, sandwiches and salads at lunch, and takeaway food (pasta and lentil salads, quiches, cold chicken) all day.

Pastore's Taste of Philly (970-923-5711, Snowmass Village Mall) This walk-up window serves pizzas with ground beef, meatballs, anchovies, salami, Italian sausage, and more—along with hoagies, burgers, and steak sandwiches.

The Popcorn Wagon (970-925-2718, 305 S. Mill St., Aspen) Don't let the name fool you: This cart (an original 1913 Cretor's Special Model), open for lunch, dinner, and late-night, serves everything from hot dogs and chips to crepes stuffed with cheese and spinach. Keep warm under the heat lamps—or next to the fire pit.

Specialty Foods of Aspen/The Cheese Shop (970-544-6656, 601 E. Hopkins Ave., Aspen) Known for its 100-strong selection of imported cheeses, like raw milk crottin, L'Etivaz gruyère, and fresh water buffalo ricotta, this lunch-only spot has salads and great paninis—including one with turkey, arugula, brie, and shaved pear. If you're planning an on-mountain picnic, stock up here.

The Stew Pot (970-923-2263, Snowmass Village Mall) Of course they serve beef stew, veggie or beef chili, and soups of the day—but also salads, tabouli, sandwiches, and chili cheese dogs.

Upside Down House (970-925-1046, 233 E. Main St., Aspen) A little hole in the wall in the center of town, Upside Down makes the cheapest lunches around (and they're good): sandwiches, subs, and wraps with fillings like egg salad, capicola, pastrami, and Genoa salami.

Farmer's Markets

Aspen Highlands Tuesday Market (aspenhighlandsvillage.com, in the main plaza of Aspen Highlands Village) Not just a food market (although they have fresh-baked bread, fruit, and veggies), Highlands' weekly summer market also has a lot of jewelry, antiques, organic skin-care stuff, and clothing.

Aspen Saturday Market (aspensaturdaymarket.com, on Hopkins Ave. next to City Hall) Organic chicken and beef, flowers, cheese, local artists, cooking demos, and even a peach harvest competition and a pumpkin-carving contest.

Frozen Desserts

Ben & Jerry's (970-920-3001, 312 S. Mill St., Aspen) Phish Food, Chunky Monkey, Chubby Hubby, Cherry Garcia—they're all here.

Boogie's Diner (970-925-6610, boogiesdiner.com, 534 E. Cooper Ave., Aspen) Buy $350 designer jeans on the first floor (brands like True Religion and People for Peace), then go upstairs for a float, malted, or milkshake. They also serve burgers, meatloaf, salads, and other good diner food.

Maggie Moo's (970-544-6668, 520 E. Durant Ave., Aspen) The best ice cream in town. Take a flavor (apple strudel, cotton candy, Southern peaches, Chocolate Better Batter), mix in fixins (cookie dough, Twix, white chocolate chips), or let them do it for you (S'more Fun Campfire, Cotton Candy Ski Jump, Cheesecake Break).

Groceries
City Market (970-925-2590, 711 E. Cooper Ave., Aspen)

Clark's Market (970-925-8046, 300 Puppy Smith St., Aspen)

Mountain Naturals (970-925-5502, 360 AABC (Aspen Airport Business Center), Suite B, Aspen)

Village Market (970-923-4444, 016 Kerns Road, Snowmass)

Nightlife

Belly Up (970-544-9800, bellyupaspen.com, 450 S. Galena St., Aspen) The best place to catch live blues, rock, country, reggae, and more: Artists like Slightly Stoopid, The Wailers, Dwight Yoakam, Joe Cocker, Tim Reynolds, and B. B. King have all played here.

Bentley's at the Wheeler (970-920-2240, 221 S. Mill St., Aspen) An English-style pub with a bar made from an old bank counter, Bentley's has Stella, Newcastle, Bass, and Guinness on tap, a weekend Bloody bar, and half-off appetizers from 3 to 6 PM.

Caribou Club (970-925-2929, caribouclub.com, 411 E. Hopkins Ave., Aspen) The most exclusive club in Aspen, this members-only spot has hosted everyone from Bill Clinton to Billy Crystal in its classic Great Room, restaurant, wine cellar, and bar. Want to join? A weeklong couples pass goes for $500; a lifetime membership for $15,000.

Club Chelsea (970-920-0066, 415 E. Hyman Ave., Aspen) Popular and swanky, this elegant nightclub has a piano bar, a cigar-smoking room, a lounge (Speakeasy) with booths you can reserve, and a dance floor—with live music and DJs. Smart dress is recommended.

Cooper Street Pier (970-925-7758, 508 E. Cooper Ave., Aspen) This is probably the closest thing Aspen has to a sports bar—loft seating with pennants hanging off the railings, sidewalk seating in summer, billiards and shuffleboard, a bunch of big-screen TVs, and ultra-cheap pitchers at happy hour.

Eric's, the Cigar Bar, Su Casa, Aspen Billiards (970-920-1488, 315 E. Hyman Ave., Aspen) A four-part night spot across from the Wheeler, this complex is always packed with people playing pool, smoking Cubans, eating Mexican, or drinking heavily while lounging on big pillows. It's a perennial favorite of ski pros and locals, too.

The J-Bar (970-920-1000, 330 E. Main St., Aspen) This watering hole has been serving Aspenites since the 1890s—and hasn't changed much, other than the big-screen TVs and the bar menu (burgers, salads, sandwiches). Though the rest of the Jerome is being renovated in 2007 (see page 17), they've promised to leave the character of the J-Bar alone.

Lava Lounge (970-925-5282, 426 E. Hyman Ave., Aspen) Buy a bottle of hard liquor for yourself and spend the night drinking it—or keep it around for tomorrow night. DJs spin here seven days a week.

The Red Onion (970-925-9043, 420 E. Cooper Ave., Aspen) Open since 1892, the Red Onion is a laid-back spot for happy hour or late-night—sit back in big, U-shaped booth seats or perch on a high stool and laugh at the posters of 1920s-era male wrestlers on the wall. If you're hungry, you can order quintessential pub food.

39 Degrees (970-925-6760, 709 E. Durant Ave., Aspen) Guests at the Sky Hotel walk around in bathrobes after taking a dip in the pool, locals recline on chaise lounges and big ottomans near the fireplace, and everyone drinks Pimptinis, Botox Martinis, and plain old martinis.

Culture

Cinema
Isis Theater (970-925-7584, 406 E. Hopkins Ave., Aspen) Usually plays mainstream movies, with four showtimes a day.

Outside at the Movies (970-925-9010, aspenchamber.org) Every Tuesday in summer, bring lawn chairs to Highlands Village for free flicks.

Stage Three Theater (970-925-2050, 625 E. Main St., Aspen) A four-screener that plays popular films.

Ghost Towns
Ashcroft Eleven miles south of Aspen on Castle Creek Road, Ashcroft was at one point bigger than Aspen—though now only nine buildings remain. By 1885, it had busted, with just $5.60 in the treasury. The Highland-Bavarian ski area was built here in the late 1930s, but development moved to Aspen after the war. Now you can take a guided tour with the Aspen Historical Society (aspenhistory.org) in the summer months, or wander around on your own.

Independence Four miles from the top of Independence Pass on CO 82, this town was short-lived—but at one point produced $190,000 of gold in a single year. During the winter of 1899, a monster storm cut off the miners' supply route, so they took apart their homes to make 75 pairs of skis and escaped to Aspen. Several buildings are still standing.

Museums
Aspen Art Museum (970-925-8050, aspenartmuseum.org, 590 N. Mill St., Aspen) A world-class museum of contemporary art housed in a historic and restored hydroelectric plant, the Aspen Art Museum is a must-stop. Take advantage of the complimentary wine-and-cheese reception every Thursday night from 5 to 7 PM—or join one of the regular talks with artists and curators.

Holden/Marolt Mining & Ranching Museum (970-925-3721, aspenhistory.org, 40189 CO 82) Back in 1891, this place was part of the Holden Lixiviation—that's "ore processing" to you and me. Later, it was used by the Marolt family for ranching. These days, the site, which includes the Sampling Building, where large machines crushed ore, is a great way to learn about how mining worked.

Wheeler/Stallard Museum (970-925-3721, aspenhistory.org, 620 W. Bleeker St., Aspen) Apparently Jerome B. Wheeler built this Victorian stunner in 1888 but never lived here (because his wife, Harriet Macy, refused to leave Manitou Springs, a town near Colorado Springs). The Aspen Historical Society finally nabbed it in 1968. Now it has rotating exhibitions about Aspen history, and it also houses the archives of the Society.

Theaters and Other Miscellaneous Venues

Aspen District Theatre (970-925-6098, 199 High School Rd., Aspen) Home of the Aspen Santa Fe Ballet (aspensantafeballet.com), a local dance troupe that performs everything from *The Nutcracker* to brand-new modern works, the District Theatre is part of the Aspen School District's Maroon Creek Road complex (on the road toward Aspen Highlands).

Crystal Palace (970-925-1455, cpalace.net, 300 E. Hyman Ave., Aspen) A dinner show that features a "revue" of the day's headlines, this cabaret theater has been running since 1957. After a meal of escargots, quail and shiitake mushroom wontons, pan-seared elk loin, Thai salmon, bread pudding, and fallen chocolate soufflé torte, sit back and take in the satire.

A modern performance by the dancers of the Aspen Santa Fe Ballet. Aspen Santa Fe Ballet

Wheeler Opera House (970-920-5770, wheeleroperahouse.com, 320 E. Hyman Ave., Aspen) When it opened in 1889, *The Aspen Times* called it "a perfect bijou of a theatre"—it was decorated with velvet drapes, a silver star–studded ceiling, gold plush seats, and 36 electric bulbs. After Aspen's bust and a 1912 fire, the Wheeler was abandoned, left dark until Walter Paepcke—as part of his "Aspen Idea"—fixed the place up. Since then, it has been refurbished several times, and now hosts everything from opera to bluegrass to author readings to movie nights.

KIDS' STUFF

Anderson Ranch Arts Center (970-923-3181, andersonranch.org, 5263 Owl Creek Rd., Snowmass) An arts center in Snowmass for all ages, Anderson Ranch has a great variety of summer workshops for kids: tree-house building, woodcarving, black-and-white photography, mask-making, clay jewelry, and kite-making.

Aspen Recreation Center (970-544-4100, aspenrecreation.com, 0861 Maroon Creek Rd., Aspen) Slide down a two-story corkscrew waterslide, float down the "lazy river," rope up and try one of 30 routes on the climbing wall, swing for the fence at batting cages, or throw an ollie in the skate park.

Aspen Youth Center (970-544-4130, aspenyouthcenter.org, 0861 Maroon Creek Rd., Aspen) Both local and visiting kids can take advantage of the offerings here: drop-in basketball, cooking classes, paintball, rafting trips, mural projects, rocket-building, movie nights, and sports tournaments.

Braille Trail On the way up to Independence Pass on CO 82, this self-guided trail has 23 interpretive panels—and the chance to experience the natural environment by taste, touch, and smell.

Gold Panning (970-923-1227) Try to sift out a few flakes at Elk Camp, up on Snowmass Mountain.

Krabloonik (4250 Divide Rd., Snowmass; see also entry under "Dining," page 31) This dogsledding outfit offers a family lunch, during which the little ones can play with sled-dog puppies (supervised by a handler).

Snowmass Recreational Center (800-SNOWMASS, 2909 Brush Creek Rd., Snowmass Village) This brand-new facility has a 145-square-foot wading pool, a water slide, a bubbling rock, tumble buckets, and an adventure cave. (There's also a 16-person hot tub for adults.)

Snowmass zip line, bungee trampoline, climbing wall (970-923-1227, Lower Blue Grouse Trail, Snowmass ski area) The only year-round zip line in Colorado, this version whizzes 1,150 feet down the mountain at heights of up to 35 feet (once you're good and strapped in). Too much? Bounce on the trampoline, or try the handholds on the wall.

The Yellow Canary (970-927-9598, 162 Midland Ave., Basalt) A small studio that offers year-round art classes for kids, from toddlers all the way up to elementary school.

RECREATION: WINTER AND SPRING

Alpine Skiing and Snowboarding

Aspen

aspensnowmass.com

Overview: When people say "Aspen," they're actually talking about four distinct ski hills: A lift ticket here gives you access to Aspen Mountain (the original), Aspen Highlands, Snowmass, and Buttermilk. **Aspen Mountain** is the one that rises straight out of town, with a bottom-to-top gondola, a diminutive 673 acres, steep bump runs, long ridges, and not a single true beginner's run. (Think those ladies in fur coats can't ski? Think again.) **Aspen Highlands,** just up Maroon Creek Road, is most famous for Highland Bowl (see "Must-ski," below), but it also has some fun steep groomers—plus an intimate base area. **Snowmass** is the behemoth of the quartet, with 3,128 acres and a sprawling layout of long blues and short, super-steep black diamonds (it's also about 10 miles from downtown, with its own village of condos, restaurants, and second homes). **Buttermilk,** the smallest of the four, sits just off CO 82 on the way into town and is home to the annual Winter X Games—with a few terrain parks, a superpipe, and good ski-school runs. In general, the snow at all four areas is feather-light and the surroundings—including views of the Maroon Bells—are spectacular.

Must-ski: On Aspen Mountain, try going from the summit to the base without stopping—through Spar Gulch, around Kleenex Corner, and down Little Nell—like they used to do in the 24 Hours of Aspen, a now-defunct and much-loved race that saw some skiers notch 270,000 vertical feet (that's 83 laps!) from noon to noon. For bumps,

Aspen: The 4-1-1

Aspen Highlands
Acres: 1,010
Summit elevation: 12,392 feet
Vertical drop: 3,635 feet
Annual snowfall: 300 inches
Percent advanced/expert terrain: 52
Percent intermediate terrain: 30
Percent beginner terrain: 18
Lifts: 5

Aspen Mountain
Acres: 673
Summit elevation: 11,212 feet
Vertical drop: 3,267 feet
Annual snowfall: 300 inches
Percent advanced/expert terrain: 52
Percent intermediate terrain: 48
Percent beginner terrain: 0
Lifts: 8

Snowmass
Acres: 3,128
Summit elevation: 12,510 feet
Vertical drop: 4,406 feet
Annual snowfall: 300 inches
Percent advanced/expert terrain: 44
Percent intermediate terrain: 50
Percent beginner terrain: 6
Lifts: 23

Buttermilk
Acres: 435
Summit elevation: 9,900 feet
Vertical drop: 2,030 feet
Annual snowfall: 200 inches
Percent advanced/expert terrain: 26
Percent intermediate terrain: 39
Percent beginner terrain: 35
Lifts: 9

Some Useful Skiing Terms

If you've never in your life clicked into a pair of skis, you might be overwhelmed with all of the jargon. Here are a few buzzwords to get you started.

Alpine skiing: Might seem obvious, but this refers to skiing with standard downhill equipment—fixed-heel bindings, stiff boots, and shaped skis designed to make everything from tight to wide turns.

Après ski: Pretty much whatever you do after you finish skiing, whether that's sitting in the hot tub or downing a few beers.

AT skiing: "AT" is short for Alpine Touring, and it designates a type of equipment that's good for backcountry skiing. The skis and boots are often lighter, and you can unlock the heel of the binding from the ski to walk uphill—then lock it back down to descend, alpine-style.

Base: The average snow depth at a ski area, sometimes measured both on the lower part of the mountain and the upper (which usually gets more snow).

Black diamond: The symbol to mark advanced ski runs. The steepest runs are sometimes marked as double-black. Remember, the rating is relative—if you're not sure whether you can handle a run, ask a patroller before you drop in.

Blue square: Same as above, only this designates intermediate runs.

Bunny slope: The part of the ski area where beginners learn—low angles, low speeds, slow chairlifts.

Climbing skins: If you're touring in the backcountry, you'll need to ascend hills—and these strips, with adhesive on one side and artifical "hair" on the other, grip the snow. (Once upon a time, they were made from actual animal skins.)

Corn snow: A particular texture of snow ("corn" refers to the size of the granules) that usually forms in the spring, when there are repeated cycles of melting and freezing during day and night.

Couloir: A steep, narrow, snow-filled chute between rocks.

Fall line: On a given run, this is the most direct line down the hill—the line on which water would flow downhill.

Glades: At its most simple, these are areas where you can ski through the trees. Sometimes they're naturally spaced, and sometimes ski resorts fell trees to make for more wiggle room.

Green circle: The symbol to mark beginner runs.

GS, or Giant Slalom: A medium-radius ski turn, great for skiing fast down groomed runs.

Line: A catch-all word for the specific route you ski down a slope (as in, "Some of the lines on Aspen Mountain reach 40 degrees").

Off-piste: A European term, off-piste just means that you're skiing off a groomed run—and sometimes on a run that doesn't even have a name.

Out-of-bounds: Refers to skiing anywhere outside the patrolled boundaries of a ski resort. Many resorts have only a few official "gates" through which you can leave the area for a backcountry ski tour; if you ski under a rope (or "duck a rope"), you could get your ticket pulled—or worse, get lost or caught in an avalanche.

Sidecut: Refers to the slight hourglass shape of an alpine ski when seen from above, and makes for easier carves when you turn.

Skier's right/left: In giving directions, this means that you're talking about things from the skier's perspective ("head skier's right into the trees"). Conversely, if you're standing at the bottom of the hill looking up, you might say, "Check out the avalanche looker's right from the top of the peak!"

Switch: Skiing, or landing a jump, backwards. (Don't try this without twin-tip skis, which have both ends turned up.)

Telemark skiing: A hybrid of cross-country and alpine skiing. So-called tele skiers keep their heels free all the time, making turns in a lunging motion. It's hard to explain in words, but if you see it, it's unmistakable.

Tuck: The aerodynamic position that racers—and everyday skiers wanting to sustain speed—use, with knees flexed close to 90 degrees and hands out in front of you.

The gondola above Aspen (summer). Aspen Chamber of Commerce

RECREATION: SUMMER AND FALL

If there's a mountain sport you want to do, it's almost a sure bet that Aspen has it—in spades. Talk about an embarrassment of riches: The valley is cleaved by the Roaring Fork, a Gold Medal trout water, and the surrounding mountains reach heights of 13,000 and 14,000 feet. In between, there are countless options for hiking, road and mountain biking, and hunting—whether the snow is just starting to melt, or the eponymous trees are turning to bright gold. There's no summer sport that Aspen is most famous for: They're all great.

Cycling: Mountain Biking

Hunter Creek Loop A 7.6-mile ring that includes a bit of everything—singletrack, double-track, paved road—this popular trail (watch out for hikers and runners) finishes with a fast downhill plunge into town.

Lincoln Creek Road About 11 miles out of Aspen on the road up to Independence Pass, this Jeep road starts out rough and rocky and then mellows out toward the end (at Grizzly Reservoir). For a bonus, keep going past the reservoir up to the ghost town of Ruby—you'll get great glimpses of the Collegiate Peaks.

Red Table Mountain This is a pretty epic ride: It takes you from Basalt Mountain to Red Table, along old Jeep roads and singletrack, on steep switchbacks and rollers, gaining 5,000 feet on the way. After starting in El Jebel, a town on CO 82 between Glenwood Springs and Aspen, you'll get to the end of the road at 11,775 feet.

Smuggler Mountain Road For this ride, you can jump on your bike right in town: Take the residential Smuggler Mountain Road, look out for the trailhead signs, head up 2 miles of gravelly switchbacks to the Iowa Mine, then join the Hunter Creek Loop and head back into town on Red Mountain Road.

Snowmass Loop You'll need a Snowmass summer trail map to piece this one together, but in a nutshell, it links the town's singletrack trails into a giant (and hard-core) circuit: Rim Trail, Highline Trail, Tom Blake, Powerline, Government, and then the Ditch Trail back to the beginning. The singletrack Rim Trail is a great ride in itself, hugging the ridge above Snowmass Village.

Sunnyside Trail Used by hikers and mountain bikers alike, this route is challenging for both: It's 10 miles one way, starting at McLain Flats Road, switchbacking through scrub oak and into aspens, crossing over Hunter Creek a few times, and finishing with a boardwalk— and some steps. You'll even get views of the Maroon Bells.

Taylor Pass Road to Crested Butte Following a rough four-wheel-drive road 27 miles one way, the Taylor route is for super-strong riders only. If you can hack it, the scenery (vistas of the Collegiate Peaks) is unbeatable.

Woody Creek to Lenado Here's a great beginner ride—or one for a relaxing outing. Park at the Woody Creek Tavern, ride up to the town-site of Lenado, then ride back down and get a couple margaritas.

Cycling: Road Biking

Castle Creek Road A beautiful ride from Aspen 12 miles to the end of the paved road (Forest Road 102), Castle Creek winds and rolls up a narrow river valley. There are a few steep climbs along the way, but nothing tortuously sustained.

Frying Pan Road Leaving from the town of Basalt, 18 miles from Aspen, this route parallels the Gold Medal trout waters of the Frying Pan River. Twelve miles in, you reach the Ruedi Reservoir, then keep climbing. There's a short descent into the town of Meredith before another 5 miles of climbing. Stop where the pavement ends.

Independence Pass Hands down, this is one of the most grueling road climbs in the entire state: It ascends from 8,000 to 12,000 feet in 17 miles around blind corners with no shoulders. At the top, you'll get spectacular views of the Collegiate Peaks, the Hunter-Fryingpan Wilderness, and the Lake Creek Valley. Return the way you came, or descend to the town of Twin Lakes for sandwiches and beer.

Maroon Creek Road Though it has a $5 fee per bike (it's $15 for cars), this ride is totally worth the dough: It's only about 11 miles, but it ends up slamming into iconic Pyramid Peak and the Maroon Bells.

Fishing

Outfitters

Aspen Flyfishing (970-920-6886, aspenflyfishing.com, 601 E. Dean St., Aspen) You can book a standard wade or float day here—with trips on the Roaring Fork and the Frying Pan—but there's also an extensive list of fishing classes: nymph fishing, dry fly-fishing, streamer fishing, casting, tying, and a three-day introductory crash course.

Aspen Trout Guides, Inc (970-379-7963, aspentroutguides.com, 520 E. Durant Ave., Aspen) They can take you on the Pan and the Fork, of course, but you can also try a few creeks (Maroon, Castle, and Hunter), some high-alpine lakes (Blue, Seller, Little Gem), and a couple reservoirs (Lost Man, Grizzly, Ruedi).

Frying Pan Anglers (970-927-3441, fryingpananglers.com, 132 Basalt Center Circle, Basalt) Wade both the Roaring Fork and the Pan in a single day, take advantage of the 60 miles of floatable water within an hour of the shop, or check out the extensive fishing reports on their Web site.

Taylor Creek Fly Shops (970-920-1128, 408 E. Cooper Ave., Aspen; 970-927-4374, 183 Basalt Center Circle, Basalt; taylorcreek.com) The oldest guiding service in western Colorado, Taylor Creek has access to 60-plus miles of Gold Medal waters and a roster of A-list guides.

Lakes and Streams

Before you fish any water in Colorado, be sure you check with a local fly shop to find out if it's public or private. Many rivers have both private and public sections, so make sure you know where you're going. For licenses and regulations, visit wildlife.state.co.us/fishing—or, again, stop into a shop. If a river is designated "Gold Medal," it officially means that there are 12 trout per surface acre that top 14 inches—or 60 pounds of trout per surface acre. Unofficially, it means that the fishing is damn good.

Crystal River Often overlooked because it lacks the Gold Medal designation of the other two rivers in the area, the Crystal has 35 miles of freestone water. Some of the best fishing is at the point where the Crystal meets the Roaring Fork in Carbondale (as rainbows and browns run up the Crystal to spawn).

Frying Pan River One of the most-loved trout waters in the country, the Pan is a don't-miss. The upper section, above Ruedi Reservoir, is a high-country stream; the 14 miles between Ruedi and the confluence with the Roaring Fork (in Basalt) is true-blue Gold Medal, with cutthroat, brown, rainbow, and brook trout. There's great fishing all year round.

High-Alpine Lakes Many of best area hikes (see page 50) also have decent to excellent fishing, including America, Josephine, and Cathedral. Carry your rod whenever you go into the high country.

Roaring Fork River Starting at Independence Pass and rolling 60 miles down to the Colorado, the Fork has it all: small pocket water, big pools, and a lower section wide and deep enough for full float trips. Steer clear of the river mid-May to mid-June, when the runoff is too heavy.

Ruedi Reservoir If the cutties and 'bows aren't doing it for you, try to land a lake trout or a Kokanee salmon in this 1.6-square-mile reservoir, 15 miles up from Basalt.

Golf

Aspen Golf and Tennis Club (970-544-1772, aspenrecreation.com, 39551 CO 82, Aspen) As a certified Audubon Cooperative Sanctuary, the Aspen Golf and Tennis Club—a municipal course—is an environmentally friendly place. It also has four sets of tees, plentiful ponds and streams, and a fee of only $45 a head.

Climb every mountain: Two hikers in the midst of Aspen's famous peaks. Robert Millman

River Valley Ranch Golf Club (970-963-3625, rvrgolf.com, 303 River Valley Ranch Dr., Snowmass Village) Designed by Jay Morrish, RVR's course has a few holes by the Crystal River, a few in the sage brush and piñons, and the majority laid out in the shadow of surrounding peaks. After 2 PM, you can play all 18 holes for $40.

Snowmass Club (800-525-0710, 970-923-9155, snowmassclub.com, 0239 Snowmass Club Circle, Snowmass Village) A private club with limited public access (call for policies), Snowmass Club opened in 2003 and won numerous awards for its architecture (thanks to designer Jim Engh). There are seven different grasses planted here, and the course undulates through the Snowmass Valley.

Hiking and Backpacking

America Lake After climbing about 2,000 feet through aspen groves, you'll be looking over the Castle Creek Valley to the abandoned town-site of Ashcroft. America Lake is a cutthroat trout spawning area.

Cathedral Lake Over the course of 3 miles, you'll follow Pine Creek to a spectacular cirque, passing below peaks that are close to 14,000 feet. If you're feeling strong and got an early start to avoid afternoon thunderstorms, continue on to Electric Pass (the highest named pass in Colorado, at 13,500 feet) for Maroon Bells views.

Continental Divide at Independence Pass Starting at the pass itself, an 18-mile drive up from Aspen, you can walk through alpine tundra at 13,000 feet.

Conundrum Hot Springs It's almost 9 miles in to this spot, but that doesn't deter the crowds from hiking up for a soak—you'll pass beaver ponds and old avalanche paths along the way.

Josephine Lake This is a great bet if you want to see wildlife—especially in the two open park areas, Henderson and Coffeepot. From the ridge above the lake (which has great fishing), take in views of the Elk Mountains: Sopris, Daly, and Capitol.

New York Creek Trail This one follows its namesake creek past several open meadows and ends up well above timberline, at 12,290 feet.

Weller Lake Just over a mile round trip, this trail is great for stretching your legs and getting a bit off the beaten path: You pass through thick forests and end up at a gemlike lake below a craggy peak.

Horseback Riding

Aspen Wilderness Outfitters (970-922-6600, aspenwilderness.com, 0554 Valley Rd., Carbondale) One-, two-, and three-hour trail rides, pony rides, a petting zoo, weeklong pack trips into the Maroon Valley and Lenado-Woody Creek, and Aspen-to-Crested Butte rides—all originating out of Snowmass Village.

Maroon Bells Lodge & Outfitters (970-920-4679, maroonbellsaspen.com, 3125 Maroon Creek Rd.) With a name like this, it has to be good: This outfitter can take you on breakfast, lunch, dinner, or full-day rides in view of the iconic Maroon Bells, Pyramid Peak, and East Maroon, stopping to nosh on the shores of Maroon Lake and winding through the wilderness. A great two-day option: Ride through the Maroon Bells Wilderness all the way to Crested Butte, spend the night in town, and ride back the next morning. Most Thursday nights, take a sleigh or hay ride and then kick up your heels at a Western-themed dinner dance.

Hot Air Ballooning

Above It All Balloons (800-282-RAFT, blazingadventures.com, 48 Upper Village Mall, Snowmass) After you land, Above It All tells the story of the first balloon flight (way back in 1783), recites a celebratory prayer, and—of course—doles out the champagne.

Unicorn Balloon Company (970-925-5752, unicornballoon.com) Celebrate your float with a champagne (or orange juice) toast and a flight certificate—and bring home a video to prove you really did it. Flights take off all year long.

Hunting

Aspen Outfitting Company (970-925-3406, aspenoutfitting.com, 315 E. Dean St., Aspen) It's all conveniently located in the lobby of the St. Regis Hotel: Three-day pheasant and partridge hunts with country-gourmet meals; two-day dove, blue grouse, goose, and duck hunts; field seminars to learn safe gun handling skills; and advanced wing-shooting clinics.

OutWest Guides (970-963-4688, outwestguides.net, 5585 County Road 3, Marble) OutWest's claim to fame (just check their Web site under the link "Kevin Costner...") was, yes, to provide horses for Costner's 2004 wedding, including staging a team-penning competition for the guests. But this Marble-based outfitter does much more—like lead clients into the Maroon Bells/Snowmass Wilderness in search of trophy mule deer, elk, blue grouse, and ptarmigan.

Mountaineering and Rock Climbing

Aspen Expeditions (970-925-7625, aspenexpeditions.com, 426 S. Spring St., Aspen) The granite rock along Independence Pass ranges in difficulty from total beginner to expert, and Aspen Expeditions leads daily guided trips there in summer. You can also sign up to climb one of the area's 14,0000-foot peaks, some of which are walk-ups (with others much more technical).

Paragliding

Aspen Paragliding (970-925-7625, aspenparagliding.com, 426 S. Spring St., Aspen) Even if you have no experience, you can take flight over Aspen Mountain with a guide—after just a few running steps off a high mountain. (You can also learn how to do it on your own.)

Rafting and Paddling

Aspen Seals (970-618-4569, aspenseals.com) Want something different from a traditional raft trip? Try whitewater sledging with Aspen Seals: This New Zealand sport involves descending rapids on specially designed boogie boards, wearing wetsuit, fins, helmet, and life jacket.

Blazing Adventures (800-282-7238, or 970-923-4544, blazingadventures.com, 48 Upper Village Mall, Snowmass) There's a raft trip for every level on the Roaring Fork: Class II and III on the lower part of the river, Class II and IV on the Upper Roaring Fork, and Class IV and V in a section called the Slaughterhouse. Blazing Paddles also runs trips down the Arkansas and the Colorado.

Rock Gardens Rafting (800-958-6737, rockgardens.com, 1308 CR 129, Glenwood Springs) Based out of Glenwood Springs, Rock Gardens has good options on the Colorado River, including half- and full-day trips through the Shoshone rapids in Glenwood Canyon. Or take an easy evening float trip to a private takeout—and feast on barbecued steak and chicken.

Driving: Scenic Drives and Byways

Castle Creek Road A short out-and-back (that many people bike), this route ends up at the ghost town of Ashcroft and the lovely Pine Creek Cookhouse (see page 33), both in an expansive valley below the Sawatch Range.

Independence Pass to Twin Lakes CO 82 runs right through downtown Aspen, then winds up and down 44 miles through the Sawatch Range to the hamlet of Twin Lakes. The highlight? Crossing the Continental Divide at Independence Pass, at 12,095 feet the highest paved pass in Colorado.

McClure Pass to Paonia From Carbondale (down the Roaring Fork Valley from Aspen), take CO 133 past Redstone over McClure (8,763 feet) through the Elk Mountains and end up in Paonia—which has some good local wineries and organic produce.

SHOPPING

Art Galleries

Aspen Grove Fine Arts (970-925-5151, aspengrovefinearts.com, 525 E. Cooper Ave., Aspen) Contemporary takes on Western scenes, prints from an assistant to Andy Warhol, paintings of Venice that look like color slides, and Baroque-style still lifes: Aspen Grove has a ton of variety and two gallery spaces.

Aspen Potters Inc. Ceramic Gallery (970-925-8726, 231 E. Main St., Aspen) Most of the pottery here—salmon-shaped platters, birch-bark-patterned mugs, aspen-leaf plates— echoes the natural world, and most of the artists are locals.

By Nature Gallery (970-544-0299, bynaturegallery.com, 605 E. Cooper Ave., Aspen) Art and furniture made from fossils, crystals, cobalt, lapis, and wood. By Nature also sells handmade jewelry (silver, turquoise, precious stones) from around the world.

David Floria Gallery (970-544-5705, floriagallery.com, 525 E. Cooper Ave., Aspen) Color prints by Michael Eastman; butterflies by Joseph Scheer; pop art by Alexis Smith; and even original lithographs by Jasper Johns.

Elliott Yeary Gallery (970-429-1111, elliottyeary.com, 419 E. Hyman Ave., Aspen) Though it concentrates on still lifes and landscapes by both national and international artists, Elliott Yeary also procures works by John James Audubon, Matisse, Picasso, Bierstadt, and more.

Galerie Maximillian (970-925-6100, galeriemax.com, 602 E. Cooper Ave., Aspen) Impressionists like Cassatt and Renoir; 20th-century legends like Miró, Matisse, and Chagall; and young and contemporary artists like Hirst and Gosti.

Huntsman Gallery of Fine Art (970-920-1910, huntsmangallery.com, 410 E. Hyman Ave., Aspen) Along with the bronzes of Don Huntsman, this gallery represents 50-plus sculptors and painters of traditional art.

Joel Soroka (970-920-3152, artnet.com/gallery/117155/Joel_Soroka_Gallery.html, 400 E. Hyman Ave., Aspen) An extensive collection of contemporary and vintage photography, with everything from Henri Cartier-Bresson and Annie Leibovitz to Man Ray and Dorothea Lange.

Magidson Fine Art (970-920-1001, magidson.com, 525 E. Cooper Ave., Aspen) A constantly rotating roster of new artists, a big stable of contemporary stalwarts, and occasional exhibitions of Annie Leibovitz photos and Marc Chagall paintings.

Royal Street Fine Art (970-920-3371, royalstreetfineart.com, 205 S. Mill St., Unit 211, Aspen) One of the most unusual kinds of artwork available at Royal Street: collage sculptures made of musical instruments and found objects. (They also sell landscape paintings, bronzes, and contemporary oils.)

Sardella Fine Art (970-925-9044, sardellafineart.com, 525 E. Cooper Ave., Aspen) Glass-blowing rock star Dale Chihuly, along with contemporary artists like Greg Gummersall, Allison Stewart, William Morris, James Shay, and Kathleen Loe.

Valley Fine Art (970-920-9193, valleyfineart.com, 414 E. Hyman Ave., Aspen) Celebrating the rich sepia-toned photos of Edward Curtis—who captured the haunting and moving faces of disappearing Native American cultures—Valley Fine Art is a must-stop, whether you're in the market or not.

Vintage Ski World (970-925-9195, vintage-aspen.com, 416 E. Cooper Ave., Aspen) If you're hunting for antique wooden skis, retro ski posters, boots, snowshoes, sleds, pins, books, or patches, you can find them all here.

Wind River Gallery (970-925-3919, windrivergallery.com, 505 E. Hyman Ave., Aspen) The place to go if you're seeking a bronze sculpture of a galloping bronc, a sleeping fawn, a noble Native American—or a painted depiction of local mountains and wildlife.

Books
Aspen Book Store (970-925-7427, 665 E. Durant Ave., Aspen) This small shop is just off the lobby of the Little Nell and sells magazines, local outdoor guides, cookbooks, fiction, and nonfiction.

Explore Booksellers (970-925-5338, explorebooksellers.com, 221 E. Main St., Aspen) Over 28,000 titles are in stock at this cozy local favorite, located in an unassuming house on Main. The bistro upstairs serves good veggie fare—tempeh satay, braised tofu, avocado omelets, and rice pudding topped with caramelized apples.

Outdoor Gear
Ute Mountaineer (970-925-2849, utemountaineer.com, 308 S. Mill St., Aspen) This local institution has been in business since 1977 and has the best-informed employees in the valley, whether you want to talk climbing, snowshoeing, hut trips, backcountry skiing routes, or scenic hikes. They sell everything from GPS units to luggage to Gore-Tex.

Western Clothing and Furs

Aspen Fur and Shearling (970-925-3300, 400 E. Cooper Ave., Aspen) A huge selection of coats in all styles, with good sales. If you're serious about your fur, you can even make an appointment.

Dennis Basso (970-925-4499, 645 E. Durant Ave., Aspen) A branch of the Madison Avenue store—which has one of the biggest fur selections in the world—this outpost in the Little Nell Hotel sells everything from the most sporty to the most luxurious.

Kemo Sabe (970-925-7878, kemosabe.com, 434 E. Cooper Ave., Aspen) Big belt buckles, big hats, beautiful boots in a rainbow of colors, snap-front shirts, and leather belts: This classy and fun store is the best place in town to walk away with a cowboy souvenir from your trip out West.

Mark Richards (970-544-6780, markrichardsaspen.com, 427 E. Cooper Ave., Aspen) If you're looking for European ankle-length fur, knitted fur, shearling, and leatherwear in one place, Mark Richards won't disappoint.

Pitkin County Dry Goods (970-925-1681, 520 E. Cooper Ave., Aspen) Since 1969, this shop has offered a good selection of jeans, shearling and leather jackets, and even free homemade fudge to fuel your shopping fire.

SEASONAL EVENTS

January: Winter X Games (970-925-1220, stayaspensnowmass.com) The top event in winter action sports, X Games turns Aspen into a huge four-day party—and showcases the best of halfpipe, slopestyle, and big-air skiing and snowboarding.

January: Wintersköl (970-925-1940) This festival has been running for 50-plus years and was founded to celebrate Aspen's Nordic heritage—with crazy canine fashion shows, snow-sculpting contests, uphill races, and the ubiquitous torchlight parade.

January: Gay/Lesbian Ski Week (970-925-1220, gayskiweek.com) For 30 years running, Aspen has hosted seven days of club nights, poker parties, group skiing, banquets, comedy nights, and downhill costume races—funding various organizations like the National Center for Lesbian Rights.

March: HBO Comedy Festival (866-350-3369, hbocomedyfestival.com) Here's a perfect example of why Aspen is so great: This event is the most prestigious comedy gathering in the country and has drawn the likes of Dave Chappelle, Billy Crystal, Robin Williams, Ellen DeGeneres, Jerry Seinfeld, Steve Martin, Chris Rock, Jack Black, and George Carlin.

April: Aspen Shortsfest (970-925-6882, aspenfilm.org) About 60 short films—comedies, documentaries, animations—are chosen from 2,000-plus entries, then juried by luminaries like Alexander Payne (*Sideways*) and Jason Reitman (*Thank You For Smoking*).

May: Ride for the Pass (970-429-2093, independencepass.org) An annual fundraiser for the Independence Pass Foundation, this bike ride (or race, if you're feeling strong) grinds up to the top of the 12,000-foot pass.

June: Aspen Summer Words (970-925-3122, aspenwriters.org) A weeklong literary festival (and just one of the events that the Aspen Writers' Foundation puts on every year),

Summer Words mixes morning workshops in fiction and nonfiction with afternoon lectures, panels, and discussions. Past themes have included Irish writers and writing about the West.

June–August: Aspen Music Festival and School (970-925-9042, aspenmusicfestival .com) A world-class tradition since the 1950s, this two-month-long festival draws the country's most talented musicians and the world's top students—and runs daily outdoor performances of both modern and well-known works.

June: Aspen FOOD & WINE Classic (970-925-9000, foodandwine.com/classic) With 5,000 attendees, 80 cooking demos and wine seminars, thousands of wines decanted, and star chefs like Emeril Lagasse, Bobby Flay, and Mario Batali, this magazine-sponsored event gives you a chance to learn from the world's best.

June: Chili Pepper and Brewfest (800-766-9627, snowmasschiliandbrew.com) A three-day event with two International Chili Society–sanctioned cook-offs (who knew they had to be sanctioned?), tastings, music, and microbrews.

June–September: Aspen Theater in the Park (970-925-9313, theatreaspen.org) In this celebration of contemporary plays, you can choose between everything from *Love, Janis* to *Dinner With Friends* to world premieres like *Seemed like A Good Idea At The Time*, by local Andrew Kole.

July: Aspen Dance Festival (877-326-2464, aspensantafeballet.com) A five-week summer series featuring contemporary dance, the Aspen Dance Festival is put on by the Aspen Santa Fe Ballet, a local 10-dancer group.

July: Snowmass Wellness Experience (800-SNOWMASS, snowmassvillage.com) The New Age settles into Snowmass for a four-day smorgasbord of yoga workshops, healthy cooking seminars, hypnosis, and exercise classes, along with appearances from Deepak Chopra and Joan Borysenko.

July: Aspen Ideas Festival (970-925-7010, aspeninstitute.com) A collection of bright minds and eager listeners, the annual Ideas Festival brings in politicians, professors, ambassadors, musicians, media types, and authors in the name of intellectual exchange. Katie Couric, Bruce Babbitt, Nora Ephron, Dianne Feinstein, Bernard Henri-Levy, and Madeleine Albright have all recently attended.

August: Aspen High Country Triathlon and Duathlon (970-544-4100, aspenrecreation.com) This sprint (short-course) event is perfect for triathlon newbies. The duathlon (2-mile run, 17-mile bike, and 4-mile run) is even better—if, of course, you don't like to swim.

September: Jazz Aspen Snowmass (970-920-4996, jazzaspen.com) With a smaller rendition in June and the big daddy over Labor Day weekend, JAS has featured Wynton Marsalis, Diana Krall, Neil Young, Sheryl Crow, David Byrne, Tom Petty, and more—all in tents or outdoor venues with views of the surrounding peaks.

September: MotherLode Volleyball Classic (motherlodevolleyball.com) This is the number-one rated Pro-Am event in North America—with 18 divisions of play, seven sites, and 700 teams, not to mention free admission.

September: Aspen Filmfest (970-925-6882, aspenfilm.org) Aspen's take on mountain-town movies has been going strong for almost 30 years. Recent attendees have included Kathy Bates, Rob Reiner, Harrison Ford, and Felicity Huffman, and the program includes independent and documentary films about everything from evangelical Christians to Sudanese refugees to dysfunctional relationships.

September: Aspen Cocktail Classic (aspenchamber.com) Local bartenders from watering holes like Elevation, Red Onion, Belly Up, and Ajax Tavern create new cocktails, competing to win the coveted "Official Drink of Aspen" title. Past winners? The Aspen Sugar Daddy (from the Range restaurant), Aspenlicious (from Bar Aspen), and Aspen Dream (from the Cantina).

October: John Denver Week (john-denver.org) If you're really into J. D., join the World Family of John Denver to bond over his music, ideas, and beliefs.

December: Storm the Stars Uphill Race (970-925-1220) Starting at the Little Nell, right near the Aspen Mountain gondola, and climbing 3,000 feet to the mountain restaurant Sundeck (where there's live music, food, and beer), this uphill ski race (competitors use AT or telemark skis with climbing skins) kicks off the season. Mortals can ride the gondola up instead.

NUTS AND BOLTS

Getting Here
You can actually get very good deals for flights into the **Aspen/Pitkin County Airport**, which is located just a few minutes outside of downtown Aspen (it's actually between Aspen and Snowmass on CO 82). There's direct service from Denver, Chicago, San Francisco, Los Angeles, Minneapolis, Memphis, and Phoenix. From the airport, there are several limo and shuttle services: **High Mountain Taxi** (970-925-8294), **Aspen Limo** (970-920-5466, aspenlimo.com), **Snow Limo** (970-544-6475), and **Aspen Snowmass Limousine and Airport Express** (970-925-5549).

If you fly into Denver, you can either drive (check Colorado road conditions at cotrip.org or 303-639-1111 and local conditions at 970-920-5454) or take **Colorado Mountain Express** (cmex.com, 800-525-6363), a van service which can cost you close to $100 each way. It's about 220 miles via I-70 through Glenwood Springs, and a good 45 minutes shorter if you drive over Independence Pass, which is closed in winter.

Ambulance/Fire/Police/Search and Rescue
For emergencies, of course, dial 911. For police assistance that doesn't require an emergency response, contact the number listed below for the city closest to your present location.

Aspen Police Department: 970-920-5400

Pitkin County Sheriff: 970-920-5310

Snowmass Police Department: 970-923-5330

Avalanche Reports
Colorado Avalanche Information Center: 970-920-1664 (Aspen hotline), geosurvey
.state.co.us/avalanche or avalanche-center.org

Roaring Fork Avalanche Center: 970-544-1058, rfavalanche.org

Hospitals and Emergency Medical Services
Aspen Valley Hospital: 970-925-1120, 0401 Castle Creek Rd., Aspen

Snowmass Clinic: 970-923-2068, 111 Trauma Lane, Snowmass Village

Valley View Hospital: 970-945-6535, vvh.org, 1906 Blake Ave., Glenwood Springs

Libraries
Basalt Regional Library District: 970-927-4311, basaltrld.org, 99 Midland Ave., Basalt

Pitkin County Library: 970-925-4025, www.pitcolib.org, 120 N. Mill St., Aspen

Media

Newspapers and Magazines
Aspen Daily News: 970-925-6445, aspendailynews.com, 517 E. Hopkins Ave., Aspen, CO
81611

Aspen magazine: 970-920-4040, aspenmagazine.com, 720 E. Durant Ave., Suite E8,
Aspen, CO 81611

Aspen Peak magazine: 970-429-1215, aspenpeak-magazine.com, 608 E. Hyman Ave., 2nd
Floor, Aspen, CO 81611

Aspen Sojourner: 970-925-7809, aspensojourner.com, 411 E. Main St., Suite 205, Aspen, CO
81611

The Aspen Times: 970-925-3414, aspentimes.com, 310 E. Main St., Aspen, CO 81611

Radio
KAJX 91.5: 970-925-6445, kajx.org. NPR and local news.

KPVW 107.1: 888-874-2656. Spanish radio.

KSPN 103.1: 970-925-5776, kspnradio.com. A "Triple A" (Adult Album Alternative) station with news and sports.

KSNO 103.9: 303-949-0140. Smooth jazz.

Public Transportation
The **Roaring Fork Transportation Authority** (970-925-8484) has free shuttle service all
around Aspen from 6:30 AM to 2:15 AM, with a hub at Rubey Park (430 E. Durant Ave.) that
sends buses to Aspen Highlands, Buttermilk, and Snowmass—as well as all the way down
the valley to Glenwood Springs. Buses between Rubey Park and the airport are also free.
The **Snowmass Village Shuttle** (970-923-2543) tools around the Village.

Ranger Stations

Aspen Ranger District: 970-925-3445, 806 W. Hallam Ave., Aspen

Sporis Ranger District: 970-963-2266, 620 Main St., Carbondale

Tourist Information

Aspen Chamber Resort Association: 970-925-1940, aspenchamber.org, 425 Rio Grande Place, Aspen

The Aspen Skiing Company: 800-525-6200, 970-925-1220, aspensnowmass.com

Basalt Chamber of Commerce: 970-927-4031, basaltchamber.com

Snowmass Village Resort Association: 800-SNOWMASS, snowmassvillage.com, snowmassmeetings.com, 16 Kearns Rd., Unit 104, Snowmass

A typical day on Main Street in downtown Breckenridge: bundling up, strolling, and shopping.
Jeff Scroggins

2

BRECKENRIDGE

The Heart of Summit County

Breckenridge is one of the most popular mountain towns in Colorado—where else can you find 250 structures on the National Register of Historic Places, lodging capacity for 25,000 people, 300 days of sunshine a year, over 100 restaurants, charming Victorian houses, a Gold Medal river (the Blue) that runs through town, and chairlifts that reach up to almost 13,000 feet? It's so popular, in fact, that winter weekends can find the place overrun with ski-schoolers, Denver day-trippers, post-grad burger flippers on their mornings off, pro-snowboarders-in-training, families flocking from condos, and college students on pub crawls. Overrun, for the most part, in a dynamic and wonderful way: You get the sense that Breck is *happening*.

The Blue River Valley was one of the first places in the state to get gold fever. The shiny stuff was first discovered in 1859, and, in the usual mining-town pattern, a bar—the Gold Pan Saloon—opened its doors soon after (they're still open, by the way). Just a year later, 8,000 miners had set up shop. General George E. Spencer, one of the first town builders, named the settlement after John Cabell Breckinridge, the vice president to James Buchanan, hoping to flatter the government into giving Breck a post office. It worked, and the first P.O. between the Continental Divide and Salt Lake City was established. But the original name didn't last long: The spelling was changed to Breckenridge after the independent town found out that their namesake opposed Lincoln's Civil War policy.

According to *The Denver Post*, Breck was known as the mining area that "turned out more gold with less work than any other camp in Colorado." The town's fame spread when a 13.5-pound gold nugget—dubbed Tom's Baby, after miner Tom Groves—was unearthed at the Fuller Placer Mine. But hindsight reveals another claim to fame: Breck was home to Methodist preacher Father John L. Dyer, the so-called "Snowshoe Itinerant," who carried mail, walked, and skied his way over passes and down valleys, spreading the gospel. Some maintain he was the first skier in the United States (but, unfortunately for proud locals, it isn't true).

Unlike some other mining towns, Breck went out with a whimper, not a bang. Gold, silver, lead, and zinc mining gradually slowed down, the population dwindled all the way down to 250, buildings were abandoned, huge dredging boats ruined the Blue River, fires tore through town, and in 1930 Breckenridge was left off maps of the United States—the closest it came to becoming a true ghost town. Speaking of maps, in 1936, residents learned retroactively that they hadn't been included in maps of the Louisiana Purchase—

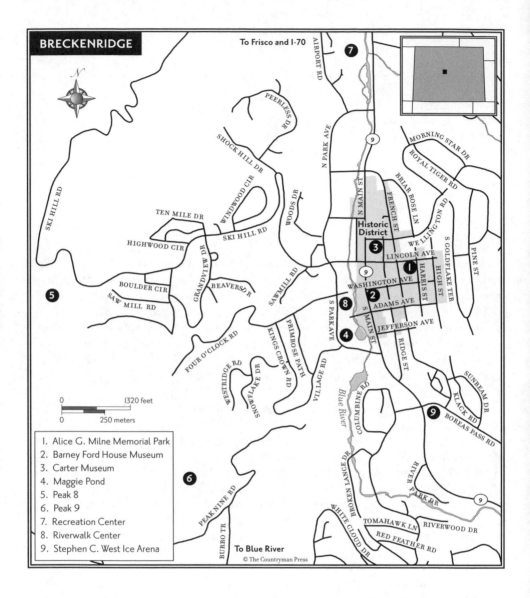

Map legend:

1. Alice G. Milne Memorial Park
2. Barney Ford House Museum
3. Carter Museum
4. Maggie Pond
5. Peak 8
6. Peak 9
7. Recreation Center
8. Riverwalk Center
9. Stephen C. West Ice Arena

© The Countryman Press

there was a missing 90-by-30-mile swath of land back when things were drawn up, so Governor Edwin C. Johnson took it upon himself to declare that Breck could be an "independent kingdom" for three days a year. Since then, "The Little Kingdom of Breckenridge" has been celebrated every August.

By the time the clock turned past 1960, fewer than 400 people called the Kingdom home, but change came almost overnight when the Kansas-based Rounds and Porter Lumber Company got a permit to build a ski area (they started on Peak 8, and now the area also includes 6, 7, 9, and 10). After a few months, 17,000 people had already paid the Blue River Valley a visit. And when the Eisenhower Tunnel opened in 1971—boring I-70 through the Continental Divide and reducing the drive time from Denver to an hour and a half—Breck's popularity was sealed.

Just a few of Breckenridge's original buildings. |Jeff Scroggins

Okay, so maybe it helped that the ski area installed the world's first high-speed quad in 1981 and decided to allow snowboarding way back in 1984. Or maybe it's the debauchery that is Ullr Fest, the annual celebration of the Norse god of snow—who, according to lore, blesses the area with heaps of snow. Or the world-class mountain biking and hiking trails. Or the number of beers available at Downstairs at Eric's. Whatever it is, Breck is consistently one of the most-visited resorts in the U.S.—if not the most visited. A million and a half people can't be wrong.

LODGING

BRECKENRIDGE

Allaire Timbers Inn
Innkeepers: Sue Carlsen and Kendra Hall
800-624-4904, 970-453-7530
allairetimbers.com
allaire@colorado.net
9511 S. Main St., Breckenridge
Price Range: $145–$390, including
    breakfast
Credit Cards: AE, D, MC, V
Children: 13 and older

Pets: N
Handicap Accessible: Y

The innkeepers here have taken the "timbers" part of Allaire Timbers to heart: Wherever you are in this sprawling, 10-room, lodge-size cabin, you'll find lodgepole pine. The king beds are made sturdy pine logs; the mantels are log beams set into river rock chimneys; the gable-roofed great room is bright with peeled wood and softened with Navajo carpets. Each room has a private bath (decorated with hand-painted tiles) and a private deck

The rustic entrance to the Barn on the River Bed and Breakfast in Breckenridge.   Evelyn Spence

with mountain views. The rooms come with thick robes and socklike slippers for lounging around; televisions and CD players; and homey touches like teddy bears. Post-slopes, catch glimpses of the Ten Mile Range from the outdoor hot tub or nibble on veggies, dips, crackers, and cheese during "social hour." Guests tuck into fruit crepes, mushroom quiches, and lofty soufflés for breakfast, which is served near the enormous picture windows.

✪ Barn on the River Bed and Breakfast
Innkeepers: Fred Kinat and Diane Jaymes
800-795-2975, 970-453-2975
breckenridge-inn.com
bnb@colorado.net
303B N. Main St., Breckenridge
Price Range: $149–$289, including
    breakfast
Credit Cards: AE, D, MC, V
Children: Y, 10 and older
Pets: N
Handicap Accessible: N

Just off Main Street and hidden behind a few Victorian houses, the timber-frame Barn, built in 1998, has the best of both worlds—it's steps away from all the action, but it's also a tranquil and charming retreat. With just five rooms, each with private balconies or patios and rocking chairs that look right over the Blue River, it's nothing if not cozy and romantic. Four of the rooms have wood-burning fireplaces, which doesn't hurt the atmosphere—nor do antique beds with eight pillows apiece, robes, fleece sockies, happy-hour wine and cheese, and a garden path right down to the water. The so-called "loafing room" is teeming with games, books, magazines, and trinkets. On powder days, Fred and Diane forgo the usual candlelight breakfast of blueberry pancakes, egg soufflés, and spinach quiches in favor of plain cold cereal—it gives everyone a better chance to get first tracks.

Beaver Run Resort
800-525-2253, 970-453-6000
beaverrun.com
620 Village Rd., Breckenridge
Price Range: $90–$1,050
Credit Cards: AE, D, MC, V
Children: Y
Pets: N
Handicap Accessible: Y

An enormous modern-ish building right across the street from the Beaver Run Superchair, Beaver Run is probably the most convenient ski-in/ski-out lodge in town: You can walk over a sky bridge straight into the day lodge, where Tiff's nightclub meets the Kinderhut day care—or ski straight to the bottom of the Quicksilver six-person lift (some people just call it the six-pack). There are 500 places to stay here—hotel rooms, studios with complete kitchens, four-bedroom suites that are big enough for two families, and executive quarters with seven queen beds. And the stats keep going: two heated pools, eight hot tubs, a tennis court, an arcade, a steam room, and in-house massage services. For the family carnivores, Spencer's, the hotel restaurant, has an all-you-can-eat prime rib every night.

Evans House
Innkeepers: Peter and Georgette Contos
970-453-5509
coloradoevanshouse.com
evans15@mindspring.com
102 S. French St., Breckenridge
Price Range: $73–$150
Credit Cards: AE, D, MC, V
Children: Y
Pets: N
Handicap Accessible: N

A cute historic home with a prime location on French Street, the Evans House has five rooms, each dedicated to a different person or period in Breckenridge's history. The

10th Mountain Room has white wicker furniture, bright bedspreads and curtains, and a claw-foot tub. The Itinerant Suite has a big pine bed, blond wood furniture, and a handmade quilt. The Colorado room has wood-paneled walls and ceilings, a bed with posts like giant chess pawns, and Victorian chairs and lamps. The common room is comfortably cluttered—soft couches with big pillows, plants, trophies—and it's where the morning crepes, apple cinnamon french toast, and belgian waffles are served. As of press time, the house was for sale; be sure to check their Web site before you get your heart set on this charmer.

Fireside Inn

Innkeepers: Niki and Andy Harris
970-453-6456
firesideinn.com
info@firesideinn.com
114 N. French St., Breckenridge
Price Range: Dorm rooms $26–$38 per
    person, breakfast not included; private
    rooms $76–$175, including breakfast
Credit Cards: MC, V
Children: Y
Pets: N
Handicap Accessible: Y

The Fireside mixes cozy B&B with dirt-cheap hostel, giving it a laid-back, youthful vibe (and great prices) just a few blocks off the main drag. The most expensive room, the Brandywine Suite, comes with a king bed, antique dresser and wardrobe, sitting area, and exclusive use of the hot tub every evening from 7:30 to 9. The most wallet-friendly option? A bed in the 10-person attic, with shared bathrooms, living room with fireplace, and ski storage. In general, the decor is homey and busy—pink-flowered wallpaper matched with plaid bedspreads, patterned quilts with patterned chairs—but some of the touches are charming: take, for example, the pay phone with

an old ski lift chair as a seat. Breakfast, which comes with B&B rooms and is available to dorm-roomers for a small charge, is usually a hearty mix of eggs, french toast, pancakes, and oatmeal.

✪ Four Peaks Inn

Innkeepers: Shannon and J. J. Bosgraaf
970-453-3813
fourpeaksinn.com
reservations@fourpeaksinn.com
407 S. Ridge St., Breckenridge
Price Range: $109–$210, including
    breakfast
Credit Cards: MC, V
Children: Y
Pets: N
Handicap Accessible: Y

The front section of the Four Peaks is historic; built way back in 1880, it has the original crown molding, the original creaks in the wood floors, and antique period furniture. The back end is much more modern (added in 1997), with bigger bathrooms, brighter paint, king beds, and a hot tub overlooking the ski resort. In fact, when excavators went to work on the addition, they found pre-1920 bottles on-site. The husband-and-wife innkeepers, who lived in Europe for four years and had 17-odd years of IT consulting experience between them, decided to make a change—having only a love for cooking and hosting friends. That love shows: Breakfast specialties include banana streusel french toast with amaretto sauce, gingerbread waffles, and spinach and sausage frittata—all served in the formal dining room. They'll even concoct a romantic in-house dinner if you request it—just tell them what you're craving. Got aches and pains? Let Shannon give you a rejuvenating reflexology massage, or let her arrange a spa treatment—for men and women both.

Grand Timber Lodge

888-783-8883
grandtimber.com
customerservice@grandtimber.com
75 Snowflake Dr., Breckenridge
Price Range: $135–$895
Credit Cards: AE, D, MC, V
Children: Y
Pets: N
Handicap Accessible: Y

An aptly named timber frame complex conveniently placed in between Peaks 8 and 9,
Grand Timber is a mega-resort that holds
on to an intimate feeling. You get spinning
classes, cocktail hours, group hikes, teen
poker nights, and movie nights, all of which
bring guests together and foster the sense
of community you might expect in a smaller
property. You also get body wraps and anti-
aging treatments at the Grand Victorian
spa; a gym, two indoor/outdoor pools, and
six hot tubs; and an in-house, family-
friendly restaurant that serves chicken in
pepper cream sauce, New York strips,
turkey and brie sandwiches, and potato
skins stuffed with Boursin. But the layout
doesn't overwhelm—it feels more like a
classy outdoorsy campus. The digs—from
studios that sleep four (tightly) to three-
bedroom condos with dining service for 10
and a full washer and dryer—are mountain-
lodge themed without being over the top
(Navajo-patterned pillows, wrought-iron
lamps, granite countertops, framed posters
of painted landscapes).

Hunt Placer Inn

Innkeepers: Trip and Kelly Butler
800-472-1430, 970-453-7573
huntplacerinn.com
info@huntplacerinn.com
275 Ski Hill Rd., Breckenridge
Price Range: $149–$270
Credit Cards: AE, D, MC, V
Children: Y, 12 and older

Pets: Y—one room available
Handicap Accessible: Y

Last year, Breckenridge Ski Area finally
built a "ski-way"—a road for skiers to get
back to their condos, cars, and second
homes—that passes right by the three-
story, Bavarian-chic Hunt Placer, making it
one of the most convenient bed and breakfasts in town. And each time you click out of
your bindings, you'll be met with après-ski
treats like smoked trout mousse, chocolate
caramel cake, or straight-out-of-the-oven
cookies. Breakfast is just as fresh and rich:
Think orange-cinnamon french toast soufflé with caramel sauce and just-squeezed
OJ. Every one of the eight rooms has a private balcony with mountain views, and the
decor is tastefully varied: dark green walls,
period walnut furniture, and flowered curtains in the Brittania suite; lodgepole pine
furniture, Santa Fe–style upholstery, and
terra cotta tiles in the corner Southwest
suite; and wicker chairs, plaid bedspreads,
and cheerful sky-blue curtains in the
Country Cottage room.

Little Mountain Lodge

Innkeeper: Linda Buchanan
800-468-7707, 970-453-1969
littlemountainlodge.com
lml@colorado.net
98 Sunbeam Dr., Breckenridge
Price Range: $140–$270, including
    breakfast
Credit Cards: AE, D, MC, V
Children: Y
Pets: N
Handicap Accessible: N

Just past town on the road up to the Lodge
and Spa (see below), Little Mountain is like
a grand cabin. The fireplace reaches up to a
three-story-high ceiling; moose and bison
trophies look down from the walls; and
Native American tapestries slouch over

Hunting lodge meets Colorado—cozy at the Little Mountain Lodge in Breckenridge. Evelyn Spence

leather couches and easy chairs. End tables resemble leather drums; some chairs are upholstered in brown-and-white cow spots. The artwork has a Western theme (horses, vast landscapes, hunting), complemented by historic black-and-white photos. Each room is different, but they all fit in with the feeling: a log four-poster and wool blanket in the Indian Point Suite, a fishing bedspread and fly-fishing memorabilia in Wolf Creek, and a twig bed with antique side tables and intricately carved lamp stands in the Trail Through Time. Want to take a walk outside or give your toes a break from ski boots? Just borrow Little Mountain's snowboots or slippers.

✪ The Lodge and Spa at Breckenridge

800-736-1607, 970-453-9300
thelodgeatbreck.com
reservations@thelodgeatbreck.com
112 Overlook Dr., Breckenridge
Price Range: $79–$508, including breakfast
Credit Cards: AE, D, MC, V
Children: Y
Pets: N
Handicap Accessible: Y

The panoramas alone at The Lodge and Spa are worth the price of admission, and worth the winding drive up Boreas Pass Road. The hotel looks over the entire town of Breckenridge and the spread of the ski area beyond, framing every season through enormous windows. Accommodations range from standard, forest-view rooms with lodgepole accents, feather duvets, and slatted shutters to oversize corner suites with king poster beds, kitchenettes, and fireplaces. An in-house spa and athletic club offers everything from aloe-cucumber wraps to earth stone massages to seaweed-herb salt glows, plus an indoor pool, cardio equipment, steam room, sauna, and outdoor hot tub. There's a great restaurant in-house (see Top of the World in "Dining," page 74) with views to match. Down in the lobby, floor-to-ceiling bookshelves display Western antiques, iron railings resemble aspen branches, and the hardwood floors are made warm with Najavo-print rugs in bright red tones. In short, the whole place is awash in high-mountain light, and it's one of Breck's most indulgent crash pads.

Mountain Thunder Lodge

888-268-8376, 970-547-5650
mountainthunderlodge.com
breckenridgelodging@vailresorts.com
50 Mountain Thunder Dr., Breckenridge
Price Range: $130–$780
Credit Cards: AE, D, MC, V

Children: Y
Pets: N
Handicap Accessible: Y

Of all the big hotel-residence-condo combos in Breck, Mountain Thunder is probably the newest—and the classiest: It has gotten luxurious, understated mountain-lodge decor down to an art. And that means rough-sawn timber exteriors and cedar accents; moss rock fireplaces in every unit; granite countertops in the kitchenettes; slate floors in the bathrooms; and balconies. There's all the service of a big hotel, too: valet, ski storage, multiple hot tubs, a brand-new gym, an outdoor pool, and a playground. It's not to say that the Lodge is oozing character—it's just too new for that. But with a five-minute walk to Main Street, a back door that opens to the Skyway Skiway, and a good DVD selection, who really needs character?

Wayside Inn
Innkeeper: Tom Gleason
800-927-7669, 970-453-5540
breckenridgewaysideinn.com
wayside@breckenridgewaysideinn.com
165 Tiger Rd., Breckenridge
Price Range: $40–$105, including breakfast
    in winter
Credit Cards: MC, V
Children: Y
Pets: Y
Handicap Accessible: N

Are you looking to plan a Breckenridge ski weekend and not break the bank? Start with a room at Tom Gleason's Wayside, where that $105 price above gets you a room that sleeps six. In the high season. Of course, rock-bottom prices mean basic rooms, but along with being spare, they're clean, bright, and even have pine beds. Bo, the resident golden retriever, tends to hang out

The Lodge and Spa at Breckenridge sits atop its own hill, with a commanding view of Breckenridge. Evelyn Spence

in front of the enormous stone fireplace while guests grab free coffee, muffins, and donuts before heading out to ski. If it's your first time to Breck in winter, Gleason himself—a longtime local—will click into his own skis and take you on a personal tour of his favorite parts of the mountain.

FARTHER AFIELD

Galena Street Mountain Inn
Innkeeper: Tammy Henry-Smith
800-248-9138, 970-668-3224
galenastreet.com
galenast@aol.com
First Ave. and Galena St., Frisco
Price Range: $89–$199
Credit Cards: AE, D, MC, V
Children: Y
Pets: N
Handicap Accessible: Y

If possible, book the King Tower at this Victorian gem of a B&B: The (naturally) four-poster king-size bed is piled high with Scandia down, and the airy and tastefully decorated room is actually a two-story turret with 270-degree views. If you can't get the King Tower, you'll still survive: Every one of Galena Street's other dozen rooms has Mission-style furniture, bright and clean colors, and lots of space. Everything about the place makes you feel at home, whether it's the built-in bookshelves and crackling fire in the living room, the house-made granola packed with fresh fruit and nuts, the hot tub, the comfy window seats, the fresh bread, the midnight snacks, or the big, secluded deck.

Guest Ranches

Aspen Canyon Ranch
Hosts: Steve and Deb Roderick
800-321-1357, 970-725-3600
aspencanyon.com
acr@rckymtnhi.com
13206 County Road 3, Star Route, Parshall

Price Range: $1,600 a week for adults;
$850–$1,100 for kids
Credit Cards: D, MC, V
Children: Y
Pets: N
Handicap Accessible: Y

Though a charmingly scant 40 people can stay at Aspen Canyon at any one time, it doesn't even feel like that many are there: Each family gets a private log cabin with covered porch, stone fireplace, gurgling river sounds, and log furniture. The group dynamics are saved for meals, all served in a main log lodge with bench seats, green tablecloths, checkered napkins, and grub like chess pie, sausage and egg casserole, barbecue ribs, and pot roast; each week ends with a cookout for the kids and a candlelight dinner for the adults. In fact, sometimes it feels like a better version of summer camp: Wranglers here create a full and rich experience for all ages, with campfires, s'mores, cowboy poetry, singing, archery, rodeos, arts and crafts, and line dancing.

DINING

Restaurants

BRECKENRIDGE

Blue Moose Restaurant
970-453-4859
540 S. Main St., Breckenridge
Meals Served: B, L
Price Range: $4.50–$10.95
Full bar: N
Reservations: N
Credit Cards: MC, V
Handicap Accessible: Y

To load up for a long day on the hill, people head over to the Moose for enormous breakfasts starting at 7 AM. Don't expect anything fancy, although the rosti (a potato and scallion patty topped with eggs) is creative. Fluffy whole wheat pancakes are made with a touch of vanilla, and french toast is packed with pecans and raisins. Think you're tough? Try to down The Boss, a top sirloin steak with two buttermilk pancakes and two eggs, or the ham and brie four-egg omelet.

Blue River Bistro

970-453-6974
blueriverbistro.com
305 N. Main St., Breckenridge
Meals Served: L, D
Price Range: Appetizers $7.25–$15.75,
    entrées $13.75–$29
Full bar: Y
Reservations: Y
Credit Cards: AE, D, MC, V
Handicap Accessible: Y

If Giampetro (see below, page 73) is home-style Italian, then Blue River is its upscale counterpart: For one, the bar stays open until 2 AM, and it offers 75 different martinis: apple, watermelon, raspberry, "Jolly Rancher," "Anti-Freeze," "Snickers," "Chocolate Monkey," and the list goes on. The walls are decorated with modern art, the dishware is colorful, and live music is scheduled every Friday and Saturday night—often Latin or Brazilian in flavor. Most people start with an order of killer calamari and continue on to one of the fresh pasta entrées: penne with rock shrimp, fettuccine with artichoke hearts and feta, or linguine with basil and cilantro pesto. The pistachio-encrusted salmon and Cajun flatiron steak are also popular.

Breckenridge Brewery

970-453-1550
breckenridgebrewery.com
600 S. Main St., Breckenridge
Meals Served: L, D
Price Range: $9–$20

Full bar: Y
Reservations: N
Credit Cards: AE, D, MC, V
Handicap Accessible: Y

Here's a place that can smooth the transition from "going out to dinner" to just plain "going out"—the Breck Brewery, with worn wood floors, silver casks, and two floors' worth of seating, serves its microbrews, like Avalanche Ale, Oatmeal Stout, Summerbright, and Christmas Ale, until 2 AM. Hungry? Try some ale-battered fish and chips, a cowboy steak (marinated in oatmeal stout), pork tamales, or artichoke dip—with a heap of mashed potatoes or a cord of skin-on French fries on the side. Opened in 1990, the company now churns out 30,000 barrels of beer a year.

Briar Rose Restaurant

970-453-9948
109 Lincoln Ave., Breckenridge
Meals Served: D
Price Range: Appetizers $6–$10, entrées
    $15 and up
Full bar: Y
Reservations: Y
Credit Cards: AE, D, MC, V
Handicap Accessible: Y

Entering the bright pink–painted, leaded-glass-windowed Briar Rose is a little bit like taking a step back in time—the walls are hung with classical paintings and historic photos of Breckenridge, the back bar is 100 years old and decorated with big-game trophies and a diamond-dust mirror, and the place was named after the Briar Rose Silver Mine up on Peak 10. Back in the day, it was a boarding house for miners, and it feels comfortably faded around the edges. The game dishes—elk, caribou, ostrich, and buffalo—are top-notch, as are the starters (baked escargot, wild game sausage). Everything comes with soup or salad, choice of starch, veggies, and warm bread.

✪ Café Alpine

970-453-8218
cafealpine.com
106 E. Adams Ave., Breckenridge
Meals Served: D; patio opens at 3 PM in
    summertime for tapas and wine
Price Range: Tapas $7.50–$11, entrées
    $25–40
Full bar: Y
Reservations: Y
Credit Cards: AE, D, MC, V
Handicap Accessible: Y

Thanks to the creativity of chef-owner
Keith Mahoney, the menu at Café Alpine
changes each day—featuring whatever is
local, seasonal, and fresh. The seating in
this historic home is on three levels,
including an attic room that seats 25 and a
second-floor tapas bar that serves a baked
crock of brie with drunken pear preserves,
a wild mushroom and bleu cheese flan, and
a hearty lump of crabmeat green chili.
Entrées could be anything from green
tea–smoked chicken breast, roasted leek
and duck confit crepes, or Creole-seared
soft-shell crabs with jambalaya risotto.
Come summer, you can take a leisurely
lunch of soup, salad, and sandwich on a
patio surrounded by wildflowers.

✪ The Cellar

970-453-4777
thecellarwine.com
info@thecellarwine.com
200 S. Ridge St., Breckenridge
Meals Served: D
Price Range: $8–$15 for small plates
Full bar: Y
Reservations: Y
Credit Cards: AE, D, MC, V
Handicap Accessible: N

From the outside, The Cellar looks like any
other cute Breckenridge Victorian: deep
rose, with blue trim and a gabled roof. The
inside is another story: It's hip, bright, and
clean, with white walls and tile accents.

Wine is the focus here, with monthly
themed tastings—and the selections on the
enormous list are stored in a 100-year-old
outbuilding. You can order a regular bottle
or glass, of course, but most people opt for
a flight: Deep, Dark, Delicious Reds
includes a merlot, a syrah and a cab; Other
White Grapes comes with a pinot grigio, a
sauvignon blanc, and a moschofilero. Sip
downstairs or climb up a story for dinner—
the intimate dining room serves up small
plates like smoked salmon Napoleon, a
vine-ripe tomato tower with shaved fennel
and basil pesto, cumin-scented venison
short loin, and seated Muscovy duck breast.
Rather splurge? The Cellar also offers a
four-course tasting menu. Either way, don't
leave without a bite of maple and mascarpone cheesecake.

Columbine Café

970-547-4474
109 S. Main St., Breckenridge
Meals Served: B, L
Price Range: $3.50–$8.95
Full bar: N
Reservations: N
Credit Cards: AE, D, MC, V
Handicap Accessible: Y

With a cozy fireplace, fresh flowers on the
tables, some quick bar-style seating, and
generous portions, Columbine can cure the
worst hangovers (it's upstairs from Downstairs at Eric's). Eggs come with steak,
trout, chicken-fried steak, pork chops,
corned beef hash, or hash browns, and you
can get your eggs Benedict with veggies,
salmon, corned beef, or turkey and avocado. Breakfast is served until 3 PM, and
the lunch menu includes burgers, soups,
salads, and sandwiches.

✪ Downstairs at Eric's

970-453-1401
downstairsaterics.com
info@downstairsaterics.com

111 S. Main St., Breckenridge
Meals Served: L, D
Price Range: Appetizers $3.75–$6.95,
    entrées $5.95–$8.95
Full bar: Y
Reservations: N
Credit Cards: AE, D, MC, V
Handicap Accessible: Y

Eric's is one of the most popular restaurants, bars, hangouts, arcades, and party spots in the Blue River Valley—it's where you go for everything from Ms. Pac-Man and Pinball to sports (it has 18 TVs) to great pub food, and the entire menu is available until midnight. Their motto: "Because everywhere else just sucks!" In fact, the walls are covered with signs that the previous owner stole from defunct businesses around town. Want pizza? A lot of it? Order a 24-inch "Gigantor" (that's 452 square inches of pie). Want beer? A lot of it? Eric's has 22 kinds on tap and 120 in bottles. The half-pound burgers come drenched in chili, smothered in American or cheddar, or topped with guac. There are 10 chicken sandwiches alone, along with pun-happy favorites like Ya Can't Tune A Fish (tuna salad), Gone to the Dogs (franks topped with sauerkraut), and Frenchy's Dive (French dip).

Fatty's Pizzeria
970-452-9802
fattyspizzeria.com
info@fattyspizzeria.com
106 S. Ridge St., Breckenridge
Meals Served: L, D
Price Range: Appetizers $2.50–$7.95,
    entrées $10.95–$16.95
Full bar: Y
Reservations: N
Credit Cards: AE, D, MC, V
Handicap Accessible: Y

The word HOTEL still remains over the Fatty's Pizzeria and Pasta sign—this white building with green trim, known as the Colorado House, is one of the oldest in Breck. And

Fatty's itself is a town institution: Since 1975, it has been serving sausage marinara sandwiches, stone-fired meatball pizzas, fettuccini Alfredo, and huge bricks of lasagna. The walls are decorated with staff photos, team trophies (some tongue-in-cheek, like a toilet seat), and NFL paraphernalia, and the TVs above the bar pull in local sports fans. The dining room is basic, with tables and booths, but it looks over town to the ski area. So does a large new patio—which gets packed in summertime.

Giampietro
970-453-3838
100 N. Main St., Breckenridge
Meals Served: L, D
Price Range: Appetizers $2.75–$7.50,
    entrées $6.75–12.50
Full bar: N
Reservations: N
Credit Cards: MC, V
Handicap Accessible: Y

On the busiest nights, the wait at this cozy, 10-table Italian eatery can push two hours—but if you come early and give the hostess your cell-phone number, you'll get a friendly call while you're browsing Main Street shops. What's the buzz all about? First, the place is cute—think red-and-white checkered tablecloths and candles in Chianti bottles. Second, the food is unpretentious and cheap: ravioli for $7.75, chicken parmigiana for $9.25, and bread-crusted deep-dish pizzas for as little as $16. The calzones are shaped like enormous donuts, with a marinara center, and start at $7.75. Really dirtbagging it? You can order a lunchtime slice at the counter and walk away just three bucks poorer.

✪ Hearthstone Restaurant
970-453-1148
hearthstonerestaurant.biz
hearthstonerestaurant@stormrestaurants
    .com

130 S. Ridge St., Breckenridge
Meals Served: D
Price Range: Appetizers $8–$14, entrées
   $17–$38
Full bar: Y
Reservations: Y
Credit Cards: AE, MC, V
Handicap Accessible: N

The much-loved Hearthstone occupies a
120-year-old Victorian house, originally
constructed for a German immigrant who
ran a butcher shop in town. Since then, it
has housed prominent business owners and
other restaurants (like the wonderfully
named Andrea's Pleasure Palace in the
1970s). In 1989, it became the Hearthstone. It still feels like a cozy home, with
period wallpaper, rich carpets, antique
light fixtures, and intimate spaces across
two stories. The food is some of Breck's
best: apps like sweet potato gnocchi with
smoked chicken and sage cream or crispy
lobster in a panko crust; entrées like elk in
a garlic granola crust with marion blackberry demi-glace or Colorado lamb with a
leek and goat cheese tart; and luscious
desserts like huckleberry bread pudding or
bourbon pecan crème brûlée.

Mi Casa

970-453-2071
micasamexicanrestaurant.com
600 S. Park Ave., Breckenridge
Meals Served: L, D
Price Range: Appetizers $5.95–$14.95,
   entrées $9.95-$15.95
Full bar: Y
Reservations: N
Credit Cards: AE, MC, V
Handicap Accessible: N

Right across from the skier drop-off for Peak
10, Mi Casa is always packed for happy hour:
From 3 to 6 PM, you can nosh on 99-cent
tacos, $3 wing baskets, and head-spinning
margaritas. Rather wait for dinner? The cantina doesn't take reservations, so expect a

wait—especially on weekends—but it's worth
being patient: Mi Casa has been around
since 1981, an eternity in ski-town time,
and there's no mystery why. It's got the
basics covered—the chicken or beef burritos, enchiladas, fajitas, and tamales—but it
also innovates with chorizo quesadillas, pork
and mango burritos, and buffalo fajitas. The
seafood is tasty, especially the grilled salmon
with avocado sauce and the snapper Veracruz.

South Ridge Seafood

970-547-0063
215 S. Ridge St., Breckenridge
Meals Served: D
Price Range: Entrées $11.95–$29.95
Full bar: Y
Reservations: Y
Credit Cards: AE, D, MC, V
Handicap Accessible: Y

South Ridge feels at once historic—with copper ceilings, a big Western-style wooden bar
accented by stained glass, and bay windows—
and playful: A school of fish is painted on
one wall, a metal fish sculpture adorns
another. The menu is divided into "Things
that swim . . ." and "Things that don't . . ."—
which means a range from Alaskan king
crab or grilled red trout with potato and
rock shrimp hash to a soy-ginger marinated
skirt steak. In fact, this cute Victorian is
where to find the greatest variety of seafood
in town—gulf shrimp, mahi-mahi, salmon,
halibut, yellowfin tuna, mussels, clam
chowder, and scallops all grace the menu.

Top of the World

970-453-9300
thelodgeatbreck.com
reservations@thelodgeatbreck.com
112 Overlook Dr., Breckenridge
Meals Served: B, D
Price Range: Appetizers $7–$19, entrées
   $18–$37
Full bar: Y
Reservations: Y

Credit Cards: AE, D, MC, V
Handicap Accessible: Y

Just like the hotel in which it lives (see The Lodge & Spa at Breckenridge, page 68), Top of the World has the best views in all of Breckdom: Huge slanted windows let in a good 180 degrees of mountains and alpine light. The decor is rustic but sophisticated—pine furniture with Navajo upholstery, river rock accents, a big brick fireplace, and cheerful red tablecloths. The French-influ-enced American cuisine ranges from tapas (mozzarella salad, polenta, flatbread pizza) and more substantial appetizers (wild mushroom ravioli with port poached apples) to entrées like ostrich filet with lin-gonberry cream and pork tenderloin Oscar—medallions of pork in a crab port cream sauce. For happy hour, swill a spe-cialty appletini, or grab a jacket and a glass of Opus One and watch the sunset from the porch.

Food Purveyors

Bakeries

Daylight Donuts (970-453-2548, 305 N. Main St., Breckenridge) The place obviously has donuts, along with fritters, donut holes, twists, maple bars, and long johns, but also has a $2.99 special (two eggs, a pancake, and bacon or sausage), biscuits and gravy, huevos rancheros, and breakfast burritos to go.

La Francaise French Bakery (970-547-7173, 411 S. Main St., Breckenridge) Every time you enter this below-street-level gem, you'll be greeted with a big "Bonjour!" The custards and creams are made in-house, and the patisserie list includes mousses, tartelettes, chan-tilly, éclairs, meringues, brioches, and croissants. You can also order sweet and savory crepes, quiches, and baguette sandwiches.

Mary's Mountain Cookies (970-547-4757, 128 S. Main St., Breckenridge) A tiny, cute storefront, Mary's sells monster quarter-pound cookies (white chocolate macadamia, peanut butter, oatmeal raisin), even more indulgent dipped quarter-pounders (like a chocolate chipper dipped milk chocolate and walnuts), and the completely sinful sandwich cookies—two quarter-pounders filled with vanilla, chocolate, or peanut butter frosting.

Coffee Shops

Cool River Coffee House and Bakery (970-453-1716, 325 S. Main St., Breckenridge) Fresh baked bagels in basic and creative flavors (apple cinnamon, parmesan pepper), breakfast wraps, egg sandwiches, and a full coffee selection.

The Crown (970-453-6022, 215 S. Main St., Breckenridge) The Crown, with cream-col-ored tiles, vines, dark wood, and chess sets, is a coffee shop—plus: Along with a full espresso bar, you can order breakfast sandwiches all day (lox and cream cheese, south-western, egg and cheese), salads, sandwiches (like the Royal Bird, chicken breast with grapes, walnuts, and red onion), spanakopita, and desserts. Martinis, wine, and micro-brews are also available.

Greta's (970-453-7275, 114 S. Main St., Breckenridge) Along with chocolate and candy, Greta's makes great coffee concoctions: The One-Eyed Jack is a chocolate mint and Irish Cream mocha with whipped cream and mint, and the Boreas Pass comes with hazelnut and honey.

Mountain Java (970-453-1874, 118 S. Ridge St., Breckenridge) A quaint and funky little café that doubles as a small book shop, Mountain Java's baristas bang out espressos and toast big bagels from dawn's light to late afternoon.

Delis

Crepes a la Cart (307 S. Main St., Breckenridge) Whether it's afternoon hunger pangs or late-night drunk munchies, Crepes a la Cart—an outdoor counter with some seating under heated lamps, white Christmas lights, and a sign hanging from a tree—can concoct something to sate you: chocolate chip and strawberry, caramel apple and cinnamon, veggies and cheese, or grilled chicken.

The Euro Deli (970-453-4473, 110 N. Main St., Breckenridge) Cheerful green-and-white checkered tablecloths, bright orange walls, artwork by locals, and a big selection of cold cuts, salami, veggies, and fresh-made breads.

Zuppa (970-453-7788, "soup hotline" 970-547-9791, 400 N. Park Ave., Breckenridge) Soups change daily between cheddar ale and sausage, Brazilian seafood chowder, Moroccan veggie tagine, and elk stroganoff, among (many) others. Sandwiches rotate, too—smoked ham and brie, smoked beef brisket, shredded pork torta.

Farmer's Markets

Breckenridge Farmer's Market (970-453-9400) A recent addition to the local food-market scene, Breck's version takes place on Sunday mornings at Main Street Station.

Dillon Farmer's Market (970-468-5100) Every Friday from June to September, 9 AM to 1 PM, this market gets set up in the Marina Park lot in Dillon (about 16 miles north of Breckenridge), between the marina and the amphitheater.

Silverthorne Farmer's Market (970-262-9239) Not the most romantic setting—near the Levi's store in the outlet mall in Silverthorne (about 15 miles north of Breckenridge)—but there's usually good live music to get you in the shopping mood.

Frozen Desserts

Cold Stone Creamery (970-453-1759, 505 S. Main St., Breckenridge) Though it's a chain, the ice cream still rules: Mix brownies, graham cracker pie crust, peanut butter, blackberries, or apple pie filling into flavors like sweet cream, peppermint, pumpkin, amaretto, and orange dreamsicle.

Rocky Mountain Fruit Shake (970-547-7690, 126 S. Main St., Breckenridge) Big, refreshing smoothies and shakes in all kinds of fruit flavors.

Groceries

Amazing Grace Natural Foods (970-453-1445, 213 Lincoln Ave., Breckenridge) This small health-food store sells soy ice cream and vegan cookies, and will make you a great sandwich to go (there's seating for just four people).

City Market (970-453-0818, 400 N. Parkway, Breckenridge)

Food Kingdom (970-453-2398, 311 S. Ridge St., Breckenridge)

Main Street Market (970-453-2253, 505 S. Main St., Breckenridge)

NIGHTLIFE

Blue River Bistro (970-453-6974, 305 N, Main St., Breckenridge) If you're a martini fan, this is your mecca: choose from close to 40 vodkas, a handful of gins, and six different stuffed olives—or let the bartender mix one for you. The Mogul Martini comes with Absolut Citron, raspberry and cranberry juices, and a raspberry garnish; the Chocolate Orange is mixed with Smirnoff Orange, crème de cacao, and Grand Marnier; and the Chocolate Cake is Smirnoff Vanilla, crème de cacao, and Frangelico—with a sugared rim.

Downstairs at Eric's (970-453-1401, downstairsaterics.com, 111 S. Main St., Breckenridge) If you haven't read the write-up on page 72, let us remind you that Eric's has 22 beers on tap and more than 120 varieties in bottles—and they serve food late.

Gold Pan Saloon (970-453-5499, 103 N. Main St., Breckenridge) This is the oldest continually operated bar west of the Mississippi: It was built in 1859, the same year that gold was discovered along the Blue River. It wasn't even shut during Prohibition. Push through the swinging doors and pull a stool up to the front or back bar (both original), warm your hands next to the old stove (called the "Big Bonanza"), or take a look at the wooden Indian, the big bison head, or the historical photos.

Salt Creek Steakhouse & Club (970-453-4949, saltcreekbreck.com, 110 E. Lincoln St., Breckenridge) By day, the downstairs dining room of Salt Creek serves steak and eggs, biscuits and gravy, beans, coleslaw, four-meat barbecue samplers, and cinnamon toffee bread

Bellying up to the bar of the Gold Pan Saloon in Breckenridge. Opened in 1859, the Pan Saloon is the oldest continually operating watering hole west of the Mississippi. Evelyn Spence

pudding. By night, the upstairs is a club, with pool tables, green leather couches, benches, and big-screen TVs. Tuesdays and Thursdays are Cheap Beer & Wings Nights; Wednesday is Country Night (with line dancing and $2 Coors!); and Fridays feature cheap Fat Tire microbrews all night.

Sherpa and Yeti's (970-547-9299, sherpaandyetis.com, 320 S. Main St., Breckenridge) Martin Sexton, Yonder Mountain String Band, Shanti Groove, DJ Logic, Blackalicious—here, even if you hang at a table in back, you can still get intimate with great live bands.

Ullr's (970-453-6060, 401 S. Main St.. Breckenridge) A dark, divey, and usually busy sports bar with grilled cheese, Bowl games, and Tuaca shots.

Culture

Cinema
Breckenridge Speakeasy Movie Theater (970-453-7243, speakeasymovies.com, 103 S. Harris St., Breckenridge) Showing documentaries, indies, foreign flicks, and some main-stream action and drama movies, the Speakeasy is open Wednesday through Sunday nights. It's located in the three-story brick building at Colorado Mountain College.

Historical Sites
Alice G. Milne Memorial Park (102 N. Harris St., Breckenridge) Flanked by two historic houses, the Eberline House—one of Breck's oldest—and the clapboard Milne House, this small Victorian lawn is open in the warmer months.

Iowa Hill (970-453-9022, off Airport Rd., north end of Breckenridge) Take a self-guided 1-mile hike of an original hydraulic mining operation, complete with boardinghouse.

Lomax Placer Gulch (970-453-9022, 301 Ski Hill Rd., Breckenridge) A 5-acre site that includes hydraulic mining equipment, an assay office, a log cabin, a stable and wagon repair shop, and a collection of period tools and clothing. Call for tour times.

Rotary Snowplow Park (Boreas Pass Rd. at French St., Breckenridge) A small park with boxcars, a restored steam engine, a tender car, a rotary snowplow, and an interpretive cabin with railroad artifacts and photos.

Valley Brook Cemetery (Airport Rd. at Valley Brook Rd., Breckenridge) The first grave-stone was placed here in 1882, and soon after the cemetery was bounded by ornate iron gates. It's still in use today.

Washington Mine (970-453-9022, Illinois Gulch Rd., Breckenridge) At its peak, Washington consisted of five shafts and 10,000 feet of underground tunnels to mine for gold and silver ore. The Summit Historial Society tour includes a shaft house, a mining cabin, a tramway, and a boatload of equipment.

Museums
Barney Ford House Museum (970-453-9022, summithistorical.org, 111 E. Washington Ave., Beckenridge) This small museum honors an escaped slave who became the first black businessman in Breckenridge—and thus a civil rights pioneer in Colorado. The original

house, constructed in 1882 and lovingly restored, was built by well-known craftsman Elias Nashold—and it's full of period furniture, historical photos, and old clocks.

Carter Museum (970-453-9022, summithistorical.org, 111 N. Ridge St., Breckenridge) In another historic building, this one a more rustic cabinlike house put up in 1875, live naturalist Edwin Carter's specimens and workshop. A rare environmentalist in the midst of the mining boom, Carter collected and documented Rocky Mountain wildlife.

Main Street Historical Museum (970-453-9022, summithistorical.org, 115 S. Main St., Breckenridge) Get a taste of what Breck was like in the late 1800s with this impressive (and free) collection of historical photos—along with fun ski artifacts.

Theaters and Other Miscellanous Venues

Backstage Theatre (970-453-0199, backstagetheatre.org, 121 S. Ridge St., Breckenridge) Based out of the Breckenridge Theater building, Backstage has been putting on plays and musicals like *As It Is In Heaven, Joseph and the Amazing Technicolor Dreamcoat,* and *The Foreigner*—as well as various workshops—since 1974.

The Riverwalk Center (970-547-3100) A big, heated tent along the Blue River in the center of Breckenridge, Riverwalk seats 770 inside, 2,000 on the lawn, and hosts parties, classical, jazz, and rock concerts, dance recitals, kids' events, and even weddings.

KIDS' STUFF

Country Boy Mine (970-453-4405, countryboymine.com, French Gulch Rd., Breckenridge) Sleigh rides or hay rides that end with s'mores and cocoa, mine tours that take you down 1,000 feet (with hard hats), panning for gold—it's all part of the experience at Country Boy, one of the biggest mines in Summit County. Started in 1887, it yielded gold and silver, as well as high-grade lead and zinc used in the World Wars.

Java Jungle (970-453-4283, java-jungle.com, 224 S. Main St., Breckenridge) Parents come for the coffee or the Mexican, African, and Indonesian art; kids love the fact that Java Jungle carries 490 different jigsaw puzzles. Some of them have up to 18,000 pieces.

Mountain Man Carriage Company (970-389-5635, corner of Washington and Main Sts., Breckenridge) For a fun ride to dinner or a half-hour historic tour, Mountain Man will pull you and your brood in a white vis-à-vis carriage behind draft horses.

Mountain Top Children's Museum (970-453-7878, 605 S. Park Ave., Breckenridge) MTCM has tons of variety: learn about marmots and black bears, touch real antlers, crawl through a bear cave, gaze up in the planetarium, dress up and put on a play, and control a robot by remote.

Peak-a-Boo Toys (970-453-4910, 117 S. Main St., Breckenridge) A toy store with a big indoor playground.

Peak 8 Fun Park (800-789-7669) Spend a summer day at the ski resort playing mini golf, racing down an alpine slide or a zip line, getting lost in a human maze, scaling a rock-climbing wall, jumping on trampolines, and grubbing on barbecue, ice cream, and cotton candy.

Rocky Mountain Snowbike (970-389-7006, 47 Fairview Circle, Breckenridge) Learn how to ride a snowbike—a hybrid cycle with skis instead of wheels—and take it out on the slopes.

Space 2 Studio (970-547-3116, 880 Airport Rd., Breckenridge) Every second and fourth Friday of the month, teens can spend a few hours doing silk painting, beading, sculpting, clay, or paper-making. The first visit is free and includes materials.

Stephen C. West Ice Arena (970-547-9974, townofbreckenridge.com, 189 Boreas Pass Rd., Breckenridge) With two NHL-size ice rinks, skate rentals, an outdoor rink that's open from mid-September to mid-April, and public skating and hockey sessions, this is a nice option when you're tired of skiing.

Recreation: Winter and Spring

Alpine Skiing and Snowboarding

Breckenridge Ski Area
breckenridge.snow.com

Overview: Spread out over four peaks, 2,358 acres, and 3,398 vertical feet, and criss-crossed with 29 lifts, Breckenridge is nothing if not sprawling. The terrain is hugely varied and offers more than enough room to move, whether you're a newbie or a wannabe pro. And the whole mountain is almost always bustling with families, locals, Front Range college kids,

> **Breckenridge: The 4-1-1**
> Acres: 2,358
> Summit elevation: 12,998 feet
> Vertical drop: 3,398 feet
> Annual snowfall: 300 inches
> Percent advanced/expert terrain: 55
> Percent intermediate terrain: 31
> Percent beginner terrain: 14
> Lifts: 29

and weekend warriors: Uphill capacity is over 37,000 skiers an hour, and even then, lines can be long. The area is fairly flat near town (think wide, mellow highways that are great for novice skiers making big wedge turns—and nightmarish for snowboarders trying to keep up their speed). It then steepens and breaks through treeline, topping out at 13,000 feet. Up on high, you get huge powderfields, cliff drops, and high winds—they sometimes call it Breckenfridge, or Breakin' Wind, for a reason. Each peak has everything from greens to double blacks, but in general, stick to Peak 7 and Peak 9 for intermediate terrain and Peak 8 and Peak 10 for the tougher stuff. New this year: a gondola, called the BreckConnect, from the town to the Peak 8 base area.

    Must-ski: Breck's longest run, at 3.5 miles, is Four O' Clock, a beginner-intermediate highway that starts at the Vista Haus warming hut and meanders all the way into town, past houses and condo complexes, dumping you straight onto Park Avenue. Anything off the QuickSilver Super6 is also good for beginners—the lift ends before the mountain has a chance to steepen. For a whole slew of intermediate cruisers, do laps on the Independence SuperChair on Peak 7: Lincoln Meadows, Monte Cristo, Pioneer, Swan City. Seeking trees? Peak 10's your place: dodge gnarled pines in The Burn, or drop off the far skier's-right side of the mountain into Trinity, Elan, and Quiver. The new Imperial Express quad—strung up to 13,000 feet on Peak 8 and the highest lift in North America—

accesses above-treeline bowls like North Bowl and 50-plus-degree shots like the Lake Chutes. Peak 8's T-bar is another great option for advanced skiers, with open steeps like Horseshoe Bowl and Cucumber Bowl. Want to hike for your turns? Hoof it up Peak 7 and drop into Y-Chute.

Grub: Where you eat depends on where you are come lunchtime—closer to Peak 8, or closer to Peak 9. On 8, the **Vista Haus** is like a food court—get burritos and soft tacos; toasted subs and soups; or an on-the-go pastry. The **Bergenhof** is the place to go for après drinks on the patio and the wafting smell of barbecue. Consume both on "Bergy Beach," an outdoor deck, if the weather gods cooperate. If you're near Peak 9, stop at **Ten Mile Station** for breakfast, lunch, and sweet crepes; barbecue; and a slightly cheesy mining theme. At the base of 9, the **Breck Burger Bar** does 'em right, complete with generous heaps of fries. Pick up your morning joe (and muffins the size of a baby's head) at the **Rendezvous.** For one-stop noshing, **Beaver Run** has a deli, a bar, a food court, a steak joint, and even a nightclub.

Cross-Country Skiing and Snowshoeing

Boreas Pass Used by mountain bikers in summer and snowmobilers, Nordos, and snow-shoers in winter, Boreas Pass is popular almost all year long—and with good reason. A for-mer wagon-train road and narrow-gauge railway, the route has a gradual and continuous grade with big S-curves and historic railroad remnants.

Breckenridge Nordic Center (970-453-6855, 1200 Ski Hill Rd., Breckenridge) Twenty-eight kilometers of classic (kicking and gliding, with your skis parallel) and skating (a highly aerobic, herringbone style) trails that cross old mining roads and beaver meadows, including the intermediate Gluteus Minimus and the advanced Gluteus Maximus, below Peak 8. For a $30 rental and ticket fee, get a free learn-to-ski lesson.

Frisco Nordic Center (970-668-0866, frisconordic.com, CO 9, Frisco) This area in Frisco, about 10 miles north of Breckenridge, has 46 kilometers of trails along the shore of Lake Dillon and another 14 kilometers of snowshoe-only trails; a log warming cabin with snack bar, rentals, and lesson information; and great beginner packages.

Gold Run Nordic Center (970-547-7889, 200 Clubhouse Dr., Breckenridge) Just north of Breck, Gold Run meanders through its namesake valley at the mouth of the Swan River, and rents skis, snowshoes, and pulks (child tow sleds). Private lessons are available.

Keystone Gulch Climbing up the southwest edge of the Breckenridge ski area, this out-and-back ends near the Outback and Wayback lifts after climbing 5 miles of gentle forested trail and then switchbacking 700 feet in 2 miles.

Lily Pad Lake A short, 3-mile trail that gains only about 100 feet in elevation, Lily Pad dips into the Eagles Nest Wilderness (so mechanized users are prohibited). You'll pass through meadows and stands of aspen and spruce, and finish at the namesake frozen lake.

North Tenmile Creek Just off of I-70 near Frisco, this popular route has a steep climb for the first half-mile before leveling off substantially, passing old mining remnants and crossing open valleys. At the junction with the Gore Range Trail, keep going straight (but the Gore Range Trail is a good option as well).

Winter Wonderland: A cross-country skier and his dog soak up the sun. Carl Scofield

Guiding and Backcountry

Summit Huts Association (970-453-8583, summithuts.org, 524 Wellington Rd., Breck-enridge) SHA runs four backcountry huts, ranging from the rustic, 1860s-era Ken's Cabin (sleeps just two to three people) to the gorgeous 20-person Francie's Cabin. They're each at least a 4-mile hike in—with skins, avalanche beacons, shovels, the works.

Ice skating

Maggie Pond (970-547-5726, 535 Park Ave., Breckenridge) This small outdoor pond is open until 10 PM most days, and it offers rental skates on-site.

Steven C. West Arena (970-547-9974, 0189 Boreas Pass Rd., Breckenridge) A full-service, year-round indoor rink with public skating hours, hockey and figure skating lessons, skate sharpening, and skating gear.

RECREATION: SUMMER AND FALL

Cycling: Mountain Biking

Boreas Pass Want to ride up to the Continental Divide? Just follow this abandoned narrow-gauge rail bed up to 11,481 feet, take it all in, then cruise back down.

Colorado Trail A mix of dirt roads and trails, the Colorado Trail hugs the woodsy hillsides above the Swan River Valley, climbing up to 11,100 feet to West Ridge, and then switchbacks down open sagebrush slopes.

French Gulch and Pass A 16-mile out-and-back that begins on mellow dirt road, rolls by mining remains, and then ascends more steeply to a 12,000-foot mountain pass.

Sallie Barber Mine An easy loop that's one of the first trails to open in the early season, Sallie Barber passes its namesake mine on dirt roads, singletrack, and doubletrack.

Summit Mountain Challenge (970-333-1159) Every Wednesday night, race in 10 different ent categories along local trails—and then party afterwards.

Cycling: Road Biking

Breckenridge to Frisco Recreation Trail At 9.5 miles one way with just a slight elevation change, this is a great way to take in the scenery, follow the Blue River, and check out the neighboring town of Frisco.

Dillon Reservoir An 18-mile, mostly flat route on paved trails and roads, this loop passes a few marinas, hugs the shoreline in spots, and opens up to beautiful vistas.

Dillon to Loveland Pass With a summit of nearly 12,000 feet, Loveland Pass is one of the highest in the state. Translation: This is a difficult ride. You'll wind through Keystone on mellow terrain, pass Arapahoe Basin Ski Area, and then switchback up and up. There's a good pullout at the top—cherish it.

Frisco to Vail Pass Climbing from 9,100 to 10,600 feet, this is a popular lung- and leg-burner that starts on an old railroad grade, passes Copper Mountain ski area, and switchbacks up to Vail Pass next to I-70.

Hoosier Pass You can hop on this 22-mile route right in the center of town on CO 9, which climbs to 11,541-foot Hoosier Pass and then drops 6 wide-open miles to Fairplay. For a shorter ride, just turn back at the pass (about 10 miles from Breck).

Fishing

Outfitters
Blue River Anglers (970-453-9171, blueriveranglers.com, 209 N. Main St., Breckenridge) Wading and float trips on the Colorado, South Platte, Blue, Williams Fork, and Arkansas—along with lake floats in a raft—with guides who've lived in Colorado for at least a dozen years.

Breckenridge Outfitters (970-0453-4135, breckenridgeoutfitters.com, 100 N. Main St., Breckenridge) If you don't want to fish all day—or even a half-day—you can just schedule a two-hour guided trip for 50 bucks. Breck Outfitters has access to private waters like Elk Fork Ranch (try your hand at Troublesome Creek) and Hartsel Ranch (four trophy ponds with brookies, browns, and 'bows up to 12 pounds).

Mountain Angler (970-453-HOOK, mountainangler.com, 311 S. Main St., Breckenridge) Summit County's oldest fly shop, Mountain Angler guides on five rivers, all within an hour's drive: the Eagle, Blue, Colorado, South Platte, and Arkansas—along with local private waters. Offers everything from beginner lessons to two-day fly-fishing schools.

Stop here before you wet your line: Blue River Anglers in Breckenridge. Evelyn Spence

Lakes and Streams

Before you fish any water in Colorado, be sure you check with a local fly shop to find out if it's public or private. Many rivers have both private and public sections, so make sure you know where you're going. For licenses and regulations, visit wildlife.state.co.us/fishing—or, again, stop into a shop. If a river is designated "Gold Medal," it officially means that there are 12 trout per surface acre that top 14 inches—or 60 pounds of trout per surface acre. Unofficially, it means that the fishing is damn good.

Blue River The stretch of water below the Dillon Dam—even the part that flows under I-70—has been designated Gold Medal; rainbows and browns gorge on Mysis shrimp and midges next to the outlet malls.

Dillon Reservoir (970-468-5100) Stocked with 50,000 rainbow trout annually, the reservoir allows fishing along almost all 25 miles of its shoreline—and you can rent boats at the Dillon or Frisco marinas to pillage the rest.

Golf

Breckenridge Gold Club (970-453-9104, breckenridgegolfclub.com, 200 Clubhouse Dr., Breckenridge) Three nine-hole courses (the Elk, the Beaver, and the Bear) are surrounded by wildflowers, mountain views, woods, creeks, and native grassland. The Elk/Beaver combo is rated the second-hardest course in the state.

Keystone Courses (970-496-4275, keystoneresort.com, 155 River Course Dr. and 1239 Keystone Ranch Rd., Keystone) The River course is a Hurdzan-Fry layout with a back nine that meaders through lodgepoles—and a front nine that matches the Snake River curve for curve. The Ranch course, designed by Robert Trent Jones Jr., hugs the shores of a 9-acre lake and dips through sage meadows.

Raven Golf Club at Three Peaks (970-262-3636, intrawestgolf.com/raven_threepeaks, 2929 Golden Eagle Rd., Silverthorne) The Raven course—one of several owned by resort developer Intrawest in the U.S. and Canada—seems to encompass the whole Colorado experience in a single location: the thirteeners, the aspens, the wetlands, the pines, the creeks. Though it's closer to Copper Ski Area than Breck, it's worth the trip.

Hiking and Backpacking

Gray's and Torrey's If you want to bag a fourteener, this is one of the most popular places in Colorado to do it—maybe because you can tag two summits for the price of one (there's a short saddle between them). The dirt road on the way in is rough-and-tumble (four-wheel drive is a good idea), but the trail to the top is well-maintained and usually quite crowded.

Mayflower Gulch A short hike with a big reward, 2-mile-long Mayflower brings you to the Old Boston Mine, with the Fletcher, Crystal, and Pacific Mountains looking on.

Mohawk Lake With a 1,700-foot elevation gain, this 7-mile-round-trip trail is one of Summit County's best, and it captures the best of the county: the old mining cabins, the ore cars, the alpine lakes, the rugged peaks, and the waterfalls. You'll get up above the tree-line toward the end, which makes for sweet panoramas.

Ptarmigan Trail A good family option—especially in fall, when the route takes you through breathtaking aspen groves—Ptarmigan climbs to a lookout and then to its namesake peak,

Golfing near Breckenridge is nothing if not a scenic experience. Carl Scofield

with lovely views of Lake Dillon, Buffalo Mountain, and the saw-toothed Gore Range. (To the lookout and back is 4.2 miles round trip.)

Quandary Peak At 14,265 feet, Quandary is one of 54 fourteeners in Colorado, and it's just 5 miles south of Breck. Make sure you get an early start (to avoid summer afternoon thunderstorms), bring a map and plenty of layers, and be prepared to lose your breath.

Salmon and Willow Lakes A 10-miler that rises a thigh-burning 2,250 feet, the trail heads into the Eagles Nest Wilderness and switchbacks to four different lakes, all spectacular—one Salmon, and three Willows—and all with good trout fishing. In between, catch views of the Gore Range.

Willow Falls Close to 5 miles each way, the trek to Willow Falls is intermediate—it gains just under 1,000 feet, passes through wildflower meadows, and finishes at the stair-stepping cascade of South Willow Creek.

Horseback Riding

Breckenridge Stables (970-453-4438, colorado-horses.com/kingdom.html, off Village Rd., Breckenridge) Cross mountain streams and meander though wildflowery meadows on the 90-minute Breckenridge Trail ride, which departs every 30 minutes. Or get up early and catch the breakfast ride: piles of pancakes, eggs, sausage, coffee, cocoa, and OJ. Steak dinners are available for big groups, by special arrangement.

Rusty Spurr Ranch (970-724-1123, rustyspurr.com, CR 387, Kremmling) About 40 miles north of Breck, Rusty Spurr offers two- and three-hour rides, "saddle and paddle" combos (a morning on a horse, an afternoon in a raft), and cattle drives on 10,000 acres of open range.

Hot Air Ballooning

Colorado Rocky Ballooning (970-468-9280, coloradoballoonrides.com, 400 N. Park Ave., Breckenridge) Rise up to 7,000 feet above ground, float for up to 10 miles, and do it all to the sound of classical music (played on board). Catch views of the Continental Divide, the Mosquito Range, the Sangre de Cristo and Sawatch Mountains, and the Collegiate Peaks.

Hunting

DAL Outfitters (970-468-0777, daloutfitters.com, P.O. Box 495, Silverthorne) DAL Outfitters, in Silverthorne, can help you bag a mule deer or elk, whether you want to go bush for a week or spend your nights in a rustic cabin built in 1934. Book a three- or five-day archery or rifle hunt while based out of the central lodge; a fully guided five-day pack hunt; or a semi-guided drop-camp hunt (during which you get some help at camp, and some independence, usually with one guide for two people).

Paragliding

Summit Paragliding and Mountaineering (970-968-0100, summitparagliding.net, 189 Ten Mile Circle, No. 110, Copper Mountain) Take off from the top of Copper in tandem with an instructor and glide down to earth.

Rafting and Paddling

Breckenridge Whitewater (970-668-1665, breckenridgewhitewater.com, 127 S. Main St., Breckenridge) From the beginner trip on the Upper Colorado to the intense, continuous whitewater of Gore Canyon (minimum age 18, strong swimming skills required), Breckenridge Whitewater has a range of trips on a half-dozen area rivers. You can also get a full day of whitewater kayak instruction.

Breckenridge Whitewater Park (970-453-1734, behind the Recreation Center between the Blue River pathway and CO 9) The longest whitewater park in Colorado—at 1,800 feet— has 15 features, including splash rocks, S-curves, eddy pools, and play holes. Depending on water flow, it's usually open mid-April to August.

Kodi Rafting (877-747-7238, 970-668-1548, whitewatercolorado.com, 503 Main St., Frisco) On the Blue River, roll through Class II rapids in the Arapaho National Forest; on the Colorado, try a 17-mile, overnight trip through Little Gore Canyon; or rent an inflatable kayak and go it alone.

DRIVING: SCENIC DRIVES AND BYWAYS

Boreas Pass Road This wide, well-maintained gravel road follows what used to be a narrow-gauge railway, passing abandoned ranches and railroad structures along the way. Finish up at Como, a ghost town where Italians used to mine for coal. A few miners still live here today.

Hoosier Pass to Fairplay If you're coming from I-70 on CO 9 and continue south through Breckenridge, you'll go through the small town of Alma, then climb up to 11,539-foot Hoosier Pass. Here, at the Continental Divide, you'll be at the northern end of Mosquito Range, where the headwaters of the Blue head one way and the headwaters of the South Platte head the other. You'll then drop into South Park, an expansive grassland basin that's almost 1,000 square miles (and sits at 10,000 feet).

SHOPPING

Art Galleries

Arts Alive! (970-453-0450, summitarts.org, 520 S. Main St., Breckenridge) Every second and fourth Wednesday of the month, take a crack at life drawing; the rest of the time, peruse the local and regional sculpture, Western painting, photography, and jewelry.

Breckenridge Gallery (970-453-2592, breckenridge-gallery.com, 124 S. Main St., Breckenridge) This was the first gallery to open in town (back in 1969), and these days it showcases prominent wildlife, landscape, and portrait painters like Gordon Brown, Shang Ding, and Leon Loughridge.

Hibberd McGrath Gallery (970-453-6391, hibberdmcgrath.com, 101 N. Main St., Breckenridge) Opened in 1982, Hibberd McGrath represents a broad range of media: papier-mâché, textiles, beading, baskets, ceramics, and jewelry, most of which are contemporary, creative, and playful.

Everything in Breckenridge's Huneck Gallery is dedicated to canines. Evelyn Spence

Highlands Gallery (970-453-1260, 224 S. Main St., Breckenridge) With a stable of 40 artists, most from the West, Glenda and Frank Bumpus's collection is extremely diverse—kinetic sculpture, fauvist landscapes, bright watercolors, and modern takes on wildlife.

Huneck Gallery (970-453-2228, 301 S. Main St., Breckenridge) A dog-friendly store with dog-themed paintings, woodcuts, and sculptures. The work of Stephen Huneck is featured.

Michael Boyett (970-453-4012, michaelboyett.us, 411 S. Main St., Suite 6, Breckenridge) Pewter and bronze sculptures in diminutive to enormous sizes, featuring subjects from Christian icons to Civil War heroes to Native American scenes to wildlife action.

Paint Horse Gallery (970-453-6813, painthorsegallery.com, 226 S. Main St., Brecken-ridge) Original artwork—like bronze sculptures of cowboys and paintings of open spaces—shares space with vintage saddles, 100-year-old Navajo rugs, antique spurs, and moccasins.

Thomas D. Mengelsen's Images of Nature (970-547-2711, 505 S. Main St., Breckenridge) Okay, he has a retail store in Denver International Airport, among other places. But Mengelsen's wildlife photos—some taken in the Rocky Mountains, some much more exotic—still dazzle.

The annual International Snow Sculpture Competition brings the world's best carvers to Breck every January.
Carl Scofield

Books

Hamlet's Bookshoppe (970-453-8033, hamletsbooks.com, 306 S. Main St., Brecken-ridge) Housed in a historic Victorian, with a cozy children's area and a big range of titles, Hamlet's is just a charming place for book lovers: high shelves, creaky wooden floors, nooks and crannies, and helpful staff.

Weber's (877-259-3237, webersbooks.com, 100 S. Main St., Breckenridge) With a great selection of Colorado-specific titles, from cookbooks (*Pie in the Sky*, about high-altitude baking) to ghost town guides to railroad histories to big coffee-table books, Weber's also has regularly scheduled readings and discussions.

Outdoor Gear

Great Adventure Sports (970-453-0333, greatadventuresports.com, 400 N. Park Ave., Breckenridge) A cycling specialty shop, Great Adventure Sports rents a wide range of bikes and sells everything from pedals to helmets to gloves.

Western Clothing and Furs

The Twisted Pine (970-453-9588, 100 S. Main St., Breckenridge; 970-453-6615, 505 Main St., Breckenridge; ttpine.com) Packed with trophies, fur coats, Native American headdresses, and Southwestern crafts, you can take home anything from a candleholder to an armoire.

SEASONAL EVENTS

January: Ullr Fest (800-936-5573, gobreck.com) The son of Sif and the stepson of Thor, Ullr is the Norse God of Winter—and Breck has been tying one on in his honor for almost 50 years. The weeklong celebration includes an enormous bonfire, a raucous Main Street parade, and close-to-nonstop partying.

January: International Snow Sculpture Competition (800-936-5573, gobreck.com) Competitors from Spain, Russia, Mexico, Canada, and elsewhere chip 12-foot-tall, 20-ton blocks of ice into temporary masterpieces.

February: Mardi Gras (800-936-5573, gobreck.com) A good excuse to put on a mask, drape yourself with beads, and eat as much Cajun food as possible while watching the Main Street parade.

March: St. Patrick's Day Pub Crawl Sometimes attracting over 400 competitors, this drinking contest involves consuming a green pint of beer at 10 different pubs and return-ing to the start/finish line.

April: Spring Massive (970-453-5000, breckenridge.snow.com) At almost a month long, this spring celebration includes the Bite of Breckenridge (with restaurant specials), celebrity weekends, and big sales at local retailers. There are also wacky competitions: The Imperial Challenge involves biking and hiking to the top of Imperial Bowl, then skiing or snowboarding down; the Bump Buffet has telemarkers tackling moguls—in costume.

June: Genuine Jazz in Breckenridge (970-418-2121, genuinejazz.com) The free daytime performances take place on Maggie Pond's floating (yes, floating) stage; come nighttime, acts like Marion Meadows, Nils, and Tim Bowman appear at various town clubs.

June–August: Breckenridge Music Festival (970-453-9142, breckenridgemusicfestival.com) An eclectic, 10-week series, Breck's music festival has featured everything from the Vienna Boys' Choir and the Von Trapp Children to the Glenn Miller Orchestra and the Breckenridge Music Festival Orchestra.

July: AMBC Firecracker 50 (970-333-1159) This cross-country mountain bike race goes for 50 miles, and climbs 12,000 feet worth of singletrack.

July: Toast of Breckenridge (877-359-5606, toastofbreckenridge.com) A high-mountain food and wine fest with tastings, seminars, and chow from local vendors.

July: July Art Festival (970-547-9326, breckartfairs.com) After almost a quarter-century, this competitive fine arts and crafts event—including metalwork, glass, photography, and jewelry—has grown to 150-plus American artists from over 20 states.

August: Colorado Gold Panning Championships (877-864-0868, gobreck.com) Watch the world's best go at it in dry-panning championships—or learn the basics yourself.

September: Breckenridge Festival of Film (970-453-6200, breckfilmfest.com) In years past, movies like *American Beauty, Frida, L.A. Confidential,* and *Being John Malkovich* have been shown here. There are also seminars, daylong workshops, and various panels.

September: Oktoberfest (970-453-5055, gobreck.com) Start off with a brewmaster's dinner (a multi-course meal paired with different beers), sample Bavarian food and German brews, gawk at the lederhosen, and dance to oompah music.

December: Holipalooza and Lighting of Breckenridge (800-936-5573, gobreck.com) Stroll among the lit-up Victorian houses, watch Santa light the town tree, listen to carolers, and get into the winter spirit.

NUTS AND BOLTS

Getting Here
Breck is a little over 100 miles from **Denver International Airport** (DIA)—a straight shot west up I-70, then a few miles south on CO 9. If you don't want to do the drive yourself, try catching a ride with the van service **Colorado Mountain Express** (800-334-7433, cmex.com). If you're in a large group (30–40 people), you can also charter a bus with **Arrow Stage Lines** (arrowstagelines.com) or **Timberline Tours** (go-timberline.com).

Ambulance/Fire/Police/Search and Rescue
For emergencies, of course, dial 911. For police assistance that doesn't require an emergency response, contact the number listed below for the city closest to your present location.

Animal Shelter: 970-668-3230

Colorado State Patrol: 970-824-6501

Poison Control: 800-332-3073

Summit County Dispatch: 970-668-8600

Avalanche Reports

Backcountry Avalanche Report: 970-668-0600

Colorado Avalanche Information Center: 970-453-6333, geosurvey.state.co.us/avalanche or avalanche-center.org

Hospitals and Emergency Medical Services

Summit County Public Health Nursing Service: 970-668-5230, 37 Summit County Road, Suite 1005, Frisco

Summit Medical Center: 970-668-3300, CO 9 at School Rd., Frisco

High Altitude Mobile Physicians: 970-389-7999

Frisco Medical Center: 970-668-3003, friscomedcenter.com, 360 Peak One Dr., Suite 240, Frisco

High Country Health Care (highcountryhealth.com):
Frisco: 970-668-5584, 300 Peak One Dr., Suite 260
Dillon/Silverthorne: 970-468-1003, 103 Main St., Dillon
Breckenridge: 970-547-9200, 400 N. Parkway, Suite 1A

Breckenridge Medical Center: 970-453-1010, vvmc.com, 555 S. Park Ave., Breckenridge

Vail/Summit Orthopedic and Sports Medicine: 970-668-3633, vsortho.com, 360 Peak One Drive, Suite 180, Frisco

Libraries

Main Branch, Frisco: 970-668-5555, 37 CR 1005

Breckenridge: 970-453-6098, 504 Airport Rd.

Silverthorne: 970-468-5887, 751 Center Circle

Media

Newspapers and Magazines

Summit County Journal: 970-668-3998, summitdaily.com, 40 W. Main St., P.O. Box 329, Frisco, CO 80433

Summit Daily News: 970-668-3998, summitdaily.com, 40 W. Main St., P.O. Box 329, Frisco, CO 80433

Ten Mile Times: 970-668-3022, 619 Main St., Frisco, CO 80433

Radio

KSMT 95.3: 970-453-2234, ksmtradio.com. Adult alternative and eclectic tunes.

KYSL 93.9: 970-668-0292, triplearadio.com. Adult alternative.

Public Transportation

The Breckenridge Transit System (970-547-3140) operates FREE RIDE, a system of buses that connects the ski resort's parking lots with the base area, downtown, the ice rink, City Market, and other perimeter stops. You can also take a **Town Trolley** in summer, which follows the transit system's Orange Route. **Summit Stage** (970-668-0999) can take you from Breck to nearby Keystone and Copper ski areas—or to Silverthorne, Frisco, and Dillon.

Ranger stations

Dillon Ranger District: 970-468-5400, 680 Blue River Pkwy., Silverthorne

Tourist information

Breckenridge Resort Chamber: 970-453-2913, gobreck.com, 311 S. Ridge St., Breckenridge

Town of Frisco: 970-668-3050, townoffrisco.com, 1 Main St., Frisco

Summit County Chamber: 800-530-3099, summitchamber.org; Information Center at 246 Rainbow Dr., Silverthorne

Making a mark in Crested Butte's white gold. Tom Stillo/Crested Butte Mountain Resort

3

CRESTED BUTTE

Welcome to Wonderland

> *It's got to be the going, not the getting there, that's good.*
> —*seen on an old hippie bus in Crested Butte*

Often called the last great Colorado ski town, Crested Butte is home to the yogis, freaks, dropouts, intellectuals, athletes, diehards, and free spirits who used to inhabit most of the state's mountain communities—it has a pride, resourcefulness, and funk that comes across as soon as you roll down Elk Avenue or click into your skis to traverse to the Extreme Limits. The whole town is a National Historic District, though some of the charmingly dilapidated buildings now house pottery studios and art galleries rather than saloons and houses of ill repute. Tucked in the midst of four drop-dead-gorgeous wilderness areas— the Raggeds, Maroon Bells, West Elks, and Collegiate Peaks—Crested Butte is also one of the most scenic towns in Colorado. The Rocky Mountain Biological Laboratory has identified more than 600 species of wildflower that call this area home. At times, the wide valley feels like the end of the world. But show up during a pagan festival, a costume-required telemark ski race, or a mushroom festival and you'll get just how warm the isolation can feel.

The first whites to explore the valley were beaver trappers. Surveyors were right on their heels, followed by miners in search of gold and silver, and English, Irish, Scottish, German, Greek, Hispanic, and Croatian laborers who toiled for mine bosses. The miners found some precious metal—but what really sustained Crested Butte, until the 1950s, was coal. Colorado Fuel and Iron, owned by John D. Rockefeller, discovered black gold in 1879; the town was incorporated in 1880; Howard F. Smith, a partner at a smelting company in Leadville, became the first mayor shortly thereafter. The Denver & Rio Grande Railroad arrived in 1881. That's when the population peaked at 1,500 (which is about what it is today), with a dozen saloons, five hotels, and a phone line to Gunnison, 30 miles away. At one point, it had a larger Slavic population than Denver.

When the demand for coal gradually decreased, so did the size of CB—and its bust was sealed when the Big Mine, the third largest in Colorado, closed down. The railroad tracks were removed. The high school closed. The population fizzled to 200.

It's hard to say whether it was the hippies or the ski area that rejuvenated Crested Butte — but it avoided the fate of dozens of ghost towns in the area (see page 116), thanks to the rowdy, steep, technical skiing at Mount Crested Butte (the official name of the ski hill, with its accompanying condo complexes and conference centers, 3 miles up the road) and the some- times freaky, often hardy, always liberal, totally inclusive personality of the town. There

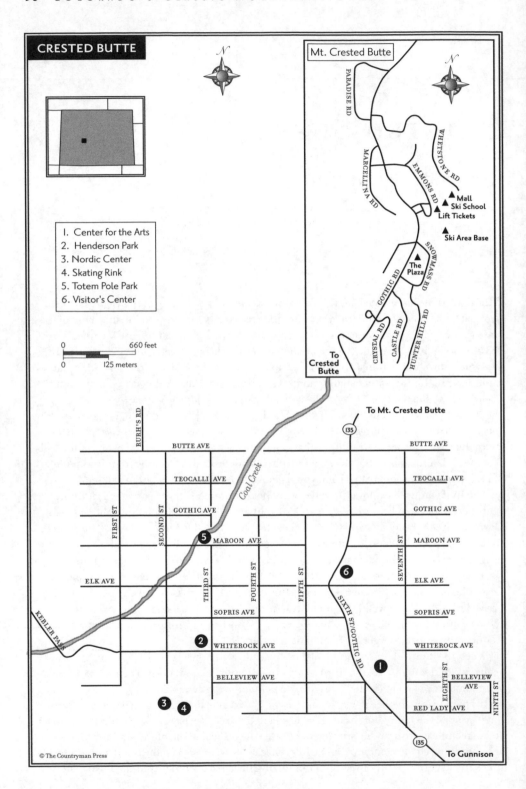

CRESTED BUTTE

Mt. Crested Butte

1. Center for the Arts
2. Henderson Park
3. Nordic Center
4. Skating Rink
5. Totem Pole Park
6. Visitor's Center

© The Countryman Press

are still locals who remember riding horses to school and watching the policemen take LSD (and while neither of these things probably happen anymore, the afterglow of both remain).

CB isn't a particularly affluent place, but it's slowly evolving like every other mountain town: new ownership, a refurbished base village, huge second homes, yuppies, slick night spots, and big hotels. Mount Crested Butte is growing steadily—and casting a spit-shined shadow over the valley below, thanks to the beginnings of a five-year, $200-million facelift. That said, the whole area still lacks the flash of Aspen and Telluride, the crowds of Vail and Breckenridge, and the cow-town character of Steamboat. Does that make it the last great Colorado ski town? The jury is out—but it is, without doubt, the most genuine.

LODGING

CRESTED BUTTE

✪ Crested Butte Club
Gary and Connie Wolf
800-815-2582
crestedbutteclub.com
info@crestedbutteclub.com
512 2nd St., Crested Butte
Price Range: $159–$299, including breakfast

Credit Cards: AE, MC, V
Children: Y, with $20–$25 per-day charge
Pets: N
Handicap Accessible: Y

The classy CB Club is the one of the more luxurious spots in town. The nine themed suites have aromatherapy tubs, steam showers, king beds, walnut furnishings and trim, pedestal sinks, and the original framed photography of the owner, Gary

An inviting common room at the Crested Butte Club (see page 102). Evelyn Spence

Wolf. Some rooms (like the Crystal River and the Summer Delight) have two-person tubs or private decks with views of Mount Crested Butte. And everything inside belies the fact that the building went up in 1886: The enormous main door is original, but the rest is totally updated—in some cases, many times over. (The Business Center used to be a squash court.) The intimate fitness center and coed spa has a lap pool, steam baths, free weights, and aerobic machines, as well as a menu of massages, body polishes, herbal wraps, facials, manicures, and pedicures—and for 15 extra bucks, you can get a massage right in your room. The hand-carved woodwork of the downstairs bar—the Wolf Den Tavern—has been there since that big main door first opened.

Cristiana Guesthaus

Innkeepers: Martin and Rosemary Catmur
800-824-7899
cristianaguesthaus.com
info@cristianaguesthaus.com
621 Maroon Ave., Crested Butte
Price Range: $65–$95, including
    continental breakfast
Credit Cards: AE, D, MC, V
Children: Y, 5 and older
Pets: N
Handicap Accessible: N

The first lodge built for the ski area, the Cristiana is a basic, economical choice— motel prices with Euro-ski-lodge character. Owners Martin and Rosemary, who have turned their rock garden in front into a prizewinner in the annual Wildflower Festival, have been running the property since 1988, when they moved to CB to "get away from the rat race." All of the 21 rooms have private baths, and either queen, king, or double-queen beds—along with floral-patterned blankets and rough wooden walls. The lobby is rustic and charming: a huge stone fireplace in the

center, with antique skis on the walls, iron sconces, and old ski boots. The railings are painted with flowers, Bavarian-style, and the continental breakfast includes home-made granola and muesli, pastries, juice, and coffee. And the view from the hot tub is one of the best in town: It looks straight into the steep faces of Mount Crested Butte.

Elizabeth Anne Bed and Breakfast

Innkeepers: Denise and Kevin Reinert
888-745-4620
crested-butte-inn.com
info@crested-butte-inn.com
703 Maroon Ave., Crested Butte
Price Range: $150–$220, including
    breakfast
Credit Cards: MC, V
Children: Y
Pets: Y, over 1 year old
Handicap Accessible: N

You could call the candy-cane Elizabeth Anne super-Victorian: The rooms are teeming with flowered wallpaper, patterned quilts, lace curtains, brass beds, and pinks, greens, light blues, and yellows. It's also super homey: Hand-knit afghans are slung over couches in the living room, stuffed

A king bed at the Victorian-style Elizabeth Anne Bed and Breakfast. Evelyn Spence

Elk Mountain Lodge: boarding house—turned—skier's retreat. Evelyn Spence

animals hold court on mantels, and mixed nuts and M&Ms are set out on end tables. The rooms are named after local peaks and bowls, like Red Lady (named for Red Lady Bowl, a backcountry favorite, and decorated with pinks, reds, and garlands), or Purple (named for 12,958-foot Purple Mountain and the most spare room of the five, with plain white walls and a beautiful cherry furniture set). The huge wraparound porch, with hanging baskets (in summer), is a great spot for a glass of wine—or a few minutes of digestion after downing cranberry-walnut-oatmeal pancakes, strawberry-stuffed french toast, or baked eggs Florentine.

Elk Mountain Lodge
Innkeeper: Mike Nolan
800-374-6521, 970-349-7533
elkmountainlodge.net
info@elkmountainlodge.net
129 Gothic Ave., Crested Butte
Price Range: $110–$160, including breakfast
Credit Cards: AE, D, MC, V
Children: Y
Pets: N
Handicap Accessible: N

With 19 rooms, Elk Mountain—two blocks off Elk Avenue—was built in 1919 as a miners' boarding house. It has all kinds of comfy crannies for you to relax with a book (there are hundreds on the various shelves), play the baby grand piano, have a drink (there's a nooklike bar open until 10:30), check local guidebooks, challenge your neighbor to Pictionary, or catch up on e-mail on an ancient computer. Yes, it's a bit cluttered downstairs, but the rooms are bright and spare, with colorful comforter covers in plaids and solids, pine furniture, and private baths. Want a view? Request one of the third-floor rooms, which come with balconies. Breakfast is deluxe continental: scrambled eggs, waffles, and french toast rotate through the menu, along with bagels, baked goods, granola, coffee, cocoa, and the like.

✪ The Ruby of Crested Butte

Innkeepers: Andrea and Chris Greene
800-390-1338
therubyofcrestedbutte.com
624 Gothic Ave., Crested Butte
Price Range: $109–$169
Credit Cards: AE, D, MC, V
Children: Y
Pets: Y
Handicap Accessible: Y

The sign at the entrance to the Ruby—a bright red B&B with red hallways—says PLEASE WIPE YOUR PAWS. It's just the beginning: Here, dogs get their own dishes for food and water, homemade organic dog treats, and dog beds; the innkeepers even offer dog sitting, hiking, spa treatments, and grooming. Says Andrea, who came here on vacation in 2004 and ended up moving to CB to run the Ruby, "We like both dogs and people who like dogs!" Rooms with names like A Daydream, The Moment, and The Proper Perspective are all painted in calming yellows, beiges, and light blues, and have radiant in-floor heating. There are fresh, hot cinnamon rolls waiting every morning in the high-ceilinged upstairs breakfast room—along with a main course of dutch apple pancakes, strawberry french toast soufflé, or caramel pecan waffles (in case the sweet roll wasn't sweet enough). With an extensive DVD and book collection (*Garden State*, *Sideways*, *Seabiscuit*, and *Finding Nemo*, or Irving, Crichton, Clancy, and Tolkien), it might be hard to leave—but just look out a window for incentive (there are mountain views everywhere).

Mount Crested Butte

✪ Crested Butte Retreat

General Manager: Jenny Roberts
970-349-1701
crestedbutteretreat.com
info@crestedbutteretreat.com
39 Whetstone Rd., Mt. Crested Butte
Price Range: $115–$400
Credit Cards: AE, MC, V
Children: Y, over 12
Pets: N
Handicap Accessible: N

Refurbished in June 2004 into a boutique inn, the Crested Butte Retreat was formerly a 10,000-square-foot home for a wealthy Texas family, and it retains the feel of a sumptuous private mansion. No expense was spared in its original construction or its remodel: hickory and maple floors, soapstone stoves, wraparound porches, slate bathrooms, international art, antique furniture, broad-beamed cathedral ceilings, and huge windows. The so-called Master Chambers have their own private decks *and* private hot tubs with mountain views—and the most opulent of them, Pearl, is a honeymooners' dream: white muslin drapes, canopied bed, ivory carpet, and a greenhouse with Finnish sauna and sunken hot tub. Though it only has nine guest rooms, the Retreat has a concierge, spa, fitness room, multiple fireplaces, area shuttles, and a private chef and sommelier for hire (for private dinners of rack of lamb and herb-rubbed salmon in the dining room). Want to watch a DVD? Their TV is 100 inches. Breakfast is no-frills and hearty, with local coffee and herbal tea, butter croissants, assorted muffins, homemade granola, yogurt, and fruit, along with eggs cooked to order, any style.

Crested Butte Trail House

Owner: Tim Stubbs
970-640-2626
cbtrailhouse.com

14 Redstone Cove, Mt. Crested Butte
Price Range: $136–$2,060 (for the whole
  house)
Credit Cards: AE, D, MC, V
Children: Y
Pets: N
Handicap Accessible: Y

Not really a bed and breakfast, but not
really a private home, either, the Trail
House is a quiet, 7,000-square-foot ski-
in/ski-out mountain mansion that sleeps
up to 18 people (but can be booked for
smaller groups). No detail has been overlooked here: radiant heat, wide pine
flooring, knotty cherry cabinets, hundred-
year-old beams, five decks, two kitchens,
and a heated garage that's 1,000 square feet
alone. Each bedroom has Italian linens,
memory foam mattresses, HDTV, down pillows, steam showers, and plush bathrobes.
The surrounding meadow teems with wildflowers in summer, then gets blanketed by
snow in winter—and you're located smack
dab at the access point for the Washington
Gulch trailhead. And that means backcountry skiing, snowshoeing, mountain
biking, and hiking (literally) right out the
front door.

Grand Lodge Crested Butte
888-823-4446
grandlodgecrestedbutte.com
info@grandlodgecrestedbutte.com
6 Emmons Loop, Mt. Crested Butte
Price Range: $69–$359
Credit Cards: AE, MC, V
Children: Y
Pets: Y
Handicap Accessible: Y

Up at Mount Crested Butte, there are a few
large-scale hotels, but the Grand Lodge is
the classiest—at least until the refurbishment of the base village is complete in 2010
and more luxe properties are built. Each of
the 200-plus rooms has wireless internet,
satellite TV, lots of complimentary bottled
water, and photos of local areas. The in-
house Wildflower Spa offers massages and
facials; the in-house WoodStone Grille has
a huge breakfast buffet and serves
Southwestern specialties for dinner. What
it lacks in character it makes up in convenience: You're minutes away from first
tracks, and
a free shuttle will drive you to town whenever you need. And its size means it can
offer packages that include both accommodations and lift tickets (check the Web site
often; these deals change frequently).

Nordic Inn
Innkeepers: Allen and Judy Cox
800-542-7669, 970-349-5542
nordicinncb.com
acox@nordicinncb.com
14 Treasury Rd., Mt. Crested Butte
Price Range: $88–$132, including
  continental breakfast
Credit Cards: AE, MC, V
Children: Y
Pets: N
Handicap Accessible: Y

If you want to stay within walking distance
of the slopes—without staying in a mammoth hotel or spending a fortune—Allen
and Judy Cox's cute Scandinavian-style
Nordic Inn is your best bet. The outdoor
railings are cut out with pine tree shapes,
there's usually a huge snowman out front
(when snowfall allows), and the fireplace is
often decorated with wreaths and stockings.
Rooms are basic—standard wooden furniture, light pink and floral upholstery, and
photos of local scenes—as is the breakfast
(bagels, danishes, cereal, juice, coffee). You
can also rent two Nordic Inn–style chalets
that sleep six to eight for $152–$310 a night.

FARTHER AFIELD

Almont Resort
Owner: Donald Gordon
970-641-4009

The Nordic Inn in Mt. Crested Butte is just steps from the slopes. Evelyn Spence

almontresort.com
stay@almontresort.com
10209 CO 135, Almont
Price Range: $55–$100
Credit Cards: AE, D, MC, V
Children: Y
Pets: Y
Handicap Accessible: N

The resident ghost of Almont Resort is named George, the town itself was named for a famous Hambletonian-caliber stallion, and in 1940 presidential nominee Wendell Wilkie—along with 10,000 guests—had a fish fry here to kick off his campaign. The upshot? There's no shortage of character in this neck of the woods. In a prime spot where the Taylor and the East Rivers come together to form the Gunnison, about 16 miles south of Crested Butte, there has been a resort or hotel here since 1893.

These days, the Almont offers rafting, hunting, horseback riding, fishing, snowmobiling, and various sizes of log cabins (20 in all). The restaurant and lounge area, Bar 47—named so because the owner's initials, D(aniel) G(ordon), are the fourth and seventh letters of the alphabet—has big wooden beams, historical photos, and varnished-wood walls, along with air hockey, pool, foosball, live music, a dance floor, and satellite TV on the big screen.

✪ Pioneer Guest Cabins

Innkeepers: Matt and Leah Whiting
970-349-5517
pioneerguestcabins.com
pioneer@crestedbutte.net
2094 Cement Creek Rd., 8 miles S. of
    Crested Butte
Price Range: $109–$159

Credit Cards: MC, V
Children: Y
Pets: Y, with advance notice
Handicap Accessible: N

Just a few miles out of Crested Butte on the road to Gunnison, the rustic but cozy Pioneer complex consists of four 1920s-era cottages and four 1960s cabins on a 7-acre spread at the base of what was once one of the first ski areas in the state, Pioneer. And outside of that are 1.7 million acres of the Gunnison National Forest, including the locals' favorite mountain bike ride, the Reno/Flag/Bear/Deadman's loop. The bright Sunshine cottage (sleeps six) has a barn-wood kitchen counter, vaulted aspen ceilings, and chinked log walls—and a private hammock out back. The Matterhorn cottage (sleeps four) has an open floor plan, a Vermont Casings wood stove, wicker furniture, and antlers on the walls. Of the newer cabins, the secluded Teocalli—remodeled in 2005—is considered the signature spot: peeled log beams, Douglas fir flooring, and views of Double Top Mountain. All accommodations come with full kitchens, gas stoves, full baths, quilts, outdoor grills, and unlimited firewood. The best perk? You can snowshoe and cross-country ski from your front porch.

Three Rivers Resort
Innkeepers: Mark and Mary Jo Schumacher
888-761-3474, 970-641-1303
3riversresort.com
email@3riversresort.com
County Road 742, Almont
Price Range: $65–$315
Credit Cards: AE, MC, V
Children: Y
Pets: Y, but inform at check-in
Handicap Accessible: Y

The riverfront cabins—named after artificial flies like Blue Dun and Green Drake—are just a small part of the Three Rivers complex. They also have their own fly shop, paddle shop, dance hall, and resources for planning anything from a Jeep tour to a rock-climbing excursion to a hot air balloon ride. You can rent a tiny, rustic one-bedroom log cabin, a two-bedroom on the river, or a four-bedroom vacation home with hot tub (ask for the George Bailey). If you'd rather pull up in an RV or just pitch a tent, sites go for $25 a night. You'll still have full access to the volleyball court, the horseshoe pit, the kids' fishing pond, and the Smokehouse—where every Friday is Catfish Fry Friday, and every remaining day means burgers, brisket, and ribs.

Guest Ranches

Harmel's Ranch Resort
800-235-3402, 970-641-1740
harmels.com
stay@harmels.com
6478 CR 72, Almont
Price Range: $95–$269 (depending on plan)
Credit Cards: AE, MC, V
Children: Y
Pets: Y
Handicap Accessible: Y

Choose the "Run of the Ranch" plan at Harmel's and you get three meals a day, unlimited trail rides, unlimited fly casting lessons, unlimited guided fishing trips, an overnight horsepack ride, swimming pool and sauna, and one rafting trip or one massage per three-day span. Not bad for about 250 bucks (and if you want to pick activities à la carte, it's even cheaper). And folks here take their eating seriously: Mondays are steak fry/crab cookout nights, with rib eye, chicken, mashed potatoes, and polka dancing. Thursdays are reserved for the Chuckwagon BBQ, including cowboy poetry and square dancing. Each of the 37 cabins, which sleep from two to nine and are brown with cheery yellow trim, has pine walls and spare decorations.

Powderhorn Guest Ranch

Owners: Greg and Shelly Williams

800-786-1220

powderhornguestranch.com

powguest@mindspring.com

1525 CR 27, Powderhorn

Price Range: $1,295 per week

Credit Cards: AE, MC, V

Children: Y

Pets: N

Handicap Accessible: N

With just 30 guests at a time (in eight peeled log cabins with front porches and patterned curtains), Powderhorn makes you feel like family—or maybe it's the friendliness of its owners, Greg and Shelly Williams. They show Western movies, with popcorn, in their main lodge; they run sing-alongs around the campfire; they call square dances; they offer free, unlimited riding instruction; and they organize cookouts on their tiny private island in the middle of the Gunnison. Kids can fish for trout in the pond right behind the lodge, and adults can walk 10 minutes to the ranch's own stocked Hidden Lake—or wet a line for German browns and brookies in Cebolla Creek, which runs right through the property. Of course, the main activity is riding, and the Powderhorn owns quarter horses, Arabians, appaloosas, thoroughbreds—and ponies for the little ones. The week wraps up with a gymkhana, in which guests compete for ribbons: a perfect souvenir.

✪ Smith Fork Ranch

Owners: The Hodgson Family

970-921-3454

smithforkranch.com

info@smithforkranch.com

45362 Needle Rock Rd., Crawford

Price Range: $5,600 (for double in
    lodge)—$19,500 (for six-person cabin)
    a week

Credit Cards: AE, MC, V

Children: Y

Pets: N

Handicap Accessible: Y

The site of a guest ranch since 1939 (then owned by Grant and Mamie Ferrier), Smith Fork is dude deluxe with a couple of capital D's. Some of the buildings date back to the 1890s, but everything—the cabins, the Old Elk Lodge, and the Dinner Bell Cookhouse—has been lovingly restored and embellished with Native American crafts and antiques, pine beds, bright-white chinking, plank floors, rocking chairs, wood stoves, slate showers, and screened-in porches. There are wonderful views of the Smith Fork River. All meals are prepared with local and organic ingredients, and the wine list pushes 250 varieties. After a day of riding through the West Elks, fishing for brookies and cutties on the water that burbles through the property, or going on a tour of area wineries, you can sit on overstuffed couches by the river rock fireplace in the parlor—where old Western saddles rest on ceiling beams and a huge elk trophy observes the goings-on. Or eavesdrop on a fly-tying demonstration. Or sing around the campfire. Or take your kids to the archery course. Of course, the luxury comes with a price—but if you can swing it, you won't be disappointed.

Waunita Hot Springs Ranch

Owners: The Pringle Family

970-641-1266

waunita.com

8007 CR 887, Gunnison

Price Range: $1,600 a week (for adults),
    $750–$1,500 (for kids)

Credit Cards: AE, MC, V

Children: Y

Pets: N

Handicap Accessible: Y

Though it's a bit of a drive from Crested Butte (it's actually 30 minutes from Gunnison), Waunita is also surrounded by the Gunnison National Forest and has access to several hundred thousand acres of territory. It makes for endless options when it comes to horseback riding—including a few rides that climb well above timberline to Baldy Mountain and Stella Mountain. The riding program starts each Monday, and you can take lessons in the arena, learn how to pen cattle, and leave the kiddies with the wranglers for riding games. Guests stay in small- to medium-size lodges, all in view of Tomichi Dome, a distinctive round-topped peak, and eat together—homemade muffins, rolls, and pies; huge pancakes and plates of fried chicken; barbecued ribs and grilled fish. And of course there's the namesake hot spring, which supplies the ranch with 300,000 gallons of water a day, fills a 95-degree swimming pool, and heats the lodges.

DINING

Restaurants

CRESTED BUTTE

Bacchanale

970-349-5257
209 Elk Ave., Crested Butte
Meals Served: D
Price Range: Entrées $13.95–$21.50
Full bar: Y
Reservations: Y
Credit Cards: AE, MC, V
Handicap Accessible: Y

It's rare for a mountain-town restaurant to stay alive for a decade—and chef-owned Bacchanale has been around for three. They must be on to something. Maybe it's the atmosphere: ornate wrought-iron railings, copper ceilings, loft seating, cruiser bikes woven with white Christmas lights, and themed photography. Most likely, it's the goods: The fave Fra Diavolo is a skillet of garlic, olive oil, jalapeño, and red sauce, with a choice of chicken, shrimp, or eggplant, topped with fresh mozzarella and served with a sidecar of linguini. The Italian staples (garlic bread, minestrone, fried zucchini, build-your-own-pasta) are all solid—and everything "a la Bacchanale" is outstanding (Pollo a la Bacchanale is a lightly breaded chicken breast topped with mozzarella and ham and baked in a Trebbiano wine sauce). Try anything with Muley's Italian sausages: They're all natural and made right in Crested Butte.

The Buffalo Grille and Saloon

970-349-9699
435 Sixth Ave., Crested Butte
Meals Served: D
Price Range: entrees $15–$38
Full bar: Y
Reservations: Y
Credit Cards: AE, D, MC, V
Handicap Accessible: Y

Don't let the name fool you: The Buffalo Grille does serve a mean bison (applewood-smoked buffalo rib eye with smashed potatoes and horseradish crème fraîche), but that's just a small slice of the classy menu. Nowhere else in town can you get anything like "3-Way Duck," a trio including foie gras with brioche french toast, duck leg confit, and duck prosciutto. Chicken comes stuffed with chèvre, the rack of venison is topped with a lingonberry demi-glace, and the salmon is rubbed with chili. Owner Jimmy Clark has been a professional bull rider since the age of 14, and he still competes in senior bull-riding championships; he's kept the cowboy influence at bay here, sticking to linen tablecloths, red-upholstered chairs, crystal, dark wood paneling, gold wallpaper, and a bar with glass-block foundations and brass railings. Unlike most of the restaurants on Elk Avenue, Buffalo Grille has grand views of Mount Crested Butte.

Ginger Café

970-349-7291
313 Third St., Crested Butte
Meals Served: L, D
Price Range: $9–$17
Full bar: Y
Reservations: Y
Credit Cards: MC, V
Handicap Accessible: N

A bright green building with purplish trim, Ginger Café is a small, storefront-style pan-Asian spot that has locals spilling out the door on weekend nights for cheap Indian and Thai. Your best bet? Wander over, put your name on the list, and have a beer somewhere down the street. But don't miss Ginger's "exotic drinks": among them, a ginger-infused martini and a mango mojito. Appetizers range from salty edamame to crispy tofu tempura, and entrées cover everything from a straight Indian aloo saag (pureed spinach and tomatoes with cumin and coriander) and pad Thai (the archetypal Thai dish, with stir-fried noodles with peanuts and tofu, chicken, or shrimp) to rogan gosht—grass-fed Colorado lamb in a tangy almond sauce. The coconut ginger ice cream, topped with mint, is so popular that some people *start* their meal with it.

✪ Izzy's

970-349-5630
218 Maroon Ave., Crested Butte
Meals Served: B, L
Price Range: $4–$8
Full bar: N
Reservations: N
Credit Cards: MC, V
Handicap Accessible: Y

Izzy's sign says it all: It's an enormous bagel rising over the mountains like a carbohydrate sun. And this red-and-blue former feed shack hasn't changed as much as you might think—it still fuels, only now it's skiers, hikers, and mountain bikers. Most mornings, townie bikes are leaning against the facade, and people are sipping lattes on the front benches. The menu puts a twist on breakfast and lunch: french toast made with challah; reubens made with potato latkes rather than bread; breakfast latkes (eggs and cheese on a latke). There's more traditional fare, too: the blueberry pancakes; the breakfast bagels with eggs, cheese, and bacon; the hummus-and-veggie wraps; the sandwiches on fresh-baked bread. Order ahead if you have summits to conquer, and it'll be ready by 7 AM sharp.

Last Steep Bar & Grill

970-349-7007
208 Elk Ave., Crested Butte
Meals Served: L, D
Price Range: $5–$14
Full bar: Y
Reservations: N
Credit Cards: AE, D, MC, V
Handicap Accessible: N

Named for a black-diamond run on the mountain's North Face, Last Steep is a great family place: cheap food (nothing over $14, and most around $10), with mini corn dogs and chicken fingers for the kids and build-your-own-Bloody-Marys for parents. Friday's an all-you-can-eat fish fry, and Saturday night is BBQ-rib night. Every night features American, Caribbean, and Cajun grub. We're not talking haute cuisine here, but the portions are generous and the choices are varied: crab cakes, egg rolls, coconut shrimp, and artichoke and cheddar soup for starters, and entrées like Cajun chicken pasta, black bean casserole, fish tacos, and chicken Caesar wraps. You can't go wrong with a sandwich (jerk chicken, Cajun-grilled ahi, crab cake) or burger (portobello mushroom, Santa Fe veggie).

✪ Lobar

970-349-0480
303 Elk Ave., Crested Butte
Meals Served: D

Izzy's in Crested Butte is a favorite breakfast stop of both visitors and locals alike, some of whom arrive on bikes, even in winter. Evelyn Spence

Price Range: $12–$20
Full bar: Y
Reservations: Y
Credit Cards: AE, D, MC, V
Handicap Accessible: N

Thought CB was only home to hippies? Think again. Lobar, a sushi joint-cum-mountain lounge, is where the hipsters come out of hiding, pull open the industrial steel door, and slink downstairs to sip Chaitinis (Godiva white chocolate liqueur, Bacardi, and green chai tea) on black sectional couches. The sushi is creative: The Green Man Roll, named after a central figure in the annual Vinotok pagan festival, combines asparagus, burdock, cucumber, avocado, scallions, sprouts, and spinach. The Rasta Roll comes with mango, avocado, tobiko, cucumber, and black sesame. With dart boards, pool tables, big-screen TVs, DJs, and live music, it isn't exactly quiet and romantic—but it's as close to Big City as you're gonna get here.

✪ **Secret Stash**
970-349-6245
thesecretstash.com
21 Elk Ave., Crested Butte
Meals Served: D
Price Range: $10–$20
Full bar: Y
Reservations: N
Credit Cards: MC, V
Handicap Accessible: Y

A pizza joint? An opium den? When you walk into the Secret Stash, it takes a second to figure out which: The interior is cozy and cavelike, with velvet cushions, couches, and funky artwork. In fact, even the outside of the Stash is compelling: The fence is made of old skis, and the eaves are always rimmed with white Christmas lights. Co-owner Kyleena Graceffa has traveled to 62 countries, and her souvenirs fill the restaurant to the rafters. Sure, you can get your pepperoni and your veggie, but what made this place tops in CB for three years

The deeper the snow outside, the cozier Soupçon will be inside.   Evelyn Spence

running is its specialty pies—concoctions like Tennessee Jed's Zaaa, with grilled chicken, barbecue sauce, burnt onions, black beans, and corn; the New Potato Caboose, topped with roasted potatoes, bacon, cheddar cheese, and green onion; and the K.G.B (Killer Greens and Bacon), with chipotle sauce, mixed greens, and feta and blue cheeses.

The Slogar Bar & Restaurant
970-349-5765
517 Second St., Crested Butte
Meals Served: D
Price Range: $15 per person (children's portions available)
Full bar: Y
Reservations: Y
Credit Cards: AE, MC, V
Handicap Accessible: Y

Looking to eat your way through (or at least surrounded by) history? There's been a building on this spot since 1882, and the Slogar's current two-story facade has been around since 1900. In fact, it was operated as a watering hole as far back as 1904, and for a while it was the town's busiest brothel; the bar and ceilings still remain. Check out the tall, double-hung windows and glazed double doors—signs of typical saloon construction—and then head in for an all-you-can-eat comfort food bonanza. For 15 bucks, you get coleslaw, half a skillet-fried chicken (the recipe supposedly dates from 1915), mashers with chicken gravy, baking powder biscuits shining with honey butter, sweet corn in cream sauce, and ice cream.

✪ Soupçon
970-349-5448
127A Elk Ave., Crested Butte
Meals Served: D
Price Range: Entrées $17–$26
Full bar: Y

Reservations: Y
Credit Cards: AE, MC, V
Handicap Accessible: Y

Occupying a historic—and tiny—miners' log cabin from the early 1900s, Soupçon's cheerful red trim, lace curtains, and hand-painted OPEN 6–10 sign are as unpretentious and friendly as the food is sophisticated. It undoubtedly concocts one of the best meals in town. And reservations are a must: There are only two nightly seatings, giving the place a vibe much closer to that of an intimate home than a showy food palace. Chef Jason Vernon, who bought the restaurant in 2006, was trained at the Culinary Institute of America and worked under Emeril Lagasse and Michael Rousse in New Orleans. He brings together French and American influences in dishes like marinated frog legs, New Zealand elk tenderloin with clove honey glaze, marinated Sonoma quail, root vegetable mélange with warm goat cheese, and Hudson Valley foie gras.

Teocalli Tamale
970-349-2005
311¼ Elk Ave., Crested Butte
Meals Served: B, L, D
Price Range: $6–$11
Full bar: N
Reservations: N
Credit Cards: D, MC, V
Handicap Accessible: Y

Don't expect to get breakfast here on certain winter days: You'll be greeted with a hand-lettered cardboard sign that reads POWDER DAY, CLOSED UNTIL NOON. PEACE. Teocalli is a casual burrito bar with quintessential chili-pepper garlands, guitars, sombreros, and even costumes hanging from the walls and ceiling. In a town where it's hard to get a late-night bite, you can get cheap margaritas and tacos until 1 AM. Teocalli offers the basics—shredded beef burritos, Baja fish tacos, huevos rancheros—along with imaginative choices like a green chili pesto burrito and a "gourmet vegetarian" burrito with roasted potatoes, onions, tomatoes, garlic, and rosemary.

✪ Timberline Restaurant

970-349-9831
timberlinerestaurant.com
201 Elk Ave., Crested Butte
Meals Served: D
Price Range: Appetizers $5.50–$9.50, entrées $14–$36
Full bar: Y
Reservations: Y
Credit Cards: AE, MC, V
Handicap Accessible: Y

Tim Egelhoff earned a BA in chemistry from Western State College in Gunnison, cooked his way through school at various restaurants in Crested Butte, and did stints in Front Range and coastal California kitchens. In 1989, he opened the New American–themed Timberline, one of the tip-top dining rooms in Gunnison County. It's bigger than it looks: The Victorian building seats 44 downstairs at bistro-style booths and round tables, 12 on the cowhair barstools, 68 upstairs in the more formal gallery and wine room, 15 on the front patio, and 45 overlooking the creek out back. But enough math: The food here shines. Come in between 5:30 and 6 PM for the $15 "early-bird special": soup or salad, choice of entrée (grilled salmon, say, or chicken baklava), and dessert. Or linger over the seasonal menu for caribou medallions with wild rice, cabbage and mushroom strudel, and blueberry-merlot demi-glace; crispy-skinned rainbow trout with honey-tequila glaze; or a Gunnison-raised beef burger with caramelized onions. Local artist Shaun Horne's work hangs on the walls.

Wooden Nickel

970-349-6350
222 Elk Ave., Crested Butte
Meals Served: D
Price Range: $12–$30
Full bar: Y
Reservations: N
Credit Cards: AE, D, MC, V
Handicap Accessible: Y

The Nickel is a CB landmark—the longest continually operated saloon/restaurant in town—and it shows (in a good way). The place is slightly cluttered with deer trophies, model ships, historical photos, flags, and beer signs; the bench seats and bar stools are covered in green vinyl; and the wood floors are worn beneath their polish. The menu is meat, meat, meat: prime rib, rack of lamb, thick pork chops, New York steaks, buffalo burgers, pork ribs, elk tenderloin, all prepared without frills. Seafood (trout, lobster, Alaskan king crab) is available, but there's not much for herbivores. The happy-hour martinis are a steal, and baseball caps and beards (if you have one) are the dress code.

MOUNT CRESTED BUTTE

Last Tracks dinner

970-349-2211
On-mountain at the Ice Bar
Meals Served: D
Price Range: $69 for a six-course meal
Full bar: Y
Reservations: Y
Credit Cards: AE, D, MC, V
Handicap Accessible: N

Only in a ski town: Sign up for Last Tracks, and you catch a late-afternoon ride up the Red Lady Express and ski partway downhill to get to dinner. Start with a signature pomotini (a pomegranate martini) at the Ice Bar, an outdoor bar made of ice blocks where the waitresses are known to wear fur bikinis. When the evening chill sets in, duck into the nearby A-frame cabin for a five-course feast complete with white tablecloths and roaring fire (just unbuckle your ski boots and hang your jacket on one of the many wall hooks). Leave your pre-conceptions about "on-mountain" mess at the door: Here, it's beef tenderloin with shiitake sauce, bouillabaisse with chanterelle risotto, venison quesadillas with huckleberry salsa, salmon with ginger demi-glace, baked brie, bottomless bread baskets, and desserts such as profiteroles stuffed with Belgian chocolate mousse and green-tea-and-port-poached pears filled with pomegranate mascarpone.

FARTHER AFIELD

Garlic Mike's

970-641-2493
garlicmikes.com
2674 CR 135 N., Gunnison
Meals Served: D, Sun. brunch

Price Range: $9–$19
Full bar: Y
Reservations: Y
Credit Cards: AE, MC, V
Handicap Accessible: Y

Chef-owner Mike Busse may have gotten his culinary start flipping burgers and scooping ice cream at Friendly's, but you wouldn't know it from the home-style Italian he cooks at this Gunnison mainstay: apps like ricotta-stuffed eggplant rolls and mozzarella caprese, entrées like seafood cannelloni, and pizzas with pesto, shrimp, artichoke hearts, roasted peppers, and fontina. The whole place reeks of Roman kitsch: red-and-white checkered table-cloths covered with white butcher paper, photos of Italian scenes hanging on the walls, and a boisterous open kitchen. On the road between Gunny and CB, it's a worthwhile stop—especially if you can get a seat overlooking the Gunnison River.

Food Purveyors

Bakeries
The Bakery at Mount Crested Butte (970-349-4757, Mt. Crested Butte Village) This convenient pre-ski stop offers fresh-baked bagels, muffins, cookies, and brownies all day long—and even has après-ski drink specials if you want a cocktail with your cruller.

Coffee Shops
Buckeroo Beanery (601 Sixth St., Crested Butte) Next to the Phillips 66 gas station as you drive into town, Buckeroo has cheerful lime-green and yellow walls, a few couches and comfy chairs, two old computers for Internet geeks, and worn wood floors. Browse among books like *The Healing Foods* and *Bad As I Wanna Be* (by Dennis Rodman) over a coffee and a croissant.

Camp 4 Coffee (970-349-5148, camp4coffee.com, 402½ Elk Avenue, Crested Butte) One of the coolest buildings in town, Camp 4's downtown location is a wooden cabin covered in old license plates. And the name? It pays tribute to Camp 4 in Yosemite, where famous climbers have dirtbagged for years. Owner Al Smith donates 5 percent of his profits to local nonprofits—and sells roasted beans, espresso drinks, gifts, and propaganda.

The facade of Camp 4 Coffee in Crested Butte is covered with license plates.   Evelyn Spence

The Daily (970-349-2800, 502 Belleview Ave., Crested Butte) If you want an Americano and your friend wants a smoothie spiked with wheatgrass, compromise at The Daily—where you can also sip organic juices, munch on baked goods, and use wireless Internet.

Delis

CB South General Store (970-349-2551, 228 Elcho Ave., Crested Butte South) More than just a deli, the General Store serves breakfast (egg sandwiches, waffles, bagels), lunch (sandwiches like the Italian Stallion, with salami, ham, hot capocollo, provolone, green peppers, and Italian dressing), and dinner (pizza with everything from shaved steak to Cajun chicken to fresh tomatoes).

Cucina of Crested Butte (970-349-7174, 425 Elk Ave., Crested Butte) Belly up to the glass countertop for asparagus and herb quiche, ham and swiss croissants, white bean and olive soup, meatball sandwiches, and chocolate banana quick bread. In winter, sit at tables with plastic flowered coverings; in summer, grab a chair on the deck.

Pitas in Paradise (970-349-0897, 212 Elk Ave., Crested Butte) "Challenge us with your freaky dietary needs," say the people at this pita shack, where the fare includes gyros, falafel, baklava, wraps, and a killer tzatziki sauce.

Why Cook?! (970-349-5858, 555 Red Lady Ave., Crested Butte) A catering business that also serves salads, sandwiches on fresh-baked bread, soups, pâtés, cheeses, and desserts.

Farmer's Markets

Gunnison Farmer's Market (gunnisonfarmersmarket.org) Open every Saturday from July 1 to mid-October on the corner of Gunnison's North Main and West Virginia Streets, Gunny's market sells local produce, baked goods, and arts and crafts, and it sometimes has live entertainment (belly dancers, guitar players).

Groceries

Clark's Market (970-349-6492, 500 Belleview Ave., Crested Butte) The town's biggest grocery store.

Mountain Earth (970-349-5132, 405 Fourth St., Crested Butte) A small grocer with natural cosmetics, vitamins, organic produce, and bulk and frozen foods.

NIGHTLIFE

The Eldo (970-349-6125, 215 Elk Ave., Crested Butte) People love The Eldo's motto: "A sunny place for shady people." It's your best bet for live music—reggae, funk, and jam bands—as well as microbrews. The copper plates on the front of the bar show the wear of patrons' boots, and the walls are crowded with beer ads. Trey Anastasio of Phish played here, which is a point of pride.

Forest Queen Pub (970-349-2099, 129 Elk Ave., Crested Butte) With a good happy hour from 4 to 6 PM, dollar scotch nights every Wednesday, and $4 pitchers of Pabst Blue Ribbon *every* day, the Queen is a dive, but it has a following. Bar food is basic—mozzarella sticks, cheeseburgers, baskets of Lay's for a buck. A few days a week, the kitchen fires up for breakfasts of blueberry flapjacks, biscuits with sausage gravy, and English muffin sandwiches.

The Eldo, a popular nightspot in Crested Butte, makes no secret of its motto—or its clientele. Evelyn Spence

Kochevar's (970-349-6745, 127 Elk Ave., Crested Butte) In an 1886 building made from hand-hewn logs and decorated with mining memorabilia—run by Yugoslavian Jacob Kochevar until Prohibition—Kochevar's tends to attract a slightly older crowd that plays pool, shuffleboard, and darts and raids the popcorn machine. Rumor has it that Butch Cassidy once drank here—and when authorities from Telluride chased him down, he ran out the front door and left his gun behind. (You can see it at the Crested Butte Mountain Heritage Museum, page 117.)

Lobar (see page 108) If you're craving the feeling of a chichi city bar, this is the only place to find it: Lobar is the anti-CB, with microsuede sectional couches, DJs, and mod lighting. Wednesday night is salsa night.

Princess Wine Bar and Café (970-349-0210, 218 Elk Ave., Crested Butte) A combination breakfast joint, coffeehouse, wine bar, and furniture store, Princess has live music nightly at 8:30 PM, tapas, wine by the glass, and a decent selection of scotches. It's also open first thing in the morning for cappuccinos, applewood-smoked bacon, quiches, baked eggs, and belgian waffles.

Talk of the Town (970-349-0210, 230 Elk Ave., Crested Butte) Talk is a no-nonsense, smoky bar with video games, pool, and foosball. One local dubbed it a "spit 'n' sawdust" kind of place. Happy hour is actually five of them (from 3 to 8 PM every day).

CULTURE

Cinema
Majestic Theater (970-349-8955, Majestic Plaza near Sixth St. and Belleview Ave., Crested Butte) Showing a mix of mainstream and independent films, the Majestic gives the movies a personal touch: During the Disney movie *Eight Below*, they brought out a real dogsled team; during *Zoolander*, there was a costume contest. The coffee is fair trade, and the popcorn is topped with pure clarified butter.

Ghost Towns
Gothic Now home to the Rocky Mountain Biological Laboratory and situated at the confluence of the East River and Copper Creek, Gothic is a classic (and well-preserved) ghost town—though it's hardly abandoned. A good 150 students spend their summers here doing research, and RMBL hosts dinners, talks, and ecological hikes. Make sure to stop by the general store for ice cream and cold drinks—and keep checking back for the museum-in-progress.

Ohio City This town probably saw the most booms and busts of any mining hub in the area—it lived and died by gold, then silver, then more gold, until it finally busted for good in 1916.

Pie Plant Named for the abundance of wild rhubarb in the area, at its peak Pie Plant only had about 100 residents, a post office, and a saloon.

Pitkin Once known as Quartzville, Pitkin (founded in 1879) was the first mining camp west of the Continental Divide. The mines around it, including Nest Egg, Cleopatra, and Swiss

Bill, yielded gold, silver, lead, iron, and copper. These days, summer residents number between 200 and 300. The Pitkin Museum, located in the Red School House on Main Street, has old newspapers, typewriters, and school seats; two other buildings, the town hall and an early home, were also moved to the museum grounds.

Tin Cup The sign on the way into Tin Cup reads, "This is God's Country. Please Don't Drive Through It Like Hell." Once one of the wildest mining towns in the state (think saloons and brothels on nearly every corner), it now has a small log cabin restaurant, Frenchy's, that serves burgers and pies. It also sits near Cumberland Pass, the highest standard car road in the country.

Museums

Crested Butte Mountain Heritage Museum (970-349-1880, 331 Elk Ave., Crested Butte) Housed in an 1883 building, Crested Butte's only museum used to be a blacksmith shop—and then a hardware store and gas station called "Tony's Conoco," after its longtime owner. The front room has dozens of portraits of locals, showing CB's international influence: English, Irish, Welsh, German, Greek, and Croatian immigrants all landed here. In back, learn about the history of mountain biking in the **Mountain Bike Hall of Fame** (mtnbike halloffame.com).

Theaters and Other Miscellaneous Venues

Crested Butte Center for the Arts (970-349-7487, crestedbuttearts.org, 606 Sixth St., Crested Butte) The Center has a 215-seat auditorium, an outdoor stage, a gallery space, and a big lawn—all of which play host to concerts (the Alpenglow summer series takes place outdoors, with wine and kids allowed), dance recitals, plays, speakers, art exhibits, and

The Crested Butte Center for the Arts hosts everything from local art exhibitions to pottery classes. Evelyn Spence

fundraisers throughout the year. The annual Tour de Forks mixes recreation with serious eating—events include "Ladies, Lures, and Lunch," "Butte Views and Bountiful Brunch," "Fun with Sushi," and "Three Rivers Run Through It."

Crested Butte Mountain Theatre (970-349-0366, cbmountaintheatre.com, 403 Second St., Crested Butte) As the longest continuously running community theater in Colorado, CBMT has produced 200 plays—both locally written and perennially popular—over the last three decades.

Rocky Mountain Biological Laboratory (970-349-7231, rmbl.org; summer: 8000 CR 317, Crested Butte; winter: 308 Third St., Crested Butte) Though it's mostly a summertime environmental residency for scientists and college students, RMBL also organizes seminars, ecology walks, and small music festivals for the public.

KIDS' STUFF

Crested Butte Parks (970-349-5338) For a small town, CB has a lot open of space to run off energy: Town Park (soccer field, sand volleyball court, tennis courts, horseshoe pits, picnic pavilion), Big Mine Park (disc golf, skate park, ice rink, sledding hill), and Three Ladies Park (playground) are just a few examples.

Pinnacle Bike Race Series (970-349-2221, ridecb.com) Feeling competitive? Both kids and adults can participate in this Thursday-evening series in July, August, and September.

Rocky Mountain Biological Laboratory Kids Nature Camps (970-349-7231, rmbl.org) With hikes and scavenger hunts, RMBL's summer sessions include "Wet, Wild & Squiggly," "Cunning Cats," and "Birds, Blossoms & Bugs." Teen science camps focus on an introduction to biology.

Torchlight Parades (skicb.com) Every Wednesday and Friday nights in winter, ski and snowboard instructors lead kids down green runs with glo-sticks in hand—then give them pizza to eat, movies to watch, and group games to play.

RECREATION: WINTER AND SPRING

Alpine Skiing and Snowboarding

Crested Butte Mountain Resort
skicb.com

Overview: The former executive editor of *Skiing* magazine, Helen Olsson, once wrote, "Whether you're skiing through a hole in Rabbit Ears Rock called the ear canal or using an old snag nicknamed the 'bat pole' to rappel into Funnel, Crested Butte is raw, unadulterated ski adventure." So raw, in fact, that there's a special trail map—featuring black-and-white aerial photos—to the Extreme Limits, an umbrella name for the most difficult inbounds skiing on the mountain: 440 acres of steeps and cliffs in the North Face, and the Headwall, Spellbound, Phoenix, and Teocalli Bowl areas. The difficulty is compounded by a sometimes less-than-stellar snowpack (leaving, uh, more "features" exposed).

Riders on a quad chairlift, Crested Butte.   Tom Stillo/Crested Butte Mountain Resort

But when Crested Butte is good, it's really good, especially if you're a bona fide expert. That said, there is plenty for the mortals, too: The front side of Mount Crested Butte has long, rolling greens and blues, a superpipe and a terrain park, and precipitous, well-manicured cruisers.

Must-ski: This, of course, all depends on your skill level. And we mean your true skill level, not how good you think you are—because at CB, you can get yourself stuck on top of 80-foot cliffs, tumble down chutes called Body Bag, and scare the s**t out of yourself without skiing very far. Beginners and intermediates should, in general, stick to what they can access by the chairlifts—long groomers like Treasury and Keystone, mellow highways like Houston and Roller Coaster. Once you catch a ride up the T-bars (the North Face Lift and the High Lift) and start hiking or traversing, make sure you know where you're going. Pick up an Extreme Limits map ($5) at one of the local shops and pay attention to signs ("cliff" really does mean cliff). Try billygoating down The Headwall, often the site of the annual Crested Butte Extremes; open it up on recently opened Teocalli Bowl; pick through the trees of Staircase; or make tight turns down front-side Forest and Peel.

> **Crested Butte: The 4-1-1**
> Acres: 1,125
> Summit elevation: 12,162 feet
> Vertical drop: 3,062 feet
> Annual snowfall: 240 inches
> Percent advanced/expert terrain: 20
> Percent intermediate terrain: 57
> Percent beginner terrain: 23
> Lifts: 15

Mid-mountain dining with a touch of class: Rustica Ristorante's chef and assistants show off lunch. Tom Stillo/ Crested Butte Mountain Resort

Grub: Grab an après-ski beer and listen to live music on the huge deck of **Route 66 Roadhouse BBQ.** Take a breakfast burrito and a latte to go from **Camp 4 Coffee.** Carboload at **Rustica Ristorante,** located in the Paradise Warming Hut. Or have yourself a chichi moment at the mid-mountain **Ice Bar** (see page 112).

Cross-Country Skiing and Snowshoeing

Crested Butte Mountain Resort Snowshoe Tours (970-349-2252) Guided snowshoe walks take off from the top of Red Lady Express at 9:45 AM and 1 PM daily—and moonlight tours are available a few times a winter (depending on what the phases are doing).

Crested Butte Nordic Center (970-349-1707, cbnordic.org, Whiterock Ave. and Second St., Crested Butte) The Nordic center has over 40 kilometers of trails for both classic and skate skiing, lessons, moonlight tours, snowshoeing, and ice skating. You can sign up for an all-day backcountry tour or a snowshoe tour to the Magic Meadows tepee for lunch. A few trails even allow dogs.

Washington Gulch to Elkton Cabins (970-349-1815, cbguide@rmi.net, Washington Gulch, Crested Butte), Though it is ungroomed, this route is more often than not very well tracked by users of all kinds, including snowmobilers. As a day trip, it's manageable—four hours of rolling hills. If you want to spend the night, be sure to reserve in advance.

Dogsledding

Lucky Cat Dog Farm (970-641-1636, luckycatdogfarm.com, 900 CR 13, Gunnison) Take a two- to three-hour lunch tour (with hot soup, bread, hot cider, and cookies) or a shorter, 1.5-hour tour with the longest continually operating dogsled business in the county.

Guiding and Backcountry

Crested Butte Mountain Guides (970-349-5430, crestedbutteguides.com) CBMG can take you on single-day tours, four-day hut trips, and spring corn tours, and they'll even provide a "sherpa service": help you carry your group's stuff to a hut, show you good places to ski, and then leave you to your own devices.

Elkton Cabins (970-349-1815, cbguide@rmi.net, Washington Gulch) This three-cabin complex, which includes the Elkton (sleeps six), the Miner's Delight (sleeps 12), and the Silver Jewel (sleeps four), was part of a mining camp in the late 1800s. Now it houses backcountry skiers. The cabins have wood-burning stoves for heat, gas cook stoves, cookware, propane lights, and bunk beds with pillows and sheets. In winter, the 5-mile ski takes about four hours and gains 1,500 feet; in summer, Elkton can be reached with a high-clearance vehicle.

Forest Queen Cabin (rmbl.org) In summer, the former mining community of Gothic is home to the Rocky Mountain Biological Laboratory; in winter, it's empty except for caretakers and backcountry skiers. One seven-person cabin can be booked by the public, and it includes electricity, wood stove, propane cookstove, cookware, outhouse, and water.

Friends Hut (970-925-5775, huts.org, huts@huts.org) Built as a memorial for 10 residents of Crested Butte and Aspen who died in a plane crash on East Maroon Pass, Friends has been open since 1985—and it's very remote (an 11-mile ski, which can take 10 hours). It sits just below Pearl Pass at 11,500 feet.

A dogsled team races over the snow with Mt. Crested Butte behind. Tom Stillo/Crested Butte Mountain Resort

Ice skating
Crested Butte Ice Skating Center (970-349-0974, Second St. and Whiterock Ave., Crested Butte) Located in Big Mine Park, this rink has skate rentals, public skating hours, and a nearby sledding hill. Best of all, it's free (skate rentals go for $5 an hour, and sleds don't cost a thing).

Sleigh Rides
Just Horsin' Around (970-349-9822, Second St. and Whiterock Ave., Crested Butte) In the winter, you can take a 30-minute ride through the streets of downtown CB, complete with historical narration.

Lazy F Bar Ranch (970-349-7593, lazyfbarranch.com, Brush Creek Rd., Crested Butte South) Every Tuesday, Wednesday, Friday, and Saturday from 5 to 7 PM, you can take a sleigh up the East River Valley for New York steak, Cornish game hens, lasagna, salmon, homemade rolls, desserts, and hot cider and cocoa.

RECREATION: SUMMER AND FALL

Cycling: Mountain Biking

Guides
Crested Butte Mountain Bike Association (970-349-6817, visitcrestedbutte.com/bikeassociation) CBMBA—the oldest mountain-bike association in the world, founded in 1983—organizes trail work days, overnight work weekends, mountain rides, parties, and the annual Fat Tire Bike Week (see "Seasonal Events," page 131).

Crested Butte Mountain Guides (970-349-5430, crestedbutteguides.com) For $125 per person per day, you can get a local guide to show you the best of CB's maze of mountain biking trails—without worrying about getting lost on your own.

Trails
401 Climbing high enough for panoramas and descending through wildflower fields that are sometimes head-high, 401 is one of the most gorgeous trails in the state. It can be done as a loop or an out-and-back—depending on the weather and your legs.

Mountain Biking Mecca
Mountain biking wasn't born here, but it has certainly made itself comfortable: Crested Butte is home to the **Mountain Biking Hall of Fame** (see page 117)—not to mention world-class trails that cleave wildflower fields and weave among fade-to-gold aspens. Fat-tire history may have started with the Buffalo Soldiers, an infantry unit that fiddled with their bikes to carry gear from Missoula to Yellowstone and back, at the turn of the 20th century. It may have started with the Velo Cross Club Parisien in 1950s France. Or it could have been John Finley Scott, who built a "Woodsie Bike" in 1953. Everyone agrees, though, that it really took off in Marin County, California, in the 1970s and spread from there. In Crested Butte, mountain biking is hugely popular, and people are passionate about it: The local Crested Butte Mountain Bike Association is heavily involved in access issues, trail maintenance, protection, and land holder trust. The result? A fat-tire experience second to none.

403 The punishing climb up Washington Gulch has a reward: riding through the old ghost town of Elkton and careening down into Gothic Valley. Snow lingers on this route well into summer, and the switchbacks are hairy; think about your abilities before you commit.

Lower Loop Starting just outside of town on the way up to Kebler Pass, Lower Loop has gentle rolling singletrack that's mellow enough for townie bikes. With several variations, it passes through Peanut Mine, next to the Slate River, and toward Gunsight Pass.

Reno/Flag Creek/Bear Creek/Deadman's Gulch The classic ride in the Cement Creek area, this loop is over 20 miles long—50 if you ride all the way from Crested Butte. But it has spectacular views, sustained switchbacking climbs, and miles-long downhills along rushing creeks.

Snodgrass Though it's on private, seasonal grazing land, Snodgrass is evidence of the enlightened relationship between landowners and the mountain-biking community. It's a good intermediate option, with well-worn singletrack, creek crossings, and clear signage at intersections.

Cycling: Road Biking

Cerro Summit The 65 miles between Montrose and Gunnison on US 50 have beautiful scenery, the road has a wide shoulder, and the route slowly gains and loses altitude. With a high point under 9,000 feet, it's also more friendly to sea level–dwellers.

Gunnison to Crested Butte There's only one paved road out of CB, CO 135, and it's busy—about 28 miles of mellow ups and downs. The other routes straight out of town are all dirt (see "Cycling: Mountain Biking," above).

Monarch Pass At 11,312 feet, Monarch Pass has a decent ski area—and to get there, it's a 32-mile haul from Gunnison that starts flat and ends with grades pushing 6 percent.

The Gate Head west out of Gunnison on US 50 for just under 10 miles and look for signs for CO 149, then start the climb up Ninemile Hill (yes, 9 miles long). Descend (steeply) to the junction with CR 26, then climb again. About 36 miles into the ride, you'll pass by The Gate itself—two cliff faces bordering the road.

Fishing

Outfitters

Almont Anglers (970-641-7404, almontanglers.com, 10209 CO 135, Almont) Along with the three main local rivers, the Taylor, the East, and the Gunnison, Almont can take beginners and experts to the San Miguel, the Arkansas, the Lake Fork, and the Rio Grande.

Dragonfly Anglers (970-349-1228, dragonflyanglers.com, 307 Elk Ave., Crested Butte) The only year-round guiding service in the area (and the oldest), Dragonfly guides on the Taylor, East, and Gunnison Rivers—and sells prints by fishing artist David Ruimveld.

Troutfitter (970-349-1323, troutfitter.com, 313 Elk Ave., Crested Butte) Float or wade through the Black Canyon of the Gunnison—or stay closer to home on private, high-mountain streams.

Willowfly Anglers (888-761-3474, 3riversoutfitting.com, 130 CR 742, Almont) Offers floating and wading trips as well as powerboat trips on the Taylor Reservoir to fish for pike and lake trout, and spin-fishing trips for the whole family.

Lakes and Streams

Before you fish any water in Colorado, be sure you check with a local fly shop to find out if it's public or private. Many rivers have both private and public sections, so make sure you know where you're going. For licenses and regulations, visit wildlife.state.co.us/fishing—or, again, stop into a shop. If a river is designated "Gold Medal," it officially means that there are 12 trout per surface acre that top 14 inches—or 60 pounds of trout per surface acre. Unofficially, it means that the fishing is damn good.

Black Canyon of the Gunnison National Park The only road to the bottom of this spectacular ditch is the East Portal Road—with a brutal 16-percent grade. But it gives you access to the Gunnison River where it flows through the National Park, with famous stonefly hatches and large rainbows. Otherwise, with a backcountry permit, you can scramble down the super-steep trails from the rim. The Black Canyon section of the Gunny is actually 50-plus miles long, but this is the primo part.

East River Meandering down from Crested Butte to Almont, the East meets the Taylor to form the Gunnison. Much of it passes through ranchland, making for limited access, but the kokanee salmon are usually worth a grip-and-grin shot.

High Lakes Irwin, Spring Creek, Mirror, Emerald, and Lost Lakes are all high-quality spots—whether you're fishing, hiking, or hiking to fish.

Taylor Reservoir Here's the place to hook a northern pike, a lake trout, a big ol' brown, or a kokanee salmon—especially in late spring, when the fishing goes off. Call **Taylor Park Marina** (970-641-2922) for information about renting pontoon boats, 14-foot fishing boats, trolling poles, and find out about the annual Taylor Park Marina Fishing Derby held each June.

Taylor River The tailwater below Taylor Dam sees some of the biggest rainbows in the state, and the half-mile right below never freezes over. In fall, try hopper/dropper combos—or nymphing.

Golf

The Club at Crested Butte (800-628-5496, theclubatcrestedbutte.com, 385 Country Club Dr., Crested Butte) Just south of town, this 18-hole, Robert Trent Jones Jr.–designed course mixes open vistas with tight aspen groves. It also has a spa, fitness center, tennis club, private homes, restaurant, and bar.

Dos Rios Country Club (970-641-1482, 501 Camino del Rio, Gunnison) The front nine of this par-71 course is flat, with narrow fairways, while the back nine is more wide-open, with more rolling terrain. And there's water, water everywhere.

Hiking and Backpacking

Guides

Alpine Meadows Hiking (970-349-0800, alpinemeadowshiking.com, P.O. 1745, Crested Butte) Want help planning a day hike, a peak-bagging trip, or an overnight backpacking adventure? Alpine Meadows pairs hikers with local guides who know the wildflowers, wildlife, and topography of everything around Crested Butte.

Trails

Beckwith Pass At 5 miles out and back, with an elevation gain from 8,820 feet to 9,970 feet, Beckwith alternates between open meadows and spruce-fir forests—and those meadows sometimes have over 70 species of wildflowers in bloom.

Crested Butte Summit Trail A moderately difficult ascent up Mount Crested Butte, this route lets you wander through forests and cross tundra to a scree field—all of which is covered (and skied over) in winter. Catch 360-degree views from the top.

Crested Butte to Aspen There are three ways to walk to Aspen from CB: East Maroon Pass Trail (14.5 miles), West Maroon Pass Trail (10.5 miles), and Conundrum Hot Springs/Ashcroft (17.7 miles). Each one-way trip is utterly stunning—vistas of the Maroon Bells/Snowmass wilderness, carpets of wildflowers, above-treeline passes, and classic Colorado scenery. You can get a ride back with Dolly's Mountain Shuttle (970-349-2620, dollysmountainshuttle@yahoo.com) for $50 a person.

Elk Creek/Gunsight Pass Just under 5 miles up Kebler Pass Road, park and head up the ravine to the right: You'll pass by a bunch of old mines and mining equipment. (Be very careful to look out for dangerous openings!)

Henry Lake Trail About 7 miles one-way, this trail starts at Lottis Creek Campground, about 15 miles up the Taylor River from Almont. It has broad views and a few very steep stretches. The fishing in Henry Lake, at 11,704 feet, is decent.

Peanut Lake/Lower Loop Great for families with young children, or people who aren't quite used to the high altitude, this loop is under 3 miles and starts right in town.

Summerville Trail To get a crash course in the wonders of the Fossil Ridge Wilderness, hike 11 miles on this trail until it meets the Fossil Ridge Trail—following a small creek and then winding through a lodgepole forest.

Various Peaks Crested Butte is a great area to notch a high peak—ranging from the fairly innocuous Mount Baldy (12,800 feet) and Ruby Mountain (12,600) to moderately exposed Purple Mountain (12,950) and Gothic Mountain (12,500) to scrambles up Mount Axtell (12,050).

Horseback Riding

Fantasy Ranch Horseback Adventures (970-349-5425, fantasyranchoutfitters.com, 29 Whiterock, Crested Butte) The featured ride with Fantasy Ranch is through the Maroon Bells wilderness from Crested Butte to Aspen. You can ride in winter as well.

Lazy F Bar Ranch (970-641-0193, lazyfbarranch.com, Brush Creek Rd., Crested Butte South) Along with big-game hunts (see "Hunting" below) and wedding cakes (yes, an odd combination), Lazy F Bar offers two-hour, half-day, all-day, and overnight horseback rides and wagon rides. Come for breakfast (bacon and sausage, pancakes, fresh-baked bread, eggs) or dinner (beef brisket, smoked turkey, baked beans, coleslaw, potatoes, and more).

Hot Air Ballooning

Big Horn Balloon Company (970-596-1008, balloon-adventures.com, 14522 Mustang Lane, Montrose) Big Horn's claim to fame? It's the world's highest hot-air balloon operation. On the three- to four-hour flight, catch glimpses of the fourteeners near Aspen and the wildflowers closer by.

Hunting

Lazy F Bar Ranch (970-641-3313, lazyfbarranch.com, Brush Creek Rd., Crested Butte South) Since they've been running hunting trips in the area since 1953, Lazy F Bar has a large National Forest permit—along with thousands of acres of private land—and a base camp of rustic cabins, a restaurant, and a shower house. They specialize in elk, deer, and bear.

Quaking Aspen Outfitters (970-641-0529, quakingaspenoutfitters.com) Hunting out of big heated tents in the Gunnison National Forest, and finding big game by riding, stalking, and waiting, QAO claims that 90 percent of its clients will get a decent shot at a buck mule deer. You can also hunt goats and bighorn sheep.

Rafting and Paddling

Scenic River Tours Inc (970-641-3131, scenicrivertours.com, 7042 CR 742, Almont) Class I and II and scenic trips on the Gunnison, Class III+ on the Upper Taylor, Class IV on the Lake Fork, and other options on the San Miguel—as well as duckie (inflatable kayak) rentals.

Three Rivers Outfitting (970-641-1303, 3riversoutfitting.com, 130 CR 742, Almont) Raft the scenic Gunnison and the rapids on the Taylor, take out a duckie on mellower stretches, or sign up for white-water kayaking lessons. Three Rivers also organizes hot air balloon rides, snowmobile tours, rock climbing, fishing, sleigh rides, and more.

Scenic flights

Gunnison Valley Aviation (888-641-2874, 970-641-0526, gunnisonvalleyaviation.com, 1 Airport Rd., Gunnison) Cruise high about the Black Canyon, the Elk range, Crested Butte, and the Gunnison Valley—or take the day to hike to Aspen and get a gorgeous ride home (for $300 a trip).

DRIVING: SCENIC DRIVES AND BYWAYS

Colorado Highway 149 Head up a narrow canyon to one of Colorado's largest natural alpine lakes, Lake San Cristobal.

Silver Thread Scenic Byway Though you'll have to take a drive just to reach the beginning of this drive (see Highway 149, above), it's worth the extra time: You'll see Slumgullion Slide, a cliff face that collapsed 700 years ago (and still creeps downhill today); the Rio Grande Pyramid, a distinctive 13,821-foot peak; the scenic former mining town of Creede; the Rio Grande River; and the volcanic Palisades cliffs.

US Highway 50 Head west of Gunnison in to Curecanti National Recreation Area, following the Gunnison River. Cross the Lake City Bridge into a high-altitude sagebrush steppe.

West Elk Loop Scenic Byway A 204-mile-long circuit of two-lane roads (including CO 135, 133, 92, and US 50), the Loop passes through Crested Butte, Gunnison, Paonia, and Crawford, hitting spectacular Kebler Pass and the Curecanti National Recreation Area—as well as canyon rims, white-water stretches, and desert plains.

SHOPPING

Art Galleries

Art Walk Evenings (970-349-6804, awearts.org) On the last Thursday of each month, stroll between Lucille Lucas, Rendezvous, Paragon, and Rijks Family galleries (see entries below for details about each).

Creekside Pottery (970-349-6459, crestedbuttepottery.com, 126 Elk. Ave., Crested Butte) Hidden along Coal Creek in downtown CB, Creekside sells raku, traditional stoneware, mica horsehair, and landscape pottery with a Southwestern or country flair—in the form of lamps, bowls, and plates.

John Ingham, Inc (970-349-7126, inghamart.com, 403 Third St., Crested Butte) John Ingham has been alternating between Crested Butte and Moab, Utah, since 1973—and painting the mountain, river, and forest scenes that surround him. He also does Native American and fly-fishing portraits.

Lucille Lucas Gallery (970-349-1903, 317 Elk Ave., Crested Butte) Want to bring home a vintage ski poster, a photo of a local scene by a local shooter like Tom Stillo, or an antique print? Lucille Lucas has some 200,000 works to choose from.

Paragon Gallery (970-349-6484, 132 Elk Ave., Crested Butte) A hugely varied co-op of 14 local artists who donate 1 percent of their sales to the Crested Butte Open Land Trust, Paragon sells mosaic mirrors, handmade paper, wine glasses, feather creations, mugs, paintings, and sculpture.

Rendezvous Gallery (970-349-6804, 427 Belleview Ave., Crested Butte) This combo frame shop and gallery represents local artists.

Rijks Family Gallery (970-349-5289, 310 Second St., Crested Butte) Rijks features the large- and small-scale plein-air paintings of local artist Shaun Horne—mostly Cezanne- and Picasso-influenced views of Elk Avenue, Victorian buildings, and the nearby mountains.

Creekside Pottery in Crested Butte, just off the beaten path. Evelyn Spence

Books

The Book Store (970-349-0504, 327 Elk Ave., Crested Butte) It's the only true bookstore in town (with a name to prove it)—and sells maps, local titles, and a decent mix of everything else.

Outdoor Gear

The Alpineer (970-349-5210, alpineer.com, 419 Sixth St., in the Bullion King Building, Crested Butte) They've been around since 1969, selling all varieties of outdoor gear—soft shells, puffy coats, climbing harnesses, snowshoes, hiking boots—and dispensing, well, indispensable advice about mountain biking, climbing, camping, and hiking in the area. You can also rent camping, skiing, and biking equipment here.

Alpine Outside (970-349-5011, 315 Sixth St., Crested Butte) Along with selling some outdoorsy stuff, Alpine Outside can also book an ice fishing trip, a snowmobile ride, a day on the river (in drift boat or white-water raft), or a bouncy 4x4 tour.

Get your Western gifts at charming Shakin' not Spurred, then pop next door for a latke at Izzy's. Evelyn Spence

Western Clothing and Furs

Shakin' not Spurred (970-349-1314, 218 Maroon Ave., Crested Butte) In a tiny, unbearably cute building next to Izzy's (see page 108), this shop sells kitschy cowboy-related gifts: T-shirts, picture frames, soaps, hats, jeans, and more. Its owner, Kris, was born and bred in Crested Butte.

SEASONAL EVENTS

January: Country in the Rockies (citr.org) For over a dozen years, CITR has brought the likes of Charlie Daniels, Robert Earl Keen, Chuck Cannon, Gretchen Wilson, Kenny Loggins, and Deborah Allen to the mountains. Bid on celeb memorabilia and jewelry at auctions, watch a fireside "guitar pull," or go for a winter horseback ride.

February: Crested Butte Winter Carnival (970-349-4950) One of the many celebrations that shut down the main drag, Winter Carnival includes competitions between avalanche dogs and humans with transceivers, ice bowling, frozen mini-golf, big air contests, disco ice-skating, and the annual Alley Loop—Nordic ski races, from 1K to 42K, through Crested Butte's narrow streets.

February: Mardi Gras (970-349-0366) A great excuse for a parade (like CB needs one!), Mardi Gras festivities start with a masquerade ball—a $75 ticket includes cocktails, a New Orleans—style meal, and live music—and end with a procession down Elk Avenue.

February: U.S. Extreme Free Skiing Championships (970-349-2222, skicb.com) Watch the sport's young and gutsy jump cliffs, do flips, and wipe out in Crested Butte's Extreme Limits to determine the best freeskier of the year.

March: Al Johnson Uphill-Downhill Telemark Race (970-349-5210, aljohnsonrace .com) A memorial for a postman who worked in the late 1800s, the Al Johnson course climbs about 600 vert near the North Face poma, then drops 1,200 feet through some of the Extreme Limits. Competitors must use telemark gear—and most wear outrageous costumes.

April: Elk Mountain Grand Traverse (970-349-5210, elkmountaintraverse.org) A grueling, 39-mile backcountry ski race from Crested Butte to Aspen, the Grand Traverse starts at midnight, passes over Death Pass, Star Pass, Taylor Pass, and by several backcountry huts before dropping down into the town of Aspen. Teams of two take anywhere between seven and 20 hours, braving often-freezing conditions.

April: Flauschink (800-814-7988) A celebration to flush out the worries of winter and welcome spring, this medieval counterpart to Vinotok (see September) starts with a coronation polka ball to crown a king and queen, and ends with (sometimes) naked skiing.

June: Fat Tire Bike Week (800-545-4505, ftbw.com) One of the oldest mountain biking festivals in the country, FTBW has been around for over 25 years—and packs in events like the Chainless (a hairy descent down Kebler Pass without your bike chain), the Poker Run (riding around town, collecting cards), a bike rodeo (log pulls, bike limbo), the Wildflower Rush (a cross-country race), "beer goggle" races, dog-and-owner look-alike contests, and guided rides and clinics.

June: Readers in the Rockies (970-349-9296, readersintherockies.com) An intimate writers' conference with workshops and lectures on both fiction and nonfiction.

July: Crested Butte Music Festival (970-349-0619, crestedbuttemusicfestival.com) Since the premiere of *Nosferatu* (an operatic interpretation by Dana Gioia and Alva Henderson of a German Expressionist drama), CBMF has earned a reputation for innovation—but it also includes bluegrass (the Transylvanian Mountain Boys), dance, big band, and traditional chamber music.

July: Crested Butte Wildflower Festival (970-349-2571, crestedbuttewildflowerfestival .com) A loving, weeklong ode to the short-lived high-mountain blooms that make CB the "wildflower capital of Colorado," this fest explores everything floral. You can eat a dinner of dandelion fritters, wild onion flower tempura, and milkweed flower clusters; take horse-and-wagon rides to bursting meadows; learn how to make a fragrance garden; and choose from over 100 guided walks and hikes.

August: Crested Butte Reel Fest (crestedbuttereelfest.com) A mountain film festival with an international bent, Reel Fest showcases animation, live-action, and documentary; the best work from Colorado film schools; video-making workshops; and panel discussions.

August: Crested Butte Wild Mushroom Festival (800-545-4505, crested-butte-wild-mushroom-festival.com) Attend workshops like "Amanitas: From Deadly to Delicious," practice taking photos of wild mushrooms, learn to cook with wild mushrooms, and go out for various forays.

August: Festival of the Arts (970-349-6438, crestedbutteartfestival.com) A street fair along Elk Avenue with 180 booths: glasswork, leather, photography, jewelry, baskets, clothing, wood, metal arts, and more.

September: Vinotok (970-641-4742) This medieval fall festival is one of Crested Butte's biggest and most famous—it's a pagan storytelling fest that takes place on the autumnal equinox and includes a raucous chanting parade, characters like the Harvest Earth Mother and the Green Man, a bonfire in which people burn a cloth figure called The Grump (who is stuffed with complaints), feasting, drinking, and dressing up.

NUTS AND BOLTS

Getting Here

Crested Butte is 28 miles from the **Gunnison Crested Butte Airport** in Gunnison, where Hertz, Budget, Avis, and Thrifty rentals are available. You can also get a shuttle ride from **Alpine Express** (alpineexpressshuttle.com, 800-822-4844), then use the free CB bus service in town when you need to get around. Driving from Denver? It can take as little as four hours with good weather; most people take I-70 a short distance west of Denver, then hop on CO 285 to Poncha Springs, drive over Monarch Pass via US 50, and hook up with CO 135.

Ambulance/Fire/Police/Search and Rescue

For emergencies, of course, dial 911. For police assistance that doesn't require an emergency response, contact the number listed below for the city closest to your present location.

Crested Butte Fire Protection District: 970-349-5333

Crested Butte Marshall: 970-349-5231

Crested Butte Search and Rescue: 970-349-5028

Gunnison County Sheriff: 970-641-1113

Mt. Crested Butte Police Department: 970-349-6516

Avalanche Reports
Crested Butte Avalanche Center: 970-349-4022, cbavalanchecenter.org

Libraries
Old Rock Community Library: 970-496-6535.

Hospitals and Emergency Medical Services
Crested Butte Medical Center: 970-349-0321, cbmedicalcenter.com, Ore Bucket Building, 214 Sixth St., Crested Butte

Crested Butte Mountain Clinic: 970-349-2525, cbmedicalcenter.com, 20 Emmons Rd. (CO 135), Mt. Crested Butte

Elk Avenue Medical Center: 970-349-1046, elkavenuemedcenter.com, 405 Elk Ave., Crested Butte

Gunnison Valley Hospital: 970-641-1456, gvh-colorado.org, 711 N. Taylor St., Gunnison

Media

Newspapers and Magazines
Crested Butte Magazine: crestedbuttemagazine.com; contact Sandy Fails at happy@crestedbutte.net, P.O. Box 1030, Crested Butte, CO 81224

Crested Butte News: 970-349-0500, crestedbuttenews.com, 432 Elk St., P.O. Box 369, Crested Butte, CO 81224

Crested Butte Weekly: 970-349-1710, cbweekly.com, P.O. Box 1609, Crested Butte, CO 81224

Gunnison Country Times: 970-641-1414, gunnisontimes.com, 218 N. Wisconsin, Gunnison, CO 81230

Radio
KBUT 90.3: 970-349-7444, kbut.org. Community , NPR, roots, bluegrass, and blues music.

Public Transportation

There are regular shuttles between Crested Butte and Mount Crested Butte, and to a lot of the major condo complexes, with three different routes (contact the **Mountain Express Bus Service**, 970-349-7318).

Ranger Stations

Cebolla/Taylor River Ranger District, 970-641-0471.

Tourist Information

Crested Butte Chamber of Commerce: 970-349-6438, crestedbuttechamber.com, P.O. Box 1288, Crested Butte 81224

Gunnison County Chamber of Commerce: 970-641-1501, gunnison-co.com, 500 E. Tomichi Ave., Gunnison

4

STEAMBOAT SPRINGS

Ski Town U.S.A.

Steamboat Springs is one of the most genuinely Western ski towns in Colorado: There are outstanding restaurants, but none smack of snootiness. There are luxury properties, but they butt up against working cattle ranches and rental homes full of lifties. Weekend events tend to be ski-joring and rodeos rather than operas and intellectual summits. Fur coats are nonexistent. Cowboy hats are common. And the snow . . . the snow! Steamboat has copyrighted the phrase "champagne powder," and the moniker is well deserved. There's nothing like floating through the trees on Closet after an 18-inch dump.

Unlike most other high-mountain towns in the state, Steamboat's foundations are in ranching rather than mining—although gold was discovered near Hahns Peak, 30 miles north of town, in 1865, drawing some 2,000 speculators into the Yampa Valley. James Harvey Crawford became Steamboat Springs proper's first homesteader in 1874, after taking a train trip to Denver and falling hard for the mountains: He struck out with his wife, Maggie, and three young kids, went up and over the Continental Divide, and used the Homestead Act to claim 160 acres where the Bear River (now the Yampa) bent through the valley. He became the town's first mayor, county judge, and school superintendent, and Maggie started the first school, church, and library.

Many of Steamboat's first visitors came for the supposed healing properties of the sulfur springs on the west side of town—which, early trappers observed, made a "chug-chug" sound (hence the town's name). By the turn of the 20th century, close to 600 people had joined the Crawfords. By 1909, the railroad had arrived; by 1913, more cattle were transported from Steamboat than from any other point in the United States; by 1914, the first road over Rabbit Ears Pass was completed. And though it took another 50 years for the ski resort to be established, doctors and mail carriers were using skis all along.

In fact, one of the first ski jumps in the United States was built in Steamboat Springs in 1915, kicking off a winter sports legacy that has no match. Steamboat is home to more past and present Olympians than any other town in America, including freestylers Ann Battelle and Nelson Carmichael; snowboarder Shannon Dunn; downhiller Buddy Werner; and four-discipline wonder Gordy Wren. We have Norwegian Carl Howelsen to thank for the legacy: He started Howelsen Hill, a 440-vertical-foot area in the middle of town that's still used for training today.

A fleet of balloons take flight at the annual Hot Air Balloon Rodeo in Steamboat Springs. Steamboat Springs Chamber Resort Association

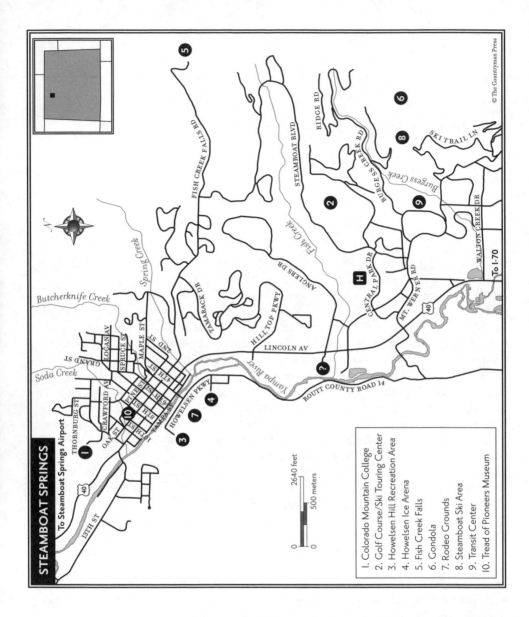

STEAMBOAT SPRINGS

To Steamboat Springs Airport

© The Countryman Press

1. Colorado Mountain College
2. Golf Course/Ski Touring Center
3. Howelsen Hill Recreation Area
4. Howelsen Ice Arena
5. Fish Creek Falls
6. Gondola
7. Rodeo Grounds
8. Steamboat Ski Area
9. Transit Center
10. Tread of Pioneers Museum

But it was when Jim Temple—with the help of Werner—decided to build a ski area on Storm Mountain (now called Mount Werner) that Steamboat really came into its own: Ground-breaking took place in the summer of 1958, and a Poma went up three years later. In 1964, Werner died in an avalanche while filming a ski movie in St. Moritz, Switzerland, and the hill's name was changed to Mount Werner Ski Area. In 1970, another Olympian—Billy Kidd—became the face of newly named Steamboat, and still is (you won't go far without seeing a photo of his cowboy hat and bandana, or a bronze sculpture of him, or sometimes even the man himself). In the 1980s, ad campaigns went something like this: "More mountain than Aspen. More powder than Vail. More lifts than Snowmass. More sun than Sun Valley. More bars than Utah. And less skiers."

Statue of the ubiquitous Billy Kidd, legendary Olympic skier, who put his stamp on Steamboat Springs starting in the 1970s—and still wears a trademark cowboy hat and bandana. Evelyn Spence

And while some of that has undoubtedly changed (the Snowmass lifts, for one, not to mention those Utah bars), the character of Steamboat hasn't: It's far enough from the Front Range to keep away day-tripping traffic; it sometimes gets slathered by 40-inch storms; its residents are cowboys and former hippies and professors and outdoorsy families; and its vibe remains mellow and full of hometown pride.

LODGING

STEAMBOAT SPRINGS

Alpine Rose Bed & Breakfast
Innkeepers: Jo and Bob Riley
888-879-1528, 970-879-1528
alpinerosesteamboat.com
bnb@alpinerosesteamboat.com
724 Grand St., Steamboat Springs
Price Range: $105–$260, including breakfast
Credit Cards: MC, V
Children: Y, over age 6
Pets: N
Handicap Accessible: N

As one of the few true B&Bs in Steamboat, the homey, Victorian-style Alpine Rose has a dedicated following. People come for its cheerful pink exterior (we're talking serious gingerbread), its flowery carpets and lace curtains, its formal dining room and elegant common areas, and its huge breakfasts (days start with biscuits and gravy, fresh fruit crepes, poached eggs on toast, bagels and lox, quiche, and mimosas or Bloodies on Sundays). They also come for a personalized vibe: There are only five guest rooms, each of which has floral comforters, fresh and dried flowers, silver trays, and fluffy robes. It's eight blocks from Lincoln Avenue—close enough for you to walk to dinner in good weather, but just far enough to feel like you're at the edge of town.

Bunk House Lodge
877-245-6343, 970-871-9121
rockymountainfun.com/bunkhouselodge.html
3155 S. Lincoln Ave., Steamboat Springs
Price Range: $64–$132, including breakfast
Credit Cards: AE, MC, V
Children: Y
Pets: N
Handicap Accessible: Y

Just a few years old, the Bunk House still feels brand-spanking new: The 38 rooms are clean, the lobby—with cathedral ceilings and a tall rock fireplace—is bright, the staff is friendly, and the rates are even friendlier. It has all the amenities of bigger resort hotels (continental breakfast, complimentary newspapers, outdoor Jacuzzi, ski lockers), and it sits on the city's free shuttle route, a few miles south of downtown. What's more, it also sits on the banks of the Yampa River (ask for a room on the back side of the hotel, away from US 40), and it's mere minutes from the slopes.

Hotel Bristol
800-851-0872, 970-879-3083
steamboathotelbristol.com
917 Lincoln Ave., Steamboat Springs
Price Range: $69–$169
Credit Cards: AE, D, MC, V
Children: Y
Pets: N
Handicap Accessible: N

Opened in 1948, the 24-room Bristol is to Steamboat what the Hotel Jerome is to Aspen or the New Sheridan is to Telluride, just not as old (or deluxe). Still, it's convenient and it's classy: The small lobby has hardwood ceilings, shelves lined with books, carved banisters, and fresh flowers. The rooms mix historic and modern—vintage photos above geometric headboards and "antique" telephones (that look rotary, but are push-button) on rustic bedside tables. Built by Steamboat's police chief, Everett Bristol, the hotel has gone through several sets of owners—including Harold Killham, whose wife, Irene, fed made-from-scratch pies to traveling salesmen. At one point, first-floor Mazzola's restaurant (see page 150) was a pool hall and geologist's lab.

The Inn at Steamboat
Innkeeper: Glen Zabel
innatsteamboat.com
innkeeper@innatsteamboat.com
3070 Columbine Dr., Steamboat Springs

Price Range: $69–$219, including
   continental breakfast
Credit Cards: AE, D, MC, V
Children: Y
Pets: N
Handicap Accessible: N

The Inn at Steamboat is a great option if
you want to stay within walking distance of
the ski area without reserving a room at a
monster hotel or booking a timeshare.
Rooms have king or queen beds, hand-
stitched quilts, landscape paintings, pine
furniture, leather reading chairs, balconies,
and views of either Mount Werner or the
Yampa Valley (the inn is up on the hill,
looking down). The building itself is a rec-
tangular lodge with an A-frame entrance,
and the lobby has pine-log railings, old
ski-run signs, wagon-wheel accents, a
stone fireplace, and a gabled roof. There's a
small outdoor swimming pool, and rates
include breakfast and access to a coffee and
tea bar in the parlor.

Mariposa Bed & Breakfast

Innkeepers: Bob and Cindy Maddox
800-578-1467, 970-879-1467
steamboatmariposa.com
mariposa@steamboatmariposa.com
855 Grand St., Steamboat Springs
Price Range: $125 per room in summer; in
   winter, it's often rented as an entire home
Credit Cards: checks or cash only
Children: Y, but notify ahead of time
Pets: N
Handicap Accessible: N

Want to stay in an inn that truly feels like
home? The Mariposa—a three-bedroom
Southwestern house next to Soda Creek—
was built by a longtime local and former ski
patroller. And the current owners have
imported a Santa Fe feeling: the stucco
exterior and interior walls, the log beams,
the handcrafted doors, the Navajo-print
furniture and keyhole windows. The wonderful sunroom, overlooking a pond,
warms in the afternoon—a great place to
read or catch a nap on one of the wicker
chairs or XL couches. The Maddoxes
(whose own home is right next door) do
everything here: give advice on where to
hike, mountain bike, or horseback ride;
serve up fresh-roasted coffee, pastries,
smoothies, and heavenly huevos rancheros;
maintain a charming garden; and keep the
place sparkling. All three of the rooms have
private baths, log or wrought-iron beds,
and local artwork.

Rabbit Ears Motel

Innkeepers: The Koehler Family
800-828-7702, 970-879-1150,
rabbitearsmotel.com
info@rabbitears.com
201 Lincoln Ave., Steamboat Springs
Price Range: $60–$185
Credit Cards: AE, D, MC, V
Children: Y
Pets: Y, with a $12 charge
Handicap Accessible: Y

When you drive into town from Rabbit Ears
Pass on US 40, the first thing you see when
you get to Old Town Steamboat is an enormous pink sign for the 65-room Rabbit
Ears Motel, complete with a dopey-
grinning and charmingly kitsch bunny.
The sign's been there since 1952 and has
become a local landmark (although some
townies, over the years, have petitioned to
have it taken down). The motel itself is in a
great location: right across from the
Steamboat Springs Health and Recreation
Association (see page 159), with some
rooms and balconies looking right over the
Yampa. The digs are basic—27-inch TVs,
wall-to-wall carpeting, polyester blankets,
in-room fridges, wireless Internet—but you
get a continental breakfast, and you're
within spitting distance of all the downtown
shops and restaurants.

The Steamboat Bed and Breakfast occupies a building that was once a church.   Evelyn Spence

Sheraton Steamboat Resort

970-879-2220
sheraton.com/steamboat
2200 Village Inn Court, Steamboat Springs
Price Range: $129–$1,799
Credit Cards: AE, D, MC, V
Children: Y
Pets: Y
Handicap Accessible: Y

Since it has one of the most convenient locations in all of Steamboat, you can forgive the Sheraton's '70s-era exterior: The lobby has nice Western and Southwestern touches like leather chairs with fringes; bronze sculptures of cowboys, horses, and eagles; the telltale antler chandeliers; and sink-in couches around the fireplace. Guest rooms are decorated in maroon, beige, and brown tones, with huge wood and wrought-iron headboards, chaise lounges, "Sweet Sleeper" beds for both humans and dogs, and slate fireplaces. And the rooftop hot tubs (there are seven of

them) are killer: You're a good eight stories up, with reach-out-and-touch views of the ski area. There's an in-house restaurant, two bar-and-grills, and a coffee shop (in case you don't want to venture outside).

✪ Steamboat Bed and Breakfast

Innkeeper: Lisa Kavadas
970-879-5724
steamboatb-b.com
info@steamboatb-b.com
442 Pine St., Steamboat Springs
Price Range: $119–$189
Credit Cards: MC, V
Children: Y, over age 10
Pets: N
Handicap Accessible: N

This building served as Steamboat's first Congregational church, but there isn't much that's churchy about it anymore: It looks more like a three-story Colonial than a house of worship. The wood floors are endearingly creaky, the common areas are filled with rocking chairs, VHS tapes, fly-fishing accents (flies on the curtains, fish on the trim), magazines, plants, and comfy pillows. The TV room doubles as a conservatory, with a piano for guests to play—and when they're not, the radio often fills in (with country and classical music). The shaded deck and expansive yard have more than enough hammocks and Adirondack chairs for the laziest of lazy Sundays, just in case the breakfast of huevos rancheros or raised pecan belgian waffles gives you a food coma. The rooms are bright and simple, with white comforters, Victorian furniture, and garden, town, or mountain views.

✪ Steamboat Grand Resort Hotel
877-269-2628
steamboatgrand.com
2300 Mt. Werner Circle, Steamboat Springs

Price Range: $116–$2,300
Credit Cards: AE, D, MC, V
Children: Y
Pets: N
Handicap Accessible: Y

A sprawling, 327-room hotel–spa–conference center–time share–fitness center near the base of the ski hill, the two-toned Grand dominates the landscape—and offers everything from valet and bell service to 5,500 square feet of ballroom space to three-bedroom penthouses on the seventh floor (with private access, slate floors, granite vanities, formal dining rooms and mountain views). Standard hotel rooms along never-ending hallways come with some of the same—the granite countertops, the black-and-white photos, the wireless Internet, and the custom cabinets. As a big resort, the Grand can offer great bargain packages: a studio with a

The Steamboat Grand Resort Hotel offers hundreds of luxe rooms and great package deals. Evelyn Spence

breakfast buffet for less than $60 a person; a one-bedroom condo with free family movie, popcorn, and cookies and milk with turndown for $38 a person; and stay-and-ski packages galore. Though its vibe leans toward the corporate (sales offices on the first-floor hallway), it's about 100 yards from the gondola maze.

FARTHER AFIELD

✪ Columbine Cabins

Innkeepers: Jan Dierks & Lyman Fancher
970-879-5522
cabinsatcolumbine.com/index.php
columbinecabins@mindspring.com
P.O. Box 716, Clark
Price Range: $75–$250
Credit Cards: AE, D, MC, V
Children: Y, under 7 stay free
Pets: Y
Handicap Accessible: N

Drive about 29 miles north of Steamboat, and you'll get to the century-old, totally endearing log cabin town-site of Columbine, where 15 cabins—ranging in size from the four-bedroom, modern Tanglewood on down to the tiny, one-bedroom Hilltop—are tucked under aspens and evergreens across from the hulk of Hahns Peak. Each one is unique (the thorough Web site has interior photos of them all), with log walls and beams, wood stoves, and front porches; most have their own bathrooms. The main lodge, with a pool table, stocked bookshelves, a community kitchen, and a wood-fired sauna, is where guests relax at the end of a hiking or skiing day. The oldest building in "town," the Columbine General Store, was built in the mid-1880s and has been an official post office since 1905; now it sells basic groceries and snacks. There's a 1-mile Nordic skiing and snowshoeing loop around the property, but that's just the beginning: Hahns Peak is steps away, as is Steamboat Lake, Pearl Lake, and the Routt National Forest.

Glen Eden Resort

800-882-0854, 970-879-3907
glenedenresort.com
eden@amigo.net
P.O. Box 908, Clark
Price Range: $95–$195
Credit Cards: AE, D, MC, V
Children: Y, 17 and under free
Pets: N
Handicap Accessible: Y

Stay at Glen Eden—a homey, sprawling family resort complex—and you have the best of Colorado at your cabin's doorstep, whether it's summer or winter: hiking in the Mount Zirkel Wilderness Area, renting a pontoon boat or sailing on Steamboat Lake, mountain biking in Routt National Forest, fly-fishing a private stretch of the Elk River, cross-country skiing near Hahns Peak, or horseback riding through the snow. If you'd rather stay inside the compound, Glen Eden has a couple of tennis courts, a campfire circle, a volleyball court, a few hot tubs, a playground, and a heated pool. Cabins—some of which overlook the Elk—have moss rock fireplaces and full kitchens, and some even have lofts, wood stoves, and sleeping room for eight. The on-site Elk River Tavern, which serves dinner nightly and lunch on weekends, has typical bar food: nachos, potato skins, Caesar salads, burgers, and steaks.

Sky Valley Lodge

Innkeeper: Martin Dennis
800-538-7519, 970-879-7749
skyvalleylodge@yahoo.com
31660 E. US 40, Steamboat Springs
Price Range: $69–$149, including
    breakfast
Credit Cards: AE, MC, V
Children: Y
Pets: N
Handicap Accessible: N

If you don't mind being a few miles up Rabbit Ears Pass (and 8 miles from downtown Steamboat), the Sky Valley Lodge is a wonderful option—especially if you're partial to panoramic Yampa Valley views and country-manor style. The vibe is a blend of Bavarian, Victorian, and modern, with brass-framed featherbeds, floral-patterned comforters, wood paneling, garlands, and an exterior that's the quintessential white with brown trim. On warm days, soak up the sun on an enormous deck—and on cold winter nights, look down on the lights below.

Guest Ranches

Dutch Creek Guest Ranch

Owner: John Hawes
800-778-8519, 970-879-8519
dutchcreek.net
16565 County Road 62, Clark
Price Range: $105–$180 per night, with a three-night minimum stay, including breakfast
Credit Cards: AE, D, MC, V
Children: Y
Pets: Y
Handicap Accessible: Y

Within walking distance of Steamboat Lake and named for the creek that trickles through the property, Dutch Creek has five two-bedroom cabins and four one-bedroom A-frame cabins with lofts available by the night. Each has views of Hahns Peak or rolling meadows, and pine-log furniture, wood stoves, stone fireplaces, Western artwork, and kitchens—if you don't want to eat a dinner of wild game, grilled salmon, chicken-fried steak, or pork loin in the main lodge and then curl up near the mossrock fireplace with a book. And if you don't have enough to do with a kids' fishing pond and playground, horseshoe pit, daily trail rides, cross-country skiing, and snowshoeing, head over to the lake and rent a pontoon boat, speedboat, canoe, or windsurfer.

Elk River Guest Ranch

Owners: Kathy and Bill Hinder
800-750-6220, 970-879-6220
elkriverguestranch.com
info@elkriverguestranch.com
29840 CR 64, Clark
Price Range: $125–$150 per night
Credit Cards: MC, V
Children: Y
Pets: N
Handicap Accessible: Y (but check for details)

Though it has a brisk trail-riding business—with wagon dinner rides, sleigh rides, and one- to six-hour rides—as well as fishing, dogsledding, and snowmobiling, Elk River also has four cozy cabins with kitchens, cooking supplies, simple Western decor, gas fireplaces, and down comforters. Although meals aren't included, you can get home-style dinners (roast chicken, salmon, duck, steak), breakfasts, or sack lunches delivered to your front door. If you want fresh flowers, they'll bring by fresh flowers. If you need a fruit basket or a cord of wood, just request it. They'll even bring by scotch, rum, cognac, brandy, beer, and wine—or you can grab a drink at the on-site Silhouette Saloon. The ranch was first homesteaded way back in 1902, and miners crashed in the main lodge while looking for precious metals; it was converted into a year-round guest ranch in the 1950s. Along with horses, there are dogs, cats, geese, and turkeys roaming the grounds—and every summer, there's a weeklong kids' camp with wilderness art projects, fishing, botany, and horsemanship skills.

High Meadows Ranch

Owners: Jan and Denny Stamp
800-457-4453
hmranch.com
highmeadows@sprynet.com
20505 RCR 16, Oak Creek
Price Range: $245–$625 per night, with a two-night minimum

Credit Cards: MC, V
Children: Y
Pets: Y, with $20 fee
Handicap Accessible: Y

Three log lodges with enough room for 26 people (the buildings sleep six, 10, and 10) make High Meadows a great place for bigger families to spend a few days near the Flat Tops and Stagecoach Reservoir—and since there's only a two-night minimum stay, you don't have to commit to a full week. Jan (who cooks and takes photos) and Denny (who fly-fishes and hunts) are both experienced horsepeople, and they've created an unpretentious, uncommercial outfit. The horses—paints, quarter horses, and thoroughbreds—are the focus here, and trail rides cover everything from the green-carpeted valley floor to 360-degree, high-alpine panoramas. Fish for brookies in High Meadows' 1 mile of Morrison Creek, or land a lunker out of the rainbow trout pond.

✪ Vista Verde Guest Ranch

Owners: The Throgmartin Family
800-526-7433, 970-879-3858
vistaverde.com
info@vistaverde.com
3100 CR 64, Steamboat Springs
Price Range: $2,700–$3,100 per week
Credit Cards: MC, V
Children: Y, over age 6 (some weeks are adults-only; check for dates)
Pets: N
Handicap Accessible: N (but depends on disability; call for details)

At Vista Verde, there are no telephones, televisions, radios, or Internet access in the guest cabins—but there's just about everything else: private porch hot tubs, rough-hewn furniture, nightly turndown service, Native American tapestries, pine-paneled walls, wood-burning stoves, and comfy rocking chairs. The 500-acre spread has been here since the 1930s, when it was

a working cattle ranch, but it now hosts cooking classes and wine-tasting nights in addition to the typical dude-ranch activities: lots of horseback riding into the Zirkels, mountain biking, fly-fishing (there are two stocked ponds with 14- to 24-inch rainbows, or you can hit the Elk River), hot air ballooning, and hiking. Unlike many ranches, where fried chicken and baby back ribs are nightly affairs, Vista Verde is nothing if not Haute Dude: Chef Jonathon Gillespie puts together dishes like free-range veal in a salt and herb crust, maple-seared Muscovy duck breast, and beef tenderloin topped with black truffle and foie gras ravioli. Ciabatta, rosemary foccacia, and pains de campagne are made in-house, and desserts are decadent (sticky toffee pudding, gingerbread cake with crème anglaise). But don't worry—there are still cowboy cookouts with checkered tablecloths, corn on the cob, and campfires.

DINING

Restaurants

STEAMBOAT SPRINGS

✪ Antares

970-879-9939
57½ Eighth St., Steamboat Springs
Meals Served: D
Price Range: $19–$35
Full bar: Y
Reservations: Y
Credit Cards: AE, MC, V
Handicap Accessible: N

If you have it in you to splurge, you'll want to reserve a table at Antares. Chef "Rocky" LeBrun masterfully blends French, Asian, and Indian influences into starters like grilled Bengali prawns (with a spicy Indian marinade and tandoori aioli), followed by entrées like Elk Capone (medallions of elk topped with Chianti crimini sauce and gor-gonzola-creamed leeks) and Cantonese baby back ribs (dry-rubbed with hoisin spices, slow-roasted, and served with a side of orange ginger Serrano sauce). And the atmosphere is just as masterfully created: The inside of the historic Rehder building, with large stone fireplaces and wood floors, has exposed brick walls covered with dozens of tiny antique mirrors, luxuriously heavy curtains, linen tablecloths, and an intimate bar and parlor where you can sip on 27 different kinds of vodka—or keep your eyes out for the friendly ghost, "Old Man Shaw," who died in the apartment upstairs way back when.

The Butcher Shop

970-879-2484
1960 Ski Time Square, Steamboat Springs
Meals Served: D
Price Range: Entrées $14–$29
Full bar: Y
Reservations: Y
Credit Cards: AE, D, MC, V
Handicap Accessible: Y

Bill Gardner has been at the helm of The Butcher Shop for almost 40 years, and the menu hasn't changed much: He seeks out the best meat he can find, whether it's buf-falo sirloin steak from King Canyon Ranch in Nebraska, trout from Utah, or king crab legs jetted in from Alaska. Start out with a Mountain Man sausage—made of black bear, elk, buffalo, and venison and topped with honey-mustard sauce—and then, if you can hack it, a 20-ounce "Bob's Cut" prime rib. Or go lighter: smoked trout with Boursin-crab spread, teriyaki chicken breast, crab cakes. The ambience of the Shop is Old West: lamps dangle with cut glass, historical photos cover the walls, and everything is made of dark wood. If the meat isn't enough, all meals come with an all-you-can-eat salad bar, fresh honey whole wheat bread, and veggies or potato.

Café Diva

970-871-0508
cafediva.com
1855 Ski Time Square, Steamboat Springs
Meals Served: D
Price Range: $21–$33
Full bar: Y
Reservations: Y
Credit Cards: AE, D, MC, V
Handicap Accessible: Y

Take a stroll in the vicinity of Café Diva and you might miss it: The restaurant is on the ground floor of an enormous condo complex. But walk into Café Diva and you know what you're in for: The entry hall is lined, floor to ceiling, with cabinets full of French, Italian, and California wines. The decor runs to burgundies and pine greens, with glass-topped tables, colorful prints, and black-and-white photos. Chef Kate Van Rensselaer, who trained at the French Culinary Institute and then cooked under Jean-Georges Vongerichten, has composed a delicious and innovative French-Asian menu: corn crème brûlée, duck confit won-ton nachos, wild boar "corn dogs," Colorado pheasant with shiitake-leek bread pudding, a Kobe pork tenderloin crusted in garam masala, and espresso-rubbed filet mignon.

Cottonwood Grill

970-879-2229
cottonwoodgrill.com
info@cottonwoodgrill.com
701 Yampa St., Steamboat Springs
Meals Served: D
Price Range: $25–$33
Full bar: Y
Reservations: Y
Credit Cards: AE, D, MC, V
Handicap Accessible: Y

The minds behind Three Peaks Grill (see page 153), Peter Lautner and Michael Fragola, started their first Steamboat restaurant in this adobe-like building, where a grand circular layout and matching circular cedar deck hold court over the Yampa River. Settle in under huge green umbrellas or duck inside under tiny hanging light fixtures for tasty Pacific Rim fusion: shrimp and Thai basil sticks (gulf shrimp with basil and ginger in a crispy spring roll wrapper), miso- and sake-marinated black cod with coconut green curry sauce, Cambodian hot pot (shrimp, scallops, and clams simmered in coconut shrimp broth), and desserts like ginger crème brûlée and steamed Chinese sponge cake. On a clear night, they'll even carry the tables—linen napkins and all—to the banks of the river, where you can dig your toes into the green grass.

✪ Creekside Café and Grill

970-879-4925
131 11th St., Steamboat Springs
Meals Served: B, L
Price Range: $8–$15
Full bar: N
Reservations: N
Credit Cards: D, MC, V
Handicap Accessible: Y

In warm weather, Creekside's patio—next to Soda Creek—is a blessed place to be. Big canvas umbrellas shade checkered tablecloths, and dogs get tied to the wrought-iron fence, which is decorated with plastic butterflies. In winter, the small dining room still makes for a summery vibe: Clouds and vines are painted on the wooden ceiling, and garlands hang over the windows and the exposed brick walls. Breakfast is served until closing, at 2 PM, and there are 10—count 'em—varieties of eggs Benedict. The Arnold comes with smoked bacon, ham, and chorizo; the Little Buddy comes with shredded corned beef; and the Big Country comes on top of buttermilk biscuits. The most ridiculous indulgence on the menu? The Waffle-laughagus—a waffle topped with sausage

gravy, melted cheese, bacon, two eggs, and potatoes. Creekside also serves good sandwiches, salads, burgers, soups, and Bloody Marys.

Dos Amigos

970-879-4270
1910 Mt. Werner Rd., Steamboat Springs
Meals Served: D (but the bar opens
    between 2:30 and 3:30)
Price Range: $12–$27
Full bar: Y
Reservations: Y
Credit Cards: AE, MC, V
Handicap Accessible: N

"Dos" is where locals go for après-ski happy hour—the apps, like black bean nachos, fish tacos, and chalupas, are half-price from 3:30 to 6 and the margaritas are stiff. Come summer, the deck is shaded by pines and aspens. Some of the employees have been tending bar for a decade—and join in while skiers trade the day's war stories. Indoors, people slump against high-backed Guatemalan chairs under Mexican-kitschy sombreros and colorful ceramic parrots. Once dinnertime rolls around, the more elaborate plates begin to fly, and the food leans toward Southwestern and Latin rather than straight Mexican: Anaheim chilis stuffed with shrimp and crab, wrapped in bacon, and served with a tomato-cinnamon sauce. Turkey in mole sauce. Grilled chicken in pumpkin seed sauce. Enchiladas stuffed with spinach, mushrooms, and cheese. Even the desserts, like candied jalapeño white chocolate truffles, get a spicy flair.

Gondola Pub and Grill

970-879-4448
2305 Mt. Werner Circle (Gondola Square),
Steamboat Springs
Meals Served: B, L, D
Price Range: $8–$18
Full bar: Y

Reservations: N
Credit Cards: AE, D, MC, V
Handicap Accessible: N

With an old gondola car hanging from the ceiling and Denver Broncos banners hanging from the walls, this is your one-stop laid-back shop for all things food when you're up on the mountain: In summer, slurp a malt, shake, or ice-cream cone. Fuel up for a day on the ski hill with chicken-fried steak and eggs, a belgian waffle, or a fried egg sandwich. Grab lunch in between laps (french dip, Philly cheese steaks, meatball sandwiches), or tuck into dinners of baby back ribs, hickory-smoked chicken, meatloaf and mashers, or rainbow trout. Just want to warm up? Sip a Hot Apple Pie (Tuaca and apple cider) or a Bailey's and coffee. The multi-level layout has two bars, TVs of various sizes, and one room that's decorated with flight suits, airplane photos, and certificates. Haute cuisine? Nah, but it'll stoke your fire.

✪ Harwigs/L'Apogee

970-879-1919
lapogee.com
911 Lincoln Ave., Steamboat Springs
Meals Served: D
Price Range: Entrées $19–$30
Full bar: Y
Reservations: Y
Credit Cards: AE, MC, V
Handicap Accessible: Y

This dual restaurant has won so many awards from *Wine Spectator* that it's no wonder the entryway and some of the dining rooms are lined with old wine crates stamped with logos from around the world: Owner Jamie Jenny, a collector, has a cellar with 10,000 bottles. Other rooms and nooks have Victorian wallpaper, wine posters, historical photos, and stained glass. The menu is as eclectic as the decor. Monday night (from May to December) is Thai Night: gaeng pao plo duook (jungle-

style curry with seafood, potatoes, coconut, and sweet basil), pad pak tao hoo (tofu, pumpkin, and veggies), pad Thai, and satay. The rest of the week, entrées range from apple- and cinnamon-rubbed pork chops with vanilla rum jus to a vegetable cassoulet with a rich truffle broth to a walleye dusted in roasted pecans. If you like white chocolate, the mousse—set on a cinnamon meringue and ringed with blackberry puree—is a winner. The Harwig Building, built in 1886, is green with purple trim and once served as a saddlery store (the enormous wine cellar came later).

Hazie's

970-871-5150
Top of the Gondola, Steamboat Springs
Meals Served: L, D
Price Range: $59 for three-course dinner, lunch $7–$14
Full bar: Y
Reservations: Y
Credit Cards: AE, D, MC, V
Handicap Accessible: Y

Named after Hazie Ralston Werner, mother of three Olympians and sometimes called the Matriarch of Steamboat, this mountain-top restaurant is a lovely spot for a long, luxurious white-linen lunch or a three-course dinner looking over the flitting lights of town. If you're planning to hit the moguls on Voo Doo, though, you might be better off with a power bar: midday meals here include Escargots au Fromage (escargot baked in herb butter and slathered in brie), conch chowder (a recipe taken from the food and bev director's experience in the Cayman Islands), spinach salads, half-pound cheeseburgers, and muffalettas. Dinner, about $60 a head and accompanied by live grand piano music, could mean a mozzarella caprese, followed by a scallop and lobster jambalaya, and finished off with a chocolate mousse pâté or a Louisiana-style bread pudding. Every

Sunday in summer, Hazie's opens up for a hedonistic summer brunch (called "Brunch on the Mountain"): smoked salmon spreads, eggs Sardou, cheese blintzes, slow-roasted beef, jambalaya, house-made éclairs and cream pies, and more.

Lucile's

970-871-6977
luciles.com
2093 Curve Plaza, C-101, Steamboat
   Springs
Meals Served: B, L
Price Range: $6–$10
Full bar: N
Reservations: N
Credit Cards: AE, MC, V
Handicap Accessible: Y

A sister to the beloved original in Boulder, Colorado, Lucile's takes breakfast to another (Cajun) level: Start out with an order of four beignets, the New Orleans–style donut—and then proceed to stuff yourself: the Eggs Ponchartrain is pan-fried trout, poached eggs, béarnaise, grits, and a buttermilk biscuit. The Cajun Breakfast is red beans, eggs, and hollandaise. And the Pain Perdu—thick french toast slices—comes with eggs, andouille sausage, and buttery syrup. Lunches continue the Louisiana theme, with shrimp po' boys, gumbo, red beans and rice, collard greens, and bread pudding with lemon rum sauce.

Mahogany Ridge

970-879-3773
Fifth St. and Lincoln Ave., Steamboat Springs
Meals Served: D
Price Range: Entrées $8–$25
Full bar: Y
Reservations: Y
Credit Cards: AE, D, MC, V
Handicap Accessible: Y

This is pub grub with an upper-crust twist: The house-brewed lagers, stouts, and porters are excellent, the tabletops are shiny, the bar is long, and the vibe is sleek. Actually, you can hardly call it pub grub—burgers come with bacon, gorgonzola, and basil pesto or guacamole, salsa, jack, and cheddar. Instead of mozzarella sticks and jalapeño peppers, you get edamame, tuna ceviche, and pan-fried kasseri cheese. Main courses—like venison osso bucco with porter cream sauce or tandoori-spiced yellowfin tuna—come with a choice of 18 dipping sauces. Add a spicy kick with the guava habanero, make it sweet with apple chutney, or stay fresh with a bright mango salsa. If you're not in the mood for beer, Mahogany mixes a mean caipiranha. And if you're not in the mood for crowds, reserve the "VIP" room—and eat in the company of huge brewing tanks.

Mazzola's

970-879-2405
mazzolas.com
917 Lincoln Ave., Steamboat Springs
Meals Served: D
Price Range: Entrées $9–$24
Full bar: Y
Reservations: N
Credit Cards: AE, D, MC, V
Handicap Accessible: Y

There are a few Italian joints in town, but Mom-and-Pop Mazzola's—started in 1970 by the Mazzola family—calls itself a "majestic Italian diner." Translation? It's small, loud, friendly, and authentic. And you'll go away feeling stuffed: apps include champagne-battered artichoke hearts and five-cheese polenta fries; pastas range from penne with shrimp, pancetta, and vodka to linguini with littleneck clams; and the pizzas can get just a little crazy (the Walkin' in Memphis comes with barbecue chicken, apple butter, pickled onions, sweet peppers, and tomatoes). They don't take reservations, which makes for long waits on weekends and holiday periods—and in

Ore House at the Pine Grove has been serving authentic Colorado cuisine for more than 35 years. Evelyn Spence

summer, it's even harder to snag one of the two sidewalk tables (with their requisite red-and-white checkered tablecloths).

✪ Ore House at the Pine Grove
970-879-1190
orehouseatthepinegrove.com
Pine Grove Center, Steamboat Springs
Meals Served: D
Price Range: Entrées $14–$30
Full bar: Y
Reservations: Y
Credit Cards: AE, D, MC, V
Handicap Accessible: Y

In 1889, this barn and silo with bright yellow trim was part of a 280-acre homestead. Since then, it has been owned by a state senator, a Russian count, and was once known as one of the best hay ranches in the area. All this history is evident once you walk through the huge red door with the heavy iron pull. There are old wagon wheels, brands burned into planks, vintage photos, chaps, and steer skulls on every wall. The banisters are draped with saddles, and the corners are filled with old wood stoves (found at the ranch). The menu is heavy on meat—steaks, baby back ribs, elk loin, steak bits, beef kabobs, all prepared with toppings like red chili pinion pesto, béarnaise, and roasted garlic. And the desserts are nice and homey: mud pie, brownie fudge sundaes, chocolate mousse. The Ore House has been around for over 35 years, making it one of the oldest—and most genuine—restaurants in the 'Boat.

Saketumi
970-870-1019
1875 Ski Time Square, Steamboat Springs
Meals Served: L (in winter), D
Price Range: $7–$20
Full bar: Y

Reservations: Y
Credit Cards: AE, D, MC, V
Handicap Accessible: Y

A small bar and restaurant near Slopeside Grill (below), Saketumi is sushi-chic: blond wood tables, black wood chairs, plasma TVs, french doors, tiny blown-glass light fixtures, big mirrors. And they have fun with their fish: There's the usual nigiri and sashimi and the California and spicy tuna rolls, but then there's also the Miles of Smiles (fried coconut panko shrimp, mango, cream cheese, and cucumber with a honey curry sauce). Or the Strawberry Fields (eel, strawberries, and cream cheese topped with honey). Or the Rad Roll (eel, crab, and cucumber, with the whole thing deep-fried tempura-style). For the less adventurous, there are teriyaki and curry bowls, seared tuna and scallops, and shrimp tempura.

✪ Slopeside Grill

970-879-2916
1855 Ski Time Square Dr., Steamboat
    Springs
Meals Served: L, D
Price Range: $7.50–$21
Full bar: Y
Reservations: Y
Credit Cards: AE, D, MC, V
Handicap Accessible: Y

Want cheap eats in the wee hours? Slopeside has a second happy hour (9 to 11 PM in summer, and 10 to midnight in winter) with $6 pizzas and $2 pints, which brings out the local color to mingle around the big square center bar. But it's even more packed right after the lifts close: Deck chairs are a stone's throw from the bunny slopes. The walls are dangling with vintage signs, cowboy hats, horseshoes, wagon wheels, and historical photos. But back to that pizza: Slopeside isn't shy with its combos. The Fish Creek has anchovy filets, green onion, feta, basil, and pine nuts; the Cyclone has Jamaican jerk chicken, black bean and corn salsa, pineapple, and cilantro; and the White Out comes with white garlic sauce, mozzarella, gorgonzola, parmesan, and provolone. You can also order chili, burgers, sandwiches, and the utterly sinful fried ravioli. Have a pooch? If you sit on the deck, you can order Purina—in chicken and rice or lamb and rice flavors.

Steamboat Yacht Club

970-879-4774
steamboatyachtclub.com
811 Yampa St., Steamboat Springs
Meals Served: L, D
Price Range: Lunch $9–$11, dinner
    $16–$28
Full bar: Y
Reservations: Y
Credit Cards: AE, D, MC
Handicap Accessible: Y

The Yacht Club is a riff on the town's name—or maybe it comes from the fact that it sits right on the Yampa River, with a huge deck and lawn that look out over the water to Howelsen Hill. (There are house binoculars available to watch the night skiers and ski jumpers.) During the summer, kayakers and inner-tubers float by, showing off and waving. The restaurateurs have taken the ocean theme and run with it: walnut dividers and cruise-ship brass railings, nautical maps and instruments, and the occasional porthole. For lunch, try a grilled salmon barbecue sandwich or the golden-brown fish and chips—or go light with a pear and stilton salad. Dinners focus on meat and seafood: shrimp and escargot linguini, filet mignon with béarnaise, and wiener schnitzel. The best seats out back are just feet away from the river, but they get snapped up first. They're worth the wait.

✪ Three Peaks Grill

970-879-3399

threepeaksgrill.com

2165 Pine Grove Rd., Steamboat Springs

Meals Served: D

Price range: $18–$35

Full bar: Y

Reservations: Y

Credit Cards: AE, D, MC, V

Handicap Accessible: Y

One of Steamboat's newest restaurants, Three Peaks is ultra-contemporary: the dining room is expansive and angular, the burnt-orange accents and mahogany furniture are Art Deco-ish and match the framed photographs of brilliant sunsets, the fireplace is surrounded by modern sofas, and a 42-inch plasma TV rules over the raw bar. This is Steamboat's only place for oysters from East and West, littleneck and cherrystone clams, and Alaskan king crab legs, flown in fresh. The menu is divided into "From the Range" (Buckhead Reserve porterhouse and top sirloin, roasted chicken, double-cut pork chops) and "From the Sea" (salmon from British Columbia, halibut from Alaska). The appetizers range from fried oysters drizzled with blue cheese to baked brie with sun-dried cherry compote. The Steamboat Quartet plays jazz every Friday night.

Winona's

970-879-2483

617 Lincoln Ave., Steamboat Springs

Meals Served: B, L

Price Range: $4.50–$10.25

Full bar: N

Reservations: N

Credit Cards: MC, V

Handicap Accessible: Y

The menu at Winona's is overwhelmingly big, but rest assured that everything on there is delicious: Just ask one soul out of the throngs of people sure to be waiting in line for breakfast every single day of the week. Omelets come with crab, lox, turkey sausage, or feta; the "french toast" is actually made of Winona's homemade cinnamon rolls, not bread, and topped with honey butter and powdered sugar; the Monte Cristo is Texas toast (basically, french toast on steroids, with thick-cut slices) dipped in egg batter and stuffed with hickory-smoked ham and swiss; and the house-made granola is packed with bran, sunflower seeds, pecans, almonds, and raisins, and baked with molasses and honey. The bakery pops out fresh muffins and scones every morning. Come lunchtime, the crowd thins a bit, but the grub is still worth a taste—wraps, quesadillas, melts, build-your-own sandwiches, and hoagies can be ordered for here or to go.

Food Purveyors

Coffee Shops

Amante Coffee (970-871-8999, Wildhorse Plaza, Steamboat Springs) An Italian-style coffee shop that sells wine, paninis, pastries, gelato, and imported mineral water along with incredible coffee (roasted in Italy by the Ghigo family), Amante is a brand-new stop on the way up to the ski hill from US 40.

Chocolate Soup (chocolatesoupcafe.com, in the Steamboat Grand Hotel, 2400 Mt. Werner Circle, Steamboat Springs) A new pastry café with high-end coffee and baked goods along with soups like carrot ginger and french onion, Chocolate Soup has silver ceilings, brick accents, and cheerful poppies outside the windows (when the weather's right). As for their namesake, chocolate soup? It's based on an Italian drink called *bicerin*—the bottom layer is melted dark chocolate, the middle is a double shot of espresso, and the top is fresh whipped cream. Yes, you need a spoon.

Gondola Joe's Café (970-871-5150, Gondola Square, Steamboat Springs) This is the perfect location for a java joint: right next to the sometimes-long gondola line. Along with coffees, Joe's sells soups, bagels, and teas—and has both indoor and outdoor stool seating.

Metropolitan Mudd Coffee Company (970-879-8015, 737 Lincoln Ave., Steamboat Springs) Free wireless, exposed brick walls decorated with 3-foot-high metal stars, antique signs, a corrugated metal counter: The new coffee house Metropolitan Mudd feels arty and hip, and the smoothies and breakfast burritos are tasty.

Steamboat Coffee Roasters (800-511-9033, steamboatcoffee.com, 1934 13th St., Steamboat Springs) Though it's not a full-service coffee shop, SCR roasts great Arabica beans—and will give you a cup if you stop by.

Delis

Backcountry Provisions (970-879-3617, backcountryprovisions.com, 635 Lincoln Ave., Steamboat Springs) Want a hearty sandwich to bring along on a long hike, a long ski tour, or a long drive? Backcountry Provisions has two dozen combinations: The Pilgrim is piled with roasted turkey, muenster, stuffing, and cranberry chutney; the Bushwhacker comes with curry chicken salad, sliced almonds, granny smith apples, and smoked gouda; and the Timberline has peanut butter, bananas, and local honey. Don't like what you see? Make your own—out of any ingredients they have lying around.

The Colorado Bagel Company (970-870-9657, Central Park Plaza, Steamboat Springs) Pick up bagels by the dozen (garlic, salt, jalapeño, chocolate chip, asiago black pepper, parmesan pesto), cream cheese (olive and pimento, honey vanilla, scallion), or make your own bagel sandwich.

The Epicurean (970-875-0997, theepicurean.us/about.html, 825 Oak St., Steamboat Springs) Marco Pauvert, the Epicurean's owner and master of meats, has been in the charcuterie business for over 30 years—and his shop is much more than a café. On the docket: house-made sausages and pâtés, duck spring rolls, lentil and feta salads, buttermilk chicken, lamb moussaka, Thai peanut soup, and cheese from every corner of the globe. Takeout is available.

Freshies (970-879-8099, 145 Trafalgar Dr., Steamboat Springs) Lunch staples include chicken club sandwiches, reubens, burgers, salads, and soups, but breakfast is served until noon on weekends—omelets, breakfast sandwiches, french toast, cinnamon rolls, and scrambles.

The Market at Gondola Square (970-871-5150, Gondola Square, Steamboat Springs) A convenient place on the mountain for breakfast, lunch, to-go dinners—things like hot paninis, wraps, chili dogs, soups, breakfast bagels, brownies, and muffins.

Mother's Deli (970-879-0798, 1940 Ski Time Square, Steamboat Springs) A tiny bar and grill, deli, and ice-cream joint that also does takeout.

Wired (970-870-0306, 1860 Ski Time Square, Steamboat Springs) With wireless access and a full coffee menu, Wired is partly a coffee shop—but it also has a huge menu of sandwiches (a muffuletta, a pastrami reuben, a roast beef garlic melt), wraps (Thai peanut chicken or Caesar), burgers, and salads. Or you can enjoy one of their generous breakfasts—the Desperado skillet comes with potatoes, chorizo, eggs, green chili, cheddar, and sour cream, and the breakfast quesadilla is a chipotle tortilla filled with scrambled eggs, tomatoes, red onion, cheddar, and bacon.

Farmer's Markets
Old Town Farmer's Market (970-846-1800, 522 Lincoln Ave., Steamboat Springs) On Saturdays in summer, stalls go up on front of the Routt County Courthouse—selling local produce, meat, and flowers.

Frozen Desserts
Ben and Jerry's (970-875-1400, 2155 Mt. Werner Rd., Suite B-6, Steamboat Springs) Need your B+J fix? Get cones, sundaes, milkshakes, smoothies, cakes, and coffee here.

Johnny B. Good's (970-870-8400, johnnybgoodsdiner.com, 738 Lincoln Ave., Steamboat Springs) Checkered floors, vinyl oldies records on the walls, a walk-up window, stool seats: Johnny B. Good's diner brings back the '50s in a big way. There's a full breakfast and lunch menu of omelets, Benedicts, hot dogs, burgers, sandwiches, pitas, and bagels, but the best part is the old-fashioned soda fountain: It cranks out ice-cream floats, hard ice-cream shakes, malts, phosphates, sundaes, and cones.

Lyon's Corner Drug and Soda Fountain (840 Lincoln Ave., Steamboat Springs) This old-time soda fountain serves malts, egg creams, phosphates, and sundaes—and has an old Wurlitzer juke box.

Mountain View Car Wash (970-870-3363, 200 Trafalgar Dr., Steamboat Springs) Get your rig cleaned up and grab a conc of soft serve while you're at it.

Groceries
The Bamboo Market (970-879-9992, 116 9th St., Steamboat Springs) Natural lotions, organic produce and baked goods, bulk foods, supplements, fresh-made juices, and a deli.

City Market (970-879-3290, 1825 Central Park Plaza, Steamboat Springs)

Gondola General (970-879-3193, Gondola Square, Steamboat Springs)

Healthy Solutions Community Market (970-879-4747, Third St. and Lincoln Ave., Steamboat Springs) A small store with yoga business cards on the bulletin board, Healthy Solutions has bulk foods, supplements, tinctures, frozen treats, and some produce.

Market on the Mountain (970-879-2965, 2500 Village Dr., Steamboat Springs)

Safeway (970-879-3766, 1400 S. Lincoln Ave., Steamboat Springs)

Sweet Pea Produce (970-879-1221, 735 Lincoln Ave., Steamboat Springs) A cute, road stand—like store with dirt floors, Sweet Pea sells multi-grain breads and quick breads, fresh fruit pies, dried fruit, plants and herbs, cheeses, locally made salami, and organic produce.

Nightlife

Elements (970-879-6830, 56 Seventh St., Steamboat Springs) Though it closes at 9 PM, Elements (located in the Off the Beaten Path bookstore, see page 173) serves wine by the taste, glass, or bottle all day long—with appetizers for two (baked brie with lingonberries, smoked salmon, dolmas, stuffed mushroom caps).

Level'z (970-870-9090, levelzonline.com, 1860 Ski Time Square, Steamboat Springs) If there's a "nightclub" in town, this is it: Level'z, which shares a building with a coffee shop (Wired, see page 155), a sports bar, and a pizza delivery service. Come here for live music, DJs, and late night.

Sunpie's Bistro (970-870-3360, 735 Yampa St., Steamboat Springs) A sandwich shop with a New Orleans bent, Sunpie's has a tiny building—and a huge yard out back that sprawls to the Yampa River. Kick back in Adirondack chairs, sip microbrews and cocktails, and—if your stomach starts growling—order some pillowy hush puppies, po' boys, muffalettas, hoagies, and Cubans.

The Tap House (970-879-2431, thetaphouse.com, 719 Lincoln Ave., Steamboat Springs) A downstairs sports bar (the stairway is lined by neon beer signs) with booth and bar seating, pool tables, and over 40 TVs—three of them 100-inchers—the Tap House stays open until 2 AM and has 21 beers on tap. On wing night (Tuesdays), mild, medium, hot, oriental BBQ, and spicy garlic wings are three for a buck. The bar grub includes soups, salads, fajitas, burgers, steak, hot fudge sundaes, and even fried ice cream.

The Tugboat (970-879-7070, Ski Time Square, Steamboat Springs) One of the few restaurants/bars to stay open late all year round, the Tugboat is a full pub and grill—with salads, sandwiches, steaks, and pasta. But because it's open until 2 AM, serves buzz-friendly things like "armadillo eggs" (deep-friend jalapeños stuffed with cream cheese), and has pool, foosball, Ping-Pong, and live music, it really gets going once the kids have gone to bed. Who can resist a motto that says, "Fast time, hard laughs, grub, suds, and liquor"? Or a hand-carved cherrywood bar that came from Baggs, Wyoming, and has bullet holes in it?

Culture

Cinema

Carmike Chief Plaza 4 (970-879-0183, 813 Lincoln Ave., Steamboat Springs) Right in the middle of Old Town, Carmike plays new releases.

Metropolitan Wildhorse Stadium Cinemas (970-870-8222, 655 Marketplace Plaza, Steamboat Springs) A new six-screener that shows both blockbuster and independent films.

Historical Sites

Carpenter Ranch (970-276-4626) twenty miles west of Steamboat, Carpenter is a working ranch that has been preserved to show the agricultural heritage of the Yampa Valley. Tour the grounds, check out the education center, and learn about the history and ecology of the area.

Routt County Courthouse (522 Lincoln Ave., Steamboat Springs) Designed by Robert Kenneth Fuller, this Beaux Arts/Classical Revival building was constructed in 1923.

St. Paul's Episcopal Church (846 Oak St., Steamboat Springs) The sandstone used to build this church, consecrated in 1913, came from the Steamboat Town and Quarry Company on Emerald Mountain.

Museums

Tread of Pioneers Museum (970-879-2214, treadofpioneers.org, 800 Oak St., Steamboat Springs) Dedicated to preserving the history of the Steamboat Springs area, the Tread of Pioneers has wonderful artifacts: a candy case (complete with 100-year-old candies) carried by traveling salesman Clay Shaw; a genuine chuck wagon; Ute moccasins; a period bedroom and kitchen; and loads of historical photos. There's a library and research center on-site, and the museum has regular workshops and classes as well as free brochures about self-guided walking and biking tours.

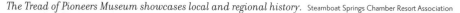

The Tread of Pioneers Museum showcases local and regional history. Steamboat Springs Chamber Resort Association

Theaters and Other Miscellaneous Venues

Depot Arts Center (970-879-9008, steamboatspringsarts.com, 1001 13th St., Steamboat Springs) Located in a historic railroad station built in 1908—which also features a Rio Grande caboose and a garden—the Depot Arts Center and the Steamboat Springs Arts Council put on art exhibits, musicals, children's dance workshops, after-school arts programs, and film series.

Emerald City Opera (970-879-1966, emeraldcityopera.org, box office at 320 Lincoln Ave., Suite H, Steamboat Springs) This local organization stages regular performances and runs numerous programs (like opera appreciation classes and resident artist programs) to educate both adults and youngsters about vocal and performing arts.

Perry Mansfield (970-879-7125, perry-mansfield.org, Strawberry Park, Steamboat Springs) Founded by Charlotte Perry and Portia Mansfield in 1913, this institution is the oldest performing arts school and camp in the country—with a 76-acre campus of cabins, open-air studios, and theaters. Children, faculty, and visiting artists perform regularly (ballet, musicals, Shakespeare, cabaret) throughout the summer.

Steamboat Springs Mountain Theater (866-707-4648, steamboattheater.com) Located just off Ski Time Square, the Mountain Theater is an entertainment smorgasbord: A recent look under "Coming Attractions" turned up a performance of *The Spitfire Grill*, music by The Samples and acoustic country group Morrison-Williams, a John Denver tribute, and a Western melodrama. Their tagline? "Comedies . . . Juggling . . . Music . . . Dance . . . Movies . . . Sports."

Yampa River Botanic Park (970-879-4300, ci.steamboat.co.us/recreation/parks/yrb-park.htm, Pamela Lane, Steamboat Springs) Open from spring until the first heavy snow of the season, this admission-free public park is a treasure: Learn about medicinal plants that Native Americans used, stroll among culinary herbs, see what the pioneers planted in their gardens, catch the short growing season in the September Charm Garden, and cross your fingers for the single-day blooms in the Daylily Garden.

Yampatika (970-871-9151, yampatika.org, Forest Service Building, 925 Weiss Dr., Steamboat Springs) In addition to kids' programs (see page 159), the conservation advocacy group Yampatika has an extensive offering of nature hikes, historical walks, wildflower treks, brown-bag lunch lectures, mushroom hunts, GPS treasure hunts, and stargazing nights.

Kids' Stuff

Amaze'N Steamboat (970-870-8682, 1255 US 40, Steamboat Springs) The closest thing Steamboat has to an amusement park, this complex will leave your inner child (or just your child) sated: mini-golf, a giant maze, squirt guns, and bumper car basketball (in which the loser gets showered with water).

Disc Golf (various locations) Throw a Frisbee-like disc into a chain-link "hole" on 9- to 18-hole disc golf courses around town, including up at the ski area, at the Colorado Mountain College Alpine Campus, and at Howelsen Hill, where rental discs are available.

Howelsen Hill (970-879-4300) Watch future Olympic ski jumpers train on a 50-meter jump, or hang out at the skate park, the tennis and volleyball courts, or the playground. Try the Howler: Jump in a plastic sled and careen 2,400 feet down a cement flume (and do good, too: It raises money for the Steamboat Springs Winter Sports Club).

Kids Adventure Club (970-879-0740) In winter, go to a Kids' Night Out for snacks, movies, tubing, pottery, pizza. In summer, come prepared with swimsuit, towel, water shoes, and jacket.

The Potter's Wheel (970-879-4944, 2780 Acre Lane, Steamboat Springs) Choose from over 200 basic ceramic shapes (bowls, cups, plates) and then decorate to your heart's content. They'll even ship your masterpiece back home.

Poulter Adventures (888-879-4816, poultercamps.com, P.O. Box 770969, Steamboat Springs) Though some of its camps (for children ages 9–17) last up to four weeks, there are 10-day adventures as well: One of them brings kids into the Flat Tops for an intro to rock climbing, backpacking, and horseback riding, and another takes them up to the Continental Divide for caving, ice-axe practice, snow travel, and Tyrolean traverses.

Steamboat Springs Health and Recreation Association (970-879-1828, sshra.org, 136 Lincoln St., Steamboat Springs) Open year-round, this complex has three hot mineral pools, exercises classes, an 82-degree Olympic-size lap pool, sauna, massage, and a 350-foot waterslide.

Yampa Valley Cutter and Chariot Racing (970-879-2820, 26480 CR 52 E., Steamboat Springs) Bring your kidlets to something truly unique: Since 1960, this association has put on quarter-mile races of two horses to one driver—all year round—in the Romick Arena in Steamboat.

Yampatika (970-871-9151, yampatika.org, Forest Service Building, 925 Weiss Dr., Steamboat Springs) A conservation group that organizes field programs, in-school workshops, specimen collections, and more, Yampatika has kids' activities for ages 3–15: lessons about different Colorado animals, backcountry skills, hiking, and ecology.

RECREATION: WINTER AND SPRING

Alpine Skiing and Snowboarding

Steamboat Ski Area
steamboat.com

Overview: The first thing you should know about Steamboat? The snow is incredible, and there is lots of it—around 334 inches of fluff a season, more than most other Colorado resorts. And we mean fluff: At 7 percent water content, it's the kind of powder that swirls around your boots and smokes up to your waist. The second thing? It's big. And decep-

Steamboat: The 4-1-1
Acres: 2,965
Summit elevation: 10,568 feet
Vertical drop: 3,668 feet
Annual snowfall: 334 inches
Percent advanced/expert terrain: 44
Percent intermediate terrain: 42
Percent beginner terrain: 14
Lifts: 25

tively so: From the base, you can't see how far back (and up) it goes, with 2,965 acres and a 3,668-foot vertical drop (one of the highest in the state). And considering the first two things, the third thing doesn't really matter (and isn't particularly true): the myth that Steamboat lacks really difficult terrain. Okay, so some people have been known to call it "Flatboat," but those people probably haven't skied the hike-to chutes off Mount Werner. Nor have they felt what it's like to float through ghostly aspen groves at a continuous 30-degree pitch. There's enough incredible snow here, and such a wide range of runs, that there's no need to be extreme: You'll be too busy choking on your buddy's contrails.

Must-ski: On a powder day, the whole mountain is a blast, from Flying Z and Ambush all the way over to Tomahawk and Ramrod. But there are a few classics: The trees of Shadow and Closet—perfectly spaced aspens and pines, with a go-forever pitch—are what skiers live for. For something more wide-open, Longhorn, Buddy's Run, and One O'Clock and Two O'Clock (referring to when the sun hits them) are good long cruisers. From the top of the Morningside triple, experts can hike about 5–10 minutes to the top of 10,568-foot Mount Werner, where narrow and short Chutes 1, 2, and 3 drop for a few good turns. Further along the ridge, No Names has supersteep and tight tree slots, and North St. Pat's opens up a bit more. Want bumps? Try Voo Doo, where the U.S. Freestyle Team often practices. The superpipe, called Mavericks (aptly named after the massive Northern California surf break), is the longest in the nation: 15-foot walls, 50 feet wide, and 675 feet long.

Grub: The swankiest place to eat on-mountain is **Hazie's** (see page 149), where reservations are required for lunch and dinner. But there are plenty of other places to grab a bite: On top of the gondola, the cafeteria-style **B. K. Corral** has burgers, pizza, salads, and barbecue, while **Stoker** has more of the same, only sit-down. Halfway down the High Noon run, **Rendezvous Saddle** has a broad selection of pastas, stews, burgers, baked potatoes, soups, Mexican dishes, and pizza. In the same building, **Ragnar's** gives fine dining a Scandinavian twist (and even serves fresh seafood). If you just want a quick bite in the Storm Peak area, stop into **Four Points Hut** for chili, hot dogs, beer, coffee, and soda.

Cross-Country Skiing and Snowshoeing

Howelsen Hill Ski Touring Center (970-879-4300, 845 Howelsen Pkwy., Steamboat Springs) Since it's considered part of the city park system, the 20 kilometers' worth of Howelsen Hill trails are free to the public—and they're also the most aerobically challenging in the valley. It's not yet a full touring center: You have to bring your own gear or rent in town.

Lake Catamount Ski Touring Center (970-871-6667, catamountclub.com, CR 18, Steamboat Springs) Though it's within a private development, Catamount has opened its trails to the public. It has passes for sale, a warming hut, rentals, dog-friendly trails, and beautiful vistas of Lake Catamount and Pleasant Valley. The terrain is flat to easy-rolling—and on Fridays, various clinics (Ladies' Days, skill-building, etc.) are taught by local athletes.

The Nordic Center at Vista Verde Ranch (970-879-3858, vistaverde.com/nordiccenter, 3100 CR 64, Steamboat Springs) With 30 kilometers of skating and classic trails across 500 acres that butt up against National Forest land, Vista Verde is normally a luxe guest ranch (see page 146)—but in winter, you can buy ski-and-lunch packages, half-day and full-day tours, and learn-to-ski sessions.

Steamboat Ski Touring Center (970-879-8180, nordicski.net, 2000 Clubhouse Dr., Steamboat Springs) With trails of all levels that wind through the neighborhoods along

Fish Creek, this Nordic area—owned by Sweden native Sven Wiik—has hosted NCAA championships, Nordic combined Olympic qualifiers, and countless local races since it opened in 1980. Group lessons, guided tours, rentals, and multi-day passes are available.

Steamboat Springs Nordic Council (steamboatxcski.org) Want to try every touring center around? Visit this Web site for overall information about the X-C scene in Steamboat. Visitors can get three- or five-day passes ($42–$65) good at any and all of the above areas—and they're also for sale at the Chamber of Commerce.

Guiding and Backcountry

Guides
Colorado's High Lonesome Outfitter & Guides (970-638-4239, cohighlonesome.com, P.O. Box 312, Yampa) High Lonesome operates a pair of fully outfitted backcountry tents (made of heavy-duty canvas, with carpeted floors and cots with thick mattresses). If you want, they'll bring in your personal food and gear so you don't have to carry a heavy pack, and shuttle it in between huts, too.

Rocky Mountain Ventures (970-870-8440, verticalgrip.com, P.O. Box 882981, Steamboat Springs) In summer, RMV takes all levels of rock climber on top-roped local climbs; in winter, they run ice climbing trips in Fish Creek Canyon and moonlight and wildlife snowshoe tours (you'll most likely see elk, deer, bison, rabbits, coyotes, and the occasional eagle).

Trails
Fish Creek Canyon Off skier's right of East Face and down, Fish Creek Canyon has deep lift-served backcountry shots—but it's easy to get lost or cliffed out (and it's a long, long traverse to get back out again). Go with a local or talk to the ski patrol before heading out of bounds.

Hahns Peak About 25 miles north of Steamboat, Hahns Peak has a small network of backcountry trails and fire roads that you can take as high as you want to go (some people climb all the way to the summit and ski back down).

Rabbit Ears Pass A playground of open meadows and gentle terrain, the Rabbit Ears area has a few loops (that, unfortunately, are also used by snowmobilers). From here, you can even follow the Hogan Park Route, which will take you to the top of Steamboat Ski Area (route-finding skills required).

Service Creek The Service Creek State Wildlife Area is closed to snowmobiles, ATVs, mountain bikes, and everything else mechanized—which makes for a quiet, isolated backcountry experience. The trail climbs gradually from 7,000 to 7,840 feet, passing by small waterfalls and crossing a bridge. It's ungroomed, so bring your trail-breaking legs.

Dogsledding
Grizzle-T Dog & Sled Works (970-870-1782, P.O. Box 772525, Steamboat Springs) Grizzle-T has been breeding huskies for the Iditarod for a quarter-century. They'll let you drive your own team along a 13-mile trail (count on it taking at least two hours).

Red Runner Dog Sled Tours (970-879-3647, 33567 US 40, Steamboat Springs) Help owner Carol Bloodworth put on her dogs' harnesses, take them for an 8-mile spin through the Yampa Valley, and finish off with hot chocolate and snacks in a tepee.

Ice Skating

Howelsen Ice Arena (970-879-4300, howelsenicearena.com, 285 Howelsen Pkwy., Steamboat Springs) This Olympic-size sheet of ice plays host to broomball, speed skating, figure skating lessons, hockey leagues, and public sessions.

Sleigh Rides

Bar Lazy L Ranch (970-879-0095, 26480 RCR 52 E, Steamboat Springs) Every night at 6 PM in winter, Gary and Hattie—whose family has owned this ranch since 1939—send off dinner sleighs packed with wool blankets and pulled by massive draft horses. Dinner is Western: ribs, chicken, beans, coffee.

Dutch Creek Guest Ranch (970-879-8519, 61565 CR 62, Clark) Of all the sleighing options, Dutch Creek has the most extensive menu choices: Entrées include coconut shrimp, pork loin, chicken-fried steak, wild game, and grilled salmon. Everything is served in a log-cabin lodge with a stone fireplace, peeled-log beams, hardwood floors, and rustic chandeliers.

Elk River Guest Ranch (970-879-6220, elkriverguestranch.com, 29840 RCR 64, Steamboat Springs) Sleigh rides in winter, carriage rides in summer, and dinners of roasted duck, New York strip, teriyaki salmon, cowboy carrots, garlic bread, and potatoes all year round. Horses pull you to a saloon for cocktails, candlelit tepees for the main meal, and back to the saloon for dessert.

Sunset Ranch (970-879-0954, sunsetranchinc.com, 42850 CR 129, Steamboat Springs) Sunset Ranch has been an outfitter in the Mt. Zirkel Wilderness Area since 1943, and they have their winter rides down pat: Glide to a tent (heated with three wood stoves) on Deer Mountain, tuck into trout, chicken, or steak, listen to cowboy poetry and singing, and head back a few hours later.

Windwalker Tours (970-879-8065, windwalkertours.com, P.O. Box 775092, Steamboat Springs) Slide along the Yampa River behind Belgians and Percherons, fill up on rib eye, rolls, beans, frosted brownies, and hot cocoa in a log cabin, and line-dance to local musician Kenny Knapp.

Snowcat Skiing

Steamboat Powdercats (800-288-0543, steamboatpowdercats.com) Think the snow at the resort is good? How about having 10,000 acres of glades, trees, steeps, and bowls all to yourself? Powdercats' terrain, near Buffalo Pass, sees 500-plus inches of snow a season, and a day of cat skiing nets up to 18 runs and 12,000 vertical feet of above-head champagne powder. Packages include a hot lunch in a backcountry cabin, cat snacks, and fat skis.

Winter Driving

Steamboat Winter Driving School (800-949-7543, winterdrive.com, 1850 Ski Time Square Dr.) At the first winter-driving school in the U.S., learn accident-avoidance techniques and rally-car driving tips on three custom-designed ice- and snow-covered courses. Work your way up to the "Scandinavian Flick," cornering, and dealing with low-grip situations.

RECREATION: SUMMER AND FALL

Boating

Steamboat Lake Marina (970-879-7019, steamboatlakemarina.com) About 26 miles away from town, 1,055-acre Steamboat Lake is open year-round, but in summertime it rents out pontoon boats (some hold up to 14 people), motorized fishing boats (the rainbows and cutties can be hog-size), canoes, paddleboats, and kayaks.

Cycling: Mountain Biking

Guides
Rocky Peak Productions (970-879-0480, rockypeakproductions.com) This local company organizes cycling events in the area, including the 24 Hours of Steamboat (a team fat-tire event) and the Tour de Steamboat (a competitive, 100-mile road tour).

Trails
Emerald Mountain You can cobble together a quick loop or a longer ride on this network of trails, and, since it's just behind Howelson Hill, it's a piece of cake to access.

Rabbit Ears Pass For 25 miles of rolling singletrack, you can either arrange a shuttle and go end-to-end, or climb all the way up US 40 (the epic option). Park

Cruising around on Steamboat Lake. Steamboat Springs Chamber Resort Association

at the turnoff for Dumont Lake and start riding north—past lakes, through meadows, and across creeks—before either continuing on to Buffalo Pass or heading past Long Lake to the Mountain View Trail (which will bring you back to the ski area).

Seedhouse/RD/Hinman/Greenville Loop This loop, on the edge of the 140,000-acre Mt. Zirkel Wilderness Area near Clark, makes for great views of nearby peaks—and has dense conifer forests that line the Elle River. It starts off Forest Road 400 (Seedhouse Road).

Two road cyclists above Steamboat Lake and the expanse of the Yampa Valley. Steamboat Springs Chamber Resort Associaton

Spring Creek Trail A short, 8-mile jaunt that starts at the intersection of Maple and Amethyst Streets near the high-school football field. Follow Spring Creek through the canyon, keep going past the second bridge, and cross the creek some 13 times (you might get soaked during runoff).

Steamboat Ski Area In summer, take the lifts up and ride 50 miles' worth of cut runs—some wide boulevards, some rocky singletrack—back down. Rental bikes are available at the ticket office at the base of the mountain.

Cycling: Road Biking
Core Trail Great for walking, jogging, or biking, this paved route follows the Yampa past outdoor artwork, waterfowl habitat, kayaking play holes, fishing spots, and downtown restaurants.

Elk River Road Heading north, follow CR 129 along the Elk River until you reach the charming little town and cabins of Columbine (and catch a view of Steamboat Lake). The ride is about 30 miles one way.

Grassy Gap For fantastic views of the Flat Tops Wilderness, turn south off US 40 at the sign for Oak Creek—then climb up and down for a total of 3,400 feet before flying into the small town of Oak Creek.

Historic Places Bike Tour Stop by the Steamboat Chamber or the Steamboat Springs Historic Preservation Advisory Commission (124 10th St.) and pick up a map to guide you past some of the town's oldest buildings.

Rabbit Ears–Muddy Pass At 52 miles one way, the route to Kremmling climbs and then descends close to 6,000 feet, but your rewards are panoramic views, consistent climbs and descents, and diverse terrain.

Stagecoach Rez This quick jaunt takes you through ranchlands from Steamboat out to Stagecoach, a small but quickly growing community alongside a big reservoir. Start the ride in Steamboat—or join CR 131 where it meets US 40.

US 40, Craig to Steamboat Springs A mellow 42-miler, this route starts in the small town of Craig and rolls up and down into Steamboat, gaining some 1,800 feet along the way and following the Yampa River on the last leg into town.

Fishing

Outfitters
Bucking Rainbow Outfitters (888-810-8747, 970-879-8747, buckingrainbow.com, 730 Lincoln Ave., Steamboat Springs) A cross between a fly shop and Western-wear store, Bucking Rainbow sells belts, hats, boots, and postcards—as well as guided trips on the Yampa, the tailwaters of the Stagecoach Rez, Sarvis Creek, Steamboat Lake, the private tailwater of Lake Catamount, Buffalo Creek Ranch, and the Colorado River.

Steamboat Flyfisher (866-268-9295, 970-879-6552, steamboatflyfisher.com, 507 Lincoln Ave., Steamboat Springs) Open since May 2005, Steamboat Flyfisher guides on the Yampa, Elk, and Colorado—or, farther afield, the North Platte and the Green. Every Saturday in summer, they run free beginner casting clinics from 10 to noon; on Wednesdays from 4 to 6, they cover more advanced techniques like double-hauling and spey casting.

Straightline Sports (970-879-7568, straightlinesports.com, 744 Lincoln Ave., Steamboat Springs) The guys at Straightline have been around since 1976, and they know where to find trophy trout in the Yampa, the high alpine lakes, and the private waters in the valley—all year round. Try a walking or wading trip, or rent gear and let them tell you where to go.

Lakes and Streams
Before you fish any water in Colorado, be sure you check with a local fly shop to find out if it's public or private. Many rivers have both private and public sections, so make sure you know where you're going. For licenses and regulations, visit wildlife.state.co.us/fishing—or, again, stop into a shop. If a river is designated "Gold Medal," it officially means that there are 12 trout per surface acre that top 14 inches—or 60 pounds of trout per surface acre. Unofficially, it means that the fishing is damn good.

Elk River Just 15 minutes from town, the Elk pours out of the Zirkels and has prolific hatches. It's good well into the fall.

Pearl Lake State Park A little under 30 miles from Steamboat, scenic Pearl Lake has native cutthroat—and is often one of the first high-country lakes to thaw each season. Try the inlets near the north end.

Stagecoach Reservoir (970-736-2436, parks.state.co.us) About 16 miles from Steamboat, Stagecoach—a small town and a big rez—has good fishing for rainbows, browns, brookies, northern pike, and the occasional cutthroat, both in the lake itself and below the dam in the tailwaters of the Yampa.

White River This waterway flows along the western slope of the Flat Tops, down through the tiny historic town of Meeker—and has excellent freestone dry fly-fishing. The whole White River Valley has over 100 miles of streams.

Yampa River A good portion of the Yampa's 150 miles are productive, especially the tailwaters under the Stillwater Reservoir—but there are some large private sections, especially from Steamboat west to Craig. Thanks to the river rock and habitat placed in the water as it passes through Steamboat, you can catch fish just two blocks from Lincoln Avenue.

Golf

Haymaker Golf Course (970-870-1846, haymakergolf.com, 34855 US 40, Steamboat Springs) Award-winning course architect Keith Foster blended 110 acres of rolling fairways and greens into 233 acres of open space, leaving native grasses and wetlands in place. The city-owned complex has a driving range, putting green, pro shop, and restaurant.

Steamboat Golf Club (970-879-4295, steamboatgolfclub.com, 26815 W. US 40) This 9-hole course borders the Yampa River and has been around since 1964; it's open to the public, and you can play for as little as $32 (9 holes) or $47 (18 holes).

Steamboat Sheraton Golf Club (800-848-8877, sheratonsteamboatgolf.com, 220 Village Inn Court) Fish Creek bubbles its way through most of the fairways along this 18-hole, 150-acre, Robert Trent Jones Jr.—designed course—which is lined with big aspens and evergreens. Staying at the Sheraton? You get a 20-buck discount.

Helicopter Tours

Zephyr Helicopter (970-879-0494) Design a custom heli tour with Zephyr: The only constraint is a minimum flight time of a half-hour (that's 200 bucks for one—two people). Fly over town or the ski area, buzz the Flat Tops or the Zirkels, or catch an express ride to the airport.

Hiking and Backpacking

Devil's Causeway The 235,000-acre Flat Tops Wilderness is Colorado's biggest, with its telltale plateaus, striated rocks, and wide-openness. Devil's Causeway is just one highlight—a 3-foot-wide, 1,500-foot-high, knife-edge wall that separates two enormous valleys.

Fish Creek Falls A 283-foot cascade that's just a quarter-mile from the road—and even handicap accessible—Fish Creek Falls is about 4 miles outside of town, and longer hikes start just across the bridge below the falls.

Howelsen Hill For quick spins, go no farther than Howelsen—a steep trail winds its way to the top of the 90-meter ski jump, where the views of Storm Peak are spectacular.

Mount Zirkel To climb the marquee peak in this namesake Wilderness Area (it's 12,180 feet high), take the south ridge to Red Dirt Pass, hiking by the ghostly Slavonia mining camp.

Rainbow Lake The Mount Zirkel Wilderness Area was one of the five original state wilderness areas founded in the wake of the 1964 Wilderness Act, and it's full of alpine lakes and

Afraid of heights? Think twice before crossing the Devil's Causeway in the Flat Tops Wilderness.

Steamboat Springs Chamber Resort Association

expansive valleys. Rainbow Lake—3.5 miles in, along a ridgeline—is the biggest in the area, with the huge cirque of Mount Ethel as a backdrop.

Sarvis Creek Wilderness A small Wilderness Area, Sarvis Creek (sometimes pronounced "service"), a sloping 47,000-acre tract south of US 40 below Rabbit Ears, has two long trails paralleling Silver and Service (still pronounced "service") Creeks, each 9–11 miles in length, one way.

Thunderhead Hiking Trail This on-mountain route climbs up Mount Werner, starting at the base area, ending at the top of the gondola, and gaining 2,180 feet in 3 miles.

Troublesome Wilderness Study Roadless Area Almost 60,000 acres in total, this roadless expanse is home to moose, elk, black bears, and rare nagoon berry plants, as well as some 50 miles of trails.

Horseback Riding

Big Rack Horseback Adventures (970-871-1427, bigrack.com) This is a true working ranch, and you can participate in spring brandings, cattle drives, cattle sorting, team penning, and Western riding lessons—or just head out on a standard breakfast, lunch, or high-country wildlife ride.

Colorado's High Lonesome Outfitter and Guides (970-638-4239, cohighlonesome.com, P.O. Box 312, Yampa) Half-day and full-day rides criss-cross Green Ridge Mountain in the Routt National Forest; in summer and fall, pack trips head into a base camp, from which you explore the Flat Tops and Pagoda Peak.

Del's Triangle 3 Ranch (970-879-3495, steamboathorses.com, 55675 CR 62, Clark) Del's has access to 114 square miles of wilderness—that's 40 lakes, countless streams and trails, and panoramic views. Ride one of their quarter horses or Arabians for just an hour, a full day, or a five-day trip complete with guide, cooker, tents, meals, and pack horses.

Elkhorn Outfitters (970-824-7392, elkhornoutfitters.com, 37399 N. Hwy. 13, Clark) Elkhorn plans day-long trips year-round—horseback rides through their 50,000 acres of private land, cattle drives, fishing rides, and photography rides. In winter, ride for part of the day, then snowshoe or cross-country ski through Dick and Cheryl Dobbs's domain.

High Meadows Ranch (800-457-4453, 970-736-8416, hmranch.com, 20505 RCR 16, Oak Creek) With a home base near Stagecoach Reservoir (about 45 minutes from Steamboat), High Meadows has prime access to the Sarvis Creek and Flat Tops Wilderness Areas and the Morrison Divide Trail. Two-hour rides depart twice daily, in the morning and afternoon, and half- and full-day rides and instruction are also available.

Saddleback Ranch (970-879-3711, saddlebackranch.net, 37350 CR 179, Steamboat Springs) Don't want a typical "nose-to-tail" trail ride? Help out with a Saddleback Ranch cattle drive. You can move strays, check for illnesses, and drive cows from place to place. Or take a dinner ride to the Double Dollar lodge and dance, learn calf roping, and eat barbecue chicken, baked beans, and bread pudding.

Sombrero Ranches (970-879-2306, sombrero.com, 835 River Rd., Steamboat Springs) Just behind the rodeo grounds, Sombrero runs one- and two-hour rides, dinner rides, fishing and hunting pack trips, and even leases horses for about 100 bucks a day.

Steamboat Lake Outfitters (970-879-4404, steamboatoutfitters.com, 60880 CR 129, Clark) The only company that operates in Steamboat Lake State Park, SLO has everything from quick one-hour spins to overnight trips into the Mount Zirkel Wilderness Area (for great trout fishing). They'll even organize pack trips up to 14 days long.

Hot Air Ballooning

Balloons Over Steamboat, Ltd. (877-879-3298, 970-879-3298) The oldest balloon service in the area, Balloons Over Steamboat has year-round flights through the Yampa Valley and over the Zirkel mountains.

Wild West Balloon Adventures (970-879-7219, wildwestballooning.com) Hourlong or half-hour floats in a balloon called *Velvet* start with continental breakfast and end with a champagne toast—and you even walk away with a flight certificate.

Hot Springs

Strawberry Park Hot Springs (970-879-0342, strawberryhotsprings.com, 44200 CR 36, Steamboat Springs) A rustic backcountry hot springs this is not: Strawberry is a 40-acre complex with two pools, one of which is 29 by 16 feet and hovers around 104 degrees. The springs remain open until midnight on weekends, and you can stay the night at tent sites, in covered wagons, and in cabins—but reserve way ahead if you want to sleep in the Train Caboose. (It's a genuine caboose with solar lights, a full-size futon, and kitchenette.) You can also get massage and watsu (a floating warm-water massage) on-site.

Soak it all in: Strawberry Park Hot Springs, Steamboat Springs. Steamboat Springs Chamber Resort Association

Hunting

Backcountry Guides & Outfitter (970-879-3977, backcountryoutfitter.net, 32670 RCR 14, Steamboat Springs) On 38,000 acres of private land, this outfit has been operating—and managing its elk herds—for over 30 years, so guides know the area like the back of their hands. Both rifle and archery elk hunts are available.

Colorado's High Lonesome Outfitter & Guides (970-638-4239, cohighlonesome.com, P.O. Box 312, Yampa) If you want to shoot an elk, High Lonesome will find you an elk. If you want a turkey, they'll find you turkey. And they'll even take you on a five-day chase for an elusive mountain lion (for $3,500 a person).

Cross Mountain Ranch (970-824-2803, crossmountainranch.com; headquarters: 1280 Industrial Way, Craig) Cross Mountain owns 70,000 acres of private land, and has more than 300,000 acres' worth of leases and permits—plus one of the biggest elk herds in the country. Take a five-day, fully guided, fair-chase trip to hunt for them, or for deer, or for antelope.

There's no shortage of challenges for skilled kayakers near Steamboat Springs. Steamboat Springs Chamber Resort Association

Del's Triangle 3 Ranch (970-879-3495, steamboathorses.com, 55675 CR 62, Clark) Choose between a full-service hunting camp (with meals, guides, wrangling, and game transport) or a drop camp, where Del's will haul in tents, cooking gear, cots, and mattresses, then leave you to your own devices.

Steamboat Lake Outfitters (970-879-4404, steamboatoutfitters.com, 60880 County Road 129, Clark) Mountain lion, elk, deer, black bear, and game birds are all possibilities when you book with SLO.

Rafting and Paddling

Backdoor Sports (970-879-6249, backdoorsports.com, Nineth and Yampa Sts., Steamboat Springs) Need to rent telemark gear? Arrange a quick float down the Yampa—by inner tube? Learn how to do an Eskimo roll? Backdoor can teach you outdoor skills and sell you the gear you need for them.

Colorado River Center (888-888-7238, 970-879-6699, coloradorivercenter .com, P.O. Box 4259, Edwards; CR 1, Trough Rd., 4 miles from State Bridge) Staged out of Rancho del Rio on the

Colorado River, the CRC is a long way from anywhere—but they offer kayaking lessons, beginner to advanced rafting trips, and duckie and sit-on-top rentals.

High Adventures Rafting (970-879-8747, buckingrainbow.com, 730 Lincoln Ave., Steamboat Springs) One of High Adventures' most requested trips heads down the Elk River, past lodgepole pine forests, with 5 miles of nonstop Class III white water. One of their most hardcore: a stretch down Cross Mountain Canyon, a 900-foot-deep gorge in the desert with huge waves and holes. For the faint of heart, the mellow Colorado is always an option.

MAD Adventures (800-451-4844, madadventures.com, 1421 E.Park Ave., Kremmling) Though it's a bit of a drive from Steamboat (the Kremmling office is the closest), MAD has permits to float the Colorado—Class I–III water that winds past old barns, hot springs, and big vistas.

Mountain Sports Kayak School (970-879-8794, 1450 S. Lincoln Ave., Steamboat Springs) With some gentle stretches, the Yampa is great for learning: Start on shore, move to a pond, and end the day paddling downriver. More advanced? Try surfing waves, riding holes, squirting, rolling, and running slalom gates.

Rock Climbing
Rocky Mountain Ventures (970-870-8440, verticalgrip.com) Offering top-roped climbs on Rabbit Ears Pass, near Fish Creek Falls, and in the Seedhouse area (just past the town of Clark), RMV caters to everyone from rank beginners to the very experienced. Both single-pitch and multi-pitch guided climbs and clinics are available.

Sporting Clays
Three Quarter Circles (970-846-5647, 3qc.net, 26185 US 40 W., Steamboat Springs) With a 40-acre, 12-station course on the historic Hogue Ranch (the 3QC brand has been around since 1899), this shooting range has 360-degree views of the Sleeping Giant, the Flat Tops, the ski area, and more. It can accommodate everyone from first-timers to expert marksmen.

DRIVING: SCENIC DRIVES AND BYWAYS

California Park After going up and over Quaker Mountain on FR 150, this half-day trip drops into grass prairie, heads north over the Slater Creek Divide, and joins Black Mountain Road.

Colorado Highway 129 For a quick two-hour loop, cruise up CO 129 from Steamboat north to Steamboat Lake State Park—rolling hills, mountain views, Elk River fishing, the historic Moon Hill schoolhouse, the tiny hamlet of Clark (the Main Street General Store has great homemade fudge), old ranches, and the lake itself. Pick up a detailed guide to the sights at the Tread of Pioneers Museum (page 157).

Flat Tops Scenic Byway This route, along CR 8, passes through what is known as the "Cradle of Wilderness," the area that inspired the 1964 Wilderness Act: It goes from Yampa to Meeker, splitting the White River Plateau Timberland Reserve and passing by canyons, Ute territory, the headwaters of the Yampa and White Rivers, and big game.

Off the Beaten Path is Steamboat Springs's oldest and biggest bookstore—and even sells wine by the bottle or the glass. Evelyn Spence

Shopping

Art Galleries

Blue Leaf Quilts (970-870-2913, davidtaylorquilts.com) So it may not be art in the traditional sense, but David Taylor's unique quilt designs are incredible: columbines, foxes, aspen trunks, leaves falling from trees, harvests, and abstracts are all sewn with rich colors and dynamic shapes.

Indian Art of Steamboat (970-870-8481, 635 Lincoln Ave., Steamboat Springs) Antler lamps, kachina dolls, dreamcatchers, Navajo rugs, sculpture, and painting: Indian Art is a one-stop shop if you're looking for Native American arts and crafts.

Mad Creek Gallery (970-875-1301, madcreek.net, 811 Lincoln Ave., Steamboat Springs) The main focus of this gallery is contemporary landscape paintings—especially from Colorado and the West—but it also sells some bronzes, pottery, pastels, and lithographs.

Schiesser Gallery 27 (970-879-6114, schiessergallery27.com, Ski Time Square, Steamboat Springs) A contemporary gallery featuring artists like Donald Berry, Cara Ober, Jonathan Kaplan, and Leah Fanning Mebane—and including painting, photography, and sculpture—Studio Gallery 27 has regular meet-the-artist openings and a hip vibe.

Thomas Mangelsen's Images of Nature Gallery (800-504-6689, mangelsen.com, 730 Lincoln Ave., Steamboat Springs) Though most of this wildlife photographer's images are from farther afield—Antarctica, Alaska, India, Tanzania—they are still stunning, serendipitous, and sometimes amusing.

Two Rivers Gallery (970-879-0044, tworiversgallery.com, 56 Ninth St., Steamboat Springs) Featuring the 19th-century images of frontier photographer Laton Huffman, along with antique horn furniture, contemporary Western art, and vintage Wild West movie and show posters, Two Rivers is a great spot to buy a genuine piece of the pioneer days.

Wildhorse Gallery (970-879-7660, wildhorsegallery.com, in lobby of the Steamboat Sheraton, 220 Village Inn Court, Steamboat Springs) With a definite Western bent, Wildhorse sells everything from bronze sculptures of cowboys on horseback to oil paintings of local lakes to wooden bowls, blown glass, jewelry, etchings, and watercolors.

Books

Books and Booty (970-870-8448, 732 Lincoln Ave., Steamboat Springs) A bizarre combination of used books, comics, trinkets, and gift cards, this atticlike bookstore feels kind of like a storeroom—but there are huge bargains to be had.

Epilogue Book Company (970-879-2665, epiloguebookco.com, 837 Lincoln Ave., Steamboat Springs) This small shop has a few new selections, but brings in the bargains with publishers' overstock at rock-bottom prices. Also has fair-trade coffees and teas and great gifts for readers.

Off the Beaten Path (970-879-6830, offthebeatenpath.booksense.com, 56 Seventh St., Steamboat Springs) Packed into a gingerbread Victorian just off the main drag is an independent bookstore (Steamboat's oldest), coffeehouse, bakery, and wine bar.

Outdoor Gear

Backdoor Sports (970-879-6249, backdoorsports.com, Ninth and Yampa Sts., Steamboat Springs) Whether you're mountaineering, kayaking, ice climbing, telemarking, rock climbing, or even just tubing down the Yampa River in summer, Backdoor has the gear for it. It has been in business since 1986.

BAP! (970-879-7507, bwear.com, 735 Oak St., Steamboat Springs) A local manufacturer of fleece jackets, pants, onesies, and more, BAP also sells Big Agnes sleeping bags, Smartwool base layers, and Honey Stinger energy gels and bars.

Western Clothing and Furs

Into the West (970-879-8377, 807 Lincoln Ave., Steamboat Springs) The proprietor of this classy shop—with a pistol grip as its door handle—is former U.S. Ski Team member and rodeo rider Jace Romick, who makes his own lodgepole furniture. Get yourself a $500 beaver-fur pillow, a cowhide mirror, a branding-iron candlestick, napkin holders, picture frames, belts, and hats.

Routt County Woolens (970-871-6363, routtcountywoolens.com, P.O. Box 770449, Steamboat Springs) Bring back a blanket, pillow, vest, oven mitt, or scarf, all made of locally spun wool—they're available at F. M. Light & Sons (see page 174).

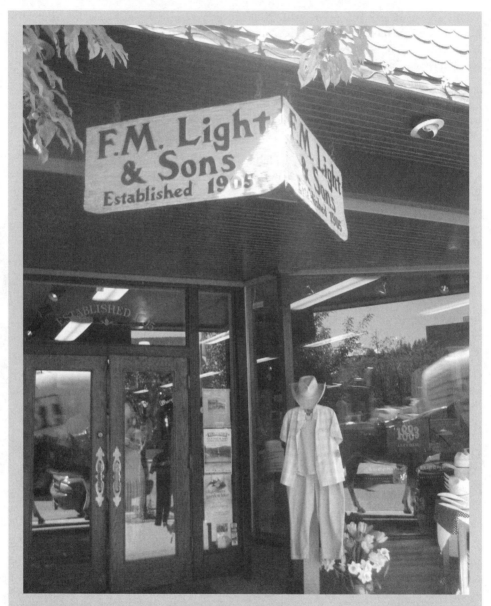

What's Up with Those Signs? The Story of F. M. Light & Sons
If you travel to Steamboat by car, you can't miss them: yellow hand-painted signs heralding F. M. Light & Sons, purveyor of cowboy hats and Western wear since 1905. First put up in 1928 by the Light brothers—Olin, Clarence, and Day—these billboards at one point numbered well over 300. The store was the first in town to sell ski clothes (in the 1920s), but today it pulls in curious tourists looking for $5 hats, Lee jeans, and a photo on the big plastic horse out front. (**F. M. Light & Sons,** 800-530-8908, fmlight.com, 830 Lincoln Ave., Steamboat Springs)

Soda Creek Mercantile (970-879-3146, soda-creek.com, 335 Lincoln Ave., Steamboat Springs) With a frontier facade and a huge open floor plan, Soda Creek is an Old West emporium extraordinaire—lassos, saddles, bridles, hats, boots, belts, Western shirts, jeans, and books.

Stephen's (970-879-1855, 1855 Ski Time Square, Steamboat Springs) There are several Western shops down on Lincoln Avenue, but this is by far the best one up at the ski hill. There's a huge selection of leather, fur, jeans, Western attire, and cowboy hats.

SEASONAL EVENTS

January: Cowboy Downhill (970-879-6111, steamboat.com) Started by Billy Kidd, a former Olympian-turned—Steamboat spokesman, this crazy race pits a hundred pro rodeo cowboys—many on skis for the first time, and wearing chaps and cowboy hats—against each other in a downhill ski race.

January: MusicFest at Steamboat (888-754-8447, bigskitrip.com) Thirty Texas and Americana bands and musicians—like Cross Canadian Ragweed, Robert Earl Keen, Susan Gibson, and Jason Boland and The Stragglers—do 40 performances over six days in a single big tent.

February: Steamboat Springs Winter Carnival (970-879-0695, sswsc.org) For almost a hundred years, Winter Carnival—which was started to help locals overcome that midwinter cabin fever—has been a hilariously eclectic mix of adventure film festival, chariot races, muzzle-loading biathlon, ski-joring, telemark skiing, shovel racing, pancake breakfasts, and Nordic dashes. Night events include snowboarding jam sessions, on-snow mountain biking races, and torchlight parades.

Flying downhill in "The Rio 24 Hours of Steamboat," a team fat-tire event. Steamboat Springs Chamber Resort Association

March: Steamboat Pentathlon (970-879-4300, steamboatpentathlon.com) A twist on the modern pentathlon, this version starts with a 400-vertical-foot climb on skis, then moves on to a 3-mile snowshoe, a 4-mile Nordic ski, a 12-mile mountain bike, and a 5-mile run.

April: Cardboard Classic (970-879-6111) People spend weeks, if not months, constructing cardboard crafts—hot dogs, Hummers, Led Zeppelin band stages, school buses, tanks, dragons, and more—and then send them sliding (or tumbling) down the face of Headwall.

June: The Rio 24 Hours of Steamboat (rockypeakproductions.com) Teams and solo riders compete to see who can mountain bike the most laps around an 11-mile, 2,100-vertical-foot loop on Mount Werner (teams of four are often strong enough to complete over 20 of them).

June: Rocky Mountain Mustang Roundup (970-879-0880, rmmr.org) Five-hundred-some mustangs—the automobile, not the wild horse—line Lincoln Avenue, competing in show-n-shine, autocross, scenic mountain tours, and popular voting.

June: Steamboat Marathon (970-879-0880, steamboatmarathon.com) Taking place in early June, this marathon has to be one of the most gorgeous in the country: rolling country roads, expansive pastureland, the usually ripping Elk River, and lots of local spirit. There's also a half-marathon, a 10K, and a kids' 1-mile fun run, all finishing on the front lawn of the courthouse.

Gridlock, Steamboat style: a Main Street cattle drive during Cowboys' Roundup Days. Steamboat Springs Chamber Resort Association

Taking in some free tunes in Steamboat Springs. Steamboat Springs Chamber Resort Association

June–August: Steamboat Springs Pro Rodeo Series (970-879-4300) The most successful weekly rodeo series in the country, this series has both Friday and Saturday night competitions in summer—in bull riding, team roping, steer wrestling, barrel racing, bareback riding, and tie-down roping.

June–August: Strings in the Mountains Music Festival (970-879-5056, stringsinthe mountains.com) Don't let the name fool you: This summer-long celebration features much more than string quartets. There's Gershwin, bluegrass, chamber music for a variety of ensembles, piano concertos, jazz, flamenco, gospel, funk, youth concerts, Tuesday concerts in a big tent, Thursday concerts at Yampa Botanic Park, garden tours and kitchen tours, and free pre concert talks—all adding up to well over 50 events.

July: Cowboys' Roundup Days (970-879-0880) This Independence Day celebration is Steamboat's oldest: It has been around for over a century. Events include a pro rodeo, a cattle drive down Main Street, tours of local ranches, fireworks, a parade, running races, and a block party.

July: Hot Air Balloon Rodeo/Art in the Park (970-879-9008) A two-day festival of leather, jewelry, glass, clay, wood, metal, photography, fiber, and fine arts, Art in the Park has more than 100 vendors, live music, food booths, performances, and kids' activities. At the same time (well, early in the morning on Saturday and Sunday), the Balloon Rodeo launches 40 huge, colorful orbs into the sky.

August: Routt County Fair (970-276-3068) About 25 miles away in Hayden, this fair has been running continuously since 1914 and now spans nine days' worth of rodeos, square dancing, pageants, country food and country music, livestock shows, pie contests, a blind man's tractor race, and a dress-your-poultry-or-beef-or-bunny-or-whatever contest.

August: Steamboat Wine Festival (877-328-2783, steamboatwinefestival.com) Bone up on oenology at daily seminars, sample inexpensive wines and expensive cheeses, listen to wine panels, stop into a local restaurant (there are many that participate) for a wine-makers' dinner, or buy a ticket to the Grand Tasting—a Lincoln Avenue affair with over 400 wines on hand.

September: Wild West Air Fest (970-879-9042) A Labor Day celebration of all things air-borne, Air Fest shows off 25 vintage planes at the local airport, remote-control aircraft shows, a flock of 30 hang gliders and paragliders launching from the top of Mount Werner and landing on the valley floor, and warbird fly-ins (a warbird is any airplane, from any era, that was once used by the armed forces of a country).

September: Fall Foliage & Steamboat Mountain Brewfest (970-879-0880, steamboat-summer.com) Peep at turning leaves, then sample beers from Rocky Mountain micro-breweries.

December: Steamboat Mountain Film Festival (970-879-6111) A small-scale action-sports film fest, this new event includes children's screenings, panels, seminars, and works by local filmmakers.

Nuts and Bolts

Getting Here
If you're driving (it's about three hours from Denver), check road conditions at 877-315-7623 or 303-639-1111. Flights land in **Yampa Valley Regional Airport,** in Hayden, with direct service from Denver, Chicago, Dallas, Atlanta, Houston, Newark, and Minneapolis. It takes about 40 minutes to get to downtown Steamboat; **Alpine Taxi** (970-879-2800, alpinetaxi.com) and **Storm Mountain Express** (970-879-1963, stormmountainexpress.com) both provide shuttle rides. Or, if you want your own wheels, you can rent from Avis, Budget, or Hertz.

Ambulance/Fire/Police/Search and Rescue
For emergencies, of course, dial 911. For police assistance that doesn't require an emergency response, contact the number listed below for the city closest to your present location.

Oak Creak Police Department: 970-736-8355

Routt County Search and Rescue: 970-879-7173, routtcountysar.org

Routt County Sheriff's Office: 970-879-1090

Steamboat Springs Fire Department: 970-879-4518

Steamboat Springs Police Department: 970-879-1144

Avalanche Reports
Colorado Avalanche Information Center: geosurvey.state.co.us/avalanche, avalanche-center.org

Hospitals and Emergency Medical Services
South Routt Medical Center: 970-736-8118, 300 S. Main St., Oak Creek

Steamboat Medical Group: 970-879-0203, 1475 Pine Grove Rd., Suite 102, Steamboat Springs

Yampa Valley Medical Center: 970-879-1322, 1024 Central Park Dr., Steamboat Springs

Libraries
Bud Werner Memorial Library (970-879-0240, steamboatlibrary.com, 1289 Lincoln Ave., Steamboat Springs)

Colorado Mountain College Library (970-870-4445, coloradomtn.edu/campus_alp/home.shtml, CMC-Alpine Campus, 1330 Bob Adams Dr., Steamboat Springs)

Media

Newspapers and Magazines
The Local: 970-875-1057, thesteamboatlocal.com, P.O. Box 881996, Steamboat Springs, CO 80477

Steamboat Magazine: 970-871-9413, steamboatmagazine.com, 1271 Lincoln Ave., P.O. Box 774328, Steamboat Springs, CO 80477

Steamboat Pilot and Today: 970-879-1502, steamboatpilot.com, 1901 Curve Plaza, P.O. Box 774827, Steamboat Springs, CO 80477

Radio
KBCR 96.9: 970-879-2270, kbcr.com. New country, ABC News, Paul Harvey, ABC sports, local news.

KFMU 105.5: 970-879-5368, kfmu.org. Classic and contemporary rock.

KIDN 95.5: 970-870-0900. Rap, pop, rock, news.

KRMR 107.3: 970-879-5368. Talk radio with Dr. Laura, Art Bell, Jim Rome, Imus, and more.

KUNC, 88.5: 800-443-5862, kunc.org. Community radio and NPR.

West Slope FM 91.7: 970-879-2591. Classical music.

Public Transportation
Steamboat Springs Transit (yampavalley.info/seniors0076.asp, 970-879-3717) runs from 7 AM until 1:45 AM during peak seasons, with frequent stops throughout town and the base of the ski area.

Ranger Stations
Hahns Peak Ranger District: 970-879-1870, 925 Weiss Dr., Steamboat Springs

Yampa Ranger District: 970-638-4516, 300 Roselawn Ave., Yampa

Tourist Information
Steamboat Springs Chamber Resort Association: 970-879-0880, steamboatchamber.com, 1255 S. Lincoln Ave., Steamboat Springs

Snow never stops bikers in Telluride. Tony Demin

5

TELLURIDE

Jewel of the San Juans

In a word, Telluride is breathtaking: refurbished gingerbread mining shacks bumping up against 2,000-foot box canyon walls. A Main Street that ends at the 300-foot cascade of Ingram Falls. Red rock dusted with winter powder. Hillsides sparkling with late-September aspen yellow. In another word, it's charming: Locals ride townie bikes carrying skis over one shoulder and holding the leash to a chocolate lab in the other. Guys with dreadlocks toss pizzas by night and rip by you on telemark skis by day. Hip artists toss Frisbees. There's a row of free cubbies to give and take gear and books and clothes. There's a set of free bikes to take around town. And the mountains—whether you're skiing them or hiking them—are steep. Very steep.

But, of course, early settlers came to mine what was first called San Miguel Park—and mine they did. After ousting the longtime Native American inhabitants with false treaties (and then pure force), characters like Linnard Remine, John Fallon, and Charles Baker found rich deposits, which attracted thousands of hopefuls. Several railroads advertised the natural splendor of the region as "a scene of beauty the imagination cannot depict"— but as soon as all the gold was panned, destructive hydraulic mining began. In 1878, a town called Columbia was incorporated, but the name soon changed (there was another Columbia out in California): Some people claim that "Telluride" comes from "to hell you ride," but it was actually named after the nonmetallic element tellurium—which, ironically, was virtually nonexistent in the area.

The golden decade for Telluride was undoubtedly the 1890s—the Rio Grande Southern Railroad arrived, the Sheridan Hotel was built, and 90-plus businesses opened. But all that paled in comparison to the arrival of Lucien Lucius Nunn, a 5'1" entrepreneur with outsized ambition who—in partnership with George Westinghouse and Nikola Tesla—decided to erect a high-voltage alternating current generator at Ames, 5 miles south of Telluride, in order to cut back on the money it took to supply power to his mines (felling trees, hauling loads with burros, paying for steam). It was the first time in history that such a setup was used for commercial purposes—and Telluride was the first town in the world to use alternating current to power streetlights.

When the U.S. government repealed the Sherman Silver Purchase Act in 1893, the bottom fell out of silver prices—but Telluride survived thanks to rich gold deposits in its high mines (in a single year, the Tomboy Mine extracted $1.2 million in gold ore). What brought it down was a succession of union fights, avalanches, electrocutions, landslides,

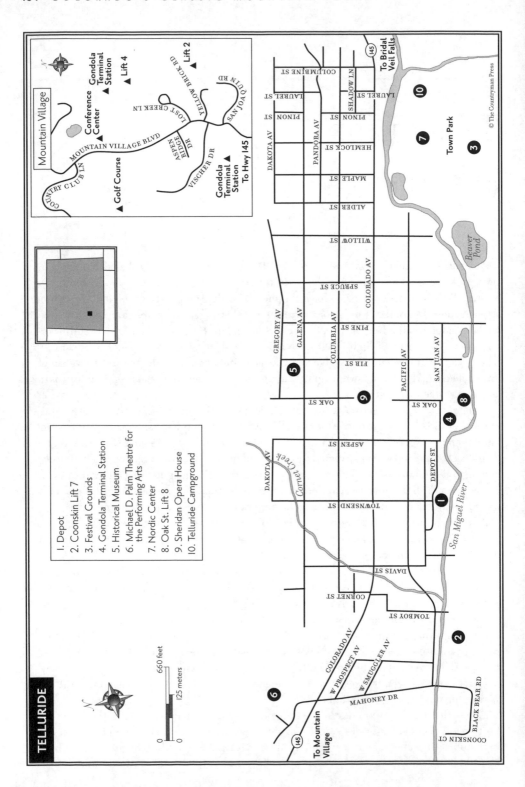

Mountain Village

Conference Center
Gondola Terminal Station
Lift 4
Lift 2
YELLOW BRICK RD
LOST CREEK LN
MOUNTAIN VILLAGE BLVD
ASPEN RIDGE DR
VISCHER DR
SAN JOAQUIN RD
Golf Course
COUNTRY CLUB LN
Gondola Terminal Station
To Hwy 145

TELLURIDE

660 feet
125 meters

© The Countryman Press

To Bridal Veil Falls
To Mountain Village

1. Depot
2. Coonskin Lift 7
3. Festival Grounds
4. Gondola Terminal Station
5. Historical Museum
6. Michael D. Palm Theatre for the Performing Arts
7. Nordic Center
8. Oak St. Lift 8
9. Sheridan Opera House
10. Telluride Campground

The spectacular backdrop of Colorado Avenue, Telluride's main drag. Doug Berry

and flus, all topped off by the stock market crash of 1929. By the 1950s, Telluride was almost a ghost town.

But, in a story familiar throughout the mountains of Colorado, it was skiing that saved the day: Bruce Palmer, an Austrian, strung up a rope tow in the late 1930s; flower children rolled into town for cheap housing; tourists followed, seeking funky festivals; the core downtown area was declared a National Historic Landmark District in 1964; and finally, Joseph Zoline—a wealthy entrepreneur and developer from Beverly Hills—took what he had learned in Aspen and turned Telluride into a true ski town, installing the first lift in 1974.

These days, the population hovers around 2,200, a mix of the super-rich (Oprah Winfrey and Tom Cruise own homes here), the latter-day hippies, the new-moneyed yuppies, and the post-college ski bums. Up over the hill from old Telluride itself (you can get there via a free gondola), there's a whole new town (incorporated and everything) called Mountain Village: a collection of huge hotels, chic condos, castle-size log cabins, and more modern amenities that brings ski-resort development to the area without compromising the character of the original settlement. There's a festival every single weekend in summer (even the Telluride Nothing Festival, to fill in the one weekend that *doesn't* have one), bringing in world-class artists, musicians, and chefs. There's consistently uncrowded, world-class skiing in winter. And no matter what, there are always the surroundings: In my humble opinion, it's the most beautiful ski town in Colorado.

LODGING

The accommodations in the towns of Telluride and Mountain Village—a gondola ride and a mountain ridge apart—are markedly different: Quirky B&Bs versus mammoth spas, boutique hotels versus multistory resorts and condo complexes, old versus new. That said, it's a piece of cake to travel between the two. Just pick your poison.

Telluride

Camel's Garden
888-772-2635
camelsgarden.com
info@camelsgarden.com
250 W. San Juan Ave., Telluride
Price Range: $275–$675, including
    continental breakfast
Credit Cards: AE, D, MC, V
Children: Y
Pets: Y, for a fee
Handicap Accessible: Y

Talk about prime real estate: Sleek Camel's Garden, named after one of Telluride's mines, is within stumbling distance of the gondola, two blocks from Colorado Avenue, and right next to the gurgling San Miguel River. From the outside, the architecture hints at mining structures and materials; from the inside, the simple lobby highlights local modern artists. The 35 roomy units (from singles on up to enormous condos) all feature cherry-oak furnishings, avant-garde light fixtures, pedestal beds, and Italian marble bathrooms—and most have balconies with town or mountain views. Downstairs, the Atmosphere Day Spa offers massages, manicures and pedicures, facials, and special high-altitude treatments.

Hotel Columbia
800-201-9505, 970-728-0660
columbiatelluride.com
columbia@telluridecolorado.net
300 W. San Juan Ave., Telluride
Price Range: $150–$460, including
    continental breakfast
Credit Cards: AE, D, MC, V
Children: Y
Pets: Y
Handicap Accessible: Y

Hotel Columbia's three friendly owners moved to Telluride in the 1970s—Jeff Campbell was a ski patroller; his wife, Marty, was a community activist; and their buddy, Jim Lincoln, was on the town council. In 1995, they opened up a 21-room hotel mere yards from the gondola, named it after what Telluride was first called, and made sure the place was lush with cherry-wood paneling, overstuffed furniture, earth tones, patterned tiles, and fresh flowers—along with extra-long claw-foot tubs, marble bathrooms, steam showers, and private balconies. The amenities listed on the brochure include boot driers and bicycle storage, "sunrises," "sunsets," and "service, service, service." And come sunrise, the adjoining Cosmopolitan restaurant (see page 194) delivers fresh-baked pastries and breads to kick-start the day.

The Hotel Telluride
866-468-3501, 970-369-1188
thehoteltelluride.com
info@thehoteltelluride.com
199 N. Cornet St., Telluride
Price Range: $399–$936, including breakfast
Credit Cards: AE, D, MC, V
Children: Y
Pets: Y
Handicap Accessible: Y

The Hotel Telluride prides itself on The Incredible Bed: 250-thread-count sheets, fluffy feather bedding, plaid down comforters, suede headboards, and piles of pillows. Each of the 59 rooms is painted in natural beiges and light yellows, with maroon furniture, 19th-century Curtis photographs, framed *Denver Post* editions from the 1930s and 1940s, and game-lodge accents (pheasant sculptures, antlers). The lobby is straight out of a Sundance catalog: leather trunks, huge candlesticks, oversize furniture, Navajo rugs, stone floors, baskets of apples on coffee tables, and a blond wood gabled ceiling. The Bistro, with Western art and huge copper pots on the walls, serves up a breakfast of omelets, belgian waffles, pancakes, cereals, and fruit each morning—and wine, beer, and apps when the lifts close. A small spa offers massages, facials, manicures, and the like.

The Hotel Telluride is one of the most luxurious spots in town. Evelyn Spence

The New Sheridan Hotel is a historic centerpiece in Telluride. Built with brick in 1895 after a fire destroyed the original building, it was restored in 1994 and filled with antique furniture and wallpaper. Evelyn Spence

The Ice House

800-544-3436, 970-728-6300
icehouselodge.com
damon@icehouselodge.com
310 S. Fir St., Telluride
Price Range: $195–$650, including
    continental breakfast
Credit Cards: AE, D, MC, V
Children: Y
Pets: Y
Handicap Accessible: Y

Tired of the ubiquitous mountain-town chic? The Ice House, sister to Camel's Garden, is a geometric combo of European and Southwestern—with light wood furniture; polished wood ceilings; Navajo-patterned rugs, cushions, and curtains; spare and roomy units; plasma TVs; and a skylit, modern mezzanine where coffee, pastries, and fruit are served each morning. Maroons, blonds, and forest greens repeat through guest rooms and common areas. Want to eat in—with class? Room service comes straight from La Marmotte (see page 196), which is housed in the eponymous ice house next door.

✪ New Sheridan Hotel

800-200-1891, 970-728-4351
newsheridan.com
info@newsheridan.com
231 W. Colorado Ave., Telluride
Price Range: $150–$425, including breakfast
Credit Cards: AE, D, MC, V
Children: Y
Pets: N
Handicap Accessible: N

The original Sheridan Hotel was built in 1891—when Telluride was a mere four years old. It burned down in 1894, was rebuilt in 1895 (smartly, in brick), operated until 1925, stood vacant for 50 years, and was meticulously restored in 1994. If you want to experience a piece of history, this is the place: Every room is decorated with period pieces, including beds, lamps, armoires, and tables; the lobby is furnished with intricately carved cherrywood; the adjoining bar (see pape 202) is the oldest in town; and the middle-of-the-action location can't be beat. The whole hotel is rich with Victorian wallpaper and scattered with antiques. Options range from Aspen Rooms, with king or queen beds and shared "Ladies and Gents" bathrooms, to Ridge Suites, with adjoining parlors and mountain views. The breakfast features cereals, fruit, yogurt, pastries, and a daily hot entrée (eggs Benedict, omelets, french toast). And the front-desk cookie jar—always full—is completely addictive.

✪ San Sophia

Innkeepers: Alicia Bixby and Keith
    Hampton
800-537-4781, 970-728-3001
sansophia.com
info@sansophia.com
300 W. Pacific Ave., Telluride
Price Range: $139–$339, including breakfast
Credit Cards: MC, V
Children: Y
Pets: N
Handicap Accessible: N

On the side, innkeepers Bixby and Hampton sponsor Telluride's annual wine festival and run a marketing firm, but they still find time to set out raspberry chocolate truffles, toffee, and baklava just in time for check-in. The 16-room San Sophia is both luxurious and charming: There's a rooftop tower with 360-degree views, a gazebo-covered hot tub, gingerbread trim, stained-glass

windows over the bathtubs, etched mirrors, and triple-sheeted king-size brass beds covered with handmade quilts. And the breakfast is the best in town—local Indian Ridge breads, divine granola, yogurt, and fruit every day, along with grilled citrus polenta, strawberry-stuffed french toast with amaretto crème, applewood-smoked bacon, homemade chocolate éclairs, and turkey apricot sausage. If you don't book a room, you can still show up for brunch daily from 8 to 10 AM.

The Victorian Inn

Innkeeper: Levi Silva
800-611-9893; 970-728-6601
tellurideinn.com
info@TheVictorianInn.org
401 W. Pacific Ave., Telluride
Price Range: $79–$249
Credit Cards: AE, D, MC, V
Children: Y
Pets: N
Handicap Accessible: Y

Believe it or not, there are deals to be found in Telluride, and the Victorian—family-operated since 1981—is one of them. Sure, prices for a basic queen room leap from $79 in early November to $249 during Labor Day's film festival, but it still comes out as a relative bargain. What you get: a basic continental breakfast (OJ, instant oatmeal or cereal, sweet rolls, tea, coffee) in the front lobby area; wrought-iron beds with fanciful headboards; in-room refrigerators, ski racks, coffee makers, and HBO; and barbecue grills, a dry sauna, and an outdoor hot tub. It's just a half-block off the main street, Colorado Avenue, which makes the deal even sweeter.

Wildwood Canyon Inn

888-728-1950, 970-728-1950
telluridemtnlodging.com/condos/
    wildwoodcanyoninnpc.htm
info@telluridemtnlodging.com

627 W. Colorado Ave., Telluride
Price Range: $169–$425, including
   breakfast
Credit Cards: AE, D, MC, V
Children: Y, 12 and older
Pets: Y
Handicap Accessible: N

Crashing at the four-bedroom Wildwood
Canyon Inn is the closest thing you'll get to
living like a (wealthy) Telluride local:
There's the location on Colorado Avenue,
just a couple blocks from downtown.
There's the stained-glass door—an elegant
calla lily. There's the decor, a tasteful mix
of antiques and modern amenities (like
blanket-size towels and 400-thread-count
sheets); views of the ski hill from the deck;
heated floors; and fresh flowers on tables,
dressers, and nightstands. That doesn't
even count breakfasts of smoothies, granola, and fluffy french toast with fresh
berries. The Silvermeadow Room has a
huge jetted tub in a bay window. The
Pinecrest Room has a private balcony. And
the common area, with cathedral ceilings,
big windows, french doors, and comfortable couches, is a bright, welcoming place.

Mountain Village

✪ Inn at Lost Creek
888-601-5678, 970-728-5678
innatlostcreek.com
reservations@innatlostcreek.com
119 Lost Creek Lane, Mountain Village
Price Range: $190–$1,895
Credit Cards: AE, D, MC, V
Children: Y
Pets: N
Handicap Accessible: Y

One of Colorado skidom's great inns, Lost
Creek walks the line between rugged and
opulent like no other Telluride crash pad,
and it's one of the most intimate options if
you want to stay in Mountain Village's land
of timeshares and massive mansions. The
Great Room lobby feels like a mountain-
home living room, crossed with huge tim-
bered ceiling beams and warmed by a
two-sided, native-stone fireplace. The
lampshades are rawhide, the flowers are
always fresh, and the glass-topped coffee
tables are strewn with magazines. Upstairs,
rooms and suites have black-and-white
landscape photographs, stone fireplaces,
chunky furniture, four-poster beds, steam
showers and marble bathtubs with mountain views, and private balconies. Need a
tune? Ski waxing and de-burring are complimentary. During holidays and festivals
(like Film and Bluegrass), prices sky-
rocket—but you can get a relative steal during the shoulder seasons.

The Peaks Resort and Golden Door Spa
970-728-6800
thepeaksresort.com
136 Country Club Dr., Mountain Village
Price Range: $99–$2,099
Credit Cards: AE, D, MC, V
Children: Y
Pets: Y
Handicap Accessible: Y

The best reason to stay in the enormous
Peaks? Can you say "Golden Door Spa"?
We're talking an oxygen relaxation room to
ease high-altitude headaches, a eucalyptus
steam room, Native American–inspired
treatments like the Turquoise Wrap (blue
cornmeal, turquoise clay, and rainstick rit-
uals performed by your friendly therapist),
and chakra balancing. You can take classes
in yoga, Pilates, spinning, and step. There's
even a Doggie Spa, with guided playtime,
doggie meals cooked by the chef and delivered to your room, "pawdicures," and
salon-caliber grooming. Okay, the hotel
itself is not too shabby: a three-story lobby
area with towering windows looking out to
Mount Wilson (think Coors cans); 174
rooms and suites with plantation shutters,
down comforters, antler chandeliers, and

french doors; both indoor and outdoor pools; and breakfast buffets, juice bars, terrace lunches, and white-linen dinners.

FARTHER AFIELD

The Blue Jay Lodge
970-728-0830
thebluejaylodge.com
kbond@thebluejaylodge.com
22332 CO 145, Placerville
Price Range: $105–$200
Credit Cards: AE, D, MC, V
Children: Y
Pets: Y
Handicap Accessible: Y

Originally just a café, this 14-room lodge opened in 2003, and is located on CO 145 on the way up to Telluride—close enough (12 miles) that it's easy to drive up to town for a show, a day on the hill, or a night on the town, but far enough away to feel like a retreat. The building is typical of Southwest Colorado architecture of late: The rough-hewn timber, metal roof, exposed beams, and forest-green window trim bring to mind old mining buildings and well-worn ski lodges. The rooms are simple and classy: king-size four-poster beds, wrought-iron sconces, down comforters, photos of local landscapes, and soothing colors. Booking a room here gets you that much easier access to the Blue Jay Café, loved among locals for its hearty breakfasts of Eggs Blue Jay (two eggs on English muffins, slathered with sausage gravy), sourdough french toast dusted with pow-dered sugar, and Frisbee-size pancakes dotted with pecans. Dinners feature com-fort food—meatloaf, pork chops—along with good pastas, pizzas, seafood, and steak.

Cascabel Club
Owners: Julie and James Thorneycroft
970-327-4832
cascabelclub.com
45045 Sanborn Park Rd., Norwood
Price Range: $325–$975
Credit Cards: AE, D, MC, V
Children: Y
Pets: Y
Handicap Accessible: N

Founded in 1991 as a members-only wilderness club, Cascabel recently opened its five cabins, two ponds, clubhouse, swimming pool, tennis courts, and San Miguel River frontage to the public. But it retains an exclusive and completely retreat-like air: Only 16 guests can play on the 320 acres at a time. Two of the cabins, the Prince and the Caddis, are single-room, with river-rock fireplaces, polished blond-wood walls, cheery red comforters, and river views; the Hopper has three bedrooms and two baths. Obviously, the fishing's the thing here—and people have been known to hook a dozen browns and rainbows an *hour*. But you can arrange heli-skiing, hunting for elk, grouse, or wild turkey, rafting, or rock climbing. The grub, prepared by Julie and served family-style in a cozy dining pavilion, is Rocky Mountain gourmet (braised elk, broiled trout with chipotle aioli, fresh-baked breads, local produce).

✪ Dunton Hot Springs
970-882-4800
duntonhotsprings.com
info@duntonhotsprings.com
52068 West Fork Rd., Dolores
Price Range: $250 per person per day and up
Credit Cards: AE, D, MC, V
Children: Y
Pets: Y, in two of the cabins
Handicap Accessible: N

Certainly one of the most unusual getaways in Colorado, Dunton Hot Springs is actually an entire 19th-century ghost town (hand-hewn cabins, a saloon, a dance hall, a book-lined library, a bathhouse, a general store, a well house, and a forge) that's been transformed into an all-inclusive retreat, surrounded by national forest and panoramic views. The cabins—which sleep two to six—are all slightly different: One has exposed chinking and vintage Western decorations, another has a private hot spring and cold plunge, a third features a Rajasthan wedding bed. Everyone eats together at long tables, and the food and wine is either grown or bottled on the premises, gathered from the mountains (chanterelles and boletos, for two), or bought from farmers on the Colorado Plateau. There's fishing, riding, and hiking out the back door—along with yoga and Pilates classes, massage, reflexology, and mineral mud wraps. You name the travel mag or newspaper, life list or adventure guide, and Dunton's been raved about in it. The accolades are well deserved.

✪ Elk Mountain Resort

970-252-4900
elkmountainresort.com
info@elkmountainresort.com
97 Elk Walk, Montrose
Price Range: $325–$1,800
Credit Cards: AE, D, MC, V
Children: Y
Pets: N
Handicap Accessible: Y

Where to begin? Elk Mountain, opened in June 2004, sits on 275 alpine acres 50 minutes from Telluride—and if you can't keep yourself occupied, you've got some issues: You can shoot skeet, trap, and five-stand at the Valhalla Shooting Club. You can rope up and scale the climbing wall. You can hop on a chopper at the resort's own helipad. You can hook trout at the spring-fed Tait's Lake. There's a full-size motocross course, a 10-acre snowmobile park, a 4.5-acre paintball course, tennis courts, barns, pottery and painting supplies, cooking classes, and a private chapel. Or you can just sample rare whiskeys in the cocktail lounge. The resort has 75 guest

rooms and cottages with enormous soaking tubs, pedestal sinks with brushed-nickel faucets, hand-stenciled headboards, 450-thread-count sheets, hand-painted parchment lamps, ocular windows, and oak floors. The resort's restaurant, Tarragon, serves an American alpine cuisine pioneered by chef Richard Chamberlain, who did time at Aspen's Little Nell and Dallas's Mansion at Turtle Creek.

Guest Ranches

Angel Ridge Ranch

Owner: Denise Fisher
970-626-4287
angelridgeranch.com
angelridge@frontier.net
177 County Road 10, Ridgway
Price Range: $175–$300
Credit Cards: MC, V
Children: Y
Pets: Y
Handicap Accessible: Y

A white picket fence, a lodge with dormer windows and a turret, panoramic views of the Cimarron and the San Juan ranges, a big wraparound front porch and a big fireplace—Angel Ridge's Victorian-style digs are at once comfortable and charming. The rooms are filled with antique furniture, and the beds are covered with homemade quilts; one bed in the Angel's Loft also has a lace canopy and an ornate brass frame. No matter which of the four rooms you choose, you'll always find fresh flowers and chocolates. Take the paddleboat around one of the two ponds, hook a few trout, and let Spot play in the "Doggie Dude Ranch"—a 16-by-24-foot shelter in a long run with shady trees. Half- and full-day trail rides stage out of neighboring Walther Ranch.

Circle K Ranch

Innkeepers: The Cannon and Brannon
    families
800-477-6381, 970-562-3826

ckranch.com
vacation@ckranch.com
27758 CO 145, Dolores
Price Range: $56–$160, with various meal
    plans
Credit Cards: D, MC, V
Children: Y
Pets: Y
Handicap Accessible: Y

Unlike many guest ranches, Circle K has an
à la carte option: You can stay in a lodge
room for $50 a night, and pay extra for
horseback riding, fly-fishing, hunting, or
pack trips. Or you can choose from among
their pre-set plans: Some include hearty
meals served at ultra-long tables with
checkered tablecloths—biscuits and gravy
for breakfast, beef stew and cornbread for
lunch, fried chicken or roast beef for dinner—but you can also purchase them day by
day. The ranch hosts a lot of reunions,
church retreats, and scout groups, so don't
expect a quiet, romantic getaway. The flip
side? No shortage of campfires, softball
games, sing-alongs, bonding, and sponta-
neous outbreaks of capture the flag.

J2F Guest Ranch

Manager: Walt Fourney
866-757-0989, 970-327-0242
j2f.com
j2f@j2f.com
1401 Thunder Rd., Norwood
Price Range: $79 for room only; $160 a
    night, including meals and riding
Credit Cards: AE, MC, V
Children: Y
Pets: N
Handicap Accessible: N

With 380 wide-open acres, mostly bor-
dered by public lands, J2F is a friendly,
intimate ranch experience: They call it "the
activities of a dude ranch with the comfort
and warmth of a bed and breakfast."
Indeed, the new lodge has just four large
bedrooms—with heavy beams, Western

decorations, and balconies with mountain
views—and everyone eats three meals a day
at one long table (unless there's a barbecue
or campfire planned). Each room, in fact, is
decorated to reflect a different period in
the history of the Old West. J2F is open
year-round, but in winter only breakfast is
provided.

DINING

Restaurants

TELLURIDE

✪ Allred's

970-728-7474
allredsrestaurant.com
Top of the gondola, Telluride
Meals Served: D
Price Range: Appetizers $9–$16, entrées
    $26–$36
Full bar: Y
Reservations: Y
Credit Cards: AE, D, MC, V
Handicap Accessible: Y

When you're at a windowside table looking
down at the winking lights of town 1,800
feet below, there's no Telluride dining
experience quite like Allred's. For starters,
you take the gondola to dinner—exiting at
the San Sophia station and walking through
a short hallway before the airy, chic dining
room and the theater-lit kitchen open up.
Then there's the 8,000-bottle wine cellar.
And finally, there's the creative food: apps
like vanilla- and apricot-poached lobster,
smoked Idaho trout, and pancetta eggs
Benedict made with quail eggs. Entrées
emphasize local or free-range produce and
game—Colorado lamb prepared with fig-
ginger puree, or a veal chop with potato-
chanterelle hash—and desserts include a
wonderful pear quartet: a Bartlett pear
mousse, a pear strudel, a pear glazed with
burnt honey, and a pear granita. If you book

the chef's table, you and five others can sit in the kitchen and try a five-course tasting menu (paired with wines) that changes nightly.

Baked in Telluride

970-728-4775
toski.com/bakedintel/index.html
bakedintel@telluridecolorado.net
127 S. Fir St., Telluride
Meals Served: B, L, D
Price Range: Salads $4.79–$9.49, pastas
   $7.99–$11.79, pizzas $9.99–$27.99
Full bar: N
Reservations: N
Credit Cards: AE, D, MC, V
Handicap Accessible: Y

B-I-T feels more like a cross between an old-school bakery and a lunchroom than a restaurant—you order at the counter, and they bring baskets to whatever table you can find. Owner Jerry Greene founded Telluride radio station KOTO in 1975, then turned his attention to baking hot-out-of-the-oven bagels, crumb-cake donuts, Frisbee-size cookies, pecan pies, éclairs, and fudge brownies—along with divine freshly made pasta, huge calzones, and sandwiches on homemade bread. Specialty pizzas are both stalwart (a combo with fresh tomatoes, olives, pepperoni, sausage, mushroom, and green pepper) and funky (Thai chicken with peanut sauce, sprouts, cheese, and carrots). Add a pitcher of microbrew for just $12.99.

✪ Chair 8

970-728-8887
chair8.com
250 W. San Juan Ave., Unit C, Telluride
Meals Served: L, D
Price Range: TK
Full bar: Y
Reservations: N
Credit Cards: AE, D, MC, V
Handicap Accessible: Y

Walking into Chair 8 is like walking onto the set of an Austin Powers movie—or maybe into a retro-groovy 1970s ski lodge: The walls are covered with white carpet, the mod sofas are swaddled with Mongolian goat-hair throws, the different dining areas are divided by mobiles and mirrors, and the bar is decorated with wooden lattice detailing. Jake Linzenmeir's menu is just as fun-loving, and it features comfort food with a twist (or two): the Truck Stop Deluxe (chili cheese fries with Muir Glen tomatoes, organic beef, and red and black beans); lobster and brie fondue with local Wildflour breads for dipping; a "PB&J" with pecan nut butter, fig jelly, and foie gras; and tempura-fried banana bread with coconut. There are 15 kinds of hot chocolate—from caramel praline with whipped cream to dark Belgian chocolate with peanut butter whipped cream. Après, order up a "group therapy" special: a pitcher of margaritas or mojitos plus nachos or fondue for $20.

Cosmopolitan

970-728-1292
cosmotelluride.com
reservations@cosmotelluride.com
300 W. San Juan Ave., Telluride
Meals Served: D
Price Range: $19–$35
Full bar: Y
Reservations: Y
Credit Cards: AE, MC, V
Handicap Accessible: Y

Urban lighting fixtures, acute angles, a cherrywood bar: the elegant Cosmo used to be a mining saloon, but it's done a 180. And chef Chad Scothorn is considered one of the most adventurous in town. Where else can you start with lobster corn dogs, move on to a Himalayan yak rib eye with golden chanterelles and bacon-braided swiss chard, and finish off with "Coffee & Donuts"—warm beignets with a choice of coffee? Of course, you're free to order standards like Caesar salad, surf-and-turf, and crème brûlée. Groups of 14 to 35 people can settle into the 2,000-bottle wine cellar—which doubles as a tasting room—for a six-course, five-wine, prix-fixe extravaganza with a wide-ranging menu that's chosen just 48 hours before dinner. Wild mushroom cappuccino, anyone?

Floradora Saloon
970-728-3888
103 W. Colorado Ave., Telluride
Meals Served: L, D
Price Range: $8–$20
Full bar: Y
Reservations: Y
Credit Cards: AE, MC, V
Handicap Accessible: Y

It's a mother and child reunion: The family-friendly Floradora—named after two of Telluride's women of, uhh, the night—was originally opened in 1972 by Florie Kane, but was rented out soon after little Roscoe was born. Thirty years and one culinary degree later, the son is back in town, and he comes bearing an extensive sandwich menu: the Duck Pocket (braised duck, spiced tomatoes, and manchego in a hollowed ciabatta), the Cuban Press (ham, caramelized onions, and chipotle aioli on a baguette), and the Tempeh Reuben (tempeh, sauerkraut, Thousand Island, and swiss on marbled rye). For dinner, the beef-tip stroganoff—on egg noodles with a red wine cream sauce—is a wonderful winter warmer.

Harmon's at the Depot
970-728-3773
300 S. Townsend St., Telluride
Meals Served: D
Price Range: Appetizers $8–$12, entrées $25–$35
Full bar: Y
Reservations: Y
Credit Cards: AE, MC, V
Handicap Accessible: Y

In 1891, the Harmon's building served as Telluride's train depot—and two passenger trains a day burped out tourists, locals, and visitors. The freight traffic was almost non-stop. These days, the joint is much more quiet and much more luxurious: The bar is made of hand-carved Honduran mahogany, the glass is etched with railroad scenes, the fireplace is heavy with stonework, and live piano music (think Rachmaninoff played by a big-bearded hippie-type) floats through the cozy space. Chef Jim Ackard composes New American mixes like rabbit veal sausage with rosemary rabbit faro pilaf; grilled red deer chop with butternut squash gnocchi, huckleberries, and sage; and moulard duck breast and seared duck liver with apricot demi-glace. Harmon Brown co-owns two wineries—and his expertise shows.

✪ Honga's Lotus Petal and Tea Room
970-728-5134
133 S. Oak St., Telluride
Meals Served: D
Price Range: $8–$24
Full bar: Y
Reservations: Y
Credit Cards: AE, MC, V
Handicap Accessible: Y

Rumor has it that hip Honga's goes through more Bacardi rum than any other restaurant in Colorado—most of which ends up in bracing mojitos. Everything served in this elegant, restored Victorian is hormone- and chemical-free, or free range, or organic, or flown in that very morning—including sushi and sashimi, blackened tofu, crunchy shrimp rolls, pot stickers, gado gado, and tom yam soup, all of which span the culinary worlds of Thailand, Japan, and Bali. Reservations are a must on weekends: Great food at un-Telluride-like prices make for a hot ticket.

La Marmotte: A touch of Provence in a 100-year-old ice-house building. Evelyn Spence

✪ La Marmotte

970-728-6232
lamarmotte.com
info@lamarmotte.com
150 W. San Juan Ave., Telluride
Meals Served: D
Price Range: $25–$40
Full bar: Y
Reservations: Y
Credit Cards: AE, D, MC, V
Handicap Accessible: Y

From the outside, La Marmotte looks unassuming: It's in Telluride's 100-year-old ice house building, made of weathered planks, and it's dwarfed by the mammoth Ice House Hotel behind it. On the inside, it's genuine Provence: wine bottles in the windows, strings of garlic bulbs, country-lace curtains, and romantic lighting. The chef-owner, Mark Reggiannini, trained under the best—Jean-Georges Vongerichten—and it shows through in dishes like coq au vin, Rocky Mountain elk with charcuterie sauce, and hot and cold foie gras with cherry chutney. Desserts range from the light (lychee, mango, or pomegranate sorbets) to the button-busting (deep-fried bananas with pistachio sauce, chocolate molten cake with espresso ice cream). The menu changes regularly, depending on what's in season; the wine list features Burgundys, Bordeaux, Rhône Valleys, and champagnes hand-picked by Reggiannini himself.

Las Montañas

970-728-5114
lasmontanastelluride.com
200 S. Davis St., Telluride
Meals Served: B, D
Price Range: Appetizers $7–$12, entrées
  $16–$24
Full bar: Y

Reservations: Y
Credit Cards: AE, D, MC, V
Handicap Accessible: Y

Whether it's 7 am on a cold, quiet winter morning or 10 pm on a hot summer Friday night, Las Montañas always feels festive. Credit the beautiful antique bar—imported from Guatemala—along with the Mexican tableware, the Spanish tiles, spiky metal star chandeliers hanging from the ceilings, and the strains of salsa and merengue in the background. Every item on the menu is labeled with its country of origin, and most people order scads of small plates to pass around the table: aolinaranja chicken (from Cuba), cumin-battered strips served with chipotle aioli dipping sauce; goat cheese, chili, and pumpkin seed nachos (from Venezuela); or chilis toreados (from Mazatlan)—soy-marinated jalapeños

stuffed with crab and feta. Don't feel like sharing? The mahimahi (from Acapulco), duck glazed in orange sauce (from Spain), and the taco and enchilada dinners (with seven choices of filling, from all over the place) are stellar. For breakfast, create your own breakfast burrito: ham, bacon, chorizo, carne seca, or tofu with green chili, potatoes, refried beans, and more.

New Sheridan Chop House
970-728-9100
newsheridan.com
233 W. Colorado Ave., Telluride
Meals Served: D
Price Range: Entrées $20 and up
Full bar: Y
Reservations: Y
Credit Cards: AE, D, MC, V
Handicap Accessible: Y

221 South Oak, a cozy Victorian, houses superb Creole cooking. Evelyn Spence

The nonthreatened fish species are flown in several times a week, the chicken is free-range or Amish-raised, the beef comes from Lombardi Meats, and the eclectic cheese course changes at least once a month. The New Sheridan takes the classic steakhouse conceit—porterhouse, filet mignon, baseball sirloin, New York, prime rib—and adds New American accents: seafood paella with andouille and red snapper, chicken breast with cinnamon citrus glaze and Himalayan red rice, and macaroni and cheese with three types of cheese. Just like the New Sheridan Bar (see page 202), the Chop House is always lively and stays open late.

221 South Oak

970-728-9507
221southoak.com
reservations@221southoak.com
221 S. Oak St., Telluride
Meals Served: D
Price Range: Appetizers $6–$15, entrées
    $20–$32
Full bar: Y
Reservations: Y
Credit Cards: AE, MC, V
Handicap Accessible: Y

In a quaint Victorian house in between the gondola building and Colorado Avenue, tasteful 221 South Oak has spotlit mustard-colored walls, modern artwork, blond-wood bench seats, and white linens. Eliza Gavin, the chef-owner, trained in Napa at the Culinary Institute of America, learned Creole cuisine on Bourbon Street in New Orleans, and trained some more at Le Cordon Bleu. Her influences come together at 221: fried oysters with bleu d'Auvergne and praline bacon, peekytoe crab and rock shrimp salad, elk short loin with a Vermont cheddar–stuffed potato, and spicy glazed scallops with sweet potato cakes. There's an extensive vegetarian menu as well—a

spinach tart with chèvre and wild mushrooms, or chive gnocchi in lemon caper brown butter.

MOUNTAIN VILLAGE

La Piazza del Villaggio

970-728-8283
lapiazzadelvillaggioristorante.com
117 Lost Creek Lane, Mountain Village
Meals Served: L, D
Price Range: Appetizers $10–$16, entrées
    $17.50–$49
Full bar: Y
Reservations: Y
Credit Cards: AE, MC, V
Handicap Accessible: Y

A roaring fireplace, mountain views, rustic decorations (like giant baskets), walls in salmon and jade tones, and a large patio: La Piazza is nothing if not romantic. And chef Luca Ramponi's cuisine is filling—whether you're skiing in for a lunch of panini with roasted rosemary pork loin and a bowl of pasta e fagioli, or settling into a multi-course dinner, the Northern Italian food is perfect for a chilly winter evening. The mushroom risotto is packed with porcini mushrooms and touched with pinot grigio; the tortelloni is filled with crabmeat and asparagus and topped with a creamy tomato-grappa sauce; and the simple lamb chops are brushed with thyme and olive oil. Don't miss the Prosciutto, Mozzarella e Carciofini: A starter of paper-thin San Daniele ham, Brindisino baby artichoke hearts, and creamy, house-made mozzarella.

9545

970-728-5678
innatlostcreek.com
Lost Creek Lane, Mountain Village
Meals Served: B, L, D
Price Range: $30–$50
Full bar: Y

The restaurant 9545 in Mountain Village proudly states its altitude. Evelyn Spence

Reservations: Y
Credit Cards: AE, D, MC, V
Handicap Accessible: Y

Named after the restaurant's elevation, 9545 is the best restaurant in Mountain Village—if only because you can exchange your ski boots for animal slippers for lunch or après-ski. And no matter whether it's breakfast or happy hour, the food is organic. Start your day with a plate of pecan sticky buns or a basket of banana bread, danishes, and muffins—or dig into duck confit hash or brioche french toast with vanilla maple syrup. Don't care about first tracks? Get a mimosa or a Bloody. Don't care about skiing at all? Take a leisurely lunch of a croque monsieur or a wild king salmon BLT. Dinners are a mouthful, in more ways than one: there's cabernet-braised Black Angus beef short ribs with mascarpone polenta and butter-braised baby beets with a red-wine demi-glace, or a line-caught, pan-roasted Alaskan halibut with lemon kalamata–braised spinach, potato gnocchi, and charred tomato and tequila fondue. The bar menu is available late into the night, and the bar itself has the biggest single malt collection for miles around.

Food Purveyors

Bakeries

Cindybread (970-369-1116, Society Business Center, Lawson Hill) A bit off the beaten track, Cindybread offers sandwiches on handcrafted bread, fresh bagels, muffins, coffee, cookies, box lunches, and soup—all in a hip industrial space.

Maggie's Bakery and Café (970-728-3334, 217 E. Colorado Ave., Telluride) For breakfast, pull apart enormous cinnamon rolls, dive into biscuits and gravy, and smother made-from-scratch pancakes with maple syrup. Come lunch, grab homemade pizza or a soup of the day.

Wildflour Cooking Co. (970-728-3701, 763 Vance Dr., Telluride) Wildflour bakes the best artisanal breads in town—along with luscious french pastries. You can order soups, sandwiches, tossed salads, and even bistro-style dinners to go.

Coffee Shops

ReStore Our World (970-728-3553, 129 W. Colorado Ave., Telluride) Part environmental bookstore, part liberal meeting place, and part coffee shop, ReStore is a New Age retailer (fair-trade T-shirts and recycled greeting cards) up front and a café in back.

Steaming Bean Coffee House (970-728-0793, 221 W. Colorado Ave., Telluride) Right in the center of things, The Bean is a cute espresso joint with a few window seats, muffins, scones, bagels, and all kinds of coffee concoctions. You can also buy their fair-trade beans at thebean.com

The Steaming Bean offers hot coffee and baked goods near the center of town. Tony Demin

Telluride Coffee Company (970-369-4400, Heritage Plaza, Mountain Village) Formerly a coffee cart, TCC is your basic coffee shop: espresso, chai, pastries, mineral water, bagels.

Tomboy Coffee Roasters (970-728-1246, S. Fir St. at Colorado Ave., Telluride) Reminiscent of a European café, Tomboy serves up both caffeinated drinks and wine and beer—along with belgian waffles and the occasional live musician.

Delis

Deli Downstairs (970-728-4004, 217 W. Colorado Ave., Telluride) It's more than just a sandwich place, though DD can make them to go when you're off for a long hike. You can also get ice cream, shakes, malts, and Mexican food for breakfast, lunch, and dinner.

Merle's Brown Bag (970-728-5556, 126 W. Colorado Ave., Telluride) A tiny sandwich shop, Merle's sells sushi rolls; baked potatoes stuffed with roasted garlic, bacon, cottage cheese, or brown sugar; paninis; and huge sandwiches like the Hippie Hater (a garden burger with bacon, avocado, and ranch) and Big Daddy's Grinder (capicola, salami, pepperoni, roasted peppers, and provolone on a hoagie).

Tortilleria Maiz (970-728-4775, Cimarron C11, at the base of Chair 7, Telluride) Run by the same team that owns Baked in Telluride (see page 194), Tortilleria Maiz isn't really a deli, or a bakery, or a restaurant, per se: Almost everything for breakfast and lunch comes on an organic corn or flour tortilla (you can take a stack home, too). Mexican baked goods and coffee are also available.

Farmer's Markets

Ridgway Farmer's Market (970-835-7600) Down the road from Telluride, Ridgway has a market every Sunday, with crafts, salsas, veggies, plants, flowers, and locally grown meats.

Telluride Farmer's Market (telluridefarmersmarket.com) Running every Friday from noon to 4 during the summer and early fall, the Telluride farmer's market sets up camp at the corner of Willow and Colorado. Depending on the season, expect organic fruits and veggies; fresh flowers; herbal tinctures; grass-fed beef, elk, and buffalo; and fresh breads.

Frozen Desserts

The Sweet Life (970-728-8789, thesweetlifeinc.com, 115 W. Colorado Ave.) A '50s-style diner with black-and-white checkered floors, aqua-colored vinyl booths, retro decorations, and Formica tables, The Sweet Life has incredible ice cream—with flavors named after locals. True to form, you can also order burgers, grilled cheese, hot dogs, fries, banana splits, and old-fashioned malts.

Groceries

Clark's Market (970-728-3124, 700 W. Colorado Ave., Telluride)

Mountain Village Market (970-728-6500, 620 Mountain Village Blvd., Mountain Village)

The Village Market (970-728-4566, 157 S. Fir St., Telluride) A small downtown store with organic produce, natural foods, and bulk items.

Nightlife

Cornerhouse Grille (970-728-6207, 131 N. Fir St., Telluride) Open until 11 PM, this cute powder-blue house one block off Colorado is a sports bar deluxe: It serves burgers, fish sandwiches, tater tots, wings, and microbrews—and plays big games on big screens—but it has a classy, polished-floor-and-industrial-spare feel.

Fly Me to the Moon Saloon (970-728-MOON, flymetothemoonsaloon.com, 132 E. Colorado Ave., Telluride) Telluride's best spot for live music, including bluegrass (of course), rock, and even the occasional rap act (2 Live Crew has appeared here).

Last Dollar Saloon (970-728-4800, 100 E. Colorado Ave., Telluride) Come here for long-neck Budweisers, a pool table, a jukebox, a dart board, and an armadillo's rear end mounted on the wall: The Buck is earthy, unpretentious, and the polar opposite of the Noir Bar (below).

The New Sheridan Bar (970-728-3911, 233 W. Colorado Ave., Telluride) Just like the hotel above it, the must-stop New Sheridan watering hole has been around since the late 1800s—and the mahogany wall paneling, light fixtures, leaded-glass divider panels, and carved wooden bar are original. With Victorian-style couches in the front windows, pool tables in back, and a crowded passageway in between, it's always packed with locals and visitors alike.

Noir Bar (970-728-8862, 123 S. Oak St., Telluride) If you're looking for a "scene" in town, this is it: The swanky Noir, downstairs from the Bluepoint Restaurant, has leather couches, leopard-print stools, faux-fur bench seats, velvet booths, and a fireplace. DJs spin while the beautiful people (often in Uggs) order primo martinis.

Smuggler's Brewpub (970-728-0919, 225 S. Pine St., Telluride) The only microbrewery in town, Smuggler's serves up Rocky Mountain Rye and Imperial San Juan Skyhop, home-made cream soda and root beer, and ribs, pastas, and burgers (like the Mountain Burger, with BBQ sauce, cheddar, and Canadian bacon).

Culture

Cinema
The Nugget Theater (970-728-3030, 207 W. Colorado Ave., Telluride) Opened in 1935, the single-screen, 186-seat Nugget shows both mainstream and indie films—and is one of the venues for the annual Telluride Film Festival.

Ghost Towns
Ames Not a ghost town per se, this was the site of the first use of alternating current for commercial purposes: L. L. Nunn wanted to reduce the operating costs of his Gold King mine above town, so he built a power plant on the San Miguel River.

Ophir Named after an Arabian city that was rich with gold, this town is actually alive and well, with residents who've left Telluride for cheaper homes and a more mellow scene. But it's been here since 1875, and some of the original buildings still stand.

Tomboy You can either hike, bike, or 4x4 this road up to Tomboy (a gain of 2,650 feet), passing waterfalls and going through a tunnel. At one point, it was one of the leading gold mines in the world: Over 900 people lived way up here; they left when the mine ran out of gold.

Historical Sites

St. Patrick's Catholic Church (saintpatrickstelluride.com, 301 N. Spruce, Telluride) In 1896, it cost just $4,800 to build this church—including bringing in carvings of the Stations of the Cross from Austria.

San Miguel County Courthouse You can't miss this Colorado Avenue building: It's right in the center of town. Built in 1885, it burned down just after construction, but they reused the bricks and built it again two years later.

Museums

Telluride Historical Museum (970-728-3344, telluridemuseum.com, 201 W. Gregory Ave., Telluride) Housed in the restored Old Miners' Hospital (built in 1896), Telluride's museum covers everything from geology to mining to health care to skiing, and recalls the days when the town was home to 12 brothels and 26 saloons.

Theaters and Other Miscellaneous Venues

Ah Haa School for the Arts (970-728-3886, ahhaa.org, 135 S. Spruce St., Telluride) A hub for all things art—including the American Academy of Bookbinding—Ah Haa hosts nature writing workshops, exhibitions, auctions, lectures, and master classes with visiting artists all year round.

Michael Palm Theater (970-369-5669, telluridepalm.com, 721 W. Colorado Ave., Telluride) Located on the Telluride Middle-High School campus, the Palm is home to ballets, films, plays—and, of course, high school musicals.

Sheridan Opera House (970-728-6363, sheridanoperahouse.com, 231 W. Colorado Ave., Telluride) Built in 1913 as a vaudeville theater for miners, the intimate, 283-seat opera house now hosts folk, blues, and bluegrass concerts, lectures, fundraisers, and films, all right behind the historic New Sheridan Hotel.

Telluride Repertory Theatre (970-728-4539, telluridetheater.com) As Telluride's only resident theater company, the Rep produces a wide variety of plays and musicals—Pinter's *Betrayal*, *The Best Little Whorehouse in Texas*, and *The Tempest*, for starters—in the Sheridan Opera House, outside in Mountain Village, and on Main Street.

KIDS' STUFF

Ah Haa School for the Arts (970-728-3886, ahhaa.org, 135 S. Spruce St., Telluride) Masks, paper-making, clay, wind chimes, painting, art bikes, collage, designer denim—Ah Haa's art classes for kids—some single-day, some weekend-long—run all summer. There are adult classes, too (painting, ceramics, welding, fabrics, even cooking and dance).

Climbing Wall (970-728-4377, Ext. 153) On Tuesday, Wednesday, and Thursday evenings in winter, the high school gym opens up for all kids to scramble up the climbing wall.

Outdoor Town Park Ice Rink A natural, nonrefrigerated rink, open seven days a week from 9 AM to 9 PM, weather permitting. There are also public skating hours at the neighboring Hanley Ice Rink (telluride-co.gov, both located at 500 E. Colorado Ave., Telluride).

Thrill Hill Up at Mountain Village, scream down snow flumes in big inner tubes or try staying upright on a ski bike.

Town Park Kid's Fishing Pond If you're under 12, have your parents put down a driver's license to borrow a rod from the Information Center—and land up to four trout.

Town Park Sledding Hill There's a footpath marked with orange cones located near the stage on the southern hillside of the park. Sleds are available for rental at the Nordic Center in the park.

Youth Link (970-728-0140, 233 E. Pacific Ave.) For 11- to 17-year-olds who need a break from Mom and Dad, Youth Link has Internet access, video editing equipment, Xboxes, air hockey, foosball, skateboard ramps, cookouts, and DJ nights.

RECREATION: WINTER AND SPRING

Alpine Skiing and Snowboarding

Telluride

tellurideskiresort.com

Overview: Thanks to the geography of the San Juans—rugged and steep, with narrow chutes and big bowls—the terrain at Telluride is some of Colorado's most challenging. From town, all you see are a few lifts climbing up and up, with a couple black-diamond routes back down. Take the gondola up to Station St. Sophia and the lay of the land starts to open up: intermediate cruisers down to Mountain

Telluride: The 4-1-1
Acres: 1,700
Summit elevation: 12,255 feet
Vertical drop: 3,530 feet
Annual snowfall: 309 inches
Percent advanced/expert terrain: 38
Percent intermediate terrain: 38
Percent beginner terrain: 24
Lifts: 16

Village, egg-carton bumps down 40-degree slopes off Chair 9, views of striated Palmyra Peak, classic panoramas on high ridges, and steep powderfields in the newer Prospect Bowl area, which opened five years ago and increased Telluride's acreage by a full third. If you're skilled enough to go into the backcountry (Bear Canyon is a buzzword you might hear), be sure to take a guide: The snowpack in the San Juans is one of the most dangerous in the world. Be smart.

Must-ski: For those panoramas we were just talking about, make your way to the Gold Hill lift and jump onto See Forever—it follows the top ridgeline all the way from 12,255 feet to the gondola station (at 10,535), with breathtaking mountain views the whole way. There are good intermediate choices on the Palmyra and Village chairs (the latter of which accesses a terrain park and halfpipe). In Prospect Bowl, drop into the narrow Little Rose or the 45-or-so-degree Genevieve for thrills. Try Buzz's Glade for trees and Bald Mountain

Telluride's free gondola rises almost 2,000 feet above town. Sven Brunso

for short hike-to shots. Two of the most famous—or notorious—runs at Telluride are on the front side, off of Chair 9: The Plunge is an incredibly steep groomer that, yes, plunges 3,000-some feet all the way into town. And Kant-Mak-Em is a bump run to end all bump runs—steep, riddled with moguls the size of Volkswagens, and seemingly never-ending.

Grub: Besides **Allred's** (see page 193), there are a bunch of on-mountain options. **Gorrono Ranch,** a historic Basque sheep-ranch building, has a sunny deck and good chili, soups, and barbecue. **Giuseppe's,** at the top of Lift 9, has views all the way to Utah's La Sal Mountains—and beer, wine, snacks, and sandwiches. Out in Prospect Bowl, you can grab a hot drink or a sandwich at the **High Camp Warming Hut.** If you'd rather share a pizza, **That Pizza Place,** down in Mountain Village, has big pies.

Cross-Country Skiing and Snowshoeing

Lizard Head Pass Because it starts up at the pass itself and finishes 500 feet lower at Trout Lake, this trail is a good one for beginners—it follows a gentle railroad bed, and the route is easy to follow. Pooped? Many people turn back at the railroad trestle, about 2.75 miles in.

Telluride Nordic Trails (970-728-1144, telluridenordic.com) With groomed trails at five locations, Telluride Nordic's territory crosses through gorgeous scenery (and high elevations). The Trout Lake railroad grade has consistent early- and late-season snow and climbs to 10,267 feet; Priest Lake is 12.5 miles south of Telluride, with all levels of trail; and Faraway Ranch's 11 kilometers sit atop Wilson Mesa. For easy access, tool around Town Park's 3 kilometers at the far end of town—or weave around Mountain Village on intermediate and advanced routes.

Telluride's friendly skies. Sven Bruns

Topaten Nordic and Snowshoe Trails (970-728-7517, tellurideskiresort.com, Mountain Village) Guided snowshoe nature tours leave from the Gondola Plaza daily at 10 AM—or ride Lift 10 up to 10 kilometers of trails, a warming tepee, and a big deck.

Guiding and Backcountry

Chamonix Alpine Adventures (970-728-3705, chamonixalpineadventures .com, P.O. Box 670, Ophir) Though he guides mostly in Europe—or leads advanced and elite rock- and ice-climbing trips in the States—Antoine Savelli can also lead you on descents from the top of Mounts Wilson and Sneffels, or from Ophir down through Bear Creek into Telluride.

Just one of the many features in the terrain park at Telluride. Aaron Dodds

San Juan Hut System (970-626-3033, sanjuanhuts.com, P.O. Box 775, Ridgway) Five huts—with padded bunks, dishes, propane stoves and lanterns, and firewood—that sleep eight people in some of the most gorgeous (and dangerous) terrain in the state. Ski in and out of a single hut, or string a few together. Warning: Be very avy savvy, or hire a guide.

Telluride Adventures (970-728-4101, tellurideadventures.com, 300 S. Mahoney Ave., Telluride) In winter, take guided full-day tours and make guided backcountry descents or take an avalanche education course. Don't ski? They'll show you where to snowshoe. Telluride Adventures can even take you on multi-day hut trips or winter camping trips.

Telluride Mountain Guides (970-728-6481, telluridemountainguides.com, 5 Lake Fork Junction, Ames) TMG has been around for three decades. They lead clients into the 50,000 acres of backcountry around Telluride—incorporating snow safety, snow science, and long skiing and snowboarding descents.

With Telluride Helitrax, you can ski or snowboard powder like this all day—and ride a helicopter to boot.
John Humphries

Heli-skiing

Telluride Helitrax (866-435-4754, helitrax.net, powder@helitrax.net) The only heli operation in Colorado, Helitrax shuttles you throughout the San Juans for an average of six runs and up to 14,000 vertical feet. Multi-day packages, with lodging and meals, are also available—as are combo packages with nearby **Silverton Mountain** (lift-accessed skiing) and **San Juan Ski Company** (snowcat skiing, about two hours away). For $250, you can even take just a single run.

Ice Climbing

Both **Telluride Mountain Guides** and **Telluride Adventures** (see page 208) teach ice climbing to kids, novices, and more experienced climbers on Bridalveil Falls and the Ames Ice House.

RECREATION: SUMMER AND FALL

Cycling: Mountain Biking

Guides

Further Adventures (800-592-6883, furtheradventures.com, 650 Mountain Village Blvd., Mountain Village) For the first-timer, Further will shuttle you to the top of Lizard Head Pass, then guide you down the Galloping Goose railroad grade past aspens, alpine lakes, and wildflowers to the Ilium Valley. For the more experienced, book a night at the timber-line Alta Observatory and explore the singletrack (with guide) from there.

Telluride Outside (800-831-6230, tellurideoutside.com, 121 W. Colorado Ave., Telluride) Plummet down 17 miles of the Galloping Goose into the South Fork Valley, or arrange a custom half- or full-day trip (the resident guides have plenty of suggestions).

Trails

Alta Lakes A multi-use, 5-mile road to the 1870s ghost town of Alta Lakes—on the National Register of Historic Places—with 1,700 feet of elevation gain (and views to match).

Deep Creek In a box canyon criss-crossed with ultra-steep climbs, Deep Creek is (relatively) mellow: 6.5 miles and a 1,600-foot elevation gain. Cross the bridge over Mill Creek, follow the Deep Creek trail to Last Dollar Road, and climb until you meet the paved airport road. Cruise back into town.

See Forever Road Starting at the Station San Sophia in Mountain Village, climb 3.4 miles to the top of Gold Hill (a thigh-busting 1,710 feet)—then hook up with the Wasatch and Bear Creek trails for an 8.7-mile loop. The reward? A 3,500-foot descent from Gold Hill to the valley floor.

Telluride-to-Moab hut-to-hut (970-626-3033, sanjuanhuts.com) Covering over 200 miles in seven days, this is one of the most spectacular mountain bike trips you could hope for: jagged peaks, epic climbs, endless vistas, 35-mile roller-coaster days, and a different hut each night. Joe Ryan, who manages the huts, doesn't guide—he merely sends out keys, directions, and advice, and supplies the hut with do-it-yourself breakfasts, lunches, and dinners.

Wasatch Trail This is an epic ride—especially if you're coming from sea level: It climbs past Bridal Veil Falls on a 4x4 road, joins a fire road, and tops out at over 13,000 feet. Expect a few sections of hike-a-bike, and don't overshoot those switchbacks on the way down.

Cycling: Road Biking

Dallas Divide Take CO 62 out of Ridgway toward Telluride, gaining 2,400 feet as you huff up to the Dallas Divide. Wrap up the climb with a stunning look at the Sneffels Range, then continue on down to Placerville, a total of 23 miles.

Lizard Head Pass Starting in Placerville and passing by the turnoffs to Telluride and Ophir, this section of CO 145 meanders through aspen groves, with ascents that are alternately mellow and lung-busting steep. From the top of the pass, it's 12 miles down into Rico.

Naturita Canyon One of the easier rides in the area (though it's still 37 miles), the Naturita route follows the San Miguel River from Placerville on down, with easygoing terrain and a single mellow climb about halfway through.

Ridgway to Silverton US 550 is probably the most beautiful road in Colorado, but it's a grueling one: Follow it from Ridgway through Ouray and you'll grind up to 11,000-plus-feet, looking over the Uncompahgre Gorge, the Sneffels Range, and the Big Blue Wilderness.

Fishing

Outfitters

Further Adventures (800-592-6883, furtheradventures.com, 650 Mountain Village Blvd., Mountain Village) Wade or float the San Miguel River, hike up to a high-alpine lake below Silver and Palmyra Peaks, or fish for pigs at the private Gurley Reservoir.

RIGS Fly Shop (888-626-4460, fishrigs.com, 555 Sherman St., Suite 2, Ridgway) Public access on the Uncompahgre, Cimarron, and Gunnison; private access at Spring Valley Ranch (spring creeks), Centennial Ranch (a private stretch of the Uncompahgre), and Double Diamond River Ranch (which includes a family-friendly 12-acre lake).

Telluride Angler (800-831-6230, tellurideoutside.com, 121 W. Colorado Ave., Telluride) If you can't swing an overnight stay at Dunton Hot Springs or the Cascabel Club (see page 191), Telluride Angler can sneak you in there for the day—or into the Lightenburger Ranch, the Gurley Rez, and the so-called "Jackson Hole," a top winter trout fishery. That's only if the 75 miles of the Dolores or the nearby San Miguel aren't enough for you.

Lakes and Streams

Before you fish any water in Colorado, be sure you check with a local fly shop to find out if it's public or private. Many rivers have both private and public sections, so make sure you know where you're going. For licenses and regulations, visit wildlife.state.co.us/fishing—

or, again, stop into a shop. If a river is designated "Gold Medal," it officially means that there are 12 trout per surface acre that top 14 inches—or 60 pounds of trout per surface acre. Unofficially, it means that the fishing is damn good.

Dolores River The 12 miles of tailwater below the McPhee dam are catch-and-release only, with decent-sized rainbows, browns, and cutties—and easy wading to riffles and bends.

High Lakes If you'd rather fish lakes than streams, you can drive right up to Priest Lake or Trout Lake, or hike into Woods Lake, Silver Lake, and the Alta Lakes.

San Miguel River This free-flowing waterway begins way above Telluride, flows through town, and parallels the road down into the canyon. It holds rainbows and browns in deep pools and freestone pockets, has good caddis and stonefly hatches, and is usually forgiving for beginners.

Golf

Fairway Pines Golf Club (970-626-5284, 117 Ponderosa Dr., Ridgway) Open to the public seven days a week, Fairway Pines is a hilly course with dense forests of ponderosa and juniper, and mountain views.

Telluride Golf Club (970-728-2606, tellurideskiresort.com, 565 Mountain Village Blvd., Mountain Village) This 18-holer is surrounded by the highest concentration of fourteeners in the Continental United States—and sits at 9,300 feet. Translation? Your ball could go 15 percent farther. Golf carts with GPS help you negotiate the aspen groves, ponds, and bubbling brooks.

Hiking and Backpacking

Guides
Herb Walker Tours (970-728-0639, herbwalkertours@earthlink.net, P.O. Box 399, Telluride) Longtime local and naturalist John SirJesse, a wild mushroom expert, can show you the area's herbs, flora, and fungi on three-hour tours—whether you're alone or in a group of 20.

Telluride Adventures (970-728-4101, tellurideadventures.com, 300 S. Mahoney Ave., Telluride) Don't want to carry your own pack? You can hire someone to do it for you—and make you a gourmet meal, roasted marshmallows included. Telluride Adventures takes individuals and small groups on various trips through the San Juans. Not comfortable hiking on your own? They can lead you.

Trails
Bear Creek Preserve A 381-acre parcel next to Town Park, Bear Creek has a 2-mile-long interpretive trail (maps available at the Town Park info center) that climbs about 1,000 feet to a cascading waterfall. From here, you can catch the Wasatch Trail for a 12-mile loop over to Bridal Veil Falls.

Bridal Veil Falls Just 2 miles east of town, CO 145 turns from paved to dirt, then climbs steeply to the top of a 385-foot cascade. Four-wheel-drive vehicles are allowed on the trail. Continue on to Bridal Veil Basin and Blue Lake (above timberline) if you have the lungs.

Golf at Telluride means spectacular views—and, because of the altitude, balls fly 15 percent farther.
Brett Schreckengost

Jud Wiebe Trail A short, steep, 2.7-mile loop that leaves from the dirt grade at Oak Street and Tomboy Road and climbs 1,300 feet for great views of town.

Lizard Head Trail The 41,296-acre Lizard Head Wilderness is named after Lizard Head Peak (13,113 feet), a jutting San Juan rock spire. Starting at the Wilson Mesa trailhead, you can follow Bilk Creek about 6 miles to the junction of the Cross Mountain trail or, if you're able to arrange a shuttle, keep going all the way to Lizard Head Pass (on CO 145).

Sneffels Highline Trail From the Jud Wiebe Trail (above), jump onto the 13-mile Sneffels Highline, which climbs a good 3,000 vertical feet along Butcher Creek and up to a saddle overlooking Mill Creek Basin. Hook up with the Deep Creek trail to make a loop back into Telluride.

Wilson Mesa About 14 miles west of Telluride on CO 145, this trail climbs 3,700 feet over the course of 13 miles, looping around the bottom of Wilson Peak.

Horseback Riding

Deb's Livery (970-626-5587, debslivery.com, debs.livery@montrose.net, 31268 US 550 S., Montrose) Summer or winter, Deb's operation leads standard two-hour rides with views of the San Juans and Cimarrons. They can also arrange longer rides, drop off supplies to a camp, or take you on a carriage ride.

Many Ponies Outfit (970-728-6278, manyponiesoutfit.com, manyponies@mindspring .com, P.O. Box 821, Norwood) Paul Finley and Lisa Foxwell lead two-hour to full-day trail rides, give hour long riding lessons in both English and Western, and let parents lead their kids around on miniature horses. For higher education, sign up for the three-day Wrangler School, held each June and September.

Telluride Horseback Adventures (970-728-9611, ridewithroudy.com, 242 Hawn Lane, Telluride) Otherwise known as Ride with Roudy, THA and Roudy Roudebush have been guiding people around the Wilson range since 1973—on everything from one-hour rides to daylong excursions to the Alta ghost town to weeklong custom pack trips.

Hot Springs

Orvis Hot Springs (970-626-5324, orvishotsprings.com, 1585 CR 3, Ridgway) You should stop at this hot spring on your way out of town to soothe those ski-weary legs. Choose from seven spring pools filled with lithium water—one of the minerals that's supposed to provide therapeutic benefits—from 98 to 112 degrees. There's lodging and vehicle and tent camping on-site.

Paragliding and Sailplane Rides

Adventure Tour Productions (970-728-1754, adventuretourproductions.com, P.O. Box 3436, Telluride) Take a running leap off the side of a 12,000-foot mountainside and soar over alpine lakes and valleys.

Telluride Soaring (970-708-0862, telluridesoaring.com, at the Telluride Regional Airport) Catch a thermal with the highest commercial gliding operation in the world. Hour long winter and summer rides leave right from Telluride Airport.

Rafting and Paddling

Further Adventures (800-592-6883, furtheradventures.com, 650 Mountain Village Blvd., Mountain Village) Leisurely half-day floats to rowdy, overnight Class IV runs on the San Miguel River, Deep Creek, Specie Creek, and Beaver Creek.

Telluride Kayak School (970-728-6250, kayaktelluride.com, info@sanjuanrivers.com, P.O. Box 2457, Telluride) Learn an Eskimo roll, practice your strokes, and then take a trip—from a half-day to 10 days—on the San Juan, Gunnison, or San Miguel Rivers.

Telluride Outside (800-831-6230, tellurideoutside.com, 121 W. Colorado Ave., Telluride) Telluride Outside's guides have lots of options—it just depends on how wild you want to get. The 28-mile Dolores River run from Dove Creek Pump Station to Slickrock is a thrill ride: 28 miles through Ponderosa Canyon, with rapids hitting the V mark. Tamer options include half-day rolls along the San Miguel and full-day trips on other sections of the Dolores.

DRIVING: SCENIC DRIVES AND BYWAYS

Guides
Silverpick Tours (970-728-5110, silverpicktours.com) Let someone else do the driving—up and over Lizard Pass to Mesa Verde, down through Ridgway and Ouray to the Black Canyon, or overnight to Canyonlands and back.

Routes
Alpine Loop You'll need a four-wheel-drive vehicle for most of this circuit, which peels off US 550 at the Engineer Mountain turnoff; winds past avalanche slopes, mine remains, and glacial valleys; goes up and over 12,800-foot Engineer Pass, with fourteener views all around; then passes by Lake City, Lake San Cristobal, the Lake Fork of the Gunnison, and Cinnamon Pass on the way back to 550.

Black Bear Road Although there isn't anything left of the Black Bear mines, this road is worth it for the journey—if you want to get scared out of your wits. It's rumored to be the most dangerous pass in Colorado—with loose gravel, steep grades, plunging drops, and even stair steps. You'll get to see the San Juans and high-mine environment at their best. Don't attempt it unless you have advanced four-wheel-drive skills.

Million Dollar Highway The portion of the San Juan Skyway on US 550 between Ridgway and Durango, this stretch of road is one of the most beautiful in the U.S. (and slightly harrowing in spots). No one's quite sure where the name came from, whether it was the high cost of building or the ore-bearing fill used in construction.

San Juan Skyway For an utterly spectacular 236 miles along CO 550, 145, and 62, the Skyway passes through Telluride, Ouray (sometimes called the Swiss Alps of the Rockies), Silverton, Durango, Cortez, and Dolores, and scales super-high passes in the San Juan, Uncompahgre, Sneffels, and Wilson ranges. Along the way, take in hot springs, Victorian houses, mining history, cliff dwellings, wildlife, and wildflowers.

Unaweep/Tabeguache Scenic and Historic Byway A 138-mile route that follows the western slope highways of CO 141 and 145 from Grand Junction to Placerville—weaving through the "redbeds" of the Dolores River canyon and onto high plains.

SHOPPING

Art Galleries
Kenshou Gallery (970-728-5787, 333 W. Colorado Ave., Telluride) Wooden wildlife carvings, hand-turned wooden bowls, prints, glicee mosaic photographs, and paintings, all with an emphasis on the Southwest and Rocky Mountains.

Lucas Gallery (970-728-1345, lucasgallery.net, 151 S. Pine St., Telluride) From representational landscapes to abstract snowscapes, from muted hues to brilliant colors, Lucas showcases contemporary paintings, sculpture, mixed media, and jewelry. Artists include Enrico Embroil, Marshall Noice, Paul Davis, Peter Roux, and Bernice Strawn.

Lustre Gallery (970-728-3355, lustregallery.com, 171 S. Pine St., Telluride) Features luminous works by Lluis Masriera (jewelry), Todd Reed (raw diamond jewelry), Ulla Darni (chandeliers), and Rick Jarvis (molten glass), plus works of sculpture and hand-built leather furniture.

Naturescapes Gallery (970-728-6359, naturescapesgallery.com, 100 W. Colorado Ave., Telluride) Local photographer Dale Malmedal has been shooting the San Juans and Telluride for a decade, and here's where to find his most iconic prints—mountainscapes, wildflowers, fall colors, and gorgeous panoramas.

Stained Glass Art Company (970-729-0495, stainedglassartcompany.com, 551 Society Dr., Telluride) Windows, small and large lamps, mosaic tables, mobiles, boxes, candle holders, and more: Glass artist Patti Childers sells made-to-order and custom-designed works in lustrous colors.

Telluride Gallery of Fine Art (970-728-3300, telluridegallery.com, 130 E. Colorado Ave., Telluride; 970-728-9884, 565 Mountain Village Blvd., Mountain Village) The oldest gallery in town, the Telluride Gallery focuses on local American contemporary art—painting, sculpture, crafts, jewelry—along with international artists. All told, the names (including Jerry Uelsmann, Sally Strand, Emmi Whitehorse, Robert Weatherford, and Lissa Hunter) number in the dozens.

Wilderness Wonders (970-369-4441, tonynewlin.com, 333 W. Colorado Ave., Telluride) A native of northern New Mexico, Newlin photographs sunsets, eagles, whales, bears, landscapes, and seascapes in Alaska, the western U.S., and Canada.

Books
Between the Covers (970-728-4504, between-the-covers.com, 224 W. Colorado Ave., Telluride) Floor-to-ceiling bookshelves, a small coffee bar in back, classics, local titles, kids' books, magazines, best-sellers, and award-winners: Between the Covers is a lovely independent bookstore—especially on a snowy, lazy day.

Outdoor Gear
Jagged Edge Outdoor Gear (970-728-9307, 129 W. Colorado Ave., Telluride) A retail store for the Telluride-based outdoor clothing company Jagged Edge, which has been in the area since 1986, this outpost also sells backcountry apparel from folks like Ibex, Moonstone, Dansko, Merrell, and Prana.

Telluride Outside (970-728-3895, 121 W. Colorado Ave., Telluride) A fly shop, adventure outfitter, and gear shop all in one.

Western Clothing and Furs
Black Bear Trading Company (970-728-6556, 218 W. Colorado Ave., Telluride) Suede pants, Western shirts, turquoise jewelry, leather belts, cowboy hats, and even home furnishings, Black Bear has almost everything "Colorado" you can think of.

The Bounty Hunter (970-728-0256, 226 W. Colorado Ave., Telluride) With an impressive collection of hats—cowboy, Panama, outback, baseball—along with cowboy boots and vests, The Bounty Hunter is owned by local boot-and-hat-maker Steve King, who's made lids for movie stars and presidents.

Hell Bent Leather & Silver (970-728-6246, hellbentleather.com, 209 E. Colorado Ave., Telluride) Hell Bent sells Native American–style beaded handbags, leather belts, and silver jewelry.

Seasonal Events

February: Telluride Comedy Fest (970-728-6363, tellurideticket.com) This increasingly popular weekend brings national-caliber jokesters into town for a few days of laughs.

February: Telluride Gay Ski Week (877-625-7535, telluridegayskiweek.com) When you get to Gay Ski Week, you can pick up a "Gaydar" armband for $35. It will track your time skiing, terrain difficulty, number of runs, calories burned, vertical feet, and more. Race in drag, mingle at an Oscar party at the Sheridan Opera House, or watch the fashion show at the Telluride AIDS benefit.

March: Plunge Music Fest (800-525-3455, plungemusicfest.com) Dedicated to underground hip-hop and rock, this new five-day festival has DJs spinning all day—whether they're at the base of the mountain, at Fly Me to the Moon, or at the Sheridan Opera House.

March: Softball Game on Skis (970-728-7432, tellurideskiresort.com) Every year, the ski patrol takes on the ski school on St. Patrick's Day—and then breaks for corned beef and cabbage.

April: Talking Gourds Spoken Word Festival (970-728-3886, sheridanoperahouse.com) Hosted by the Telluride Writers Guild, Talking Gourds has poetry readings, word shows, discussions, poetry slams, and "late-night carouses" at local bars.

May: Telluride Mountainfilm (970-728-4123, mountainfilm.org) A film festival that concentrates on the environment, nature, travel, mountains, and mountain sports, Mountainflim premieres a range of short and long flicks every Memorial Day—then sends them off on a world tour.

June: Telluride Balloon Festival (tellurideballoonfestival.com) Watch colorful balloons rise into the air each morning, ask to be part of a crew, or grab a cup of coffee and a muffin to benefit local schools.

June: Telluride Bluegrass Festival (800-624-2422, bluegrass.com) In a town that's known for great summer festivals, this is hands-down the biggest—and most famous. Over the years, acts like Bonnie Raitt, Bela Fleck, Lucinda Williams, the Sam Bush Band, Jerry Douglas, Willie Nelson, David Grisman, Lyle Lovett, Alison Krauss, and Natalie Merchant have all come here, and fans camp in Town Park to the sound of late-night jam sessions.

June: Telluride Wine Festival (970-728-3178, telluridewinefestival.com) Take classes like "Wines of Northeast Italy and Slovenia," taste scotch and cigars, sit down to multi-course meals, sample chocolate truffles and learn what to pair with them, and bid on wines in a grand finale auction.

June: Wild West Fest (970-728-6363) This weeklong event brings inner-city youth from around the country to Telluride to learn horsemanship skills, trick roping, fly-fishing, golf, drama, and dance.

July: Hard Rock 100 (run100s.com/HR) A brutal endurance run that loops through Silverton, Ouray, Telluride, Lake City, and Ophir, the Hard Rock course is 100 miles long, gaining 33,000 feet of elevation and reaching a high point of 14,048 feet on Handies Peak.

July: Plein Air Festival (970-728-6363, telluridepleinair.org/events.html) Every year, 30 artists come to Telluride to paint mountains, wildflowers, historic buildings, and big landscapes—then exhibit their works for the public. Observe artists at work, watch a one-hour "Quick Draw" competition, and bid on your favorite plein-air piece.

July: Telluride Nothing Festival (telluridenothingfestival.com) More of an inside joke than a true festival, the Nothing Festival takes place on the only free weekend all summer— no staff, no passes, no schedule, no T-shirts, no nothing.

August: Culinary and Arts Festival (877-359-5606, tellurideculinaryart.com) There are art festivals and food festivals, and then there's the Telluride Culinary and Arts Festival, where you can stop by an exhibition of contemporary artists and then swing by the "Beer, Sausage, and Cheese Seminar with Jorge de la Torre." Both local and internationally known chefs teach master classes all weekend.

August: Mushroom Festival (970-708-0289, mushroomfestival.com) Fungophiles unite in this celebration of the 'shroom, with workshops on growing, cooking, identifying, preserving, and finding the fungi. The highlight: a mushroom parade down Colorado Avenue.

August: Telluride Chamber Music Festival (970-728-8686, telluridechambermusic.com) The free outdoor concerts are perfect for picnicking. The children's concerts introduce kids to classical music. And the featured concerts—horn trios, sextets, arias, Mozart, Shostakovich, Brahms, Verdi, and even Thelonious Monk—are held at venues all around town.

August: Telluride Jazz (970-728-7009, telluridejazz.com) Going strong for over 30 years, this jazz fest has multiple indoor and outdoor venues, and has hosted the likes of John Mayall, Regina Carter, Herbie Hancock, Soulive, and Nnenna Freelon.

September: Blues and Brews (866-515-6166, tellurideblues.com) Fifty microbreweries pour their latest favorites, and musicians like Bruce Hornsby, Lou Reed, and John Mayer perform at Town Park—then jam into the night at local bars.

September: Imogene Pass Run (970-728-0251, imogenerun.com) A 17.1-miler that connects Ouray and Telluride, this race goes up and over 13,114-foot Imogene Pass along the way—straight up some 5,000 feet, and then straight down.

September: Telluride Film Festival (603-433-9202, telluridefilmfestival.org, mail@ telluridefilmfestival.org) One of the top film fests in the country, Telluride's festival has been going strong since 1974. The schedule is kept secret until opening day, but recent flicks have included *Brokeback Mountain, Capote, Walk the Line, Roger and Me,* and *The Crying Game.* The festival has brought in the likes of Peter Sellars, Errol Morris, Peter Bogdanovich, and Francis Ford Coppola.

NUTS AND BOLTS

Getting Here

Telluride has the highest commercial airport in North America, at 9,078 feet, with direct service from Denver and Phoenix (tellurideairport.com). You can also fly into Montrose, an hour away, from LA, Salt Lake, Houston, Dallas, Atlanta, Chicago, and Newark. From Montrose, you can rent a car with Dollar, Budget, National, Hertz, or Thrifty—or book a shuttle ride with **Telluride Express** (970-728-6000) or **Mountain Limo** (970-728-9606). Otherwise, it's about six hours from Denver.

Ambulance/Fire/Police/Search and Rescue

For emergencies, of course, dial 911. For police assistance that doesn't require an emergency response, contact the number listed below for the city closest to your present location.

San Miguel County Search and Rescue: 970-728-1911

In Telluride, even the phone booths are funky. Evelyn Spenc

San Miguel County Sheriff: 970-728-1911 (dispatch) or 970-728-3818

Telluride Fire Protection District: 970-728-3801

Telluride Marshall's Department: 970-728-3818

Avalanche Reports

Colorado Avalanche Information Center: 970-247-8187, geosurvey.state.co.us/avalanche and avalanche-center.org

Hospitals and Emergency Medical Services

Telluride Medical Center: 970-728-3848, telluridemedicalcenter.org, 500 W. Pacific Ave., Telluride

Libraries

Wilkinson Public Library: 970-728-4519, telluride.lib.co.us/index.htm, 100 W. Pacific Ave., Telluride

Media

Newspapers and Magazines
Telluride Daily Planet: 970-728-9788, telluridegateway.com, 283 S. Fir St., Telluride, CO 81435

Telluride Style Magazine: 970-728-3422, telluridestyle.com, 300 S. Mahoney, C-8, P.O. Box 577, Telluride, CO 81435

The Telluride Watch: 970-728-4496, telluridewatch.com, 125 W. Pacific Ave., P.O. Box 2042, Telluride, CO 81435

Radio
KOTO 89.3, 91.7, 105.5: 970-728-8100, koto.org. Community radio, bluegrass, NPR, BBC, reggae.

Public Transportation
The Galloping Goose: 970-728-5700, Telluride's free shuttle service has several loops around town.

Ranger Stations
BLM's Uncompahgre Field Office: 970-240-5300, www.co.blm.gov/ubra

Dolores Ranger Station: 970-882-7296

Mount Sneffels and Lizard Head Wilderness Areas: 970-327-4261

Norwood Ranger Station: 970-327-4161

San Juan National Forest: 970-247-4874

Tourist Information
Telluride Chamber of Commerce: 970-728- 3041, telluridechamber.com, telluride today.com

Telluride and Mountain Village Convention and Visitor's Bureau: 888-605-2578, visittelluride.com, 630 W. Colorado Ave., Telluride

6

VAIL/BEAVER CREEK

The Making of a Dream

Wrote Fred R. Smith in *Sports Illustrated* in 1964: "It is difficult to believe, but three winters ago there was no Vail. Truckers or skiers bound for Aspen coasting west from the 12,000-foot heights of Loveland Pass might have paused to admire this tree-lined trout stream, a herd of mule deer, or even a Rocky Mountain bighorn ram, silhouetted on a rim of red rock. They would have seen little else."

Vail is a case of a few people really wanting to found a ski area—and then going right ahead and founding it. Yes, there were some mines here (Irishman "Lord" George Gore and American Jim Bridger were among the first prospectors). Some sheep ranchers. A legacy of Utes. But Vail, unlike Aspen or Breck or Telluride, was started from scratch with ski turns and chairlifts in mind, and built into a world-class resort and town. Forty years ago, it was a pasture—and now it's one of the biggest and busiest ski resorts in North America, with 1,676,118 skier-days last year.

And we basically owe it all to the vision of one man, Pete Seibert. Seibert, a 10th Mountain Division soldier in World War II, a member of the 1950 U.S. Ski Team, and manager of nearby Loveland Pass ski area, had long harbored ambitions to found a great American ski area. In 1957, he was tipped off by his friend, Earl Eaton—a ski patroller and snowcat driver who thought he saw some potential in a certain area west of Vail Pass. One day, the two men skied up from old US 6 to scope things out. When they reached the top of the ridge—and the 4,000 acres of what are now the Back Bowls unfolded before them— Seibert knew he'd found his place.

From then on, things moved quickly—very quickly. Seibert and crew started building in 1962, and in just 20 months, they'd cut 3,000 vertical feet of trails, erected three chairlifts and a gondola (the first in the United States), and constructed a restaurant, parking, shops, and even lodging. As *Denver Post* writer Cal Queal wrote, "The Vail area . . . looks to be a honey."

Although opening day only attracted a few curious locals, by its third season Vail had piled up more skier-days than any other resort in the state. By 1969, there were seven chairlifts, two gondolas, 20 restaurants, and a ski school with 70 instructors. And its fame was sealed when Gerald Ford started vacationing here in the 1970s. In 1981, Beaver Creek— Vail's even-more-upscale sister resort 10 minutes west on I-70—was opened: It's a smaller resort, but superlative in its own right, with a World Cup downhill course, a Ritz-Carlton,

Cookies—the ultimate fuel for a winter's day at Beaver Creek. Chris McLennan/Beaver Creek Resort

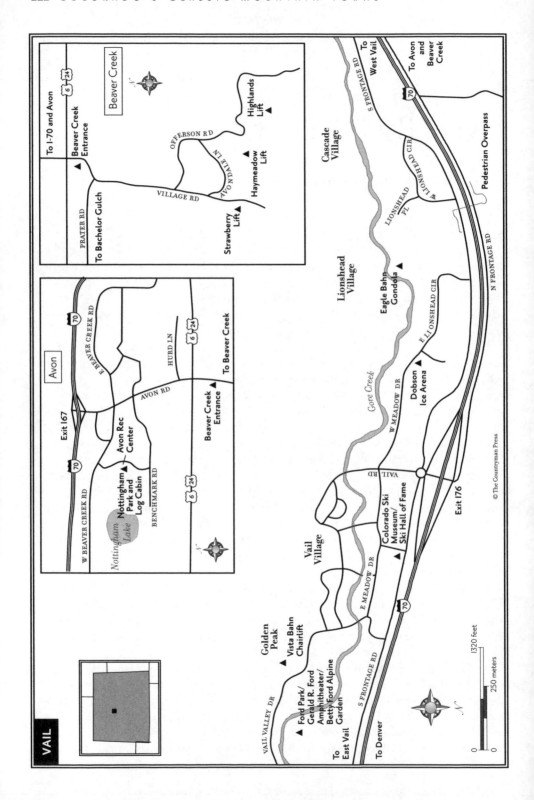

and a spit-shined vibe (not to mention covered escalators in the base village and free hot chocolate-chip cookies handed out by staffers).

As a newer community, Vail lacks some of the genuine historical feeling that you might get in Telluride or Aspen; it was modeled after a high-Alpine ski town, and sometimes feels, well, modeled. As of press time, the base area was undergoing a major overhaul—and we mean major. Between a Four Seasons slated to open in 2008, a few residence hotels, more shops, refurbished older properties, and a brand-new plaza, the whole shebang will cost $1 billion. In this chapter, more than any other, keep in mind that businesses move, close for remodeling, and open. What might be a family-run motel as we write could be a Relais & Châteaux spa by the time you read.

LODGING

VAIL

Austria Haus Hotel
877-644-7625, 970-477-4200
austriahaushotel.com
info@austriahaushotel.com
242 E. Meadow Dr., Vail
Price Range: $125–$625, including
    breakfast
Credit Cards: AE, D, MC, V
Children: Y
Pets: N
Handicap Accessible: Y

Of all the Alps-style hotels in Vail, Austria Haus is the most elegant. Its exterior is bright white with dark wood eaves, hanging flower baskets, and candy-cane shutters. Its lobby is sleek without being sterile, with tiled floors, oversize velvet chairs and ottomans, and loads of fresh flowers. And with just 25 rooms, it's much more intimate than the larger, more opulent hotels. But it still has luxurious touches: bathrooms with heated marble floors, hand-troweled plaster walls, Bose radios, french balconies, and fabrics in rich reds and greens. Especially nice are the beamed cathedral ceilings and large, slope-facing windows of the Bellflower Junior Suites. The continental breakfast is chock full of fresh seasonal fruit, breads, hot cereal, and muesli—and the Lobby Lounge's plush leather couches,

huge pillows, and wrought-iron reading lamps are perfect for an après-ski chess match (there are a couple sets available if you're up for it).

Christiania at Vail
800-530-3999, 970-476-5641
christianiaatvail.com
chrlodge@vail.net
356 E. Hanson Ranch Rd., Vail
Price Range: $115–$650, including
    continental breakfast in winter
Credit Cards: AE, D, MC, V
Children: Y
Pets: N
Handicap Accessible: Y

The cute Bavarian Christiania is one of the few true ski-in/ski-out properties in Vail—just steps from both the Riva Bahn and the Vista Bahn lifts—which makes its rates that much more of a good deal. It has all the ubiquitous Alpine trappings: carved wooden railings, flags flying over the entryway, multiple gabled roofs, stucco walls. The rooms—suites or standard spaces facing either the mountain or the village—have a wide variety of styles, from the busy (cheery checkerboard pillowcases and floral-patterned duvets that match floral-patterned walls) to the plain (white duvets, beige upholstery). Some are more Austrian than others, with knotty pine beds and paintings of Alpine scenes, some have fireplaces and jetted tubs, and some have private balconies. The breakfast and après area, Sarah's Lounge, has hand-carved Tyrolean chairs, garlands painted over the doorways, and a small bar.

Gasthof Gramshammer

800-610-7374, 970-476-5626
pepis.com
info@pepis.com
231 E. Gore Creek Dr., Vail
Price Range: $105–$780, including
    breakfast
Credit Cards: AE, D, MC, V
Children: Y
Pets: N
Handicap Accessible: Y

Because of former internationally known ski racer Pepi Gramshammer, the name "Pepi" is a legendary one in these parts: There's Pepi's Bar, Pepi's Restaurant (see page 237), and Pepi's Sports Shop. There's a Pepi's ski training camp series called Wedel Weeks (named after a short and stylized Euro ski turn). And then there's Pepi's hotel, the 39-room Gasthof Gramshammer, a cute Bavarian affair in the heart of town that's been around since 1964—making it one of the oldest lodges in all of Vail. In a town of Austrian-wannabes, this is the genuine article, both in service and in style: The rooms and suites all have original oil paintings, pastel tones, and big armoires; some of them overlook the creek, and some look over the happenings at the children's fountain in the middle of Vail Village. In keeping with its European roots, Gasthof's breakfast is made up of fresh-baked breads, cheeses, meats, muesli, and fruit. The location can't be beat, although it can get a tad loud on weekend nights (if you're worried, ask for a room that isn't over Pepi's Bar).

✪ The Lodge at Vail

800-367-7625, 970-476-5011
lodgeatvail.rockresorts.com
174 E. Gore Creek Dr., Vail
Price Range: $135–$1,100
Credit Cards: AE, D, MC, V
Children: Y
Pets: Y, $25 a night
Handicap Accessible: Y

First, the accolades: The Lodge at Vail has been picked as the best ski resort hotel in North America by *Condé Nast Traveler.* It made *Travel & Leisure's* 500 Greatest Hotels in the World. It was chosen as the top hotel by the 138-hotel luxury group Preferred Hotels. Second, the location: Stay here, and you're just 150 feet from the liftline maze of the Vista Bahn. And third, the past: The Lodge has a long history in a town where history tends to be short. This place opened in 1962, at the same time fledgling Vail did, when lift tickets cost $5 and a room cost $10. Since then, they've racked up amenities along with awards—Wi-Fi in all rooms, four hot tubs, an outdoor pool, ski valets, a piano bar, complimentary ski waxing, two restaurants (including Wildflower, page 239), and an 8,000-plus-foot, rustic Colorado spa, Avanyu, that's slated to open in winter 2007. Modeled after the Lodge at Sun Valley, Vail's version is deceptively sprawling, with 165 rooms (49 of which are suites) of varying styles and sizes. Some have in-your-face views of the slopes, balconies, kitchens, wood-burning fireplaces, and bathrooms with heated marble floors.

✪ Savory Inn and Cooking School of Vail

866-728-6794, 970-476-1304
savoryinn.com
info@savoryinn.com
2405 Elliot Ranch Rd., Vail
Price Range: $150–$360, including
    breakfast
Credit Cards: AE, D, MC, V
Children: Y, 10 and older
Pets: N
Handicap Accessible: N

The Savory Inn, alongside Gore Creek near Vail, combines an intimate inn with a cooking school. Evelyn Spence

Rather stay in an intimate B&B than a chichi, ski-in/ski-out resort hotel? Looking for real character? This 12-room, barnlike log cabin on Gore Creek is one of the most unusual properties in the area—and not just because there's a demonstration kitchen to the left as you walk in the big front door (though that helps). Yes, there's a definite homage to cooking here: Rooms are named after herbs and spices (the big four-poster bed and warm chocolate tones of the Jasmine room, the velvet duvet and bay window of Paprika, the chaise lounge and pair of country quilt–clad queens in Basil), but they are tasteful, not gimmicky, with log walls, spruce beams, and simple decorations. In the afternoon, guests take the inn's shuttle back from the slopes and relax with snacks by the stone fireplace. Of course, it can't hurt that the Savory Inn is also a cooking school—not only can you take "The Oaxacan Kitchen: Authentic Mexican" or "Finger Lickin' Down-Home Southern Barbecue" without leaving the building, but you also reap the benefits come breakfast.

Sonnenalp Resort

Innkeepers: The Faessler family
800-654-8312, 970-476-5656
sonnenalp.com
info@sonnenalp.com
20 Vail Rd., Vail
Price Range: $240–$2,950, including
    breakfast
Credit Cards: AE, D, MC, V
Children: Y
Pets: Y, $35 per night
Handicap Accessible: Y

The Tivoli Lodge: big, brand-new, slopeside rooms. Tivoli Lodge

Sonnenalp fits Vail's European-style architecture and service to a T: The exterior echoes Bavaria without imitating, with candy-striped shuttles and gabled roofs, and the lobby and bar are more bierstube than Great Room (cavernlike spaces, stucco walls, low arches, wood beams, antiques, thick dark-green curtains). Most of the guest rooms are actually spacious suites, from the 350-square-foot Junipers to the 1,600-square-foot Castle Peaks. Whatever the layout and size, they all have a calm and classy decor: pastel plaid duvets in sages and blues, pine-wood and stucco walls, sepia photos, gas log fireplaces, and huge bathrooms with heated marble floors and double vanities. And, being a resort, Sonnenalp has resort amenities: two pools (one indoor, one outdoor), a fitness center, three hot tubs, an in-house spa and ski shop, a bar, two restaurants, and a library.

Tivoli Lodge
800-451-4756, 970-476-6601
tivolilodge.com
reservations@tivolilodge.com
386 Hanson Ranch Rd., Vail
Price Range: $229–$1,599, including breakfast
Credit Cards: AE, D, MC, V
Children: Y
Pets: N
Handicap Accessible: Y

This beloved slopeside lodge, which opened in 1968 and has been run by the Lazier family ever since, just reopened after a $30 million facelift: It has been transformed from kitschy Bavarian crash pad to truly classy European boutique hotel. It's still a stone's throw from the Vista Bahn lift and the Golden Peak base area, but that's about all that's the same. All 62 rooms have luxurious touches worthy of the bucks that were sunk into it: leather sofas, Turkish towels and robes, double showers, and fireplaces. The rooms in the tower areas are octagonal, all with wraparound views of the ski resort and some with vaulted ceilings; the village-view rooms are cheaper, but still have all the same amenities. The lobby is totally new, too: a massive stone fireplace, a few tastefully placed sets of antique skis and poles, oils of mountain scenes, and 15-foot-high windows looking out to the mountains.

Vail Mountain Lodge and Spa

866-476-0700, 970-476-7721
vailmountainlodge.com
reservations@vailmountainlodge.com
352 E. Meadow Dr., Vail
Price Range: $99–$525, including breakfast
Credit Cards: AE, D, MC, V
Children: Y
Pets: Y, in selected rooms
Handicap Accessible: Y

This 24-room lodge is actually best known for its athletic club, which has an extensive menu of classes—Anusara yoga, Pilates, rock-climbing on an indoor wall, spinning, outdoor training for summer and winter sports—and state-of-the-art fitness contraptions. It's also home to a spa (which just got a $250,000 renovation), where you can immerse yourself in 20,000-year-old Moor mud, get scrubbed by mineral salts, and soak in a mandarin and chamomile milk bath. Even the in-house restaurant, Terra Bistro, is healthy: Everything is free-range, organic, or local. The accommodations are clean-cut, in reds and creams, with big armoires, black-and-white photos, wrought-iron lamps, and sunken, four-fixture tubs. The lobby is full-on ski lodge: bronze sculptures of elk, tables with antler legs, leather couches, pairs of antique skis leaning against the wall, an old wooden canoe hanging from the ceiling, and stone floors covered in rich Persian carpets.

BEAVER CREEK

Beaver Creek Lodge

970-845-9800
beavercreeklodge.net
info@beavercreeklodge.net
26 Avondale Lane, Beaver Creek
Price Range: $179–$2,799
Credit Cards: AE, D, MC, V
Children: Y
Pets: N
Handicap Accessible: Y

With a total renovation just completed, Beaver Creek Lodge is now a modern, mountain-chic place to stay: All of its 72 suites (every room is a suite) are decorated with commissioned artwork and come with granite vanities, huge flat-screen TVs, Bose radios, pillow-top mattresses, gas fireplaces, humidifiers, overstuffed leather couches, and separate bedrooms. And all the common areas echo the same themes: scarlet-red ceilings, walnut baseboards, leather chairs, and original modern art. That includes the Grand Bohemian Gallery, which showcases dozens of paintings under a playful chandelier strung with large bronze rock climbers and mountaineers—both heading toward a skylight several stories above. Walking in here is like getting a breath of fresh air: There are no antler chandeliers or hanging pelts in sight.

Park Hyatt Beaver Creek

970-949-1234
beavercreek.hyatt.com
50 W. Thomas Place, Beaver Creek
Price Range: $112–$925
Credit Cards: AE, D, MC, V
Children: Y
Pets: N
Handicap Accessible: Y

A big wedding cake of a slopeside building, the 274-room Hyatt has the best location of any hotel here: It's right in the heart of the village, and you can ski right up to the back

With its grand-lodge architecture, the Ritz-Carlton Bachelor Gulch near Beaver Creek brings together unparalled luxury and a classic mountain feel. Evelyn Spence

terrace. The lobby, with overstuffed leather and plaid furniture, a grand piano, two-story windows, and wildflower prints, is grand and welcoming. The rooms are all spacious and simply accented, with leather headboards on the beds, fluffy comforters in beige and red patterns, marble bath-rooms, and views of the resort, the village, or the ice skating rink. Guests lean back in rustic Adirondack-style chairs around a fire pit in winter, or soak in the hot tubs (surrounded by natural stones and cascading water). There's an in-house spa, Allegria, that has ginger-peach body scrubs and hydration facials on the menu (and a calm Southwestern decor)—and underwent major improvements in 2006. Ask about the Aqua Sanitas ("healing waters"), with a

coed mineral pool, calderiums, tepidariums, and cool rain showers.

✪ Ritz-Carlton Bachelor Gulch on Beaver Creek Mountain

970-748-6200, 800-241-3333
ritzcarlton.com/resorts/bachelor_gulch
0130 Daybreak Ridge, Avon
Price Range: $150–$6,000
Credit Cards: AE, D, MC, V
Children: Y
Pets: Y
Handicap Accessible: Y

If there's a question you have or a service you need, the 237-room Ritz-Carlton in Bachelor Gulch has a person employed just for it: There's a wildlife concierge to help with animal tracking and plant identification. There's a bath butler to draw a soak of wildflowers and lavender flower goat milk soap for you, or for your little one, a fly-fishing bath complete with miniature rod, reel, and magnetic fish. There's a technology butler to solve your computer issues. Need a canine companion? Sign up for the Loan-A-Lab program and get the resident yellow dog for a half-day of hiking and playing. With an architecture that harkens back to the great National Park lodges, this Ritz—and its peaked roofs, three-story great room stone fireplace, leather-topped tables and leather-walled elevators, complimentary après-ski slippers (so you don't have to drink in ski boots), pillow-top mattresses, Vahlrona chocolate turn-down service, and marble baths—gives a whole new meaning to Rocky Mountain luxury. If you feel like skiing, the Bachelor Gulch quad is a few steps from the building (just past the outdoor fire pit). If you feel like spending the afternoon getting pampered, the 21,000-square-foot spa has rock grottos, eucalyptus steam rooms, plunge pools, and services ranging from altitude facials to four-handed massages to peppermint pedicures. If you'd rather just lounge around, order a cocktail and sit back in a leather chair in the fly-fishing library or roast a marshmallow out back—with a stick provided by the Fireside Concierge, of course.

Trappers Cabin

970-845-5788
trapperscabin-beavercreek.com
On top of Beaver Creek Mountain
Price Range: $850–$1,050 per person per night, including breakfast and dinner; $1,100–$4,584 per night for the whole cabin without services
Credit Cards: AE, D, MC, V
Children: Y
Pets: N
Handicap Accessible: N

Trappers Cabin on Beaver Creek Mountain is only reachable by skis or snowcat. Jack Affleck/Beaver Creek Resort

You get the sense (correctly) that some people will stop at nothing to have a luxurious, exclusive experience at Beaver Creek—and Trappers Cabin is the epitome: It's a mountaintop cabin that sleeps 10, comes with a private butler and 24-hour maid service, a personal chef, a champagne welcome, a Jacuzzi, a group snowcat tour, and (obviously) the best ski-in/ski-out location imaginable. The bedrooms, with peeled-log beds, country-chic comforters and curtains, bare pine walls, and bright windows, are spacious; the common area has wooden floors, hanging quilts and furs, a river rock fireplace, overstuffed couches, built-in bookshelves, window seats, an open kitchen, and big log beams. But back to that private chef: He might surprise you with pan-seared foie gras with Grand Marnier french toast, smoked pheasant and corn chowder, watercress salad with bacon and Asian pears, trout crusted with Colorado pine nuts, cinnamon pheasant with peach compote, braised short ribs in chocolate demi-glace, and maple syrup crème brûlée. For an extra charge, they'll send a massage therapist or a personal ski instructor.

FARTHER AFIELD

The Lodge & Spa at Cordillera
970-926-2200
cordillera.rockresorts.com
2205 Cordillera Way, Edwards
Price Range: $199–$1,199
Credit Cards: AE, D, MC, V
Children: Y, 12 and younger free
Pets: N
Handicap Accessible: Y

To get to the Lodge & Spa at Cordillera, you wind your way up and up from US 6 west of Beaver Creek, check in at a security gate, pass 7,000-square-foot mansions perched on hillsides, and keep on climbing until you see the white chateau. Not surprisingly, the Rocky Mountain views from every single one of the 56 rooms here are spectacular, whether you book a standard Lodge Room or a spacious, two-bedroom Cordillera Suite; most also have vaulted ceilings, wood-burning fireplaces, french doors to private patios, and tumbled-stone-and-glass baths. Once you settle in, you have free rein of four (yes, four) different golf courses, a 20,000-square-foot spa and fitness center, indoor and outdoor pools and Jacuzzis, a Nordic center with 17 miles of trails, two tennis courts (with those same spectacular views), a shuttle to either Vail or Beaver Creek, and four different, and excellent, restaurants. Try Mirador for an avant-garde French-Asian fusion and Grouse on the Green, an Irish-style pub, for buffalo burgers, beef hot dogs with waffle fries, and fish and chips.

✪ Minturn Inn
Innkeepers: Tom and Cathy Sullivan
800-646-8876, 970-827-9647
minturninn.com
info@minturninn.com
442 Main St., Minturn
Price Range: $99–$319
Credit Cards: AE, D, MC, V
Children: Y, over 12
Pets: N
Handicap Accessible: N

Just a few miles off the beaten path in the former mining hamlet of Minturn, the quiet and charming Minturn Inn—a combination of a 1915 hewn log home built by a railroad family, and two Eagle River–side lodges behind it—is a laid-back alternative to the scene that is Vail Village, especially if you tend to like intimate, family-run establishments rather than hundred-room multiplexes. Whichever building you're in, you'll find handcrafted log or cast-iron beds, river-rock fireplaces, Egyptian-cotton sheets and towels, antler chandeliers, handmade quilts, bright white ceilings

The Minturn Inn, in a small town just a few miles from Vail, sits right on the Eagle River. Evelyn Spence

criss-crossed with thick beams, and tasteful antiques. Some rooms even have their own two-person Jacuzzis. In the afternoon, pick one of three common areas and enjoy wine and cheese on the house. Breakfasts tend to be deliciously filling, but simple: waffles, berries, eggs and bacon.

Piney River Ranch

970-477-1171
pineyriverranch.com
pineyreservations@yahoo.com
Forest Service Road 700, Vail
Price Range: $55–$175
Children: Y
Pets: Y
Handicap Accessible: N

Piney River isn't a full-service guest ranch —you can stay for a night or for a week, you can just come for a Wild West dinner show, you can roll in and rent a canoe for plashing around Piney Lake—but it might as well be. You can rent a cabin (with full kitchen, loft, floor-to-ceiling wood walls, peeled log furniture, and homey plaid curtains), a cottage (same decor, but no private bath or kitchen), or even a tepee that sleeps up to eight people and costs a total of $55 (it's outfitted with cots, but you have to bring your own bedding). You can fish the Piney River, which runs right through the property; hike straight into the Gore Range, which overlooks it; or paddleboat around gorgeous Piney Lake. And, of course, you can ride horses for a half-hour or a half-day. The Piney River Bar—with checkered tablecloths, Western artwork on the walls, exposed beams—serves home cooking.

Bart & Yeti's serves great home-cooked food—and honors the owner's dogs while they're at it. Evelyn Spence

DINING

Restaurants

VAIL

Bart & Yeti's

970-476-2754
553 E. Lionshead Circle, Vail
Meals Served: L, D
Price Range: $8–$18
Full bar: Y
Credit Cards: AE, D, MC, V
Handicap Accessible: N

Bart, of Bart and Yeti, was a golden retriever and a dog of some renown: He was the father of puppies that went on to belong to Nelson Rockefeller, Henry Kissinger, and Clint Eastwood. Now, the big dog in the house is Woodrow (a spaniel). This home-style American spot feels like a rustic log cabin, decorated with stuffed fowl, wagon wheels, old chairlifts, dozens of patches from clubs and fire departments, and team photos. It's a small space, and almost always packed: People come for the Irish stew (thick with carrots, onions, and beef medallions), the fried chicken (served with mashers and gravy), and the fiery green chili. In summer, there are a few tables on a sunny deck; in winter, there's usually NFL on the telly.

Blu's

970-476-3113
blusrestaurant.com
blusrestaurant@aol.com
193 E. Gore Creek Dr., Vail
Meals Served: B, L, D
Price Range: $8–$26
Full bar: Y
Reservations: N
Credit Cards: AE, D, MC, V
Handicap Accessible: Y

With its (of course) blue awning and road-house script, Blu's might at first look like a diner—and yes, it doles out its share of comfort food. Yes, it serves breakfast (green eggs and ham, banana nut bread french toast, corned beef hash) until 5 PM. And yes, its prices are reasonable (more so at lunch than at dinner). But its exposed brick walls, framed art posters, black and blond chairs, cork wreaths, and a hip little bar belie its true calling: a true restaurant with a wide-ranging menu, a loyal local following, and a laid-back vibe. There's nowhere else in town where you can order meatloaf with onion gravy, your spouse can order steak salad with jicama fries, your friend can order penne arrabiata with wild boar sausage, and your kids can have SpaghettiOs. In summer, ask for a table on the patio so you can watch the beautiful people walk by.

Bully Ranch

970-479-5460
sonnenalp.com/dining/bully.html
20 Vail Rd., Vail
Meals Served: L, D
Price Range: $10–$29
Full bar: Y
Reservations: N
Credit Cards: AE, D, MC, V
Handicap Accessible: Y

One of several restaurants in Sonnenalp (see page 225), casual, cozy, saloon-style Bully Ranch is known, first and foremost, for its mudslides—that dessertlike mix of Kahlúa, Bailey's, vodka, and cream. It's also a good family choice: classy without being prohibitively expensive, with lunch options like fish and chips (with a Fat Tire beer batter), slow-roasted barbecue pork sandwiches, chicken Caesar wraps, and grilled ham and cheese with tomato-cheddar soup. Dinner notches it up a bit, with New York steaks, Colorado lamb shanks, trout, and

Breakfast, lunch, and dinner, the whole family can get comfort food (plain and fancy) at Blu's. Evelyn Spence

Roquefort-encrusted beef burgers. You can't go wrong with chocolate fondue (hazelnut chocolate with piles of fruit and sponge cake) or bourbon sauce—slathered bread pudding. What would go with that? Hmmm . . . perhaps another mudslide.

Chap's Grill and Chophouse
970-479-7014
vailcascade.com
1300 Westhaven Dr., in Vail Cascade Resort & Spa
Meals Served: B, L, D
Price Range: $26–$45
Full bar: Y
Reservations: Y
Credit Cards: AE, D, MC, V
Handicap Accessible: Y

Only in a place like Vail would an executive chef—in this case, Randy Belanger—list his three favorite hobbies as skiing, dirt-biking, and hang gliding. But Belanger hasn't neglected his true calling (which actually started in high school at an exclusive summer camp in Maine): Only in Chap's can you get such good steak and game, whether it's the Colorado trio (lamb, elk, and venison), or a buffalo rib eye served with four sauces (béarnaise, red wine demi-glace, lingonberry reduction, and steak sauce), or Colorado lamb chops. This is where you go for an upscale mountain-town vibe, where the walls are dark wood, the upholstery is horsehair, and the accents are wrought iron. Of course, there's more than meat here, like a house-made tagliatelle with mussels, littlenecks, rock shrimp, and lobster sauce, for one. As with many restaurants in Vail, you can pony up for a multi-course tasting menu (here, it's $75), which could net you a cauliflower soup with peeky toe crab, a scallop and foie-gras sweet-potato hash, and a chateaubriand.

✪ Game Creek
970-479-4275
vail.snow.com
Game Creek Bowl, Vail
Meals Served: D, Sun. brunch in summer
Price Range: $90 for the prix-fixe menu
Full bar: Y
Reservations: Y
Credit Cards: AE, D, MC, V
Handicap Accessible: Y, but notify in advance if possible

Talk about a culinary destination: To get to Game Creek, you have to ride the Eagle Bahn gondola, jump in a snowcat, and trundle down Game Trail cat track—a snowy road you may well have skied that very morning on your way to the blues and blacks of Game Creek Bowl. In fact, you probably skied right past this sprawling, Bavarian-style lodge without realizing it, for Game Creek is tucked into the hillside and couched in exclusivity. It's members-only for lunch, but dinner opens up to the masses—a prix-fixe affair, whether you choose four courses or seven. Chef Thomas Newsted brings together American and French themes into apps like cauliflower velouté with Osetra caviar, chervil, and chives, or almond-crusted venison loin with green apple compote; mains like grilled Colorado lamb chops with lamb cheek cassoulet or white bean pierogi with truffle vichyssoise; and desserts like a port-poached pear with a gorgonzola flan. Everything takes place in dining rooms that cross rustic, mountain-lodge style with European elegance: high-backed leather chairs, Persian carpets, arched doorways, antique skis, artwork depicting wild game. Everything looks out toward Battle Mountain, Beaver Creek Mountain, and the vast valley to the west.

Kelly Liken
970-479-0175
kellyliken.com
12 Vail Rd., Vail
Meals Served: D
Price Range: $29–$38
Full bar: Y

Reservations: Y
Credit Cards: AE, D, MC, V
Handicap Accessible: Y

Rumor has it that Kelly Liken—the 30-year-old chef-owner of this namesake hot spot—wanted to be an astronaut when she went to college in Boulder, Colorado, but lucky for Vail, she switched gears and ended up at the Culinary Institute of America instead. Her pedigree includes stints at Virginia's Inn at Little Washington and Beaver Creek's Splendido, no less. And in Kelly Liken (the restaurant), she's hit a home run: The dining room is metropolitan and modern, with slate floors, glass tile–lined banquettes, modern art, burnished wood tables, and classic motifs of burgundy and cream. The menu changes frequently with the seasons and features local meat and produce, whether it's an elk carpaccio with whole-grain mustard crème, potato-crusted trout filets with caramelized brussels sprout leaves, or duck breast glazed with honey and Colorado wildflowers and served with cornmeal crepes. Liken isn't afraid to play games, like when she serves "dueling maple leaf duck salads": duck confit and brioche toast points versus duck proscuitto lardons with a poached quail egg over petite frisée. Nor does she shy away from the down-home: The sticky bun sundae—baked fresh each morning, topped with vanilla ice cream and caramel sauce—is comfort food at its sweet-toothed best.

Larkspur
970-479-8050
larkspurvail.com
458 Vail Valley Dr., Vail
Meals Served: L, D, Sun. brunch
Price Range: $27–$50
Full bar: Y
Reservations: Y
Credit Cards: AE, MC, V
Handicap Accessible: N

Larkspur's cuisine has been called "contemporary American with a French soul," thanks to chef Thomas Salamunovich's résumé—he's done time in Lyon and at Paris's famed Lucas Carton, Elysée Lenôtre, and Boulangerie Poilâne. And it shows: Starters include a wild rocket salad with foie gras mousse and black truffles, a Hudson Valley duck breast with mascarpone-roasted peaches and brioche french toast, and corn bisque with tobiko caviar. The dessert list is just as long as the entrée list—with everything from a cherry and plum cobbler with buttermilk and cherry swirl ice cream to a swooningly teeth-rotting peanut butter and chocolate cheesecake with Cracker Jack and caramel sauce. The dining room walls, painted in warm pale yellows and decorated with a flock of small, wooden birds, are whimsical; the kitchen is wide open and dynamic; and you can get great (and cheaper, like under $17) food at the bar—Texas chili with hominy and tortillas, wild mushroom pizza with truffle oil, short ribs with Tuscan bread salad. You can also reserve the Chef's Table and get a custom, multi-course meal for $125 a head.

✪ La Tour
970-476-4403
latour-vail.com
122 E. Meadow Dr., Vail
Meals Served: D
Price Range: $21–$34
Full bar: Y
Reservations: Y
Credit Cards: AE, D, MC, V
Handicap Accessible: Y

If you're going to drop names in Vail Valley, drop this one: Paul Ferzacca. La Tour's award-winning chef has headed up this contemporary French dining room since 1998, and it's beloved by locals and visitors alike. No wonder: It's chic but not stuffy—a Provençal bistro with sunny yellow walls, wine glasses that are a rich, clear blue, and a river-rock fireplace to keep the place cozy. Ferzacca, who did time at Spiaggia and the Ritz-Carlton in Chicago under French masters, then headed up Vail's Game Creek Club, has retained his French foundations, but he doesn't shy away from being playful: His grilled wild salmon comes with opal basil coulis and a red Thai curry sauce, the yellowfin tuna poke is accompanied by red and black tobiko (flying fish eggs), and the maple and buttermilk pudding cake is matched by a black pepper vanilla ice cream. Of course, the standards are all here, too: escargots in sauce persillée with vermouth and cream, cheese fondue, lobster bisque, Dover sole meunière, veal sweetbreads with haricots verts and caper brown butter sauce, and a Vahlrona chocolate and hazelnut terrine. On Sundays in summer, you can sit out front, drink Bloodies, and watch the farmer's market crowd go by.

Osaki's Sushi

970-476 0977
100 E. Meadow Dr., Vail
Meals Served: D
Price Range: Sushi and sashimi $5–$25,
     entrées and combos $10–$45
Full bar: N
Reservations: Y
Credit Cards: MC, V
Handicap Accessible: Y

This tiny, eight-table restaurant with a polished blond-wood sushi bar is tucked in among hotel rooms, condos, and construction, but it's worth seeking out: The chef, who comes from a few generations of sushi makers, honed his skills at Matsuhisa Aspen. Fish is flown in fresh every day, the rice—a short-grain Tamanishiki—comes straight from Japan, and the soy sauce is made in-house for a rich, earthy flavor. Along with sushi standards, including sea urchin, unagi, smelt egg, and blue fin tuna,

there's a good dinner menu: broiled black cod with miso, Kobe beef sashimi, king crab tempura, teriyakis, and spicy tuna tataki.

Pepi's Restaurant

970-476-4671
pepis.com
info@pepis.com
231 E. Gore Creek Dr., Vail
Meals Served: L, D
Price Range: $31–$50
Full bar: Y
Reservations: Y
Credit Cards: AE, D, MC, V
Handicap Accessible: Y

It's hard to walk by Pepi's and not want to sit down and eat: There's the extra-Bavarian exterior, the orange umbrellas, the wildflowers rimming the deck, and the crowds (it's popular both for dinner and for après drinks). The inside is no less charmingly Austrian—the shelves are stacked with copper pots, and the walls are hung with portraits of old-school mountain men. Pepi Gramshammer and his wife, Sheika, have been running the restaurant and the attached (equally Bavarian) hotel, Gasthof Gramshammer (see page 224), for 40 years, and they've stuck to what they know. In the main dining room, that's Graubundner Teller (air-dried meat and gruyère), Tafelspitz Innsbruck (boiled beef brisket with apple horseradish and lingonberries), and sauerbraten braised in burgundy. And in the Antlers Room, where wild game is the star, you can order the Wilddieb Platter—a selection of braised quail, buffalo, wild boar, elk, and venison—or stick to one species (the caribou cutlet with wild boletus mushroom sauce is especially tasty).

Sapphire Restaurant and Oyster Bar

970-476-2828
sapphirerestaurant.com
223 Gore Creek Dr., Vail

Pepi's has been a Vail institution for 40 years and is owned by a former Austrian ski racer. Evelyn Spence

Meals Served: L, D
Price Range: Lunch $8–$13, dinner
  $18–$34
Full bar: Y
Reservations: Y
Credit Cards: AE, D, MC, V
Handicap Accessible: Y

Think you can't have a raw bar a thousand miles from the nearest ocean? Think again—Sapphire not only has the best (and most) oysters and crack-and-peel shrimp this side of the Divide, but also has the sea-themed decor to match: fish artwork, metal cutouts of fish, and a great wraparound deck above Gore Creek. If you don't trust anything on the half-shell, the rest of the menu seamlessly blends French with Asian with Southwestern—Prince Edward Island mussels with green Thai curry, chicken breast baked with fontina cream and complemented by a sweet fried banana, and poblano- and pistachio-crusted New York steak with chipotle mashed potatoes. True to form, all the seafood here is good, from yellowfin to trout to rock shrimp.

✪ Sweet Basil

970-476-0125
sweetbasil-vail.com
info@sweetbasil-vail.com
193 E. Gore Creek Dr., Vail
Meals Served: L, D, brunch Sat. and Sun.
Price Range: Lunch $12–$17, dinner
  $25–$39
Full bar: Y
Reservations: Y
Credit Cards: AE, D, MC, V
Handicap Accessible: Y

Someone in a recent edition of Zagat had one word for this restaurant: "supernova." Sleek and modern, with blond-wood chairs, tiny pendant light fixtures, contemporary paintings, and tables overlooking Gore Creek, Sweet Basil has an outsized reputation here—and, in fact, has since it opened in 1977, a couple chefs and remodels ago. But it's not without basis: The food, which fuses the Asian with the Mediterranean, is beautifully presented and made from fresh local ingredients—so the menu changes often. What doesn't change? Current kitchen master Bruce Yim's creative and rich combinations. Take the housemade granola, served on weekend mornings: It comes with grilled watermelon. Starters include calamari stuffed with sausage and golden tomato gazpacho with hot coriander oil. And dinner entrées? Well, they're the prototypical works of art—Hawaiian snapper with shaved radish and saffron vanilla butter, Colorado lamb with chick-pea fries and artichoke and fennel salad. You may hear people raving about the hot sticky toffee pudding cake with Myer's rum sauce, which has been on the menu in one form or another since the beginning. Believe the hype (or be a rebel and opt for mascarpone cheese cannoli).

The Wildflower

970-476-5011
lodgeatvail.rockresorts.com/info/din
   .wildflower.asp
174 E. Gore Creek Dr., Vail
Meals Served: L, D, Sun. brunch
Price Range: $25–$40
Full bar: Y
Reservations: Y
Credit Cards: AE, D, MC, V
Handicap Accessible: Y

The enchanting Wildflower takes its name to heart: In summer, the path leading to the restaurant on the east side is spilling over with flowers and plants, and the dining room—part of which is an airy gazebo—looks down on the garden. Even when the snow covers the colors in the dead of winter, the place is still cheery and light: The interior is done up in mint greens, light pinks, and yellows, with floral-patterned booth seats and enormous arrangements of real blooms. Every diner starts off the meal with a complimentary glass of champagne and an amuse bouche that changes nightly with the whim of the chef, Englishman Steven Topple. Many of the dishes use herbs and veggies grown right outside the window—pork with sweet potato puree and glazed sugar snap peas, braised Kobe short rib with tarragon polenta, an ostrich breast soaked in cabernet and served with mustard spaetzle and summer squash. And many are made rich not by butter and cream and salt, but by reduced stock, making for a lighter eating experience. Come Sunday, brunch is a three-crepe affair: While you sip bubbly, choose two savory and one sweet option, from cream cheese and chive to smoked lobster to blackberry and apple.

BEAVER CREEK

Foxnut

970-845-0700
bcfoxnut.com
phil@bcfoxnut.com
122 The Plaza, Beaver Creek
Meals Served: L, D
Price Range: Sushi and sashimi $6–$16,
   entrées $9–$21
Full bar: Y
Reservations: Y
Credit Cards: AE, MC, V
Handicap Accessible: Y

Foxnut, the newest sushi restaurant in the valley, is hip, kitschy, and bright: The clusters of papery cutouts over the light fixtures are magenta and lime green, the bench seating is lime green, the tables are shiny and silver, the ceiling is magenta, the chairs are upholstered in flowers, and the walls are hung with Japanese posters and advertisements. But the loudness is somehow endearing, and it does nothing to take away from the great sushi: the nigiri and sashimi are practically off-the-boat fresh and the rolls are creative (the Butterfly Roll comes with tuna, eel, smelt, cucumber, avocado, banana kabayaki, and sesame seeds, and Kenny's Roll is a combo of albacore, yama gobo, daikon, smelt, and soy paper). If you'd rather skip raw fish, try the Shanghai Meatloaf: It's a pork and beef mix, served with mashed potatoes and sambal ketchup. Or go with some standards (udon noodle bowls, pad Thai, miso black cod, or cashew chicken).

Grouse Mountain Grill

970-949-0600
grousemountaingrill.com
info@grousemountaingrill.com
Pines Lodge, 1141 Scott Hill Rd., Beaver
    Creek
Meals Served: B, L, D
Price Range: Lunch $10–$18, dinner
    $31–$43
Full bar: Y
Reservations: Y
Credit Cards: AE, MC, V
Handicap Accessible: Y

Grouse Mountain is a BC favorite, and no wonder: Almost everything in the kitchen is either artisan (fontina cheese from Italy, bacon from Wisconsin, lamb from Colorado) or made in-house—and that includes house-whirled condiments, house-cured prosciutto, and house-churned cream. The dining room is intimate (three-way fireplace, green carpeting, fresh flowers, overstuffed chairs) and lively (it's usually packed, and there's live jazz music almost every night). It's European in bent without being too stuffy. Unlike many of the upper-crust restaurants in the valley, it serves three square meals a day. Start your morning with a lobster and mascarpone omelet or a buttermilk waffle with apple cinnamon compote, pop in for a lunch of duck enchiladas or Colorado heirloom tomatoes with balsamic honey, or a long, elegant dinner—chef Rick Kangas prepares originals like pretzel-crusted pork chops with orange mustard sauce, Yukon River salmon with crab bread pudding, and duckling with smoked blackberry jus. If you have room, make sure to order the plate of artisan cheeses accompanied by brioche and fig jam.

✪ Mirabelle

970-949-7728
mirabelle1.com
info@mirabelle1.com
55 Village Rd., Beaver Creek
Meals Served: D
Price Range: $25–$40
Full bar: Y
Reservations: Y
Credit Cards: AE, MC, V
Handicap Accessible: Y

Most of the top restaurants in the Vail/Beaver Creek area are either in hotels, on plazas, or next to rental shops and ticket windows—which makes Mirabelle, a former family farmhouse (and one of the first buildings in Beaver Creek), a very special experience. It still feels like a turn-of-the-20th century Victorian home: The entrance is under a covered porch that's decorated with garlands and white lights; the dining area is divided into smaller rooms, each differently decorated, giving it great intimacy; and the vibe is classically understated. Chef Daniel Joly was born and trained in Belgium—in fact, he started cooking at 14 and never looked back, and he was named the best young chef in Belgium in 1988. That influence shows in a cuisine that's best classified as European with a French bent—Yukon gold potato vichyssoise, roasted lamb loin with a vegetable tartlet and garden thyme jus, roasted duck breast with spice caramel and quince compote, a fromage blanc meringue with a red fruit marmalade gâteau.

Rocks Modern Grill

970-845-1730
rocksmoderngrill.com
26 Avondale Lane, Beaver Creek
Meals Served: B, L, D
Price Range: $10–$29
Full bar: Y
Reservations: Y
Credit Cards: AE, D, MC, V
Handicap Accessible: Y

Part of the refurbishment of Beaver Creek Lodge (see page 227) was the opening of this hip, cosmopolitan bar and grill, with a hammered copper entryway, zebra-print benches, flat-screen TVs, and red motifs (in napkins, lighting, and patio umbrellas). The centerpiece of the restaurant is the bar, which serves watermelon, peach, and espresso martinis along with $2 Pabst Blue Ribbons (on S.I.N., or Service Industry Night) and $2 Tommyknocker brews (on Tommy Tuesdays). The salads and sandwiches are big—the rotisserie chicken Cobb comes with lots of avocado, bacon, egg, blue cheese, and creamy herb dressing, and the grilled portobello burger is piled with roasted red peppers and Haystack Mountain chèvre. There's always a decent nightly special, too, from lavender honey–glazed Sonoma duck to a rack of pork brined in allspice. Breakfasts are tried-and-true favorites: granola parfaits, buttermilk pancakes, Denver omelets, steak and eggs.

Splendido

970-845-8808
splendidorestaurant.com
17 Chateau Lane, Beaver Creek
Meals Served: D
Price Range: $29–$48
Full bar: Y
Reservations: Y
Credit Cards: AE, D, MC, V
Handicap Accessible: Y

At most ski-town restaurants, no matter how expensive the menu, you can walk in wearing Sorels, jeans, and a fleece—and fit right in. Splendido is one of the few places where that might not fly: The dining room is Old World–opulent, with warm yellow and orange walls, Chagall prints, high-backed European chairs, rich curtains, an open kitchen, and nightly piano music by local Bob Finnie (who takes requests). And it's housed in no less than a luxe residence club called The Chateau. Here's where to get your caviar service (with corn blini and crème fraîche), your Maine lobster (with cognac herb sauce), your elk loin (with Anson Mills white grits and huckleberry jus), and your Valrhona chocolate fudge soufflé (with Grand Marnier crème anglaise). Chef David Walford first moved to Vail in the 1970s as a ski bum, then worked in Napa, St. Helena, at La Côte d'Or in Saulieu, France, and at Masa's in San Francisco before moving back to the Colorado mountains. The wine list is award-winning and mind-blowing, whether you want to drop $30—or $1,500.

FARTHER AFIELD

The Gashouse

970-926-3613
34185 US 6, Edwards
Meals Served: L, D
Price Range: $10–$25
Full bar: Y
Reservations: Y
Credit Cards: AE, MC, V
Handicap Accessible: Y

This rustic log cabin was actually the first building, a gas station, in Edwards (which, you'll see, is growing faster and faster)—and from the moment you step through the swinging saloon-style doors, you step into

The Gashouse in Edwards was once a gas station, and now serves meat, seafood, and cheap margaritas.
Evelyn Spence

another era. There are old license plates from around the country lining the rough-hewn interior walls, dozens of elk and deer and trout and water buffalo trophies hanging above, tables crowded together, and a dark and pleasantly divey bar with names etched into the wood. There's a huge selection of meat (buffalo rib eye, quail, boar sausage, elk tenderloin, filet mignon, porterhouse) and seafood (soft-shell crabs, lobster tails, baked oysters, mahi, trout, littleneck clams, king crab). At happy hour, the margaritas are only two bucks apiece, and the apps list—teriyaki "tidbits," Rocky Mountain oysters, and onion rings—is totally unpretentious. If you want a laid-back lunch or a casual dinner out, this locals' favorite is a great option.

Juniper Restaurant

970-926-7001
juniperrestaurant.com
dine@juniperrestaurant.com
970 Main St., Edwards
Meals Served: D
Price Range: $26–$32

Full bar: Y
Reservations: Y
Credit Cards: AE, D, MC, V
Handicap Accessible: Y

If you feel the need to get out of Vail or Beaver Creek for a night, this gem in Edwards—just a few miles west of Avon—is worth a special trip: Juniper has served wonderful contemporary American cuisine to a mostly local crowd since it opened in 2002. Credit chef Mike Irwin, who worked at Vail's Larkspur and Sweet Basil before moving downriver. He pairs seared foie gras with funnel cake, strawberries Foster, and chantilly cream; glazes Colorado lamb with peaches and adds a curried potato samosa; and combines lemon pea ravioli with carrot ginger sauce. In summer, they open up a big metal garage door out back and set up the best seats in the house on a small deck looking over the Eagle River in the shade of evergreen trees. The interior is slightly industrial (black corrugated metal ceilings, tiny track lights) and slightly sunny (pale golden walls, a bright glassed-in kitchen).

Minturn Country Club
970-827-4114
131 Main St., Minturn
Meals Served: D
Price Range: $15–$35
Full bar: Y
Reservations: Y
Credit Cards: MC, V
Handicap Accessible: Y

The motto of this Minturn mainstay: "The only thing missing is the golf course." Indeed, there's no pool, no tennis courts, no putting greens—only a butcher's case full of protein, a couple 1,000-degree fires, and your own devices. Yes, here at Minturn CC, you grill your own meal, whether it's a Kobe beef steak or a breast of chicken. If you're not sure whether to add lemon pepper, garlic powder, or teriyaki sauce, the staff is on hand to give advice—but it's up to you to cook it right. Of course, there's more than just meat here: start out with jalapeño poppers, smoked trout, or stuffed mushrooms, and end with a Minturn Tater (a lump of cookies and cream ice cream rolled in cocoa and topped with whipped cream, almond slivers, and chocolate sauce). If you're a pyro, you can roast dessert, too: Ask for s'mores fixins and char sugar to your heart's content.

✪ Minturn Saloon
970-827-5954
minturnsaloon.com
146 Main St., Minturn

Meals Served: D
Price Range: $8–$29
Full bar: Y
Reservations: N
Credit Cards: AE, D, MC, V
Handicap Accessible: Y

The Minturn Mile (see page 252) is a back-country ski run from the top of Vail Ski Resort down into Minturn, ending up right here—the most historic restaurant and bar in the valley (it was built in 1901, and has seen a century of drinking and gambling and, according to the history on its Web site, "additional uses"). The back bar in the dining room area was originally built in Missouri during the 1830s; it was moved here from its prior home in Leadville. At one point, the Minturn was literally called "The Saloon Across the Street from the Eagle River Hotel." It has a slightly abandoned, ghost town–like look from the exterior (at least when it's too cold for people to drink on the patio), but don't let that turn you away. The inside is cluttered with pennants, posters, hats, trophies (sports and wildlife alike), vintage ski signs, and historical photos, and the fireplace crackles all winter long. Though the vibe is Old West, the food is all Mexican: chili con queso, arroz con pollo, charbroiled quail, combo fajitas. And the tequila (and therefore, margarita) menu is extensive—everything from Cuervo and Sauza to Corazón Reposado and Don Eduardo Añejo.

Food Purveyors

Bakeries
Avon Bakery & Deli (970-949-3354, 0025 Hurd Lane, Avon) The artisan breads here—ciabatta, olive and rosemary, potato dill, rye—are all made with organic flour, and sandwiches are packed full and wonderful: chicken salad made with walnuts, golden raisins, and thyme; smoked bratwurst with sauerkraut and grainy mustard; eggplant parmesan with tomato basin sauce. The egg and cheese breakfast sandwiches come on foccacia, and the breakfast burritos are stuffed with fiery chorizo.

Bonjour Bakery (970-926-5539, 97 Main St., Edwards) Fresh-out-the-oven bread is Bonjour's claim to fame, but you can also get coffee drinks, homemade pastries, and sandwiches here.

Coffee Shops

Covered Bridge Coffee (970-479-2883, next to covered bridge in Vail) Tucked below Bridge Street, this joe joint has a big pastry case full of muffins, scones, and bagels; breakfast burritos with eggs, cheese, sausage, and veggies; deli sandwiches and wraps; and a long smoothie menu.

Crescendo (970-845-5577, Beaver Creek Plaza) Get a coffee drink, a snack, or a scoop of ice cream at this walk-up window.

Loaded Joe's Coffeehouse Lounge (970-748-1480, loadedjoes.com, Benchmark Shopping Center, Avon) A hip combination of coffee shop, dance floor, Internet café, and lounge, Loaded Joe's has events almost every night of the week: movie nights, trivia nights, karaoke nights, DJs, and battles of the bands.

Vail Coffee Company (970-476-1287, 470 E. Lionshead Circle, Vail) In one corner of a T-shirt/ski shop, this counter sells ice cream, coffee, cookies, croissants, sodas, and bagel sandwiches.

Delis

Blizzard's Mountain Deli (970-476-1755, 304 Hanson Ranch Rd., Vail) This brightly colored, dog-friendly spot has sandwiches like the Gondola (ham, turkey, salami, cheddar, provolone) and the Mediterranean Turkey Melt (with feta, roasted red peppers, and olive tapenade). They also serve big salads, soups—and pancakes for breakfast.

Flying Burrito (970-479-6356, 520 E. Lionshead Circle, Vail) Though it's not a deli per se, Flying Burrito is a good place for a quick bite—wraps, salads, burrito bowls, and soft tacos filled with everything from potatoes to tofu to chicken.

Joe's Famous Deli (970-4790-7580, 288 Bridge St., Vail) This downstairs deli and ice-cream counter has the biggest breakfast-sandwich menu in town—whether you want to start the day with Canadian bacon, smoked Norwegian salmon, portobello mushrooms, or corned beef.

Les Delices de France (970-476-1044, 531 Lionshead Mall, Vail) This small, charming French bakery and lunch spot has been here since 1984, with a mix of the European (pâté plates, quiches, baked brie) and the standard American (omelets, sandwiches).

The Market (970-479-8050, 458 Vail Valley Dr., Vail) The brains behind Larkspur (see page 236 run this boutique deli, with artisan-bread sandwiches (oil-cured yellowfin tuna on olive batard), house-made soups (Yukon gold potato and keel soup), big salads, rotisserie chicken and duck, chèvres, and specialty coffees.

Rocks on the Run (970-845-1730, 16 Avondale Lane, Beaver Creek) A small sidewalk-side deli and snack shop with breakfast wraps (egg, green chili, and cheddar), cold and hot sandwiches, and sweets (scones, cookies, candy bars, ice-cream bars).

Farmer's Markets

Edwards Farmer's Market (rockymountainmarkets.com/edwards/index.html, Edwards) A Saturday morning collection of fresh bread, local veggies and fruit, Colorado beef and lamb, Alaskan seafood, and organic dog treats at Edwards Corner.

Minturn Market (downtown Minturn, Exit 171 off I-70, Minturn) Multiple entertainment tents (featuring things like Accordion Man), fresh fruit and flowers, local produce, crafts, and a cool small-town vibe—every Saturday in summer.

Vail Farmer's Market (vailfarmersmarket.com, on Meadow Dr., Vail) This Sunday affair is probably the biggest you'll find in this book—with crepe carts, baked goods, handmade baskets, used books, bronze sculptures, dried pastas, fresh Colorado peaches, local meat and produce, street food, pony rides, reindeer rides, and live music.

Frozen Desserts

Marble Slab Creamery (970-479-1705, 242 E. Meadow Dr., Vail) Get standard conefuls of banana rum, cinnamon, chocolate amaretto, birthday cake, honey, pumpkin, or bubble gum ice cream—or mix in everything from Ding Dongs to gummy bears to granola.

Rocky Mountain Chocolate Factory (970-476-7623, 304 Bridge St., Vail) Caramel apples, truffles, chocolates, hot cocoa, coffee—and 25 flavors of ice cream.

The Vail Farmer's Market takes place Sundays during the warmer months. Evelyn Spence

Groceries

City Market (970-276-1017, 2109 Frontage Road, Vail; 970-949-5409, 260 Beaver Creek Place, Avon)

Crossroads Market (970-476-8222, crossroadsmarketvailvillage.com, Crossroads Center, Vail) With a deli/café that sells soups, salads, sandwiches, and takeout, and a grocery that stocks all the basics, Crossroads will be around for part of 2007 before moving to a space at One Willow Bridge Road, across the street, as part of the base village reconstruction.

Freshies Natural Foods (970-926-8622, 34500 US 6, Unit B6, Edwards)

The General Store (970-476-3223, 610 W. Lionshead Circle, Vail)

Safeway (970-476-3561, 2131 N. Frontage Rd., Vail)

Shop & Hop Food Stores (970-748-9660, 150 Beaver Creek Rd., Avon)

NIGHTLIFE

The Club (970-479-0556, theclubvail.com, 304 Bridge St., Vail) The motto of this self-proclaimed world's greatest ski bar? "If you don't come to party, don't f**king come." There's live music, debauchery, body shots, dancing, scantily clad women, wasted lifties, and drink specials seven nights a week.

Coyote Café (970-949-5001, coyotecafe.net, 210 The Plaza at Beaver Creek) Neon lights, townie bikes and kayaks above the bar, exposed brick walls, big screen TVs, rows of ski-patrol photos, and a cheesy ski mural—the Coyote is where locals and lifties come for a marg (from a lengthy list), a beer, or a heaping plate of nachos.

8150 (970-479-0607, club8150.com, 143 E. Meadow Dr., Vail) For a night of dancing to resident and visiting DJs under colored lights, 8150—named after the club's elevation—is your best bet, especially if you want a spring-loaded dance floor. They also have occasional tribute bands (AC/DC, Zeppelin) and after-parties for Vail events.

Garfinkel's (970-476-3789, garfsvail.com, 536 E. Lionshead Circle, Vail) With an enormous deck right over the Eagle Bahn gondola building and right across from the Bwana run, Garf's is consistently named "Best Patio" in town polls. There are wooden ski racks for leaning your gear, heat lamps, and long tables outside. Inside you'll find old license plates; signed photos of Bob Hope, Buddy Hackett, and Frank Sinatra; and a spinning "shot wheel." Check for nightly après specials, especially in winter ($5 wing baskets, buck-fifty drafts).

Red Lion (970-476-7676, theredlion.com, 304 Bridge St., Vail) Local—and super popular—musician Phil Long plays at the Lion on a regular basis, and whether he's playing or not, the place gets pretty rowdy with tourists and locals alike. This is Vail's first free-standing restaurant (built in 1962, an eternity ago around here), and it still serves food—spinach artichoke dip, chicken quesadillas, spaghetti and sausage, blue cheese burgers—and local microbrews.

Sandbar Sports Grill (970-476-4314, sandbarvail.com, 2161 N. Frontage Rd., West Vail) Yes, the Sandbar is a sports bar, with 28 TVs (nine of them plasma big-screen), booth

With a slopeside view, the patio at Garfinkel's is always voted as among Vail's best. Evelyn Spence

seats, and neon signs, but it's a sports bar that serves food (burgers and fries and other late-night staples) until 1:30 AM. Don't miss White Trash Wednesday, when you can get 24-ounce PBRs for $3 and huge buckets of fried chicken and ribs.

The Tap Room/Sanctuary (970-479-0500, taproomvail.com, 333 Bridge St., Vail) This split-personality nightspot is divided into two atmospheres, which in turn are divided into even more spaces, each with a vibe of its own: The Sanctuary is sleek and chic, with a fireside lounge, a couple of VIP suites, and a penthouse dance floor. The Tap Room is more rustic and more raucous—Mondays, the Coors pints are two bucks; Tuesdays, you can get a burger and a beer for five bucks; and on Thursdays, "Strip Night," a NY steak and a pint go for $15.

CULTURE

Cinema
Capitol Theater (1140 Capitol St., Eagle) A four-screen theater, Capitol is down in Eagle, but might be worth a trip if there's an indie film you just have to see.

Cascade Village Theatre (970-476-5661, vailmovies.com, 1310 Westhaven Dr., Vail)

Crossroads Cinema (970-476-5661, vailmovies.com, 141 E. Meadow Dr., Vail)

Lakeside Cinema (970-748-4060, avonrec.org, 400 Benchmark Rd., Avon) In summer, watch free outdoor movies (classics and new releases both) on the grass of Nottingham Park. Bring the kids early for paddle boating and scavenger hunts.

Riverwalk Theater (970-476-5661, vailmovies.com, 34253 US 6, Edwards)

Museums
Betty Ford Alpine Gardens (970-476-0103, bettyfordalpinegardens.org, 183 Gore Creek Dr., Vail) At 8,200 feet, this is the world's highest botanic garden—with areas like the International Alpine Crevice Garden (inspired by those in the Czech Republic), Alpine Pools (surrounded by sedges, rushes, and willows), the Water Garden (with waterfalls, irises, marigolds, and water lilies), and a children's garden.

Colorado Ski Museum (970-476-1876, skimuseum.net, 231 S. Frontage Rd., Vail) Learn about the history of snowboarding and skiing, check out exhibits on the evolution of gear, and gawk at clothes worn by Olympians Nelson Carmichael and Billy Kidd.

Theaters and Other Miscellaneous Venues
Gerald R. Ford Amphitheater (888-920-2787, vvf.org, 530 S. Frontage Rd. E., Vail) A big outdoor venue (1,200 guests under cover, and another 1,300 on the hillside above), the Gerald Ford plays host to Australian roots rock, big band swing, hip-hop, Jamaican jazz, and folk music, all in view of Gore Creek and the Gore Range.

Gore Range Natural Science School (970-827-9725, gorerange.org, 82 E. Beaver Creek Blvd., Suite 202, Avon) Gore Range has outdoor and naturalist programs for kids and adults alike—weekend-long orienteering, edible plants, botanical illustration, and mushroom hunting seminars; kids' overnights in backcountry huts; parent-child classes like "Claws and Paws" and "Busy Beavers"; and winter "SKE-cology" (environmental awareness in combination with Vail ski schools).

Vail Symposium (970-476-0954, vailsymposium.org, P.O. 3038, Vail) For 35 years, this grassroots group has been organizing writing workshops, economics forums, political speakers, tours of neighboring historic towns, geology seminars, origami exhibits—anything and everything to enrich and educate the Vail community.

Vilar Center for the Arts (800-920-2787, vilarcenter.org, Avondale Lane, Beaver Creek) Ballet, stand-up comedy, classic rock, flamenco guitar—if there's a major performer coming to Beaver Creek, he'll come to Vilar, a 530-person semicircular theater tucked below BC's main plaza.

Kids' Stuff
Adventure Ridge (970-476-9090, vail.snow.com) Located at the top of the Eagle Bahn gondola, Adventure Ridge has tubing, snow-biking, snowmobiling on kid-size machines, orienteering, and laser tag in winter—and volleyball, horseshoes, trampolines, sandboxes, Frisbee golf, and mountain biking in summer.

The Art Factory (970-926-7444, theartfactory.biz, 41 Silver St., Edwards) Sign up for paper-, kite-, mask- and piñata-making classes—or learn how to make jewelry, tie-dye, or work with mosaic tiles.

Beaver Creek Children's Museum (970-845-9090, Beaver Creek) Put on a play at the J.B. Tucker Showman's Theater, learn about building and construction at Professor Quackenbush's Workshop, or get in touch with your inner Einstein at Banana Jones's Jungle Science Lab. Open in summer only.

Beaver Creek Children's Theatre (970-926-5855, bluecreek.com, Beaver Creek) On-stage interpretations of fairy tales, poems, and folk tales from around the world like "The Green Hobgoblin and "The Amazing Adventures of Robin Hood."

Beaver Creek Climbing Wall (970-845-7531, Beaver Creek) Scale this 25-foot-high out-door wall on four different routes.

Beaver Creek Summer Rodeo Series (beavercreek.snow.com) Every Thursday in June, catch team roping, mutton busting, bull riding, and barrel racing, take a pony ride, visit the petting zoo, or grab a barbecue dinner.

Eagle County Skate Park (53B Eagle Rd., Avon) A 29,000-square-foot spread of stairs, railings, pools, and ramps, this new park in Edwards is usually packed.

Imagination Station (970-479-2292, vailrec.com, in the Lionshead Parking Structure) A small children's museum for ages 2–12, Imagination Station has activities in both the arts and the sciences—including a giant kaleidoscope and a sound exhibit.

Lionshead/Beaver Creek Miniature Golf (970-476-1121 in Vail; 970-845-7531, located at the base of the Centennial Express lift in Beaver Creek) Both of these 18-hole courses are in beautiful settings—and they're as sculpted as some of the big boys.

Vail Nature Center (970-479-2291, vailrec.com, 841 Vail Valley Dr., Vail) A small white farmhouse on Gore Creek, the Nature Center organizes wildflower walks, stargazing and s'mores-making nights, beaver pond tours, bird walks, and day camps. There are also several good interactive displays inside.

RECREATION: WINTER AND SPRING

Alpine Skiing and Snowboarding

Vail
vail.snow.com

Overview: Let's dispense with the numbers first. Vail is the biggest ski resort in the United States, and second only to Whistler Blackcomb in all of North America—that's 5,289 acres, seven huge bowls, four terrain parks, and 33 lifts. Those lifts can carry 53,381 skiers uphill an *hour*. It's 7 miles wide. It's so sprawl-ing, in fact, that you can ski here for a week and still feel like there are whole swaths you missed. The best way to

Vail: The 4-1-1

Acres: 5,289
Summit elevation: 11,570 feet
Vertical drop: 3,450 feet
Annual snowfall: 348 inches
Percent advanced/expert terrain: 53
Percent intermediate terrain: 29
Percent beginner terrain: 18
Lifts: 33

Going deep into a dose of Vail's cold smoke. Jack Affleck/Vail Resorts

conceive of it? Think of Vail as three areas: The Front Side (everything facing I-70), the Back Bowls (an incomprehensibly huge set of drainages on the back side), and Blue Sky Basin (the newest runs on the mountain, which are beyond the Back Bowls). Within each, there's everything from steep powder shots to sustained bump runs to endless, roller-coaster cruisers. And to get from one to the other, there are cat tracks that are miles long—tough on boarders trying to get from one end of the mountain to the other. Your best strategy? Pick an area and spend a day exploring it, without folding to the temptation of trying to see—and ski—the whole thing.

Must-ski: Where to begin? Front Side first: On looker's left, the old-school Highline lift has long bump runs, as does Northwoods (try Prima for moguls, Prima Cornice for steeps). From Mid-Vail, do laps on Mountaintop Express—Expresso and Cappuccino are both short, intermediate cruisers that won't induce too much leg burn. Some people spend an entire morning in Game Creek Bowl, with its mix of blacks and blues. For big Giant Slalom turns and sustained vert, take Born Free or Bwana from the top of the gondola all the way down to Lionshead.

The Back Bowls are probably what made Vail famous, and no wonder: There are 3,000-plus acres of skiing here, in bowls that range from mellow to steeper (though there's isn't a lot of what you'd call extreme here). On a powder day, there's nothing quite like finding a pristine line—and on those days, it doesn't matter whether you're in Sun Up, Sun Down, China, Outer Mongolia, or Tea Cup Bowl. Just remember: They're all quite affected by exposure and can get sun-baked, so you might have to experiment with your aspect.

Finally, there's Blue Sky Basin—there are several lifts way back here, but it's so far from the base area that it almost feels like backcountry. Come here for gladed skiing through Iron Mask, Little Ollie, and the Pete's and Earl's Bowl areas—or jump the cornice on Lover's Leap.

Grub: There's no shortage of options, and no matter where you're skiing, food and drink aren't far away. For quicker bites, ridgetop **Two Elk** (made famous by ELF eco-terrorists during its construction) is a huge timber lodge with salad and soup bar, burgers, pizzas, wraps, and sweets. Cozy and often-crowded **Buffalo's** has chili in bread bowls, coffees, and sandwiches. At the top of the gondola, **Eagle's Nest** has a huge cafeteria with pretty much any lunch option you can think of. If you're out in Blue Sky Basin, **Belle's Camp**, a rough-hewn, mining-style building, has sandwiches, candy bars, hot drinks, and soda—and if you bring your own meat, you can use the outdoor grills. The **Mid-Vail** complex has three different restaurants serving everything from barbecue to baked potatoes to bagels. If you'd rather sit for a full-service lunch, try **Blue Moon** in Eagle's Nest—a publike spot with salads, sandwiches, and beer.

Beaver Creek
beavercreek.snow.com

Overview: Though Beaver Creek is sometimes overshadowed by its upmountain sister, Vail, it's a wonderful resort in its own right. In fact, some say the experience is even better here—smaller crowds, a more intimate and more manageable mountain (though it's all relative, because Beaver Creek is anything but small, with 16 lifts and 1,805 acres), and steeper sustained runs. Some Front Rangers make it a habit of driving right past Vail and skiing here all winter. The terrain is varied, with

Beaver Creek: The 4-1-1
Acres: 1,805
Summit elevation: 11,440 feet
Vertical drop: 4,040 feet
Annual snowfall: 310 inches
Percent advanced/expert terrain: 34
Percent intermediate terrain: 35
Percent beginner terrain: 31
Lifts: 16

plenty of well-manicured top-to-bottom highways, winding beginner tracks, and quad-torching double-blacks. Sure, the Beav sometimes has a rep as a super-upscale resort, but don't let that dissuade you. The skiing here is, in a word, awesome.

Must-ski: For bragging rights, you have to try the Birds of Prey (sometimes called Golden Eagle)—it's the site of an annual World Cup race, with fallaway turns, 40-degree sections, and huge rollers. In fact, you'll earn bragging rights for tackling any run off the Birds of Prey lift: Peregrine and Goshawk are steep bump runs that go and go and go. Grouse Mountain has a nice mix of moguls (Ruffed Grouse), glades (Royal Elk), and groomers (Raven Ridge), and Larkspur has the same mix—only at lower angles. Some people like going over to quiet, secluded Rose Bowl for a couple laps on a powder day; many of the runs meander through the woods before dropping down for dozens of steep turns. If you're in the mood for speed, both Centennial and Latigo are cured to perfection—hit them in the morning before they get scraped up.

Grub: Most people meet up at one or two places: The grand and centrally located **Spruce Saddle,** with a food court of chili, burgers, stews, salads, pizzas, and huge cookies and brownies, or **Red Tail Camp**, a smaller cabin at the base of the Birds of Prey terrain. Come here for smoked barbecue, brisket, and chicken sandwiches cooked on an outdoor grill—and great deck seating in sunny weather. To splurge, reserve a spot at **Beano's Cabin** for lunch: This hand-hewn building, nestled next to the runs on Larkspur, serves multi-course meals of Colorado cuisine.

Cross-Country Skiing and Snowshoeing

Cordillera (866-650-7625, cordillera.rockresorts.com, 2205 Cordillera Way, Edwards) This smallish area (11 kilometers of ski trails, 18 kilometers of snowshoe trails) is usually uncrowded, has great views of the Sawatch Range, and offers both rentals and private instruction.

McCoy Park (970-845-5313, beavercreek.snow.com/info/winter/ss.nordic.asp) At the top of the Strawberry Park lift at the Beaver Creek Ski Area, there are some 20 miles of cross-country and snowshoe trails tucked between Beaver Creek and Bachelor Gulch; you can sign up for Nordic lessons and snowshoe nature tours (complete with lunch).

Vail Nordic Center (970-476-8366, 1778 Vail Valley Dr., Vail) Located on the Vail Golf Course and running up and down the gut of the valley, this Nordic area has 17 kilometers of skating and classic trails, 10 kilometers of snowshoe-specific trails, rentals and demos, a retail shop, and a waxing room.

Dogsledding

Nova Guides/Winterhawk Dogsled Adventures (888-949-6682, novaguides.com) These morning or afternoon tours circle around Camp Hale, the former home of 10th Mountain Division soldiers in the Pando Valley, about a half-hour from Vail (the package includes door-to-door transportation). Steer your own team—or sit back and enjoy the flight.

Guiding and Backcountry

Guides

Paragon Guides (970-926-5299, paragonguides.com, P.O. Box 130, Vail) If you want to do a hut trip but you're not sure you can do it alone, Paragon can take you. This all-purpose outdoor guiding company organizes three- to six-day excursions to all 15 of the famed 10th Mountain Division backcountry huts.

Trails

Commando Run At 18 miles one way from Vail Pass all the way back down to Vail, Commando is a challenging and exhilarating ski tour—and requires route-finding and avalanche skills to climb, contour along ridges, descend, and climb again. You'll end up within the resort boundaries for a last screaming push to the Golden Peak parking lot.

Minturn Mile This famous backcountry run (which is way longer than a mile) starts at a gate at the top of Vail, then winds its way down a drainage through powder pockets and down narrow, lugelike conditions all the way to Minturn—where tradition dictates downing a stiff margarita at the Minturn Saloon (page 243).

Shrine Pass Though it's pounded by the motorized and nonmotorized alike, Shrine is still a good three- to five-hour jaunt, with views of Mount of the Holy Cross and deep powder-fields to play in. The route ends at the Shrine Mountain Inn—which is actually three cabins run by the 10th Mountain Division Hut Association (go to huts.org to make reservations).

10th Mountain Division huts (970-925-5775, huts.org) This organization operates 20-plus huts in the Rocky Mountains, with 2- to 8-mile approaches. Book early, especially if you want to come up for a weekend.

Ice Climbing

Vail Rock and Ice Guides (970-471-1173, vailrockandice.com) Driving on I-70 in winter past East Vail, you'll notice numerous frozen waterfalls on the south side of the highway—that's where Vail Rock and Ice will take you, whether you're climbing up a low-angle slab or trying to get to the top of a 120-foot-high standing pillar. There are classes from beginner all the way up to lead climbing.

Ice Skating

Black Family Ice Rink (970-845-5248, Beaver Creek Village) Spin around and around the middle of the village at this public outdoor rink.

Dobson Ice Arena (970-479-2270, 321 E. Lionsgate Circle, Vail) An indoor arena that has public skating times and cheap rentals.

Sleigh Rides

Bearcat Stables (970-926-1578, bearcatstables.com, 2701 Squaw Creek Rd., Edwards) Ride in a two-horse sleigh through snowy glades and open meadows, then sit down to a meal of duck with Bing cherry chutney, bacon-wrapped filet mignon, or ruby red trout with andouille corn bread stuffing at the Timber Hearth Grille in Cordillera.

4 Eagle Ranch (970-926-3372, 4eagleranch.com, 4098 CO 131, Wolcott) With 4 Eagle, you can take a private ride, a midafternoon spin, or a trip to the cozy, circa-1890 Nelson Cabin for dinner, where the fire roars, the tables are covered in checkered tablecloths and lit by lanterns, and the grub includes a chili bar, a buffet of steak, ribs, and chicken, and roasted marshmallows.

RECREATION: SUMMER AND FALL

Cycling: Mountain Biking

Guides

TrailWise Guides (970-827-5363, trailwiseguides.com) If you're a beginner, TrailWise can teach you mountain biking techniques on dirt roads, Jeep trails, and mellow single-track; if you're experienced, they can guide you to the gnarliest rides in the area. Trips include a front-suspension bike, water, biking gloves, lunch, and rain poncho.

Vail Bike Tech (970-476-5995, vailbiketech.com, 555 E. Lionshead Circle, Vail) These guys will take you up to Vail Pass for an epic descent down into Lionshead (or the other way, east to Frisco), or lead you on a full-day tour through Glenwood Canyon along the Colorado River.

The other side of Vail, showing its colors. Vail Image/Jack Affleck

Trails

Beaver Creek Get a head start with a ride up Centennial, or just start climbing from the base: There are trails that will get you all the way up to 11,440 feet. You can ride all the way over to Bachelor Gulch and Arrowhead Village, too.

Lost Lake to Buffeher Trail This ride has a mix of everything: hard and fast singletrack, dirt roads, a great lunch spot by Lost Lake, a technical descent, and a winding finish through aspen groves. But it ain't easy: You'll gain 3,500 feet in a sustained climb on the way up.

North Trail Just above I-70, North Trail isn't where you go for peace and quiet (you can often hear the freeway below). But it contours the north hillsides above town with steady climbs and manageable descents—and connects to a lot of other local trails.

Nottingham Ridge and Davos You'll need a map or detailed instructions for this cross-country combo: The route utilizes several area trails for both easy and steep rutted climbs. Avoid it during hunting season.

Shrine Pass to Upper Lime Creek Road Start down Road 709 from Vail Pass and take in views of the Sawatch Range, then join Road 728 to 728C for a glimpse of Mount of the Holy Cross. Retrace your tracks (it's a total of 15 or so miles round trip).

Son of Middle Creek Trail Smooth, covered with pine needles, and breathtaking in the fall, Son of Middle Creek is a 9-mile forested route of singletrack, dirt road, and pavement. Expect switchbacks—and creek crossings, especially in spring.

Two Elk Trail Starting at the Gore Creek Campground in East Vail and ending in Minturn, Two Elk traverses the Back Bowls, with epic climbs and technical descents almost the whole way.

Vail Mountain Vail has hosted several mountain-biking world championships, and there's a huge variety of trails here. Take the Vista Bahn quad or the Eagle Bahn gondola, then climb up to the ridgeline Grand Traverse, negotiate the technical '94 Downhill, or mosey down the mellow Gitalong Road.

Cycling: Road biking

Tennessee Pass Just off the beaten path from Vail, the small town of Minturn is the jumping-off point for this ride, which gains a painful 2,500 feet and then drops (barely) into the high-altitude former mining town of Leadville.

Vail to Eagle via US 6 The ride is just what it says it is: Follow US 6 the 20 miles from Vail to Eagle, rolling downhill along the Eagle River.

Vail to Glenwood Springs On this mostly downhill route that sticks to frontage road alongside the interstate, you'll pass through Wolcott, Eagle, and Dotsero, where a lovely bike path keeps you up close and personal with the Colorado River. Glenwood Canyon—the last 17 miles—has spectacular jagged walls.

Vail to Vail Pass Many locals do this ride on a regular basis: It climbs 14 miles and 3,700 feet on a bike path that parallels I-70, topping out over 10,500 feet. If you just want to ride the downhill portion (wimp!), **Charter Sports** (888-295-9797, chartersports.com) can shuttle you to the top, bike and helmet rental included, for $35.

Fishing

Outfitters

Fly Fishing Outfitters (970-476-3474, flyfishingoutfitters.net, Westgate Building on US 6, Avon) Along with wade and float trips on the Colorado and Eagle, FFO can take you to 3,000-acre Sweetwater Ranch for a chance to nab trout in three alpine lakes or along a 2-mile stretch of Sweetwater Creek (where 30-inch browns have been caught in the past).

Gore Creek Flyfisherman (970-476-3296, 193 E. Gore Creek Dr., Vail; 970-845-5418, Beaver Creek Village; gorecreekflyfisherman.com) These folks have been guiding in the Vail Valley for 20-plus years, have a slew of National Forest permits, and do wade and float trips on the Colorado, Eagle, and Roaring Fork Rivers.

Gorsuch Outfitters (877-926-0900, gorsuch-outfitters.com, Edwards Riverwalk) Gorsuch books everything from half-day wading trips to spring creeks to fishing at private ranches and streams. If you want a multi-day excursion, you can float, wade, camp, and let your guide cook dinner for you right next to the water.

Lakes and Streams

Before you fish any water in Colorado, be sure you check with a local fly shop to find out if it's public or private. Many rivers have both private and public sections, so make sure you know where you're going. For licenses and regulations, visit wildlife.state.co.us/fishing—or, again, stop into a shop. If a river is designated "Gold Medal," it officially means that there are 12 trout per surface acre that top 14 inches—or 60 pounds of trout per surface acre. Unofficially, it means that the fishing is damn good.

Colorado River If you head west from Vail, you'll get to where the Colorado meets the Eagle, at Dotsero; upstream from here, the river cuts through beautiful Gore Canyon. The best time of year is June–October.

Eagle River Jackson Streit, in *Fly Fishing Colorado*, called the Eagle a "meat and potatos kind of trout stream." It's a freestone waterway that stretches over 70 miles, much of it public—and you can float it from early June until the water drops too low.

Gore Creek For convenience, there's no beating Gore Creek—it cuts right through Vail, and there's Gold Medal water from Red Sandstone Creek to where it joins the Eagle River. It's fairly narrow and brushy, with a lot of private water; check a local shop for kosher access points.

Nottingham Lake Whether you want to use your float tube or cast from the perimeter, Nottingham—run by the Town of Avon—has solid and consistent fishing (it's stocked by the Colorado Division of Wildlife).

Golf

Beaver Creek Golf Club (970-845-5775, beavercreek.snow.com, 103 Offerson Rd., Beaver Creek) If you're staying at Beaver Creek, Bachelor Gulch, or Arrowhead, you can play here all season long; otherwise, it's open to the public until June 15 and after September 15. The Robert Trent Jones Jr. course runs up and down Beaver Creek between the resort and the bottom of the canyon.

Taking in the scene high above the Vail Valley. Vail Image/Jack Affleck

Eagle Ranch Golf Course (970-328-2882, eagleranchgolf.com, 0050 Lime Park Dr., Eagle) Arnold Palmer–designed, with five sets of tees ranging from 5,504 to 7,575 yards, Eagle Ranch can handle golfers of many abilities.

Eagle Vail Golf Course (970-949-5267, 431 Eagle Dr., Avon) Six miles west of Vail and situated along the Eagle River and Stone Creek, this course has 50-plus bunkers and is full of elevated tee shots.

Red Sky Golf Club (866-873-3759, redskyranch.com, Red Sky Rd., Wolcott) There are two full courses here, one designed by Tom Fazio and the other designed by Greg Norman, and both in between a wildlife migration corridor and a mountain ridge. Walk up and down sage-covered hills, traverse aspen forest, and catch views of Castle Peak and the Back Bowls.

Vail Golf Club (970-479-2260, 1778 Vail Valley Dr., Vail) The highest-elevation public course in the valley, this club has been open since 1966—and it's just a mile or two from the center of Vail Village. It parallels Gore Creek and I-70.

Hiking and Backpacking

Guides
Beaver Creek Hiking Center (970-854-5373, The Plaza, Beaver Creek) Join regularly scheduled hikes with local naturalists, learn map and compass skills, get a workout with Nordic walking, or let a guide lead you up a local fourteener.

Paragon Guides (970-926-5299, paragonguides.com, P.O. Box 130, Vail) Want to sharpen your mountaineering skills? Sign up for one of Paragon's four- to six-day mountaineering camps. Want to top out on a local peak? Paragon can guide you up 13,670-foot Mount Jackson in the Holy Cross Wilderness or 13,575-foot Mount Powell, the highest peak in the Gore Range.

Vail Nature Center Hiking Club (970-479-2291, 841 Vail Valley Dr., Vail) Every hike with this group has an educational component, whether it's wildflowers or wildlife. Go on three or more hikes with the club, and the membership pays for itself (it's $130).

Trails

Grouse Lake Trail A popular trail in the Holy Cross Wilderness, Grouse Lake crosses its namesake creek several times and finishes at the foot of Grouse Mountain (it's about 4.6 miles one way, with close to a 3,000-foot elevation gain).

Lost Lake Trail You can walk this 3.75-miler in the Eagles Nest Wilderness end to end (with a shuttle), or walk from the west trailhead to the east and back again. Either way, you'll climb moderately and pass through wildflower meadows and aspen groves.

Meadow Mountain Gaining about 2,000 feet over 4.5 miles, this trail ends at a small cabin, with good views of the Gore Range and a look at cuts in the land from old, abandoned ski runs.

Horseback Riding

Bearcat Stables (970-926-1578, bearcatstables.com, 2701 Squaw Creek Rd., Edwards) For one of the most beautiful pack trips in Colorado, book a four-day, three-night ride from Vail to Aspen—spending the night in 10th Mountain Division backcountry huts and guest ranches along the way. Bearcat also has short trail rides year-round.

Beaver Creek Stables (970-845-7770, vailhorses.com, 45 W. Thomas Place, Avon) Choose from one- or two-hour rides through the White River National Forest, a three-hour picnic ride, a half-day jaunt up to Beaver Lake (with a chance to catch a trout), or a wagon or horseback ride up to Beano's Cabin for dinner (see page 251). They'll also arrange hunting and fishing trips for you.

Lazy J Ranch (970-926-34720, lazyjranch.net, 001 Sporting Clay Way, Wolcott) Lazy J's "Horse Flies and Caddis Flies" package combines two hours of riding with two hours of fly-fishing, and its 10-station sporting clays course lets you get in some target practice. Standard one-, two-, and three-hour rides available.

Triple G Outfitters (970-926-1234, tripleg.net, Wolcott, 4098 CR 131) Along with standard nose-to-tail trail rides, Triple G has advanced horsemanship rides, half-day cattle roundups, winter rides, "Saddles & Paddles" combos (ride in the morning, raft in the afternoon), and high-country fishing and photography trips.

Hot Air Ballooning

Balloon America (970-468-2473, balloonridesusa.com, Miller Ranch Rd. soccer field, Edwards) Sit on leather seats (most balloon trips are standing only) and sip Dom Pérignon with this first-class outfit, which has both 40- and 90-minute sunrise floats.

Renowned kayaker Nikki Kelly takes the plunge near Vail. Vail Image/Jack Affleck

Camelot Balloons (970-328-2290, camelotballoons.com, P.O. Box 1896, Vail) Camelot sends up balloons with groups of four to eight people all year round—and they've been doing it for 18 years.

Hunting

A.J. Brink Outfitters (970-524-7344, 3406 Sweetwater Rd., Gypsum) A.J. Brink does multi-day guided and drop-camp trips in a huge range of permit areas: the Maroon Bells, the White River National Forest, the Roosevelt National Forest, and the Rawahs.

Rafting and Paddling

Alpine Quest Sports (970-926-3867, alpinequestsports.com, 34510 US 6, Suite A-1, Edwards) One of the largest kayak schools in the state, Alpine Quest takes on anyone from absolute white-water beginners to squirt-boating experts, with classes on local rivers, creeks, and lakes. Both group and private lessons are available.

Colorado River Guides (800-938-7238, raftcolorado.com, P.O. Box 391, Yampa) Book trips on rollicking sections of the Eagle or sign up for relaxing runs down the Colorado, with everything from Class I to Class IV trips.

Lakota River Guides (970-845-7238, lakotariver.com, 41466 US 6, Eagle-Vail) Lakota can take you down the Colorado River's Gore Canyon, considered one of the top three gnarly commercial runs in the United States—or stick with less heart-racing options on both the Colorado and the Eagle. They're the only outfitter in the area with so-called "Night Vision" tours, Class I–II floats through the calm of twilight.

Nova Guides (719-486-2656, novaguides.com, P.O. Box 2018, Vail) Just a couple miles from Vail and Beaver Creek, the Eagle River has a great variety of rapids: Dowd Chute, starting in Minturn, reaches Class IV status, and the Lower Eagle is usually a mellow Class II–III. Nova runs half-day trips here—and also does full-day excursions to the Arkansas, up past Leadville.

Timberline Tours (970-476-1414, timberlinetours.com, P.O. Box 131, Vail) With some 35 years of experience, Timberline's guides know Vail's waterways like the backs of their hands—and they've won world rafting championships for men and women to boot. They're even in the Guinness Book of World Records for most miles rafted in 24 hours.

DRIVING: SCENIC DRIVES AND BYWAYS

Glenwood Springs, Aspen, and Independence Pass Got all day? This 188-mile loop is one of Colorado's great drives, hitting the historic mining town of Leadville, the breath-taking climb up (and narrow descent down) Independence Pass, the idyllic and chic town that is Aspen, the Roaring Fork Valley, the deep cleft of Glenwood Canyon, and the open spaces near Gypsum, ending up back where you started.

Top of the Rockies Scenic and History Byway Along this byway, you'll get to see 10 of Colorado's 14,000-foot peaks, including the states two highest, Elbert and Massive. You'll also cross the Continental Divide twice (at Tennessee Pass and Fremont Pass), get a chance to check out Minturn, Camp Hale, Leadville, and beautiful Twin Lakes, and see whether you can spot the telltale feature on Mount of the Holy Cross.

Wolcott to Kremmling Follow CO 131 past endless vistas of sagebrush, through the tiny hamlet of State Bridge, and up to where the Colorado River begins its trickle to the Gulf of California.

SHOPPING

Art Galleries

Beaver Creek/Vail Fine Art Gallery (970-845-8500, St. James Place, Beaver Creek; 970-476-2900, 141 E. Meadow Dr., Vail; vailfineart.com) If you want to walk away from your mountain vacation with a Chagall, Picasso, Miró, Rembrandt, or Renoir, make sure to stop by one of Vail Fine Art's branches in the valley. But that's not all—Western bronze sculptors like Walt Horton and painters like Fedor Zakharov and Robert Hagan are also represented.

By Nature Gallery (970-949-1805, bynaturegallery.com, Market Square, Unit C-10, Beaver Creek) Everything in this gallery originated in nature, whether it's a rock-slab table with imprinted fossils, marble animal sculptures, huge quartz cross-sections, agate geode bookends, or turquoise jewelry.

Claggett/Rey Gallery (970-476-9350, claggettrey.com, 100 E. Meadow Dr., Suite 10, Vail) With an emphasis on historical Western scenes and wildlife sculptures by close to 50 American artists, Claggett/Rey can also arrange for a monumental sculpture or a fountain installation if you need one. Kenneth Bunn, Terri Kelly Moyers, Oreland Joe, Herb Mignery, and Wayne Wolfe are just a small part of the roster.

DeMott Gallery (970-476-8948, demottgallery.com, 183-3A Gore Creek Dr., Vail) Landscape painters John Phillip Osbourne and Skip Whitcomb, sculptors Gary Lee Price and Hollis Williford, wildlife artists Tim Shinabarger and Luke Frazier, plus a large collection of traditional American frontier art.

Gore Creek Gallery/Travellers Books (970-477-4621, gorecreekgallery.com, 158 E. Gore Creek Dr., Vail) This small gallery displays Western art, bronzes, some jewelry, and a selection of antiquarian books and maps.

Knox Gallery (970-949-5564, knoxgalleries.com, 123 Beaver Creek Plaza, Beaver Creek) Knox is best known for monumental sculpture (they've even installed sculpture gardens in public spaces), but they also sell etchings, watercolors, and paintings if you'd rather walk away with something smaller.

Masters Gallery at Vail (970-477-0600, mastersgalleryvail.com, 100 E. Meadow Dr., Suite 27, Vail) An eclectic mix of modern, Western, sculptural, and pop art, Masters represents artists like Arkhipov, Morante, Pierson, Stiltz, and Terakedis.

Pismo Gallery (970-949-0908, Village Hall, Beaver Creek; 970-476-2400, 122 E. Meadow Dr., Vail; pismoglass.com) Dazzling displays of glass vases, chandeliers, wall pieces, miniatures, abstracts, and jewelry: There's a $250,000 Chihuly, a stunning Lino Tagliapietra, a futuristic Jon Kuhn, and works by several dozen other glass masters.

The Verbatim Bookstore, with its resident doorkeeper. Evelyn Spence

Sportsman's Gallery (970-949-6036, sportsmansgallery.com, 6 Avondale Lane, Beaver Creek) The perfect place to outfit your log cabin, mountain house, or fishing lodge, Sportsman's Gallery has paintings, prints, and sculptures of trout, hunting dogs, lakescapes, ducks, cowboys, hunters, moose, and all things outdoor-related. Artists include Arthur Shilstone, Roger Blum, Al Barnes, Lynn Bogue Hunt, and Frank W. Benson.

Vail International Gallery (970-476-2525, vailgallery.com, 100 E. Meadow Dr., Suite 17, Vail) The Russian expressionist Alexey Merinov, Dutch-influenced Ron Hicks, and landscape painter Leon Loughridge are all exhibited here.

The Vickers Collection (970-845-7478, vickerscollection.com; St. James Place, Beaver Creek; 122 E. Meadow Dr., Vail) Here's the place to get Lyman Whitaker kinetic sculptures in floral, helix, lily, and flame shapes, some of which you'll see around town—as well as the paintings and bronze, obsidian, wood, and marble creations of 50-plus artists.

Wilderness Wonders (970-845-7230, tonynewlin.com, Gallery Row, Market Street Building, Beaver Creek) Large color photos of grizzlies, eagles, caribou, Alaska and Rocky Mountains, and golden aspenscapes—they're all shot by outdoor photographer Tony Newlin, and they're all here.

Books

The Bookworm (970-926-7323, bookwormofedwards.com, 0105 Edwards Village Blvd., Edwards) For 10 years, Nicole Magistro and Neda Jansen have stocked this indie store with fiction and nonfiction, kids' books, reference titles, and even out-of-print books. They'll gift wrap and special order, too.

Verbatim (970-476-3032, 100 E. Meadow Dr., Suite 23, Vail) A charming, small shop with french doors and a resident English sheepdog, Verbatim has a good selection of travel guides, fiction, and personalized staff recommendations.

Outdoor Gear

Bag and Pack Shop (970-476-1027, 122 E. Meadow Dr., Vail) Vail's biggest outdoor store, Bag and Pack carries hard-core brands like The North Face, Marmot, Prana, Patagonia, and Mountain Hardwear.

Ptarmigan Sports (970-926-8144, ptarmigansports.com, 0137 Main St., Edwards) Get your camping, hiking, and travel wear, guidebooks, and maps here. The knowledgeable staff can recommend day hikes and overnight activities, too.

At Axel's in Vail, you can buy cowboy boots in a rainbow of colors. Evelyn Spence

Western Clothing and Furs

Axel's (970-476-7625, axelsvail.com, 201 Gore Creek Dr., Vail) From the outside, Axel's has a rich, elaborately carved wood facade—and the store itself is full of classy handmade boots, leather belts, fur-trimmed jackets, and Western wear. The examples of footwear lining the walls are practically works of art—in bright colors and intricate stitched patterns—and come from bootmakers like J.B. Hill, Liberty, Arditti, Zelli, and Tres Outlaws.

Fantasia Furs (970-845-9111, 258 Beaver Creek Plaza, Beaver Creek; 970-476-5099, 286 Bridge St., Vail) Fur coats and fur hats in both traditional and contemporary styles.

The Fur Club of Vail (970-476-2889, 194 Gore Creek Dr., Vail) Fur boots, ankle-length coats, thin leather jackets, and more.

Kemo Sabe (970-479-7474, kemosabe.com, 230 Bridge St., Vail) Looking for a cowboy hat? Kemo Sabe, a hip Western boutique, has a huge selection in all styles—as well as silver spurs, Pendleton blankets, leather belts, and staff members who fully dress the part.

SEASONAL EVENTS

February: Beaver Creek Winter Culinary Classic and Celebrity Ski Race (970-845-9090, beavercreek.snow.com) Watch Eric Ripert of New York's Le Bernardin race downhill against Elizabeth Falkmer of San Fransico's Citizen Cake, or a tag-team cake-decorating contest, or a vodka-tasting seminar—or just show up for the finale Grand Tasting, with food from dozens of visiting and local chefs.

February: Mardi Gras (vail.snow.com) Costumes, Cajun and Creole cuisine, street parties, a parade, and—of course—lots and lots of beads.

March: Vail Film Festival (970-476-1092, vailfilmfestival.org) An eclectic mix of documentaries, short films, features, animated films, TV pilots, screenplay competitions, panels, and workshops, Vail's fest has been in business for four years—and already attracts some of the industry's best.

April: Beaver Creek Snowshoe Shuffle (970-569-7511, snowshoeshuffle.com) One of the largest snowshoe races in North America, this one raises money for the Women's Cancer Coalition. Races are 1 mile, 5K, and 10K.

April: Spring Back to Vail (vail.snow.com) The highlight of this two-week end-of-season bash? Depends who you talk to, but most people would say it's the World Pond-Skimming Championships—during which people ski down a ramp and try to get across a long pond without biffing. There are concerts, parties, and lodging and lift ticket deals, too.

May: Beaver Creek BB&B (beavercreek.snow.com) The three B's stand for Blues, Brews, and BBQ—it's a weekend of 'cue tasting from local and visiting chefs (from Denver and KC), grilling demos, blues music, and brewmasters' dinners.

June: Beaver Creek Summer Culinary Classic (970-845-9090, beavercreek.snow.com) Chefs from around the country lead cooking demos and wine, tequila, and scotch seminars—then let everyone sample the goods.

Street dancing at Vail's Oktoberfest. Vail Image/Jack Affleck

June: TEVA Mountain Games (970-926-4799, tevamountaingames.com) Pros and amateurs alike compete in kayaking, rafting, mountain biking, climbing, fishing, trail running, adventure racing, photography, filmmaking, and even who has the Mountain Dog of the Year. When the sun goes down, the concerts and parties begin.

June–August: Bravo! Vail Valley Music Festival (970-827-5700, vailmusicfestival.org) Over the course of this summerlong festival, some 60,000 audience members listen to the Rochester Symphony Orchestra, the Dallas Symphony Orchestra, the New York Philharmonic, chamber music, youth ensembles, morning concerts, and choruses.

July: Triple Bypass Cycle Tour (970-748-4032, teamevergreen.org) A 120-mile road ride from Evergreen (just outside of Denver) all the way to Vail, the Triple Bypass gains 10,000 feet in elevation and scales Squaw, Loveland, and Vail passes on the way.

July: Rocky Mountain Antique Festival (970-845-1113, rmafest.com) It's an antique-lover's dream: tent after tent of country furniture, Chinese collectibles, antiquarian maps, vintage rugs, Victorian glass, and estate jewelry—all in Beaver Creek's big main plaza.

July: Vail International Dance Festival (970-845-8497, cvf.org/cultural/dancefest.php) Companies from around the world come together for a month of innovative performances, world premieres, and classical and contemporary numbers. In 2006 there were dancers from China, Mexico, and Quebec.

August: Eagle County Fair and Rodeo (970-328-3646, eaglecounty.us/fair/fair.cfm) Almost 70 years old, this fair is by now an institution. It brings in world-class bronc and bull riders, barrel racers, and calf ropers. Check out the winners of the 4-H poultry contest, enter a cookie into the Cookie Jar Contest, compete in a salsa-dancing contest, or just gorge on funnel cake.

August: Vail Arts Festival (970-376-3756, vailartsfestival.com) A three-day outdoor exhibition in Lionshead Village, the Vail Arts Festival has everything from watercolor and woodworking to metalwork and mosaics. Hobnob with artists, watch live music, and eat street food.

September: Vail Jazz Festival (970-479-6146, vailjazz.org) Over a 24-hour period on Labor Day weekend, this festival schedules performances morning, noon, and night—with big names like the Clayton Brothers Quintet, the Monty Alexander Trio, Dr. Lonnie Smith, Dee Dee Bridgewater, and Diana Krall.

September: Vail Mountain School Home Tour (970-476-3850, vms.edu) Want a chance to tour some of the biggest, most exclusive homes in Vail Valley—and contribute money to Vail Mountain School scholarship coffers at the same time? Sign up for this annual circuit, which includes a catered lunch and van transportation from front door to front door.

September: Vail Oktoberfest (970-476-6797, vailoktoberfest.com) Yodeling demos, bratwurst-eating competitions, keg bowling, alpenhorn tooting, official keg tappings, oom-pah music, and lots of beer.

November: Beaver Creek Cookie Competition and Gingerbread Competition (970-845-9090) One day, you can enter your favorite cookie recipe or taste everything and cast a vote; the next, you can bid by silent auction on elaborate edible abodes constructed by local chefs.

December: Birds of Prey World Cup Week (970-845-9090) Watch world-class skiers like Hermann Maier and Bode Miller compete in GS, slalom, super-combined, and downhill—in which men ski from the top of the near-vertical, icy-slick Birds of Prey run to the bottom in two minutes. (Try it yourself once the course has cleared.)

NUTS AND BOLTS

Getting Here

If you're traveling by air, you can either fly into **Denver International Airport** and drive the 110 miles over Loveland and Vail passes on I-70, book a shuttle ride with **Colorado Mountain Express** (800-525-6363, ridecme.com), or fly into the **Vail/Eagle County Airport**, about 30 minutes west of town. There are a good number of direct flights straight into Vail from Newark, LaGuardia, Charlotte, Miami, Los Angeles, Minneapolis, Atlanta, Cincinnati, Chicago, Dallas, Houston, and Philly, and rental cars are available when you land. If you're curious about Colorado road conditions, dial 303-639-1111 or visit cotrip.org. Remember that weekend morning and afternoon traffic on I-70 can be brutal in winter, especially in bad weather, so be sure to leave enough time (a good reason to choose Eagle over DIA).

Ambulance/Fire/Police/Search and Rescue

For emergencies, of course, dial 911. For police assistance that doesn't require an emergency response, contact the number listed below for the city closest to your present location.

Avon Fire Department: 970-748-9665

Avon Police: 970-748-4040

Eagle County Sheriff: 970-328-8500

Edwards Fire Department: 970-748-9665

Edwards Police: 970-479-2200

Minturn Police: 970-827-4272

Vail Fire Department: 970-479-2250

Vail Police: 970-479-2200

Avalanche Reports

Colorado Avalanche Information Center: geosurvey.state.co.us/avalanche or avalanche-center.org

Libraries

Avon Public Library: 970-949-6797, evld.org, 200 Benchmark Rd., Avon

Vail Public Library: 970-479-2185, vaillibrary.com, 292 W. Meadow Dr., Vail

Hospitals and Emergency Medical Services

Colorado Mountain Medical: 970-476-5695, 181 W. Meadow Dr., Suite 200, Vail; 970-949-3222, 71 Beaver Creek Place, Avon

Medical Center of Eagle: 970-328-1650, 232 Broadway, Eagle

Vail Valley Medical Center: 970-476-2451, vvmc.com, 181 W. Meadow Dr., Vail, with other branches in Avon, Beaver Creek, Edwards, Frisco, Keystone, Eagle, and Silverthorne

Media

Newspapers and Magazines

Eagle Valley Enterprise: 970-328-6656, eaglevalleyenterprise.com, P.O. Box 450, Eagle, CO 81631

Vail-Beaver Creek Magazine: 970-476-6600, Ext. 10, vailbeavercreekmag.com, 160 W. Beaver Creek Blvd., Suite 102, Avon, CO 81620

Vail Daily: 970-949-0555, vaildaily.com, 40780 US 6 and 24, Avon, CO 81620

Vail Trail: 970-328-7245, vailtrail.com, 40780 US 6 and 24, Avon, CO 81620

Vail Valley Magazine: 970-926-3969, P.O. Box 3423, Vail, CO 81658

The 10th Mountain Division

Most backcountry skiers in Colorado know the 10th Mountain Division because of the hut system named after it (see page 253). This group of soldiers—created during the lead-up to U.S. involvement in World War II (and inspired by Finnish success against Soviet invasions, or perhaps the less-successful Italian campaign in Albania, in which 10,000 froze to death)— was founded in 1941 with the help of Charles Minot Dole ("Minnie" Dole), the head of the National Ski Patrol. Dole recruited thousands of expert skiers and mountaineers from his ranks. In 1942, Camp Hale—in a valley in Pando, Colorado, below Tennessee Pass— was established as a training ground, where the soldiers learned downhill skiing, winter survival skills, rock climbing, cross-country skiing, and endurance ski-mountaineering. The 10th proved key in advancing through Italy's Po Valley and eventually forcing a German surrender in Italy: In February 1945, the 86th Regiment scaled a feature called Riva Ridge and surprised the Germans, moving on past Mount Belvedere, Mount della Spe, and Tole. In the end, the 10th had 4,888 casualties— and a place in the history of mountain warfare.

Radio

KPRE 89.9 FM: 800-722-4449. Public radio programming.

KTUN 101.7, 97.3, 95.3: 970-949-0140, ktunradio.com. Everything from the Eagles and Elvis to Marilyn Manson and Nirvana.

KZYR 97.7: 970-845-8565. Adult alternative music.

Public Transportation

Eagle County Regional Transit (ECO): 970-328-3520, eaglecounty.us/eco_transit/. This network serves Eagle, Avon, Edwards, Minturn, Beaver Creek, and Vail.

Vail Transit: 970-479-2178. This is the country's largest free, year-round bus service.

Ranger Stations

Holy Cross Ranger District/White River National Forest, Minturn: 970-827-5715

White River National Forest, Eagle: 970-328-6388

Tourist Information

Vail Chamber and Business Association: 970-477-0075, vailchamber.org, 241 S. Frontage Rd. E., Suite 2, Vail

Vail Valley Chamber and Tourism Bureau: 970-476-1000, visitvailvalley.com, 100 E. Meadow Dr., Suite 34, Vail

Vail Visitor Information Center: 970-476-4790 (fourth floor of the parking lot, Vail Village); 970-476-4941 (Lionshead)

The Winter Park area has more than 600 miles of mountain biking trails. Winter Park/Fraser Valley Chamber of Commerce

7

Winter Park

Denver's Playground

The 9,000-foot-high valley bounded by the Continental Divide and the Vasquez Mountains and threaded by the Fraser River has been called many things over the years: "Little Switzerland," "Somewhere Between Purgatory and Heaven," and "The Icebox of the Nation" (the local record for freezing temps is minus 65 degrees Fahrenheit). But don't let that—or the Mini Cooper–size moguls on Mary Jane Mountain—scare you off: Winter Park is one of the most unpretentious, laid-back, and oldest ski towns in the entire state. And it's only 67 miles from Denver.

Way back when, the area was seething with bear, bison, antelope, and elk, attracting French trappers and Native American tribes, from the Utes to the Sioux, the Blackfeet to the Arapahos. Their legacy? The nearby Indian Peaks Wilderness, which is topped by summits honoring Navajo, Apache, Shoshoni, and Pawnee. It wasn't until the 1860s—when survey parties arrived in the valley, searching for the shortest possible railroad route over or through the Divide—that development begin (albeit slowly) in the form of a horse trail over Berthoud Pass, south of today's Winter Park, and a few ranching and lumber operations. The first stagecoach from Georgetown to Hot Sulphur Springs scaled the pass in 1874, but it took decades before railroad tracks were laid.

And that only happened thanks to one visionary. Down in Denver, David H. Moffat—who started as a Woolworth's clerk, worked his way up to owning gold mines and heading banks, and became the richest man in Colorado—had a yen to build tracks over the Divide. Construction started in April 1903; by June 1905, the route reached Hot Sulphur Springs, with 33 tunnels, countless bridges, and a 4 percent grade in places. Trains were sometimes delayed by avalanches or storms for weeks. Winter Park (then still called Middle Park, or Old Park) remained an island in the sky.

Everything changed for the Fraser Valley in 1927, when crews completed the Moffat tunnel (Moffat himself died in 1911, his fortune depleted), a 6.2-mile, $15.5 million passage that cut through 15,000 feet of bad rock and cost 19 lives—and took the place of 33 miles of track above. The previous route from the east portal to the west took five hours at best; the tunnel took 12 minutes, no matter what. Soon, the towns of Fraser and Tabernash sprang up.

At around the same time, the City of Denver was deeded about 90 acres for a mountain park; a ski area officially opened in 1940, with three runs and two jumps. The Mary Jane Trail—which followed an old sheep path—was cleared, and a ski legend was born: Not only

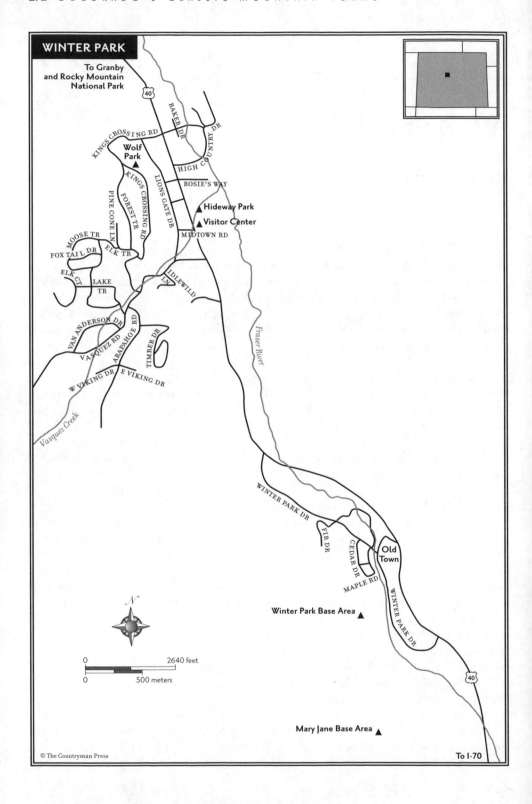

WINTER PARK

To Granby
and Rocky Mountain
National Park

40

KINGS CROSSING RD

BAKER DR

HIGH COUNTRY DR

Wolf
Park

KINGS CROSSING RD

LIONS GATE DR

ROSIE'S WAY

Hideway Park

Visitor Center

PINE CONE LN

FOREST TR

MIDTOWN RD

MOOSE TR

FOX TAIL DR

ELK TR

ELK CT

LAKE TR

IDLEWILD LN

VAN ANDERSON DR

ARAPAHOE RD

VASQUEZ RD

TIMBER DR

W VIKING DR

E VIKING DR

Fraser River

Vasquez Creek

WINTER PARK DR

FIR DR

CEDAR DR

Old
Town

MAPLE RD

WINTER PARK DR

N

0   2640 feet

0   500 meters

Winter Park Base Area ▲

40

Mary Jane Base Area ▲

© The Countryman Press

To I-70

did it become synonymous with bone-rattling moguls, but it was also named after the Mary Jane placer gold claim, which in turn was named after a lady of ill repute. Shortly after, a small community known as Hideaway Park developed around a gas station, motel, and restaurant on US 40.

Since then, Hideaway Park has turned into Winter Park, and has slowly grown—the ski area has expanded over to Parsenn Bowl and Vasquez Ridge and now encompasses 2,770 acres, and the town has accumulated a few swanky hotels, a sushi joint, a covered parking garage, and some new condo complexes. It still retains the most rustic, sometimes run-down, always friendly vibe of any town in this book. But, as locals will tell you, the town is truly at a crossroads: In late 2002, the City of Denver struck a deal with ski-resort developer Intrawest (think Whistler, Mammoth, Stratton, Copper), which promised to invest $50 million in on-mountain improvements—including a pond for ice skating, 500-plus housing units, a glass observation area for nonskiers to watch skiers, and even a possible widening of the Fraser River. The question remains: Will The Man end up changing WP's low-key, fleece-and-Carhartt vibe? Or just make a good thing better? Stay tuned. In the meantime, the bumps beckon.

A side view of Byers Peak. Winter Park Resort

The Arapahoe is a family-style lodge. Evelyn Spence

Lodging

Winter Park

Arapahoe Ski Lodge
Innkeepers: The Holzwarth and Roman families
800-754-0094, 970-726-8222
arapahoeskilodge.com
skilodge@arapahoeskilodge.com
78594 US 40, Winter Park
Price Range: $150–$321 in winter, including breakfast and dinner; $59–$101 in summer, including breakfast
Credit Cards: AE, D, MC, V
Children: Y
Pets: N
Handicap Accessible: N

Family run for 32 years, the Arapahoe Ski Lodge is a family place: Guests seem to return year after year. It could be the food—hearty breakfasts and dinners, with prime rib, spinach soufflé, seafood gumbo, and homemade cheesecake, all served in a dining room decorated with steins and baskets. It could be the game room—kept cozy by a large fireplace and packed with comfy old chairs and couches, toys, sombreros, ancient ski gear, Ping-Pong, pool, and Legos. It could be the in-house bar, where cheese and crackers await tired skiers as they get off the shuttle from the ski area. With just 11 rooms—none of which have TV—everyone gets to know one another. The Arapahoe also has a serviceable, if dank, indoor hot tub, sauna, and swimming pool.

Beaver Lodge

Manager: Mark Johnson
970-726-5741, 800-666-0281
beavervillage.com
info@beavervillage.com
79303 US 40, Winter Park
Price Range: $35–$120, including breakfast
and dinner
Credit Cards: MC, V
Children: Y
Pets: Y
Handicap Accessible: N*

Part of Beaver Village's holdings of condos,
ski-in/ski-out townhomes, and private
houses for rent, the steep-roofed and iconic
Beaver Lodge was opened on Thanksgiving
Day in 1940—Winter Park's first lodging
establishment. The Beav's location—just a
mile and a half from the ski area (on a free
shuttle route) and a few blocks from the
heart of downtown—makes it one of the
most convenient (and budget-wise) crash
pads in the valley. The rooms are basic, with
bathrooms, beds, and a tiny shelf for the
telephone; the wood-paneled hallways are
dark and warrenlike. Everyone who stays
here has access to the on-site ski shop, hot
tubs, sauna, game room, and the James Peak
Saloon, with an entrance framed by elaborately painted skis. Not only that, during ski
season, both breakfast and all-you-can-eat
dinner are included—which might mean
roasted chicken, lasagna, pot roast, baked
beans, scalloped potatoes, hot dogs, or a
fajita bar, depending on the night—and
everything is served in the 1970s-alpine
dining hall at one end of the lodge. Kids
under 5 eat and stay free all winter long.

    *About 300 yards from the Main Lodge,
the Lake Lodge has some handicap-accessible
rooms, but they are usually rented out to
larger groups or long-term renters.

✪ Gasthaus Eichler

Innkeepers: Joan and René Weder
800-543-3899, 970-726-5133
gasthauseichler.com
78786 US 40, Winter Park
Price Range: $69–$250, including
breakfast and free ski wax
Credit Cards: AE, D, MC, V
Children: Y
Pets: N
Handicap Accessible: N

The only traditional European hotel in the
valley, Gasthaus Eichler was established
in 1987 by German mason Hans Eichler—
then decorated sparingly, with a downstairs
restaurant serving, well, heavy German
food. Everything changed in 2003, when
Joan (former corporate human resources
director) and René (former executive chef
for places like the Beaver Creek Hyatt and
the Boca Raton Hotel & Resort) decided
they had had it with city life. They bought
the 15-room Gasthaus, added homey and
luxurious touches like colorfully patterned
duvet covers, down comforters, Jacuzzi
tubs, and sheer shower curtains—and
transformed the cuisine from German to
Continental. From the outside, the place
still looks like it had been transplanted
from a Zermatt hillside, complete with a
Swiss flag and Bavarian trim (René was
born in Switzerland's Rhein Valley).
Vasquez Creek bubbles right past the
outdoor hot tub, and room rates include a
free ski wax. Come morning, you're met
with a spread of fresh breads, cheese,
cold cuts, fresh fruit, and a daily hot
entrée (belgian waffles, swiss scrambled
eggs).

Iron Horse Resort

800-621-8190, 970-726-8851
ironhorse-resort.com
101 Iron Horse Way, Winter Park
Price Range: $69–$699
Credit Cards: AE, D, MC, V
Children: Y
Pets: N
Handicap Accessible: Y

Beaver Lodge was Winter Park's first lodging establishment—and is still one of the best deals in town.

Evelyn Spence

This modern complex, tucked in the woods on the front side of the mountain between the Mary Jane and Winter Park base areas, is technically ski in/ski out—but skiing in requires a trip down difficult Mary Jane runs or a shuttle ride up from the base, and skiing out often involves pushing through a cat track covered in at least a few inches of snow. That said, Iron Horse has all the amenities of a full ski-resort hotel: indoor-outdoor pool, fitness center with steam rooms, a poolside barbecue deck, covered parking, and ski storage. The studio units are cramped (the Murphy bed, when pulled down, takes up a good portion of the room), but two- and three-bedroom options are more spacious; all have full kitchens, private balconies, and homey touches like novels propped up on the mantel and dishtowels folded on the countertops. The on-site restaurant, Jane Creek Grille, is decent (with nightly specials on things like prime rib and Dungeness crab), but if you're around on a Friday night, don't miss the performance of local country-western singer Washboard Annie, complete with wine and cheese.

The Pines Inn of Winter Park

Innkeeper: Teri Cline
800-824-9127, 970-726-5416
winter-park-lodging.com
mountaingirls04@yahoo.com
115 Timber House Rd., Winter Park
Price Range: $85–$150, including breakfast
Credit Cards: AE, D, MC, V
Children: Yes
Pets: Negotiable
Handicap Accessible: N

Tucked away at the edge of the ski area, just 600 yards from the base, the eight-room, ski-in Pines has been a B&B since the 1960s—but, since 2004, it has been run by a former Boulder, Colorado, native and her three daughters. Expect to be greeted by Cline's two dogs, Gidgit (a Yorkie) and Harley (a Yorkie/Dachshund mix). The living room is dark, cozy, and full of tchotchkes; the breakfast room is large and airy—with instruments in the corner for impromptu marimba concerts. Each room has a theme: The Mountain Room has two sturdy pine beds, bright red comforters, and old snowshoes hanging on the wall; the Victorian Room has a four-poster bed and frilly pillowcases. Two rooms have Jacuzzi tubs. Cline, whose cinnamon rolls "were killer at church bake-offs," does all the cooking and serves up everything from eggs Benedict with homemade English muffins to biscuits with sausage gravy. She'll even make dinner for you, if requested. Don't want to walk to the lifts each morning? A free shuttle can take you there.

Timberhouse Ski Lodge

Innkeepers: Sheri and Todd Waldron
800-843-3502, 970-726-5477
timberhouseskilodge.com
End of Timberhouse Rd., Winter Park
Price Range: $58–$103
Credit Cards: MC, V
Children: Y
Pets: N
Handicap Accessible: N

At the very top of Timberhouse Road, the namesake lodge is only open in winter—and offers everything from six-person dorm rooms with shared bath to economical private rooms (that are still just over a hundred bucks). In the entryway, the wall is covered with Polaroids and a U.S. map annotating just how far many of the guests have come. Just 700 yards from the lifts, you can ski in—but not out. The Timberhouse is reminiscent of a traditional ski lodge, with Bavarian touches on the trim, a rambling layout, a casual common area with crackling fire, a game room with pool and Ping-Pong, a selection of ski videos, a large outdoor hot tub for star-gazing, and long wooden tables in the dining room. A chalkboard announces each night's family-style meal, which starts promptly at 6 PM (listen for the dinner bell): tomato Florentine soup, dinner rolls, roast turkey, glazed carrots, and pumpkin pie one night; chicken cordon bleu or barbecue ribs another. For après, chai, cocoa, and spiced tea are served with muffins or brownies. Rooms are spare, with floor-to-ceiling wood paneling, bedside table, and lamp (no telephone).

Viking Lodge

Innkeepers: Chris and Sue Seamann
800-421-4013, 970-726-8885
skiwp.com
skiwp@rkymtnhi.com
78966 US 40, Winter Park
Price Range: $50–$300, including light
    continental breakfast during ski season
Credit Cards: AE, D, MC, V
Children: Y
Pets: Y
Handicap Accessible: N

If you want a basic, convenient place to crash, the Viking—built in 1956, which is relatively old for any ski town—is your place. These days, it's owned by former U.S. Ski Team aerialist Chris "Sea-Dog" Seamann, who's put old skis on the walls and offers special ski-tune deals in the downstairs shop. The simply furnished rooms have dark green carpets, thick curtains, and wood paneling; some come with lofts and kitchens. Guests congregate in the fireplace lobby, TV room, and game room for wireless Internet access, pool, Ping-Pong, and board games. Not enough entertainment? The Viking is steps away from the Cooper Creek outdoor mall, with a half-dozen restaurants, scads of trinket shops, and a few night spots—and it sits right on Winter Park's free shuttle route.

Woodspur Lodge

Innkeepers: Jimmy and Jeannine Lahrman
800-626-6562, 970-716-8417
woodspurlodge.com
woodspurlodge@woodspur.com
111 Van Anderson Dr., Winter Park
Price Range: $75–$115, including breakfast
    and dinner
Credit Cards: D, MC, V
Children: Y
Pets: N
Handicap Accessible: N

The secluded, 32-room Woodspur Lodge feels like a huge family ski home, if all family ski homes had a big deck with Adirondack-style chairs; a living room with exposed beams, cathedral ceilings, and floor-to-ceiling windows; a covered outdoor hot tub; a library; a bar; a sauna; and a meal plan that includes all-you-can-eat dinners of prime rib, pork tenderloin, baked rigatoni, and salmon, and breakfasts of biscuits and gravy, pancakes, and french toast. And if all family ski homes had a 112-person capacity, with a dining room big enough to serve everyone on thick, well-worn wooden tables. Après ski, guests lounge on the couches near the fireplace and kids play games in the rec room.

Zephyr Mountain Lodge

866-433-3908, 970-726-8400
zephyrmountainlodge.com
201 Zephyr Way, Winter Park
Price Range: $249–$983
Credit Cards: AE, D, MC, V
Children: Y
Pets: Y
Handicap Accessible: Y

Zephyr Mountain provides a glimpse into what Winter Park's base village might look like in a decade: a huge, new ski-in/ski-out lodge with rustic-chic, Intrawest-style architecture (if you've been to Whistler, British Columbia, or Mammoth, California,

Friendly dogs await visitors at the Outpost Bed and Breakfast. Evelyn Spence

you know what we mean). There's heated, underground parking. There's an on-site ski shop and ski storage. There are four outdoor hot tubs. There's a free hotel shuttle to take you the mile downhill into town. The condo-style rooms, in woodsy greens and rich burgundies, have full kitchens, gas fireplaces, balconies (be sure to request one with a mountain view), big armoires, and spacious common areas.

FRASER

Outpost Bed and Breakfast
Innkeeper: Barbara Parker
800-430-4538, 970-726-5346
winterpark-inn.com
info@winterpark-inn.com
687 County Road 517, Fraser
Price Range: $95–$130, including breakfast
Credit Cards: D, MC, V

Children: Y
Pets: N
Handicap Accessible: N

"If I ever got hitched, I'd do it here!" So says Barbara Parker, innkeeper at the Outpost, a seven-room B&B well off the beaten path of US 40. In summer, the enormous garden is a playground: horseshoes, volleyball, a putting green, an open fire pit—and hammocks for lazy afternoons. And yes, weddings are big here: The views of the Indian Peaks are stunning. Inside, the inn is homey, with stuffed animals, antiques, real saddles, and a huge video library. Breakfasts—of eggs Florentine or french toast stuffed with cream cheese, banana slices, and honey—are served by candlelight, and the rooms are named after "my bratty kids, my siblings, and my

The Snowberry is a French Country–style inn tucked deep into the woods. Winter Park Resort

mom." The Susan Carol is busy, with floral patterns on the bedspread, lamp stands, painting, and upholstery; the Kenneth Anthony, with the best view in the house, has more understated pine-green wallpaper, a rich red carpet, and a roll-away bed. All rooms come with TV/VCR, plush robes, and a private bath.

Snowberry Inn

Innkeepers: John and Chris Cribari
970-726-5974
thesnowberry.com
info@thesnowberry.com
1001 CR 8, Fraser
Price Range: $155–$225, including breakfast
Credit Cards: AE, D, MC, V
Children: Y, over 12 years old

Pets: N
Handicap Accessible: Y

A sister inn to the Wild Horse (see below), hidden up a long, winding driveway, the French Country–style Snowberry feels more like a posh mansion than a mountain cabin: The grand living room has hardwood floors, walnut bookcases, leather furniture, and french doors that open to the front porch. Off the back deck, chairs sit facing a panorama of the Indian Peaks. None of the five rooms have phones or TV, and each is graced with classy, unique decorations. Book the Adobe for a Mexican pine queen bed, Southwest colors, and earthen pottery; for a more cabinlike style, request the Pine Grove, with twig chairs and a green cedar wardrobe with evergreen-tree cutouts. The largest room at the Snowberry is the Mountainview: It comes with a whirlpool tub, a cozy reading nook, a private deck, and four-poster king bed. And no matter what digs you choose, your day will start with quiches, french toast, blue corn pancakes, frittatas, fresh-baked scones, and loads of fruit.

✪ Wild Horse Inn

Innkeepers: John and Chris Cribari
970-726-0456
wildhorseinn.com
info@wildhorseinn.com
1536 CR 83, Fraser
Price Range: $165–$235, including breakfast
Credit Cards: AE, D, MC, V
Children: Y, over 12 years old
Pets: N
Handicap Accessible: N

No question, the Wild Horse is the best B&B in the Fraser Valley: The lodge is handcrafted from 400-year-old logs, the fireplace is constructed from river rocks, the rooms are enormous—with vaulted ceilings, classic Western, Southwestern, and mountain decor—and the breakfast is second to none. Depending on the day, you might wake up to apple, brie, and bacon frittatas, whole-wheat peach and pecan pancakes, homemade brioche rolls, or blue-corn crepes with asparagus filling. In the afternoon, nosh on chocolate gingerbread or snowball cookies. You can choose from seven lodge rooms or three cabins, each with unique furnishing and feels: The Mariposa Cabin has a kiva fireplace, stained glass windows that echo Navajo rug patterns, Spanish tile accents, leather-topped tables, and a rustic pine king bed. The Saddleblanket Cabin has more of an

A four-poster bed graces a room in the Wild Horse Inn. Evelyn Spence

Old West–chic theme, with a denim down duvet, cast-iron wood stove, rocking chair, wrought-iron bed, and cow skull keeping watch over the living room. Back at the main house, the rooms feature overstuffed reading chairs, log accents, private balconies, Pendleton blankets, and jetted tubs. In summer, the buildings are surrounded by a rambling wildflower garden.

FARTHER AFIELD

✪ Devil's Thumb Ranch

800-933-4339
devilsthumbranch.com
3530 CR 83, Tabernash
Price Range: $175–$795
Credit Cards: MC, V
Children: Y
Pets: N
Handicap Accessible: Y

You can call Devil's Thumb a cross-country skiing area: There are 125 kilometers of groomed trails here. You can call it a spa: Ranch Creek Spa, opened in 2005, specializes in treating the problems of high altitude, sun, and winter weather with natural products. You can call it a world-class dining experience: The Ranch House Restaurant serves apps like rainbow trout smoked over hickory chips and antelope satay; entrées like Niman Ranch lamb lightly dusted in lavender salt, and cowboy-cut steaks with ranchero beans; and desserts like the "Slice of the Mountain," a chocolate pound cake heaped with whipped cream. And yes, you can call it a ranch, too: The stables offer riding and cattle-work lessons, hay rides, and half- and full-day trail rides. You can fly-fish the Williams Fork, the Fraser, and the Blue, hike 9 miles up to the namesake Devil's Thumb (a unique rock formation), or just head over to Winter Park for a day of skiing. In 2007, they're opening a new lodge in "Parkitecture" style—complete with a

three-story fireplace and bowling alley—in addition to the already-existing classy (and romantic) cabins, which all have wood-burning fireplaces, antiques from around the world, and tasteful Rocky Mountain decor. To top it off, Devil's Thumb has won numerous awards for environmental responsibility: geothermally heated buildings, food from local vendors, and a main lodge (the Broad Axe Barn) that's made of beams from trees harvested during the Civil War.

Guest Ranches

✪ C Lazy U Ranch

Owners: The Murray Family
970-887-3344
clazyu.com
ranch@clazyu.com
3640 CO 125, Granby
Price Range: $2,350–$2,525 per week
Credit Cards: AE, MC, V
Children: Y
Pets: N
Handicap Accessible: Y

Before Willow Creek—which runs through C Lazy U—was dammed in the late 1940s, it meandered in the shape of a *C* with a *U* underneath, and thus provided inspiration for the ranch's long-standing brand. In fact, there's been a dude ranch on these 8,000 acres since 1946, and it has always emphasized horsemanship skills along with the typical trail rides (there's a 12,000-square-foot indoor arena and a "Shodeo" at the end of each week). The rooms and suites, which mix a contemporary simplicity with Western and Southwestern touches like bold-print comforters and overstuffed leather chairs (and all get a nightly chocolate-mint turndown service), are scattered in a few buildings within walking distance of the main lodge. And that's where you go when the dinner bell rings: chef Mike Schneider—who's been on *Emeril Live*—

cooks up rosemary rack of lamb, antelope frittatas, and goose rouladen for dinner. On Friday mornings, breakfast takes place at a campfire near the Willow Creek Reservoir—with blueberry pancakes, eggs, and bacon cooked over the flames. Besides horseback riding, C Lazy U has tennis courts, a basketball court, skeet shooting, paddle boats, an outdoor pool, a game room, an on-site bar, and—if you're not exhausted yet—an exercise room.

Drowsy Water Ranch

Owners: Ken and Randy Sue Fosha
800-845-2292, 970-725-3456
drowsywater.com
dwr@drowsywater.com
Off US 40, 6 miles W. of Granby
Price Range: $325–$345 daily, $1,525–$1,590 weekly; children and nonriders have reduced rates
Credit Cards: MC, V
Children: Y
Pets: N
Handicap Accessible: Y

All 100 or so horses at Drowsy Water have been bred, raised, and trained by the Fosha family, who have been running the ranch since 1977. (It has been a guest ranch for something like 70 years—and apparently the first owner marketed himself so well that he got a train station built here and re-christened the creek running through the property.) Their activities list reads as follows: "horseback riding, swimming, horseshoes, steak fryes [sic], trout fishing, Western dancing, Jeep trips, song fests, campfires, hay rides, carnival, pack trips, staff entertainment, gymkhana rodeos, raft trips, children's programs, nearby golf, hunting, and much more." Translation? There's plenty to do here. And you'll be fueled by hearty Western food (dinner rolls, ribs, cowboy coffee, fried chicken), sometimes served in the wood-paneled dining

room, sometimes served out at the barbecue, and sometimes just dished out the back of a chuckwagon. Both cabin and lodge rooms are decorated with elk trophies, Navajo rugs, wagon-wheel chandeliers, stone fireplaces, and exposed beams.

DINING

Restaurants

WINTER PARK

Carlos & Maria's

970-726-9674
Cooper Creek Square, Winter Park
Meals Served: D, with L on weekends and holidays
Price Range: Appetizers $4.75–$8.95, entrées $7.95–$15.25
Full bar: Y
Reservations: Y
Credit Cards: AE, D, MC, V
Handicap Accessible: Y

Carlos & Maria's is named after its husband-and-wife owners, Chuck and Marie Huston, who play chef and hostess, respectively—and have lived in Winter Park since 1984. When you enter from the top walkway of the Cooper Creek mall, you cross a threshold into a cozy and genuine gem: The walls are a cheerful orange and hung with Mexican beer ads, piñatas swing from the ceiling, and the bulletin board near the kitchen is tacked with photos of staff river trips. With a cheap happy hour and a good children's menu, C&M is perfect for families looking for a post-ski, post-hike feast of spicy beef fajitas, chili rellenos, and cheese enchiladas with spinach filling. Maria's recommendation? The carnitas, a dish of marinated pork that's sautéed in butter and orange juice until it's caramelized and sweet.

Carver's Bakery Café serves healthy, hearty breakfasts and lunches with fresh-baked bread. Evelyn Spence

Carver's Bakery Café

970-726-8202
carversbakery.com
carversbakery@netscape.com
Behind Cooper Creek Square, Winter Park
Meals Served: B, L
Price Range: $6–$11
Full bar: N
Reservations: N
Credit Cards: MC, V
Handicap Accessible: Y

Through various owners, Carver's has stood behind the three-story Cooper Creek shopping complex for 30-odd years; its latest custodians, Simon (a biologist and Cordon Bleu chef) and Candy (who started running her own restaurant at age 17), eliminated all shortenings, food colorings, and additives in favor of natural yeasts, whole eggs, and Grade-A butter. The cute and comfortable seating area is decorated with vintage skis, and the pastry case is full of homemade breads, bagels, and muffins. Breakfast brings traditional eggs Benedict, Denver omelets, and fresh-squeezed grapefruit juice; lunch ranges from healthy to heart-attack hearty, with big salads, fresh soups, green chili, chicken stew, Frito pie (Fritos covered with beans, green chili, cheddar, and lime sour cream), and the Oh-My-Goodness (grilled-cheese sandwich with cheddar, swiss, and bleu).

Deno's Mountain Bistro

970-726-5332
denosmountainbistro.com
denos@rkymtnhi.com
78911 US 40, Winter Park

Meals Served: L, D
Price Range: $11–$30
Full bar: Y
Reservations: Y
Credit Cards: AE, D, MC, V
Handicap Accessible: Y

Opened in 1946 as the Village Inn—when there used to be a nickel juke box inside and hitching post out front—then renamed the Swiss House in 1967, and finally dubbed Deno's in 1973 (after owner Deno Kutrumbos), this local institution is a mix of formal and casual. The dining room, thanks to Culinary Institute of America grad Debbie Lewis, serves up artichoke au gratin, jagerschnitzel, twin-cut pork chops, and Voodoo Calypso Chicken (spiced chicken over linguini Alfredo), with a wine list that boasts an Excellence Award from *Wine Spectator*, one of only 11 restaurants so

honored in the entire state of Colorado. The bar, with nine big-screen TVs and a pub menu of pizza, quesadillas, soups, sandwiches, and burgers, is homage to Deno's true love: the Denver Broncos. And it's always packed with true Winter Park natives, catching games and catching up with each other. As 30-year veteran waitress Edie says, "We treat the locals like gold." Not to mention visitors.

✪ Fontenot's Fresh Seafood & Grill

970-726-4021
Kings Crossing Rd. and US 40, Winter Park
Meals Served: L, D
Price Range: Lunches $5–$10, dinner
    entrées $15–$25
Full bar: Y
Reservations: Y
Credit Cards: AE, D, MC, V
Handicap Accessible: Y

It's not far from the Rockies to Cajun Country when you visit Fontenot's—po' boys, catfish, and crawfish are part of the cuisine. Evelyn Spence

Chris Moore, the owner of Fontenot's, is originally from New Hampshire—but that doesn't stop him from cooking like he's straight out of Cajun country. And a new location—with picture windows, balcony seating, and a two-story-high gabled ceiling—makes for an airy, happening atmosphere. For lunch, the po' boys—ham and cheddar, shaved sirloin and provolone, scallops with ginger lime mayo, turkey meatball with marinara—bring in a regular lunch crowd. Or perhaps it's the French Silk Pie, a graham-cracker-crusted creation with a rich dark chocolate filling. For dinner, you won't leave hungry: The Atchafalaya Catfish is deep-fried in cornmeal batter; the crawfish ettoufée is smothered in rich pepper, garlic, and tomatoes; and the bone-in French-cut rib eye swims in jalapeño bleu-cheese cream sauce. Don't want to roll down the slopes the next day? Try a hearty bowl of gumbo (with crawfish, okra, tomatoes, and chicken) or the blackened tilapia.

✪ Gasthaus Eichler

970-726-5133
gasthauseichler.com
info@gasthauseichler.com
78786 US 40, Winter Park
Meals Served: B (for inn guests only), D
Price Range: Appetizers $8.50–$10, entrées
$15.50–$29.50
Full bar: Y
Reservations: Y
Credit Cards: AE, D, MC, V
Handicap Accessible: Y

On the ground floor of its namesake inn, Gasthaus Eichler (the restaurant) is known for Old World, Continental cuisine. We're talking vegetable strudel, chateaubriand for two, rindsrolladen (a braised beef roll filled with veal, bacon, and pickle), kassler rippchen (cured and smoked pork chops with sauerkraut), and paprika goulash. Chef René Weder, a native of Switzerland, did

stints as executive chef at the Brown Palace and the Palace Arms before moving to Winter Park full time—and he brings his pedigree with him. The meat is butchered on the premises, the breads are homemade, a pianist plays nightly, and the tables are set with crystal and charger plates.

Fondue Stube at the Gasthaus

For $19–$25 a head, you can settle into what Joan Weder calls the "living room" of the Gasthaus and make a meal of fondue. On weekends, you'll even be accompanied by live acoustic guitar. The traditional Swiss Matterhorn fondue, a rich blend of Emmentaler, Gruyère, and Appenzeller cheeses and white wine, kirsch, and garlic, comes with french bread, vegetables, and apple slices. The Gasthaus fondue is for carnivores: venison, beef, shrimp, and chicken with assorted dipping sauces. For dessert, don't skip the Chocolate Decadence, a bubbling cauldron of melted Swiss goodness in which to drench cake and fresh fruit.

✪ Hernando's Pizza Pub

970-726-5409
hernandospizza.com
hernandos@rkymtnhi.com
78199 US 40, Winter Park
Meals Served: D
Price Range: Appetizers $1.75–$9.95, pizzas
$8.25–$17.25, pasta $6.95–$7.50
Full bar: Y
Reservations: N
Credit Cards: AE, D, MC, V
Handicap Accessible: Y

When a server sets down a honey bear along with your thick-crusted pie, here's a tip: at Hernando's, you eat your way to the edge of the pizza, then drizzle honey on the crust for a built-in dessert. Sound bizarre? Trust us—when the dough is as good as this, whether it's regular or whole wheat, you'll wonder why other pizza joints haven't thought of it. Hernando's, a Winter Park stalwart since 1967, is always packed; while you wait, decorate a dollar bill and donate it to the wallpaper (as of 2005, there was $22,000 worth of Washingtons in the restaurant). The vibe is crowded but cozy, with several roaring fireplaces and stained-glass windows. As for the pies? Choose from one of three styles (pizza sauce and mozzarella; olive oil, basil, and minced garlic; double cheese, extra garlic, olive oil, basil, and black pepper), and then a set of toppings: The Sonoma is piled with sun-dried tomataoes, artichokes, and grilled chicken, and the Column 1 is, well, even more piled—with pepperoni, sausage, meatballs, salami, ham, and bacon. You also can order spaghetti and lasagna, but at Hernando's, the pizza's truly the thing.

✪ Lodge at Sunspot

970-726-1446, 800-510-8025
skiwinterpark.com
On top of Winter Park Mountain
Meals Served: L, D
Price Range: Prix-fixe dinner Thurs.
    through Sat. $39–$59
Full bar: Y
Reservations: Y
Credit Cards: AE, MC, V
Handicap Accessible: N

During the winter, you can step into the Lodge at Sunspot—a massive log cabin on the 10,700-foot summit of Winter Park, with practically 360-degree views of the Continental Divide—for a lunch of baked potatoe, soup, salad, or sandwich. Or you can indulge in a five-course dinner, taking the seven-minute ride up the Zephyr Express under clear Rocky Mountain skies to tuck into entrées like Hawaiian opah marinated in miso and wrapped in wontons, or four-cheese and walnut ravioli with roasted artichokes and candy-striped beets. The lobby, decorated with big wreaths and antique skis and snowshoes,

has a stone fireplace to warm your toes, a library in which to lounge, and richly patterned carpets more conducive to slippers than ski boots. The dining room's heavy log columns frame floor-to-ceiling windows. According to local legend, this used to be the site of a shepherd's hut—not a bad place to look out for the flock.

Smokin' Moe's Ribhouse & Saloon

970-726-4600
smokinmoes.com
smokinmoes@coweblink.net
Cooper Creek Square, Winter Park
Meals Served: L, D
Price Range: Appetizers $6.50–$8.50;
    entrées $10.99–$19.99
Full bar: Y
Reservations: Y
Credit Cards: AE, D, MC, V
Handicap Accessible: Y

The entryway to Smokin' Moe's is a black-and-white (fake) photographic history of the joint—with characters like "Joe 'Baby Face' Carter, Rib-Rubber and Personal Hair Groomer to Moe" and "Moe's Pal, David 'The Pencil' Palmer, Moe's Most Literate Friend." The decor is over-the-top Western—think saloon doors, wagon wheels, old mining photos, a sign over the bathroom door that reads "Used Beer Department," and a cowboy mannequin sitting quietly at the end of the bar—but Moe's also brings in top blues acts like Tommy Castro and James Cotton once a month. Tuck your napkin under your chin for prize-winning pulled pork, chicken, hot links, saucy ribs, beef brisket, baked beans, Texas toast, and Oreo pie, then play a round of pool or pinball.

The Sushi Bar

970-726-0447
ineedsushi.com
info@ineedsushi.com
78941 US 40, Winter Park

Meals Served: D
Price Range: Special rolls $5.25–$19.99,
   two-piece nigiri $3.99–$5.99
Full bar: Y
Reservations: Y
Credit Cards: AE, D, MC, V
Handicap Accessible: N

Every ski town needs a spot for sushi, and
Winter Park is no exception. Sushi Bar has
the requisite goldfish aquariums, bamboo
window coverings, and neon Kirin signs,
but its red-painted walls and thin iron
stools make it the most urban-feeling spot
in the valley. And they don't rest on their
laurels: Their $20 Aquarium Roll, packed
with veggies and soft-shell crab tempura
and topped with salmon, ahi, octopus,
hamachi, shrimp, unagi, and tobiko—is
practically a meal in itself. Just as creative
is the Spicy Monkey Roll, a concoction of
spicy tuna and unagi topped with banana
and sweet soy sauce. They offer the usual
nigiri and sashimi, as well as a menu
fraught with sexual references: appetizers
are "Foreplay" and sushi combos range
from the "69" to the "Sushi Orgy." In the
end, the fish is fresh, and that's all that
matters.

Untamed Steakhouse

970-726-1111
untamedsteakhouse.com
78491 US 40, Winter Park
Meals Served: D
Price Range: Appetizers $11.95–$13.95,
   entrées $7.95–$23.95
Full bar: Y
Reservations: Y
Credit Cards: AE, D, MC, V
Handicap Accessible: Y

The use of produce from Morales Farms, an
organic operation in nearby Granby that's
been humming along since 1943, is one
reason to pull up a comfortable wooden
chair to a white tablecloth at Untamed.

Another? The 30-foot vaulted ceilings,
river-rock fireplace, and exposed lodge-
pole-pine beams. Need more? Add in
friendly service, a sports bar, 9-foot billiards tables, darts, and live music on
weekends, and you get the upscale-casual
mountain-town vibe that Untamed has
perfected. First and foremost, it's a steak
house, with Angus sirloin slathered in
hollandaise, mini filet mignons sautéed
with brie, peppered strip on a bed of
caramelized onions, and surf-and-turf.
But don't leave without sampling the
roasted-corn cheese chowder or the ancho-
crusted buffalo carpaccio. Here's a place
where Guinness-battered catfish is
considered "Tame Fare" on the menu and
dessert reaches the sinful heights of a
caramel apple crème brûlée.

FRASER

The Hungry Bear

970-726-0069
thehungrybear.com
5 CR 72, Fraser
Meals Served: B, L, D
Price Range: Breakfast $4.95–$8.95, lunch
   $4.25–$11.25, dinner $12.50–$15.25
Full bar: N
Reservations: N
Credit Cards: MC, V
Handicap Accessible: Y

In 1885, pioneer rancher Lewis Dewitt
Clinton Gaskill lived and ran the post office
here. These days, the Gaskill House is now
home to the Hungry Bear, a Fraser favorite
that serves up huge portions all day long.
For breakfast, locals dig into chicken-fried
steak, malted pancakes, and chorizo scrambles. Dinner offerings include steaks, pork
chops, Kobe beef burgers, focaccia pizzas,
house-made soups, and daily dessert specials like Lemon Dream Bread Pudding and
PBJ Cheesecake.

✪ **Ranch House Restaurant at Devil's Thumb Ranch**
970-726-5633
devilsthumbranch.com
3530 CR 83, Tabernash
Meals Served: L, D
Price Range: Appetizers $7–$12, entrées
    $17–$37
Full bar: Y
Reservations: Y
Credit Cards: MC, V
Handicap Accessible: Y

The menu at the Ranch House changes constantly, depending on what local organic produce is available. All the meat comes from Niman Ranch or Diestal Ranch. All the seafood is flown in daily. And the restaurant—with large, curtain-framed windows that look toward the Indian Peaks—is housed in a 1937 homestead that used to be located along a stagecoach trail which crossed the Continental Divide. In short, it's one of the best dining experiences in the Fraser Valley. Start with the Bags of Gold—Boulder's MouCo Camembert baked in homemade pastry—or the elk carpaccio, pounded melt-in-your-mouth thin and accompanied by whiskey marmalade. Entrées run the gamut of game, from free-range antelope steaks with prickly pear sauce to pan-seared Colorado bison, but make someone in your party order the lavender rack of lamb: It's a Niman Ranch cut that's dusted with lavender sauce and complemented by a summer fruit chutney. The Saloon, a gable-roofed log cabin with exposed wood beams and historical photos, takes the food down a notch from highbrow: mac and cheese, meatloaf, ribs, burgers.

Food Purveyors

Bakeries
Base Camp Bakery and Café (970-726-5530, 78437 US 40, Winter Park) Crowded, with high stools and blond wood tables, Base Camp bakes its own croissants, scones, beignets, nut bars, and enormous cinnamon rolls. Their breakfast sandwiches are made with house-baked bagels and have a camping theme: The Winnebago comes with two eggs, grilled veggies, and jack and cheddar cheeses; the Bedroll is filled with eggs, avocado, tomato, and swiss.

Coffee Shops
Mountain Grind Coffee and Bistro (970-726-0999, 47 Cooper Creek Square, Winter Park) A combination Internet café/ice cream shop/lunch spot with big windows and bright red leather couches, Mountain Grind can serve up anything from a Byers (a latte with cocoa, caramel, white cocoa, and whipped cream) to a pomegranate gelato to a bowl of sausage and potato soup.

Rocky Mountain Roastery (970-726-4400, 78723 US 40, Winter Park; 543 Zerex St., Fraser) The Fraser branch of RMR adjoins Totally Wired Cyclery and has couches and a few public computers, but both branches blend hot drinks like the Peaches and Cream (peach syrup and steamed milk) and the Mexican Mocha. You can also order their beans online (rockymountainroastery.com).

Delis

Rudi's Deli (970-726-8955, winterparkdeli.com, Park Plaza Center, US 40, Winter Park) Rudi's has just five round tables and wire-backed chairs, so most people take their food to go: Holiday on a Bun (turkey breast, cream cheese, cranberry sauce, sprouts) or Bacon Boy (three slices of marble rye with bacon, ham, and turkey) or the WACC (walnuts, avocado, cream cheese). Rudi's also serves paninis, daily soup specials, and sack-lunch combos.

Farmer's Markets

Granby Farmer's Market (granbychamber.com, Fri. nights in Sept. in the parking lot next to Ian's Bakery) Local vendors Morales Farms, Sweet Pea Products, Hungry Mother Foods, and Basecamp Bakery sell produce, fresh eggs, dressings, fruits, pastries, and whole-grain breads.

Frozen Desserts

Mountain Grind (see "Coffee Shops," above) Gelato flavors include spiced caramel apple, spumoni, and eggnog.

Groceries

Safeway (970-726-9484, 40 CR 804, Fraser)

Stop & Save (970-726-5836, 78415 US 40, Winter Park)

Winter Park Market (970-726-4704, 78336 US 40, Winter Park) Located in the King's Crossing shopping area, this store sells organic produce, herbal tea, frozen food, protein powders, flower essences, natural food books, and gifts. They also prepare lunches to go.

Nightlife

Buckets Saloon and Laundry (970-726-3026, 78415 US 40, Winter Park) A short lesson on the origin of Buckets: "In 1998, two couples got together and came up with the idea of creating a fun spot in Winter Park where adults could do laundry, play video games, and become dangerously drunk all at the same time." They soon added *South Park* TV nights, karaoke, pool tables, arcade games, and live music.

Crooked Creek Saloon (970-726-9250, 401 Zerex St., Fraser) An old-school saloon on US 40 in Fraser (in fact, the oldest in Grand County), Crooked Creek serves burgers, wings, and steaks until late—thus the motto "Eat Till It Hurts, Drink Till It Feels Better." Rosie, the woman reclining above the entrance to the bar, practiced the world's oldest profession about 100 years ago. Mondays are poker nights, and there are drink specials and 25-cent wings during all NASCAR races.

Derailer Bar (800-979-0332, base of Winter Park) Get them to honk the real train whistle, try a serving of deep-fried pickles, or just kick back to daily après-ski food and drink specials at this base-area bar.

Randi's Irish Saloon (970-726-1172, 78521 US 40, Winter Park) Owned by a former world-class rower, Randi's has Irish beers on tap, Irish food on the menu (Dublin beef stew, shepherd's pie), and live music in summer. Stools encircle the square center bar, and old beer cans line the shelves next to big-screen TVs.

Randi's Irish Saloon is owned by a former world-class rower—and has plenty of Guinness to go. Evelyn Spence

Verso Cellars (970-726-9417, versocellars.com, Cooper Creek Square, Winter Park) Taste the goods from this boutique Colorado winery, or reserve a table for 10 and try various "wine bites" paired with Verso's wines: figs stuffed with Colorado Haystack goat cheese and accompanied by a Verso cab, phyllo duck purses with a Plum Creek Riesling, or a brandy peppercorn terrine of pork with a Woody Creek merlot.

Willow Creek Bar and Grill (970-887-0885, 903 W. Agate Ave., Granby) Pool tournaments on Wednesdays, karaoke on Thursdays, and live music on most weekends.

The Winter Park Pub (970-726-4929, 78260 US 40, Winter Park) Open until 2 AM on weekends, The Pub is decorated with old ski-area trail signs, photos of massive wipeouts, and collages of snapshots of drunk people (taken at The Pub). It's dark and divey, with worn wood tables, high rafters, and a cozy fireplace.

CULTURE

Cinema
Silver Screen Cinema (970-726-5390, Park Plaza Shopping Center, US 40, Winter Park) Shows the biggest of Hollywood's blockbusters.

Historical Sites

Phoenix Gold Mine (303-567-0422, phoenixgoldmine.com, Trail Creek Road, Idaho Springs) Head underground to see what mining was really like at this 1871 claim, look at veins, learn about gold milling and refining, and finish up by panning for gold (they let you keep what you find).

Museums

Cozens Ranch Museum (970-725-3939, grandcountymuseum.com, 77849 US 40, Fraser) About 115 years ago, this was a stagecoach stop run by William Zane Cozens and his wife, Mary Elizabeth—and it now contains original furniture, historical photos, mining paraphernalia, along with a "pioneer garden" that showcases flowers that were grown during Winter Park's beginnings.

Pioneer Village Museum (970-725-3939, grandcountymuseum.com, 110 E. Byers Ave., Hot Sulphur Springs) Though it's a bit of a drive from Winter Park proper, this museum complex—just off US 40—has a blacksmith shop from the 1890s, a jail with original graffiti, a collection of tools, and an exhibit highlighting the role of women on the frontier.

Theaters and Other Miscellaneous Venues

Fraser Walk Through History Park (970-726-5491, frasercolorado.com, 120 Zerex St., Fraser) A collection of 20 Jim Hoy sculptures depict "The American Experience" through bronze portrayals of pioneering female physician Doc Susie, outlaw Jeremiah Johnson, a mountain lion, a rancher, and more.

Grand Theatre Company (970-726-5048, grandtheatreco.com, 78415 Park Place 203) Local crews stage plays and musicals ranging from G-rated (*A Year with Frog and Toad*) to R (*All in the Timing*). Desserts and cocktails are available, and some nights even include a wine tasting.

KIDS' STUFF

Amaze'n Winter Park (980-726-0214, amazenmazes.com) See how fast you can get through this two-story labyrinth, located at the base of the ski resort.

Beaver Village Fishing Ponds (beavervillage.com) Affiliated with historic Beaver Lodge, these family-friendly waters are filled with trout.

Fraser River Valley Lions Club (fraservalleylions.org) This organization has a wheelchair-accessible pond that's open to children, locals, and tourists alike—and it's just off US 40 near the Fraser Safeway.

Fraser Tubing Hill (970-726-5954, behind Alco shopping center in Fraser) Made smooth and slippery from tube after tube, this hill is perfect for achieving huge crashes at high speeds.

Georgetown Loop Railroad (888-456-6777, georgetownlooprr.com) Open in summer, this historic narrow-gauge railroad steams up from Georgetown (on I-70, west of the turnoff up Berthoud Pass to Winter Park) to Silver Plume, passing the remains of gold and silver mines along the way.

Trail Ridge Art Company (970-726-4959, trailridgeart.com, Cooper Creek Square) In this art gallery/pottery studio, you can pick a plain ceramic piece, decorate it to your heart's content, and walk away with a custom-made artwork of your own.

Winter Park Alpine Slide (970-726-1564, winterparkresort.com) Ride a plastic sled, bobsledlike, as you careen down a twisting, 3,000-foot-long, 610-vertical-foot cement flume—the longest of its kind in Colorado.

RECREATION: WINTER AND SPRING

Alpine Skiing and Snowboarding

Winter Park

skiwinterpark.com

Overview: Year after year, in magazines like *Skiing* and *Ski*, Winter Park has been voted the best area for moguls in the country: The bump runs here are long, relentless, and look (and feel) like egg cartons. But with 2,762 acres and a 3,060-foot vertical-foot drop, there are plenty of other options—including good kids' areas, above-treeline bowls, steep tree shots, and long cruisers.

> **Winter Park: The 4-1-1**
> Acres: 2,762
> Summit elevation: 12,060 feet
> Vertical drop: 3,060 feet
> Annual snowfall: 359 inches
> Percent advanced/expert terrain: 70
> Percent intermediate terrain: 21
> Percent beginner terrain: 9
> Lifts: 24

Winter Park is technically divided into two areas—Winter Park and Mary Jane—with two base areas, each of which has parking lots, restaurants, rental shops, lockers, and the like. In general, The Jane is a tougher hill, with the biggest moguls and the steepest slopes, and some die-hards never cross over to the Winter Park side.

Must-ski: Beginners should stick to the Eskimo Express, Prospector Express, and Olympia Express chairs, with wide green runs like March Hare and Allan Phipps. Intermediates can make huge GS turns on the likes of Hughes (off the Zephyr Express) and Sleeper (off Challenger). For wide-open, high-alpine runs, head up the Timberline double chair: It drops you off at 12,060 feet, where an apron of powder (sometimes windblown) covers lines like Forget-Me-Not and Larkspur. The best bump runs are either off Challenger (Railbender, Derailer, Brakeman) or between Mary Jane and Winter Park (Outhouse, Drunken Frenchman). The relatively new Vasquez Cirque area, opened in 1997, has a few short and steep chutes, but it requires both a long traverse/hike in and a long, long traverse out. The Rail Yard terrain park has big tabletops and a variety of rails to slide.

Grub: The **Moffatt Market**, at the base of the mountain, is a huge food court with multiple offerings—fried chicken, pizza, burgers, soups, salads, Asian food, breakfast burritos, bagel sandwiches, mac and cheese, coffees, hot chocolate, and tea. The nearby **Derailer Bar** serves up traditional pub grub (burgers, beer) and nontraditional apps like fried pickles. Over at the Mary Jane base area, the **Club Car** has sushi Fridays, Bloody Marys on Sunday, and killer seafood chowder every day. Up on the summit, the **Lodge at Sunspot**

(see page 287) has both a full-service dining room and a smaller food court. The tiny warming hut and bigger deck at the top of the Super Gauge Express, **Lunch Rock,** has snacks and hot drinks if you don't want to head all the way back to the base areas. Over near the halfpipe, **Snoasis,** open from 10:30 AM until 3 PM, grills up burgers and pours cocktails on a deck overlooking the new-schoolers.

Cross-Country Skiing and Snowshoeing

Devil's Thumb Ranch (970-726-8231, devilsthumbranch.com, 3530 CR 83, Tabernash) Devil's Thumb is the most extensive Nordic system in the area, with 63 trails totaling 125 kilometers, 4,000 acres of terrain, and three warming huts. They even have 2.5 kilometers of lighted trails that close at 9 PM and 8 kilometers of trails designated for skijoring (when your dog pulls you along on your skis). Learn-to-ski packages, kids' lessons, and private lessons available. (For more information, see "Lodging" and "Dining" entries on page 282 and 289.)

Snow Mountain Ranch (970-887-2152, ymcarockies.com, 1101 CR 53, Granby) Rolling over 5,200 acres of meadows, Snow Mountain Ranch's trails stretch to 100 kilometers. This YMCA branch offers group lessons, children's programs, snowshoeing, and dog-sledding.

SolVista Basin at Granby Ranch (970-887-3384, granbyranch.com, 1000 Village Rd., Granby) Over 25 kilometers of groomed trails for all abilities, equipment rentals, and wide-open scenery at this small combination cross-country/downhill area.

Winter Park Tour Center (800-729-7907, winterparkresort.com) Daily snowshoe tours depart from the base of the mountain in winter.

Dogsledding

Dog Sled Rides of Winter Park (970-726-8326, dogsledrides.com/winterpark, Kings Crossing Rd., Winter Park) A team of dogs—in this case, Siberian and Alaskan huskies, some of which have competed in big-time races—can reach up to 20 miles per hour on tours ranging from a half-hour to two hours, all weaving through 1,800 acres of wilderness.

Guiding and Backcountry

Berthoud Pass This former ski area, one of the first in Colorado, has some of the steepest, most varied, and most easily accessible backcountry terrain in the state: You can skin up either side of US 40 at the top of the pass, ski down chutes, bowls, and glades to the road, and hitch a ride back to your car. The avalanche danger can be extreme—so bring your beacon, shovel, probe, partner, and ideally a knowledgeable local.

Second Creek Cabin to Winter Park Resort You have two options here: a mellow out-and-back to Second Creek Cabin, an old backcountry hut, that's just 3 miles total—or a shuttle trip that continues past the cabin all the way to the ski area (5.5 miles one way). If you go for option two, you'll pass through avalanche terrain, so be prepared.

Other backcountry areas Over 70 percent of Grand County is public land, which means there are endless opportunities for earning your turns: the **Indian Peaks**, the **Never Summer Wilderness**, the **Medicine Bow/Routt National Forest**, and the **Byers Peak Wilderness.** Check with a local shop or a ranger station (see page 303) for routes and conditions.

Ice Skating

Cooper Creek Square Right near the parking structure at this outdoor mall in Winter Park is a small, free rink. Rent skates at nearby **Christy Sports** (970-726-8873).

Devil's Thumb (800-933-4339, devilsthumbranch.com, CR 83, Tabernash) Rent skates for $5 and get a rink pass for $5, then enjoy the idyllic setting of this guest ranch and Nordic ski area.

Fraser Valley Recreation Rink (970-726-4708, CR 5, Fraser) There's no fee here, but you need to bring your own skates.

Snow Mountain Ranch (970-887-2152, ymcarockies.com, 1101 CR 53, Granby) Snow Mountain recently opened an outdoor rink near its Nordic facilities, with $3 admission and $5 skate rental. Kids under 9 and YMCA members, get in free.

Sleigh Rides

Dashing-Thru-The-Snow (970-726-0900, dashingthruthesnow.com, 85 CR 5105, off CR 5, Fraser) Wrap yourself in wool blankets and take an old-fashioned sleigh on a dinner ride (steak, chicken, salmon, salad, veggies, dessert) or dessert ride, or book a bonfire ride and roast marshmallows under the stars.

RECREATION: SUMMER AND FALL

Cycling: Mountain Biking

Buck Creek and Broken Thumb A mix of single- and doubletrack that follows part of the Fraser River Trail before branching off and climbing the steep Buck Creek path (complete with Winter Park views). On the way down, the Broken Thumb Trail is steep and rocky—and hooks back up with the Fraser River Trail.

Flume/Creekside Loop From the St. Louis Creek campground, follow the creek up (keeping an eye out for beaver ponds and moose) and the Flume Trail, a mellow descent, back down. The loop is just over 5 miles.

Fraser River Trail A paved bike path parallels the river and US 40 between Fraser and Winter Park Resort for 5-odd miles, gaining about 600 feet and passing through Old Town and the Idlewild campground.

Rogers Pass The only nonmotorized trail above treeline that's open to mountain bikers, this challenging 6.3-mile trail starts at Corona Pass Road, ascends almost up to the 12,000-foot mark, and drops you at the Continental Divide. Start this ride early in the morning to avoid dangerous summer-afternoon thunderstorms—you're well above any shelter.

Snow Mountain Ranch (970-887-2152, ymcarockies.org, 1101 CR 53, Granby) With on-site rentals, 30 miles of family-friendly single- and doubletrack, and affordable rooms, Snow Mountain Ranch can be as all-inclusive as you want it to be.

The Tipperary Race Course Ranked as one of the top five mountain bike race courses in the world, this 26-mile cross-country route passes through meadows, near springs and creeks and ponds, and up and down steep hills. Ask a local bike shop for directions (they're kind of complicated).

Winter Park Resort (970-726-1564, winterparkresort.com) Within the resort boundaries alone, there are over 50 miles of trails—and they connect to come 600 more miles in the Fraser Valley. A ride up the Zephyr Express gets you to high-alpine intermediate routes like Icarus and Upper Roof of the Rockies; gravity-fueled free-for-alls like The Downhill; and the creek crossings, rock drops, and narrow tree passes of Mountain Goat. At the base, rent full-suspension bikes from **West Portal Bike Rentals.** Several coffee shops, bars, and patios are open all summer long.

Cycling: Road Biking

With the exception of US 40, the paved roads here see few cars—and the high elevation makes any of them a challenge.

Granby to Grand Lake A series of rolling hills on US 34.

Trail Ridge Road For the toughest ride around, leave from Grand Lake and climb into Rocky Mountain National Park—it's 28 miles and 3,100 feet of elevation to Rock Cut. You'll need to pay a park entrance fee (or bring your pass).

Willow Creek Pass on CO 125 From Granby, this relatively unpeopled road rises 1,770 feet over 26 miles.

Winter Park to Berthoud Pass Recently widened, US 40 is congested but safe. It's 11 miles one way from town with a 1,920-foot elevation gain. Want a real challenge? Go up and over, down to I-70, and then return—you'll gain 6,000 feet of elevation.

Winter Park to Granby Eighteen miles on the main highway, this route is busy—but it's lined with coffee shops (and bike shops).

Fishing

Outfitters

Devil's Thumb Ranch (970-726-8231, devilsthumbranch.com, 3530 CR 83, Tabernash) From beginners' lessons on-site to half-day wade trips to overnight float trips on private water (like the Colorado River at Miller Ranch) and public water (the Fraser River), Devil's Thumb has a full menu—plus an in-house fly shop.

Grand County Fishing Company (970-531-9988, grandflyfishing.com, 234 CR 803, Fraser) Among their many options, GCFC has exclusive access to a 4-mile stretch of the Fraser River—and you can fish it either guided or unguided. If you opt for a guide, owners Jeff Ehlert and Dave Parri have a combined 65 years of experience.

Mo Henry's Trout Shop (970-726-9754, mohenrys.com, 540 Zerex St., Fraser) Over 700 fly patterns. Guide-owned and open at 6 AM, every single day. Mo Henry's (named after two brothers) is the best shop in the valley, selling tying materials, clothing, float tubes, licenses, maps, and a full range of guided trips.

Lakes and Streams

Before you fish any water in Colorado, be sure you check with a local fly shop to find out if it's public or private. Many rivers have both private and public sections, so make sure you know where you're going. For licenses and regulations, visit wildlife.state.co.us/fishing—or, again, stop into a shop. If a river is designated "Gold Medal," it officially means that there are 12 trout per surface acre that top 14 inches—or 60 pounds of trout per surface acre. Unofficially, it means that the fishing is damn good.

Colorado River If you follow US 40 northwest past Hot Sulphur Springs, there's a great 3-mile stretch of public water—full of browns and rainbows. Just check with a local fly shop about access issues.

Meadow Creek Reservoir Look for the signs on US 40 near Tabernash. The 168-acre reservoir contains rainbows (stocked), and brookies haunt the creek above and below. Hoof it up to Columbine or Caribou Lakes (a few miles) for cutties.

St. Louis Creek Turn onto CR 73 at Fraser's Eisenhower Drive, then drive 2 miles to the Forest Service boundary. Starting here, there's 7 miles of public water swimming with brook and rainbow trout. Hike 3 miles past the end of CR 73 to St. Louis Lake for a shot at cutthroat.

Upper Fraser River One mile south of Winter Park, parallel to US 40, there's open fishing for rainbow trout—and the river is stocked annually. Check with the Forest Service or a local fly shop for where the private sections are.

Vasquez Creek Head west from Winter Park on Vasquez Road to the Forest Service boundary for native brookies and stocked rainbows.

Willow Creek and Willow Creek Reservoir Just west of Granby. The rez has a picnic area, campground, boat ramp, and decent fishing for pan-size rainbows; the creek has 14 miles of public water, and more often than not, you'll have the place to yourself.

Golf

Grand Elk Ranch & Club (877-389-9333, 970-887-9122, grandelk.com, 1321 Ten Mile Dr., Granby) A rolling, 18-hole, par-71 course designed by Craig Stadler and Tripp Davis, Grand Elk is the newest spread in the valley—and has four sets of tees, making it user-friendly for all abilities.

Headwaters Golf Course (866-765-8478, 970-887-2709, headwatersgolfcourse.com, 1000 Village Rd., Granby) Headwaters has the largest practice facility in Grand County, a 2,000-square-foot deck, GPS-equipped carts, and an 18-hole course designed by Michael Asmundson.

Pole Creek Golf Club (800-511-6838, 970-887-9195, polecreekgolf.com, 5827 CR 51, Tabernash) Opened in 1983, Pole Creek—the closest course to Winter Park—has 27 holes (three 9-hole courses), views of the Continental Divide, two ponds and five lakes, a chipping area, and a restaurant (the Untamed Grill, brother to Winter Park's Untamed Steakhouse).

A long vista and a large green at the Headwaters Golf Course. Headwaters Golf Course

Hiking and Backpacking

Over a half-million acres of national forests, wilderness areas, and parks surround Winter Park, including the Continental Divide–split Indian Peaks, Rocky Mountain National Park (farther afield at 35-odd miles away), the Arapaho National Recreation Area, and the Vasquez Peak Wilderness. There are just a few suggestions.

Berthoud Pass Trailhead At the top of the pass, US 40 meets the Continental Divide Trail; take it either way (as far as you want) for rolling ridges and vast views in all directions.

Byers Peak Trail With spectacular views and a climb from 10,080 feet to 11,906 feet, the Byers Peak Trail gives you good bang for the buck: The trailhead is about 8 miles west of Fraser, and the 3-mile (round trip) route passes through spruce and fir old-growth on the way up to the summit.

Columbine Lake Just past the Meadow Creek Reservoir, this trail starts at the Junco Lake Trailhead and climbs just under 3 miles to a tiny high-mountain lake.

High Lonesome Trail With several access points and panoramic views, High Lonesome follows the Continental Divide. Though it doesn't gain or lose significant elevation, the trail reaches almost 11,700 feet at points.

Indian Peaks trails There are numerous trailheads on the eastern side of the Indian Peaks (the Western side, reachable from Denver and Boulder, tends to be more crowded) that access high-alpine lakes, 13,000-foot peaks, and above-timberline passes.

James Peak Finishing up at a breathtaking 13,294 feet, this is just a small piece of the Continental Divide Trail.

Lake Evelyn A 4-mile loop that follows the Kinney Creek Trail in the Byers Peak Wilderness through lodgepole forests and ends at little Lake Evelyn, tucked below the Vasquez Mountains.

Horseback Riding

Blue Sky Outfitters (970-726-1099, devilsthumboutfitters.com, 3530 CR 83, Tabernash) BSO (formerly known as Devil's Thumb Outfitters, hence the Web site) offers the gamut: one- and two-hour rides, lunch rides, half-day rides, and full-day excursions. They'll even take you out on horseback for fishing and hunting trips.

Monarch Stables (970-726-0900, 1400 CR 5, Fraser) Take a wagon ride, a pony ride, or a chuck wagon-BBQ ride (steak, chicken, soup, salad, and s'mores in a rustic cabin in the woods).

Samuelson Outfitters, Inc (970-726-8221, samuelsonoutfitters.com, P.O. Box 868, Fraser) In addition to offering hunting trips, Samuelson runs multi-day horse pack trips and daylong rides in the Medicine Bow-Routt National Forest.

Sombrero Stables (970-722-0100, sombrero.com, 1101 CR 53, Granby) Staged out of the YMCA's Snow Mountain Ranch in Tabernash, Sombrero—a nine-stable Colorado chain—offers one- to four-hour rides, breakfast rides (pancakes, eggs, fresh-squeezed OJ, coffee), and steak-fry rides (grilled meat, Dutch-oven potatoes, baked beans).

Hot Air Ballooning

Grand Adventure Balloon Tours (970-887-1340, grandadventureballoon.com, 79303 US 40, Winter Park) Float up at the crack of dawn, contour over peaks and valleys, and climb up to 3,000 feet AGL (Above Ground Level) for 100-mile views. Flights last an hour, landing where the wind takes you—and include a continental breakfast, a ride back to where to you started, and a champagne toast.

Hunting

Samuelson Outfitters, Inc (970-726-8221, samuelsonoutfitters.com, P.O. Box 868, Fraser) Operating out of the Troublesome Basin since 1967, Samuelson guides clients by horseback and on foot to a remote base camp that includes a cook tent with running water and electricity, sleeping tents with cots and mattresses, wood-burning stoves, and a trout stream just steps away—to hunt for deer and elk. Already have experience? They can pack your gear to a designated spot and pick you up later.

Rafting and Paddling

Clear Creek Rafting Company (800-353-9901, 303-567-1000, clearcreekrafting.com, 350 Whitewater Rd., Idaho Springs) Head back up and over Berthoud Pass toward Denver for steep and narrow runs on Clear Creek that parallel I-70. The burliest trip drops 1,300 feet and hits 30 Class IV–V rapids in 18 miles.

Mad Adventures (800-451-4844, 970-726-5290, madadventures.com, 1421 E. Park Ave., Kremmling) Another Clear Creek outfit, Mad's half-day trips come in at under $50 a head. Some rafting experience is recommended.

DRIVING: SCENIC DRIVES AND BYWAYS

Colorado River Headwaters This route can be driven either way (about 70 miles), or as an out-and-back. Start at the edge of Rocky Mountain National Park on US 34, then join US 40 to Kremmling, criss-crossing the Colorado and passing through huge vistas. Look for signs to Road 1 (which will become Road 11), and drive through piñon pine–juniper woodlands and Dakota sandstone to State Bridge.

Trail Ridge Road A spectacular, 48-mile stretch of road between Grand Lake (about 35 miles from Winter Park) and Estes Park that cuts through the heights of Rocky Mountain National Park, Trail Ridge reaches a height of 12,183 feet, passing by tundra, wildlife, and wildflowers and winding past classic Colorado mountain views.

The Ski Train
If you don't want to rent a car or take a shuttle up from Denver, catch a ride on the only ski-specific train in the States: The Ski Train has been carrying people from the city to the very base of Winter Park since 1940. In the 1950s and 1960s, most of the riders were teen-aged ski club members, but now it's filled with families and tourists—up to 750 people, the largest capacity of any scheduled passenger train in the country. The route, which takes about two hours, climbs 4,000 feet, chugs through 28 tunnels (including the 6.2-mile-long Moffat Tunnel), and provides glimpses of Boulder's Flatirons, Coal Creek Canyon, and Pine Cliff (once a popular resort town). A $74 Club ticket gets you reclining seats, a continental breakfast, après snacks and drinks; a Coach ticket, at $49, is the pared-down option. For more savings, you can buy discounted lift tickets when you make your reservations. (**Ski Train,** 303-296-4754, skitrain.com, askskitrain@skitrain.com)

SHOPPING

Art Galleries
Belerique Gallery (970-726-2362, beleriquegalleries.com, 78727 US 40, Winter Park) Bronze sculptures of Native Americans, paintings by Nancy Lund, Aaron Harker, and Gordon Foulger, enamels by Daphne Keskinis, and ceramics by Luiz Salvador.

Elk Horn Art Gallery (970-726-9292, elkhorngallery.com, 7-Eleven Shopping Plaza, 78878 US 40, Winter Park) This gallery focuses on Native American, Western, landscape, and wildlife works by artists like Winter Park local Karen Vance, illustrator Carl Cassler, and ceramicist Mata Ortiz.

Naked Aspen Designs (970-726-1039, nakedaspendesigns.com, 208 Eisenhower St., Fraser) Owner and designer Rob Peeters hikes through the Colorado high country looking for standing dead aspen, then shapes it into coffee tables, benches, beds, lamps, coat racks, stair railings, and much more.

Trail Ridge Art Company (970-726-4959, trailridgeart.com, Cooper Creek Square, Winter Park) This gallery features the work of Colorado artists (over 60 of them) in media ranging from glass, gourds, and wood to fabric, batik, pencil, and photography.

Outdoor Gear

The Viking Ski Shop (970-726-8885, skiwp.com, 78966 US 40, Winter Park) Located in the Viking Lodge, this shop has a good selection of skiing and biking gear.

Winter Park Sports Shop (970-726-5554, winterparkski.com, Kings Crossing, Winter Park) A mostly ski-specific shop with sportswear, snowshoes, demos, and gifts.

SEASONAL EVENTS

January: Grand Lake Snowshoe Festival (grandlakesnowshoefestival.com) Sign up for 5K and 10K races, moonlight walks, and "geocaching" events (a timed scavenger hunt using your GPS), along with technique talks, chili lunches, and live music.

January: Three Lakes Ice Fishing Contest (granbychamber.com) Win thousands of dollars in cash and prizes while fishing for the biggest rainbow, brown trout, or mackinaw (there's even a division for kids 5 and under).

February: Grand County Sled Dog Classic (rmsdc.com/granby.htm) Catch local teams in action.

April: Golden Bunny Classic Fun Race & Candy Hunt (970-726-1564, skiwinterpark .com) For over 30 years, kids have been hunting for candy eggs—and then racing down the bunny slopes—in this Eastertime tradition.

June: Fat Tire Classic (303-722-7474, denver-redcross.org) The FTC's motto is, "It's not about the beer. But it's a nice addition." This Red Cross benefit/mountain bike festival includes six catered meals, organized rides and hikes, prizes for fundraising, and not a single competitive race.

July: Blues from the Top (970-531-1641, grandblues.org) Organized by the Grand County Blues Society, a small but dedicated group of blues lovers in the Fraser Valley, the annual daylong festival lasts from 10 AM to 10 PM.

July: 103.5 The Fox Hawgfest (800-977-6198, skiwinterpark.com) Rock out with the likes of ZZ Top, Vince Neil, Hell's Belles, RATT, and Eddie Money at the outdoor stage at the base of Winter Park.

July: Winter Park Art Affair (970-726-9492, winterpark-info.com) Proceeds from the sale of fine art, jewelry, crafts, photography, used books, and sculpture help fund art scholarships for Grand County students.

July: Winter Park Folk Festival (970-726-4118) Catch acts like Shawn Colvin and John Gorka at downtown Hideaway Park.

August: Famous Flamethrower's High Altitude Chili Cookoff Weekend (winterpark.org) A regional cook-off to qualify for the world championships; awards go out to Best Red Chili, Best Salsa, Most Creative Chef, and more. Taste tickets for public sampling are two for a buck.

August: Rocky Mountain Wine, Beer & Food Festival (970-726-4118, nscd.org/events/winebeerfood.htm) Pay $40, get a sampling tray and a commemorative stein, and eat and drink all the local gourmet grub you can for three hours.

September: Road Kill Trail Half-Marathon (877-573-6654, kremmlingchamber.com/roadkilldescription.htm) Starting and finishing in the nearby town of Kremmling, the course climbs up the back of the Kremmling Cliffs, crosses creeks, follows cow tracks, and ends on rolling singletrack. The post-race lunch? Barbecued elk, deer, and bear.

December: Jingle Rails (800-903-PARK) Spend New Year's Eve watching 50-odd pro and newbie riders sliding rails for $3,000 in prize money.

Nuts and Bolts

Getting here
Most people come up from Denver and the Front Range, whether they live there or just landed at **Denver International Airport.** From DIA, it takes around two hours to drive up I-70, then up and over Berthoud Pass on US 40 (a total of about 90 miles). For Colorado road conditions, check out cotrip.org or call 303-639-1111. If you'd rather not drive, **Home James Airport Shuttle and Taxi** (970-726-5060, homejamestransportation.com) can take care of you—they offer up to 22 daily departures from the airport to Winter Park. Or you can take the historic **Ski Train** (see box on page 300).

Ambulance/Fire/Police/Search and Rescue
For emergencies, of course, dial 911. For police assistance that doesn't require an emergency response, contact the number listed below for the city closest to your present location.

Colorado State Highway Patrol: 970-824-6501

East Grand Fire Protection District No. 4: 970-726-5824

Fraser and Winter Park Police Department: 970-722-7779

Granby Police: 970-887-3007

Grand County Search & Rescue: 970-725-3343

Grand County Sheriff's Department: 970-725-3343

Avalanche Reports
Colorado Avalanche Information Center: 303-499-9650, avalanche-center.org

Hospitals and Emergency Medical Services
Granby Medical Center/Centura Health: 970-887-2117, 480 E. Agate Ave.

Grand County Public Health and Nursing: 970-724-3288, 150 Moffatt Ave., Hot Sulphur Springs.

Kremmling Memorial Hospital: 970-724-3442, 214 S. Fourth St., Kremmling

7-Mile Medical Clinic: 970-887-7470, 145 Parsenn Rd., Winter Park

Winter Park Medical Center: 970-726-8989, Kings Crossing Center, Winter Park

Libraries
Fraser Valley Library: 970-726-5689, gcld.org, 421 Norgren Rd., Fraser

Media

Newspapers & Magazines
Daily Tribune: 970-887-3334, grandcountynews.com, 424 E. Agate, Granby, CO 80446

Grand Lake Prospector: 970-887-3334, grandcountynews.com, 424 E. Agate, Granby, CO 80446

Middle Park Times: 970-724-3350, grandcountynews.com, 111 Central Ave., Kremmling, CO 80459

Sky-Hi News: 970-887-3334, grandcountynews.com, 424 E. Agate, Granby, CO 80446

Winter Park Manifest: 970-726-5721, grandcountynews.com, 78622 US 40, Winter Park, CO 80482

Radio
KRKY 930 AM: 970-887-1100, highcountryradio.com. Talk radio, weather, road reports, local news, and tidbits.

Public Transportation
"The Lift," a Winter Park–area shuttle system, has eight different routes around WP and between Winter Park and Fraser, stopping near most major hotels and at several places downtown on a regular basis, even at night (970-726-4163).

Ranger Stations
Arapaho and Roosevelt National Forests: 970-498-2770, 240 W. Prospect Rd., Fort Collins

Clear Creek Ranger District: 303-567-2901

Kawuneeche Visitor Center: Off US 34 in Grand Lake, 970-586-1206

Rocky Mountain National Park information: 970-586-1206, nps.gov/romo

Sulfur Ranger District: 9 Ten Mile Dr., Granby, 970-887-4100

Tourist information

Greater Granby Area chamber: 970-887-2311, granbychamber.com, P.O. Box 35, Granby

Winter Park/Fraser Valley Chamber of Commerce: 970-726-4118, winterpark-info.com, 78841 US 40, Winter Park

BIBLIOGRAPHY

Want to read more about the character and history of Colorado's mountain towns? The best place to find the most obscure and detailed memoirs, biographies, nature guides, and collections of historical photos are in each town's local museum or library—where tiny brochures share the shelves with self-published labors of love. Most books about general Colorado history have something about mining, ranching, and skiing, but the tomes written by longtime locals have much more specific information (if that's what you're looking for). Here's a selection to get you started.

Biography and Reminiscence

Arlen, Caroline. *Colorado Mining Stories*. Montrose, CO: Western Reflections Publishing Co., 2002.

Bird, Isabella L. *A Lady's Life in the Rocky Mountains*. Norman, OK: University of Oklahoma Press, 1999.

Clifford, Hal. *Falling Season: Inside the Life and Death Drama of Aspen's Mountain Rescue Team*. Seattle, WA: Mountaineers Books, 1999.

Clifford, Peggy. *Aspen, Dreams & Dilemmas: Love Letter to a Small Town*. Athens, OH: Swallow Press, 1970.

Clifford, Peggy. *To Aspen and Back: An American Journey*. New York: St. Martin's Press, 1980.

Conover, Ted. *Whiteout: Lost in Aspen*. New York: Vintage, 2001.

Cornell, Virginia. *Doc Susie: The True Story of a Country Physician in the Colorado Rockies*. Carpinteria, CA: Manifest Publications, 1991.

Fish, Harriet. *Tomboy Bride: A Woman's Personal Account of Life in Mining Camps of the West*. Boulder, CO: Pruett Publishing Co., 2000.

Hayes, Mary Eshbaugh. *The Story of Aspen: The History of Aspen as Told Through the Stories of Its People*. Aspen, CO: Aspen Three Publishing, 1996.

Kinkade, Stuart. *Aspen Bummin': Aspen Ski Bum Stories from the Sixties*. Self-published, 2000.

Smith, P. David. *Mountains of Silver: Life in Colorado's Red Mountain Mining District*. Montrose, CO: Western Reflections Publishing Co., 2000.

Western Voices: 125 Years of Colorado Writing. Golden, CO: Fulcrum Publishing, 2004.

Wirth, Kelsey. *Reflections on a Western Town: An Oral History of Crested Butte*. Crested Butte: Oh-Be-Joyful Press, 1996.

History & Cultural Studies

Auge, Ed. *Ed Auge's History of the Breckenridge Mining District*. Oak Park, IL: Marion Street Publishing, 2003.

Barlow-Perez, Sally. *A History of Aspen*. Aspen, CO: Who Press, 1999.

Bie, Tom. *Steamboat: Ski Town USA*. Boulder, CO: Mountain Sports Press, 2002.

Black, Robert C. *Island in the Rockies: The Pioneer Era of Grand County, Colorado*. Country Printer, 1977.

Buys, Christian. *A Brief History of Telluride*. Montrose, CO: Western Reflections Publishing Co., 2003.

Champion, Ruth. *Breckenridge Gold*. Fort Collins, CO: Old Army Press, 1977.

306 Colorado's Classic Mountain Towns

Fiester, Mark: *Blasted, Beloved Breckenridge*. Boulder, CO: Pruett Publishing, 1973.

Lavender, David. *The Telluride Story*. Ouray, CO: Wayfinder Press, 1987.

Rohrbough, Malcolm. *Aspen: The History of a Silver-Mining Town, 1879-1893*. Boulder, CO: University Press of Colorado, 2000.

Seibert, Pete W. *Vail: Triumph of a Dream*. Boulder, CO: Mountain Sports Press, 2002.

Shelton, Peter. *Aspen Skiing: The First Fifty Years, 1947–1997*. Aspen, CO: Western Eye Press, 1996.

Smith, Duane A. *Crested Butte: From Coal Camp to Ski Town*. Montrose, CO: Western Reflections Publishing Co., 2005

Smith, Duane and John L. Ninnemann. *San Juan Bonanza: Western Colorado's Mining Legacy*. Santa Fe: University of New Mexico Press, 2006.

Vandenbusche, Duane. *The Gunnison Country*. Self-published, 1980.

Wyckoff, William. *Creating Colorado: The Making of a Western American Landscape, 1960–1940*. New Haven: Yale University Press, 1999.

Nature Guides

Andersen, Paul. *Elk Mountains Odyssey: The West Elk Loop Scenic and Historic Byway Guide*. Carbondale, CO: Redstone Press, 1998.

Clarke, Herbert and Mary Taylor Gray. *The Guide to Colorado Birds*. Englewood, CO: Westcliffe Publishers, 1998.

Folzenlogen, Robert. *Colorado's Year: A Guide to Nature's Highlights*. Littleton, CO: Willow Press, 1996.

Foutz, Dell R. *Geology of Colorado Illustrated*. Grand Junction, CO: Your Geologist, 1994.

Guennel, G. K. *Guide to Colorado Wildflowers: Mountains*. Englewood, CO: Westcliffe Publishers, 2005.

Jacobs, Randy and Robert M. Ormes. *Guide to the Colorado Mountains*. Golden, CO: Colorado Mountain Club Press, 2000.

Jones, Stephen R. *Colorado Nature Almanac: A Month-By-Month Guide to the State's Wildlife and Wild Places*. Boulder, CO: Pruett Publishing, 1998.

Kavanaugh, James. *Colorado Trees & Wildflowers*. Phoenix, AZ: Waterford Press, 2001.

——. *Colorado Wildlife: An Introduction to Familiar Species of Birds, Mammals, Reptiles, Amphibians, Fish, and Insects*. Phoenix, AZ: Waterford Press, 2003.

Warren, Kathy Darrow and Katherine D. Warren. *Wild About Wildflowers: Extreme Botanizing in Crested Butte, Wildflower Capital of Colorado*. Fort Collins, CO: Heel & Toe Publishers, 1998.

Photographic Studies

Barbour, Elizabeth. *Telluride (Images of America)*. Mount Pleasant, SC: Arcadia Publishing, 2006.

Benjamin, Eileen. *Telluride: Landscapes and Dreams*. Telluride, CO: Montoya Publishing, 2000.

Buys, Christian J. *Historic Aspen in Rare Photographs*. Montrose, CO: Western Reflections Publishing Co., 2000.

——. *Historic Telluride*. Montrose, CO: Western Reflections Publishing Co., 1998.

Fails, Sandy. *Crested Butte: The Edge of Paradise*. Crested Butte, CO: Crested Butte Publishing, 1989.

Fielder, John. *Colorado: Lost Places and Forgotten Words*. Englewood, CO: Westcliffe
  Publishers, 1989.
———. *Colorado Wildflowers*. Englewood, CO: Westcliffe Publishers, 1996.
Muench, David and Marc Muench. *Colorado*. Portland, OR: Graphic Arts Center Publishing
  Co., 2001.
Ohlrich, Warren. *Aspen in Color*. Aspen, CO: Who Press, 1990.
Ohlrich, Warren and Paul Anderson. *Aspen, Portrait of a Rocky Mountain Town*. Aspen, CO:
  Who Press, 1994.
Wentworth, Frank. *Aspen on the Roaring Fork: An Illustrated History of Colorado's Greatest
  Silver Camp*. Northborough, MA: Sundance Publications, 1976.
Whitlock, Flint and Bob Bishop. *Soldiers on Skis: A Pictorial Memoir of the 10th Mountain
  Division*. Boulder, CO: Paladin Press, 1992.

INDEX